Three sisters who are fans sent
me some handmade items. They
even included the gag item that
Asta tried to buy at the black
market! It's so heartening to look
at! Thank you very much!!

—Yūki Tabata, 2017

YŪKI TABATA

was born in Fukuoka Prefecture
and got his big break in the 2011
Shonen Jump Golden Future Cup
with his winning entry, *Hungry
Joker*. He started the magical fantasy
series *Black Clover* in 2015.

BLACK CLOVER
VOLUME 10
SHONEN JUMP Manga Edition

Story and Art by YŪKI TABATA

Translation ♣ TAYLOR ENGEL, HC LANGUAGE SOLUTIONS, INC.

Touch-Up Art & Lettering ♣ ANNALIESE CHRISTMAN

Design ♣ SHAWN CARRICO

Editor ♣ ALEXIS KIRSCH

Printed in the U.S.A.

Published by VIZ Media, LLC
P.O. Box 77010
San Francisco, CA 94107

10 9 8 7 6 5 4 3 2 1
First printing, February 2018

RATED T FOR TEEN

PARENTAL ADVISORY
BLACK CLOVER is rated T for Teen and is recommended for ages 13 and up. This volume contains fantasy violence.

ratings.viz.com

SHONEN JUMP www.shonenjump.com

VIZ media www.viz.com

SHONEN JUMP MANGA

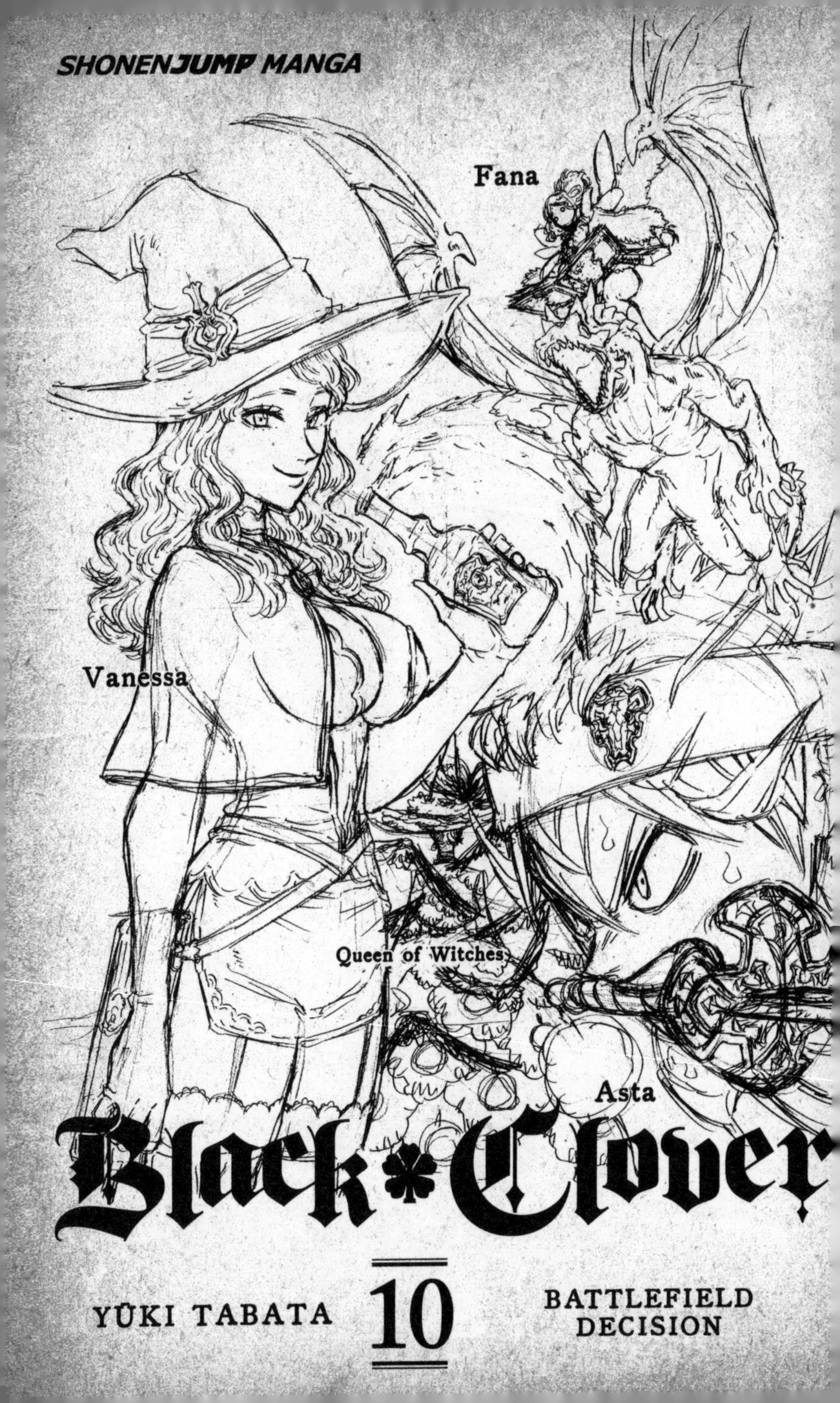
Fana
Vanessa
Queen of Witches
Asta

Black Clover

YŪKI TABATA

10

BATTLEFIELD DECISION

Characters

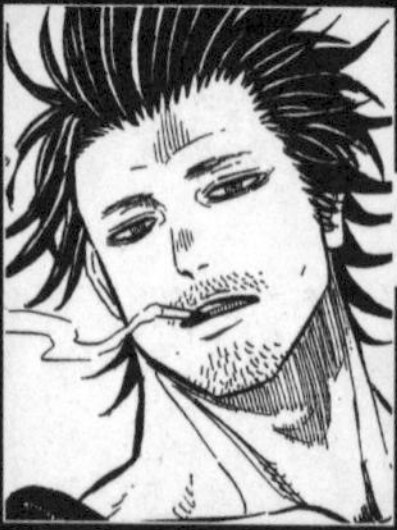

Yami Sukehiro

Member of: The Black Bulls
Magic: Dark

A captain who looks fierce and has a hot temper, but is very popular with his brigade.

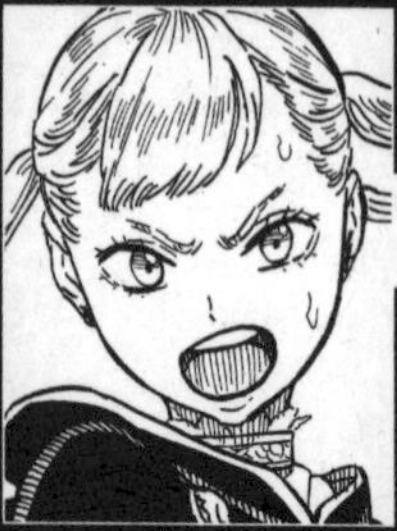

Noelle Silva

Member of: The Black Bulls
Magic: Water

A royal. She's really impudent, but can be kind, too.

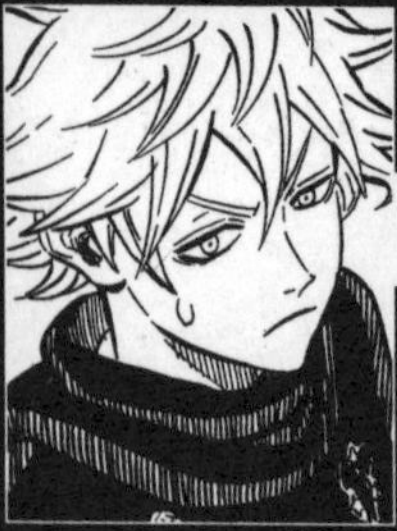

Finral Roulacase

Member of: The Black Bulls
Magic: Spatial

A flirt who likes girls so much it gets in the way of his missions.

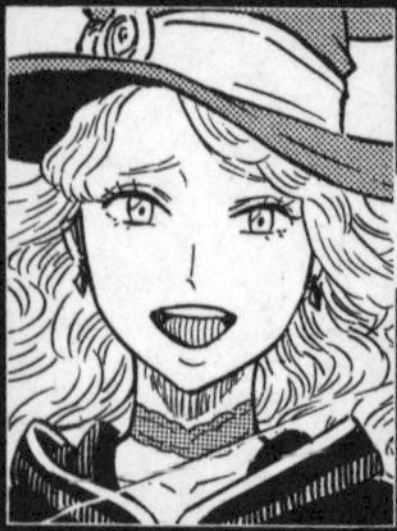

Vanessa Enoteca

Member of: The Black Bulls
Magic: Thread

A witch with an unparalleled love of liquor who was exiled from a distinguished family.

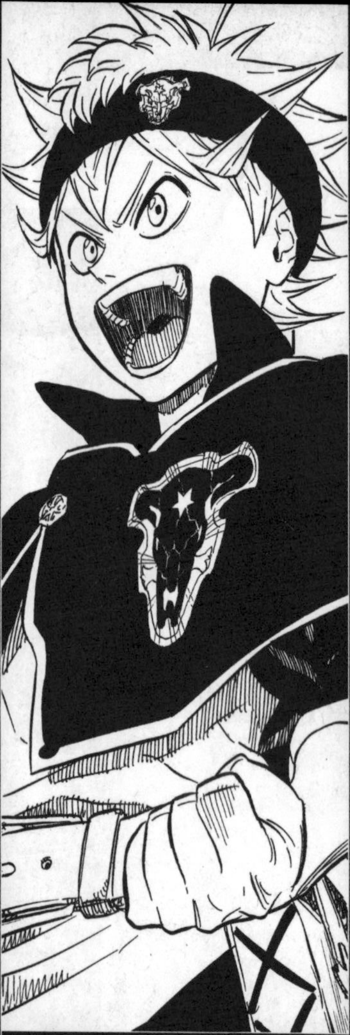

Asta

Member of: The Black Bulls
Magic: None (Anti-Magic)

He has no magic, but he's working to become the Wizard King through sheer guts and his well-trained body.

Luck Voltia

Member of:
The Black Bulls
Magic: Lightning

A battle maniac who smiles constantly and has a problematic personality.

Magna Swing

Member of:
The Black Bulls
Magic: Flame

He has the temperament of a delinquent, but he's quite manly and good at taking care of others.

Gauche Adlai

Member of:
The Black Bulls
Magic: Mirror

A former convict with a blind, pathological love for his little sister.

Charmy Pappitson

Member of:
The Black Bulls
Magic: Cotton

She's small, but she eats like a maniac.

Gordon Agrippa

Member of:
The Black Bulls
Magic: ?

Incredibly bad at communicating. He wants to get closer to everybody else, but he can't say it.

Grey

Member of:
The Black Bulls
Magic: Transformation

She has a shy personality, and she constantly transforms to look like someone who's near her.

STORY

In a world where magic is everything, Asta and Yuno are both found abandoned on the same day at a church in the remote village of Hage. Both dream of becoming the Wizard King, the highest of all mages, and they spend their days working toward that dream.

The year they turn 15, both receive grimoires, magic books that amplify their bearer's magic. They take the entrance exam for the Magic Knights, nine groups of mages under the direct control of the Wizard King. Yuno, whose magic is strong, joins the Golden Dawn, an elite group, while Asta, who has no magic at all, joins the Black Bulls, a group of misfits. With this, the two finally take their first step toward becoming the Wizard King...

After the battle at Kiten, the top healing mage in the kingdom examines Asta's wounded arms and tells him that, because of an ancient curse, the wounds can't be healed, and there's no hope for treatment. However, Asta's friends in the Black Bulls want to save him no matter what!

CONTENTS

BLACK ✤ CLOVER

10

♣ Page 81: Because He's Like That

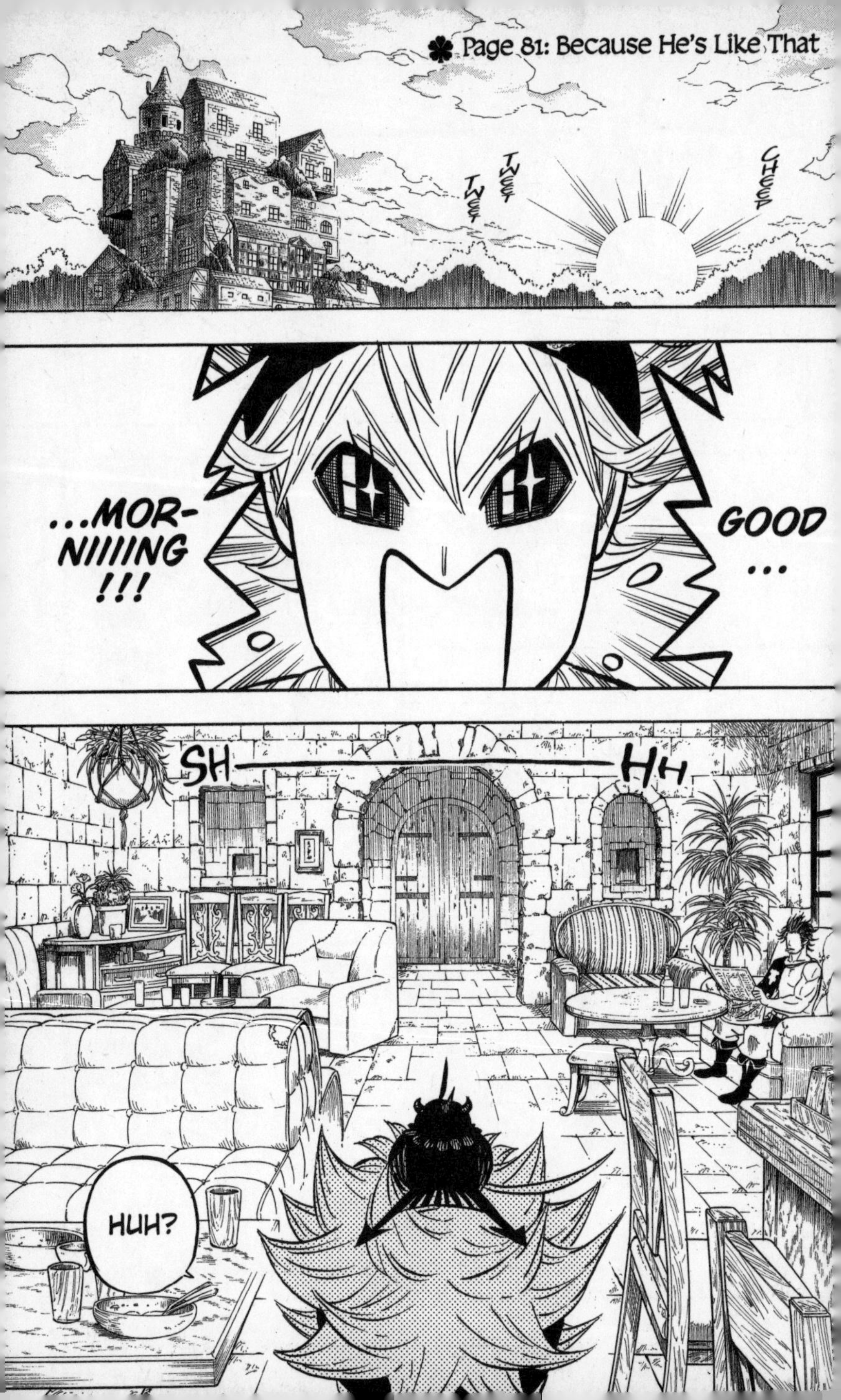
CHEEP
TWEET
TWEET
GOOD...
...MOR-NIIIING!!!
SH——————HH
HUH?

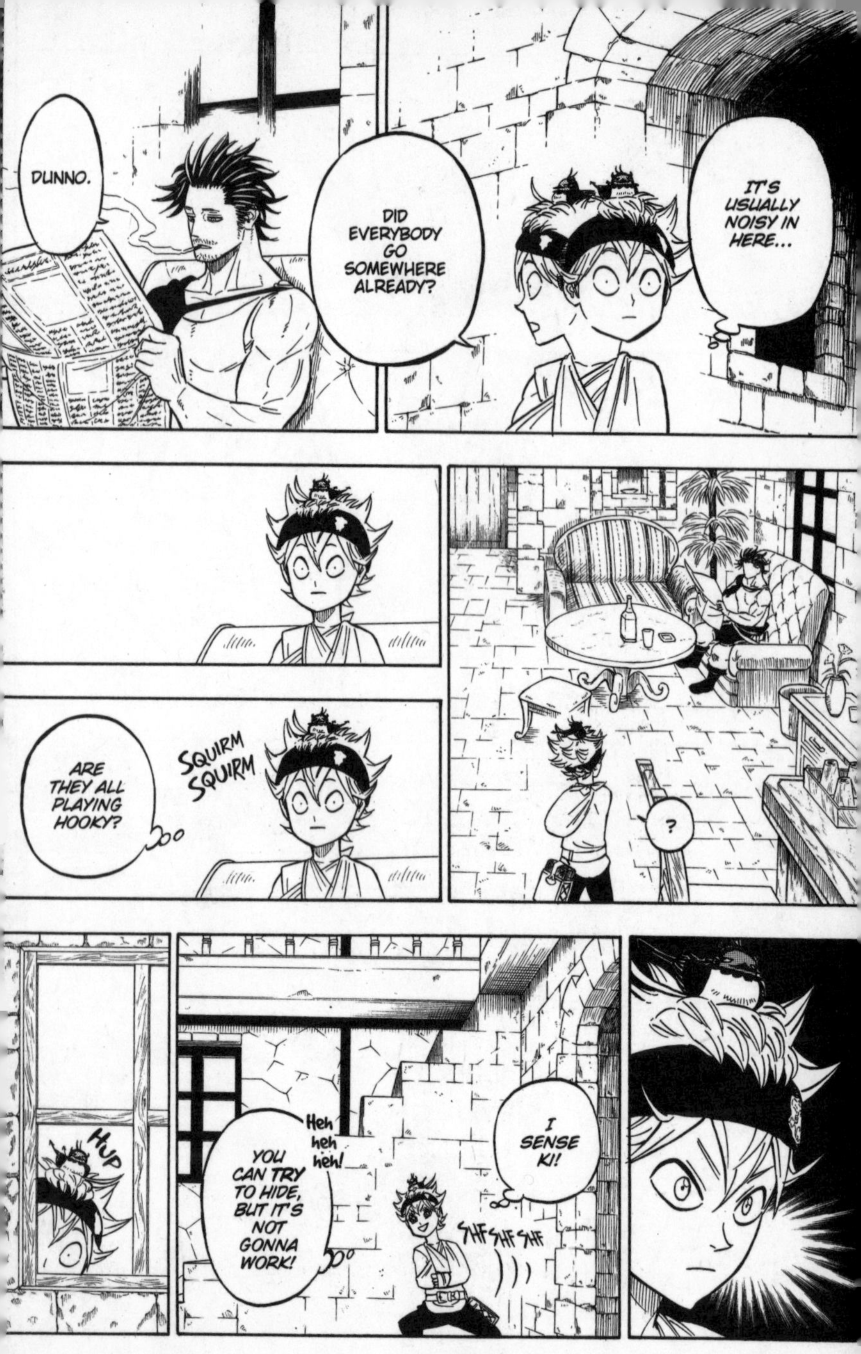
IT'S USUALLY NOISY IN HERE...
DID EVERYBODY GO SOMEWHERE ALREADY?
DUNNO.
?
SQUIRM SQUIRM
ARE THEY ALL PLAYING HOOKY?
I SENSE KI!
Heh heh heh!
YOU CAN TRY TO HIDE, BUT IT'S NOT GONNA WORK!
SHF SHF SHF
HUP

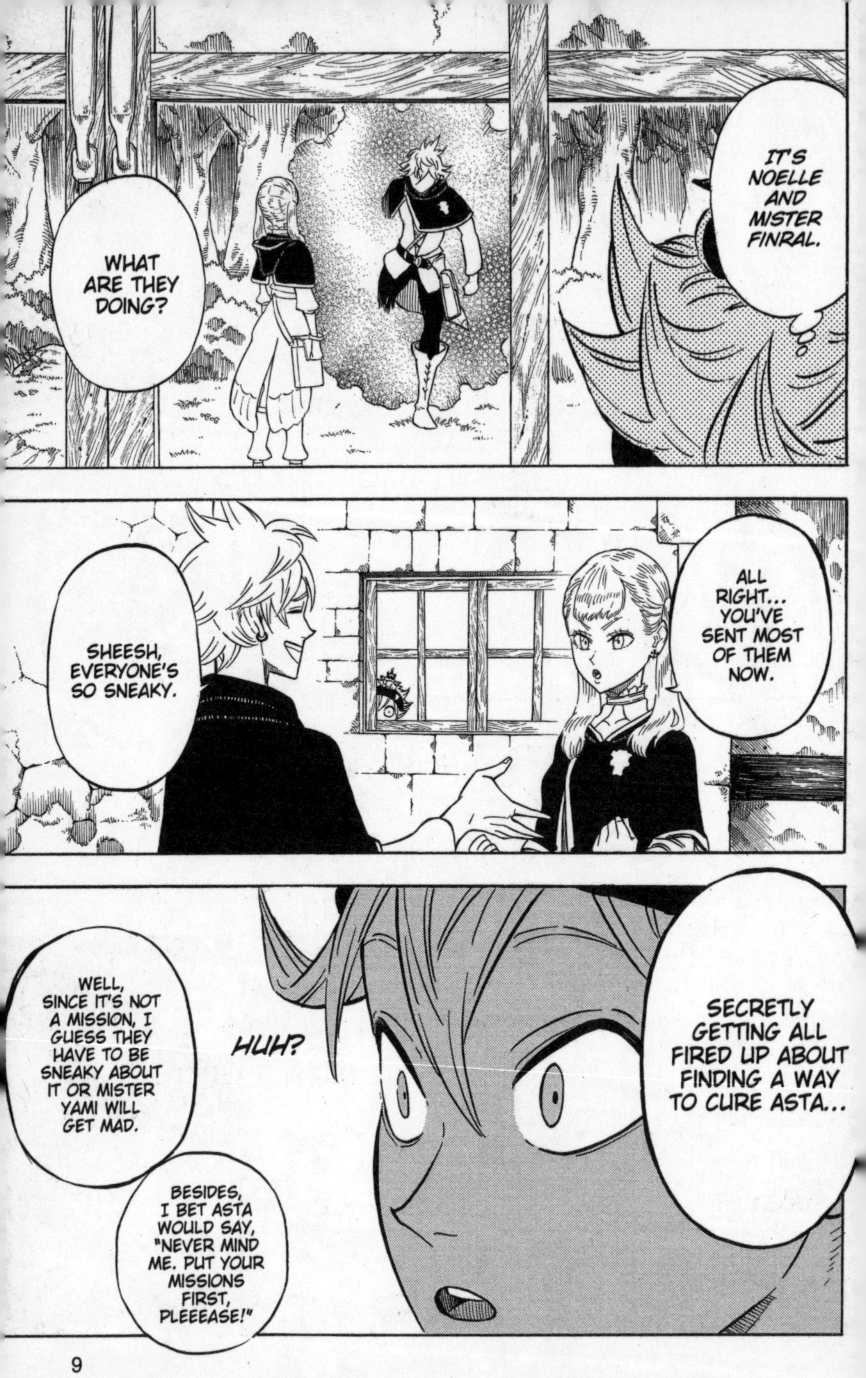
IT'S NOELLE AND MISTER FINRAL.
WHAT ARE THEY DOING?
ALL RIGHT... YOU'VE SENT MOST OF THEM NOW.
SHEESH, EVERYONE'S SO SNEAKY.
SECRETLY GETTING ALL FIRED UP ABOUT FINDING A WAY TO CURE ASTA...
HUH?
WELL, SINCE IT'S NOT A MISSION, I GUESS THEY HAVE TO BE SNEAKY ABOUT IT OR MISTER YAMI WILL GET MAD.
BESIDES, I BET ASTA WOULD SAY, "NEVER MIND ME. PUT YOUR MISSIONS FIRST, PLEEEASE!"

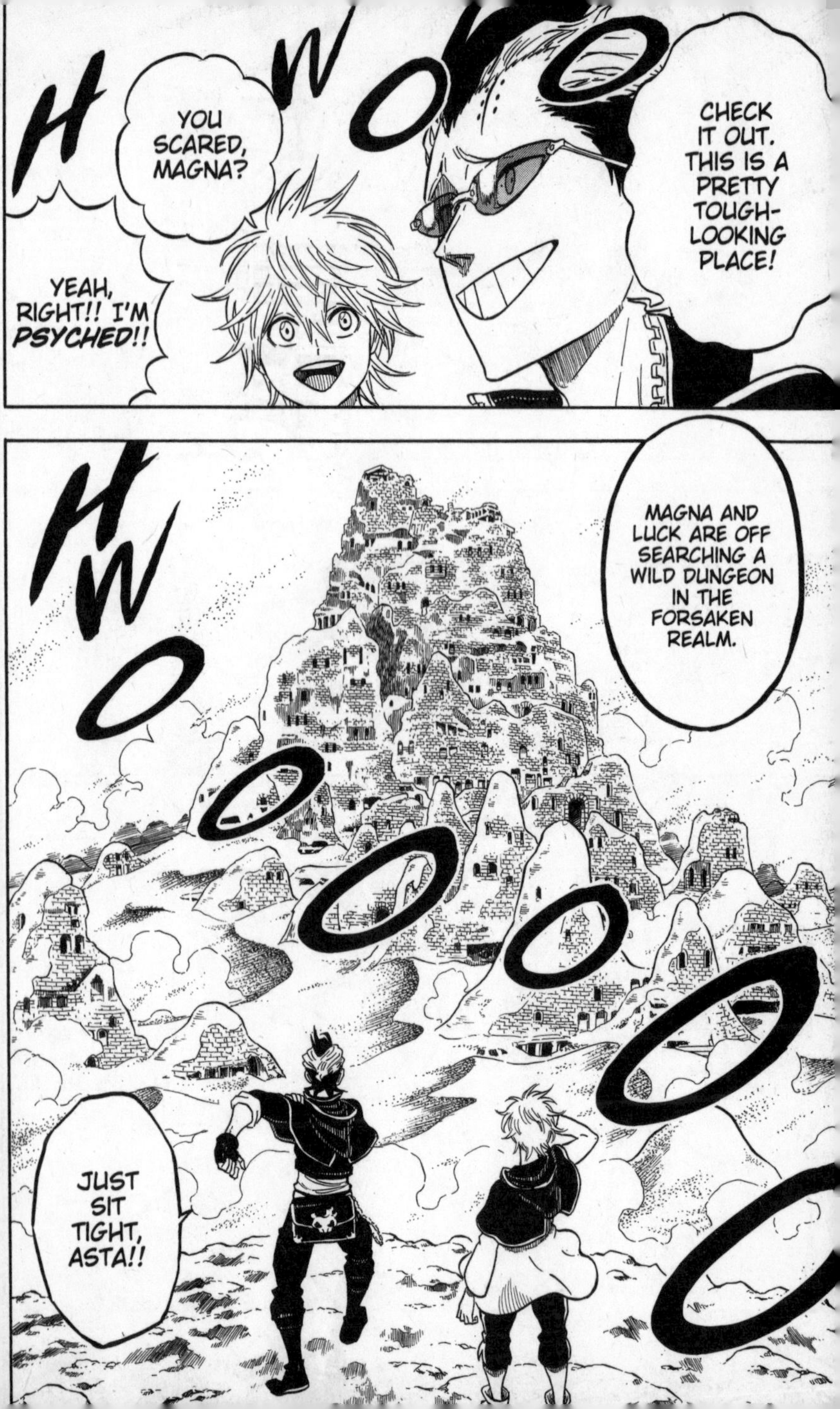
HOWOO
CHECK IT OUT. THIS IS A PRETTY TOUGH-LOOKING PLACE!
YOU SCARED, MAGNA?
YEAH, RIGHT!! I'M *PSYCHED*!!
MAGNA AND LUCK ARE OFF SEARCHING A WILD DUNGEON IN THE FORSAKEN REALM.
HWOOOOOOO
JUST SIT TIGHT, ASTA!!

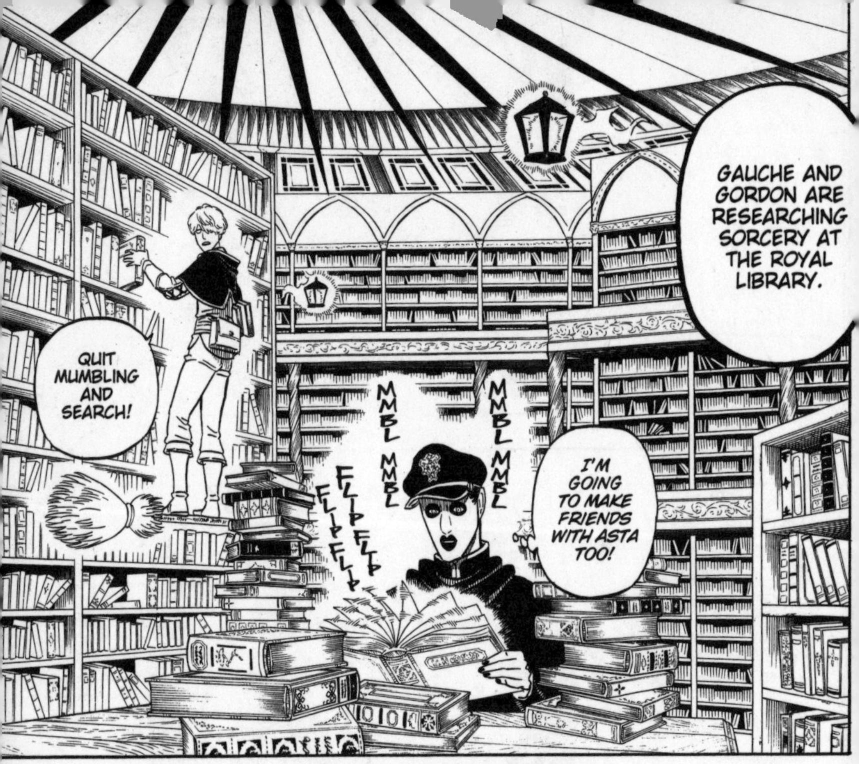
GAUCHE AND GORDON ARE RESEARCHING SORCERY AT THE ROYAL LIBRARY.
I'M GOING TO MAKE FRIENDS WITH ASTA TOO!
MMBL MMBL
MMBL MMBL
FLIP FLIP
FLIP FLIP
QUIT MUMBLING AND SEARCH!
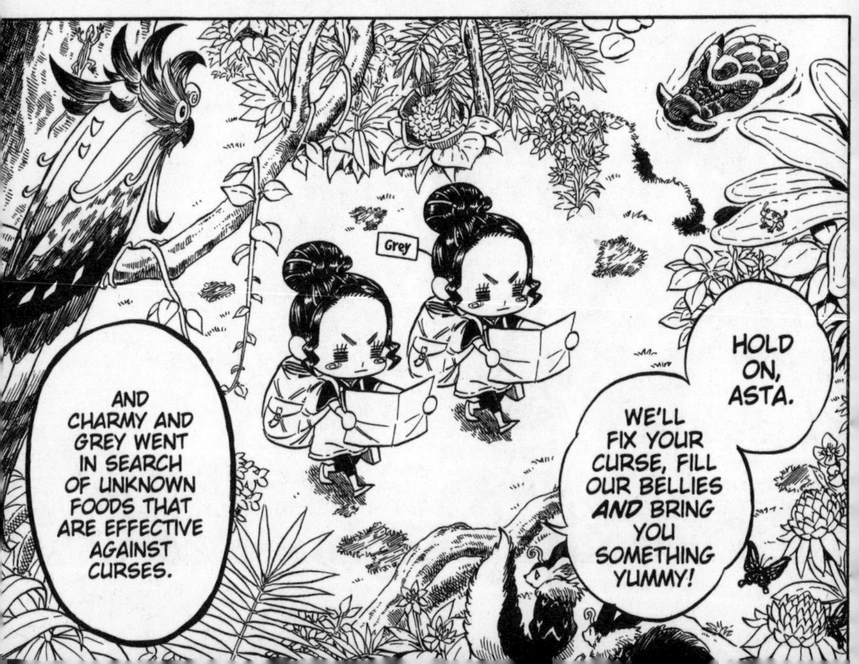
HOLD ON, ASTA.
WE'LL FIX YOUR CURSE, FILL OUR BELLIES AND BRING YOU SOMETHING YUMMY!
Grey
AND CHARMY AND GREY WENT IN SEARCH OF UNKNOWN FOODS THAT ARE EFFECTIVE AGAINST CURSES.

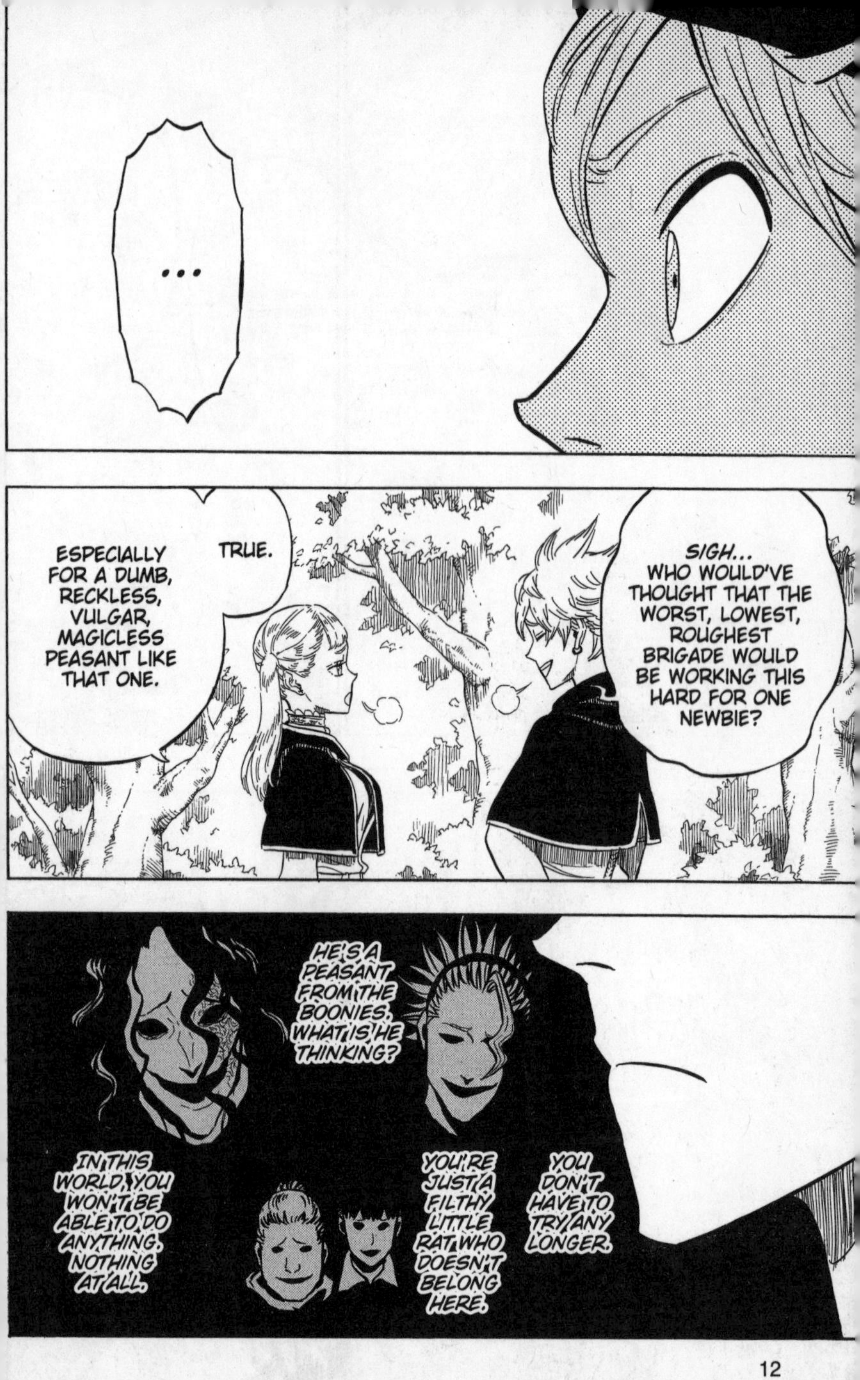
...
SIGH... WHO WOULD'VE THOUGHT THAT THE WORST, LOWEST, ROUGHEST BRIGADE WOULD BE WORKING THIS HARD FOR ONE NEWBIE?
TRUE.
ESPECIALLY FOR A DUMB, RECKLESS, VULGAR, MAGICLESS PEASANT LIKE THAT ONE.
HE'S A PEASANT FROM THE BOONIES. WHAT IS HE THINKING?
YOU DON'T HAVE TO TRY ANY LONGER.
YOU'RE JUST A FILTHY LITTLE RAT WHO DOESN'T BELONG HERE.
IN THIS WORLD, YOU WON'T BE ABLE TO DO ANYTHING. NOTHING AT ALL.

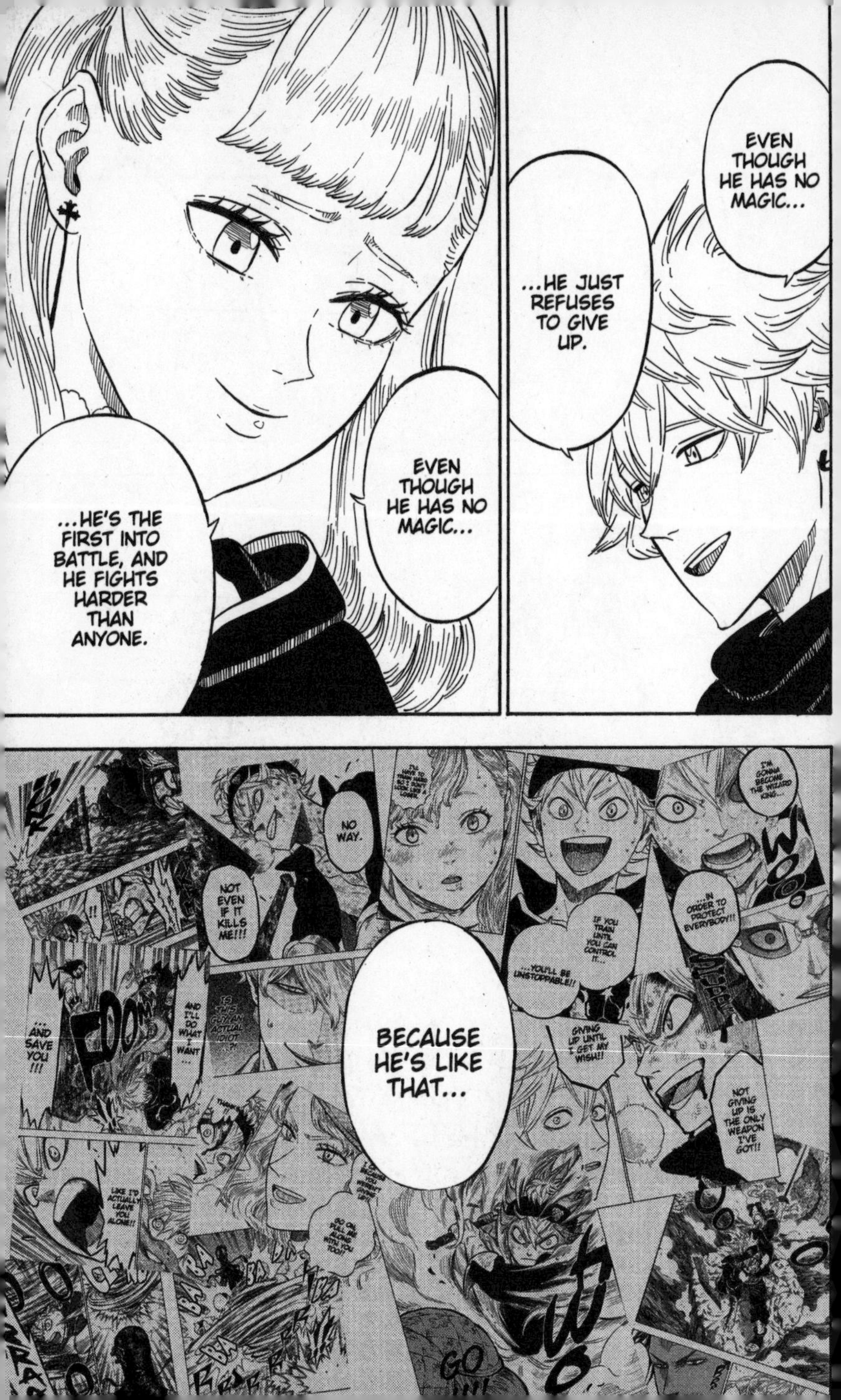

EVEN THOUGH HE HAS NO MAGIC...
...HE JUST REFUSES TO GIVE UP.
EVEN THOUGH HE HAS NO MAGIC...
...HE'S THE FIRST INTO BATTLE, AND HE FIGHTS HARDER THAN ANYONE.
I'M GONNA BECOME THE WIZARD KING...
NO WAY.
NOT EVEN IF IT KILLS ME!!!
...IN ORDER TO PROTECT EVERYBODY!!
IF YOU TRAIN UNTIL YOU CAN CONTROL IT...
...YOU'LL BE UNSTOPPABLE!!
BECAUSE HE'S LIKE THAT...
NOT GIVING UP IS THE ONLY WEAPON I'VE GOT!!
FOOM
GO

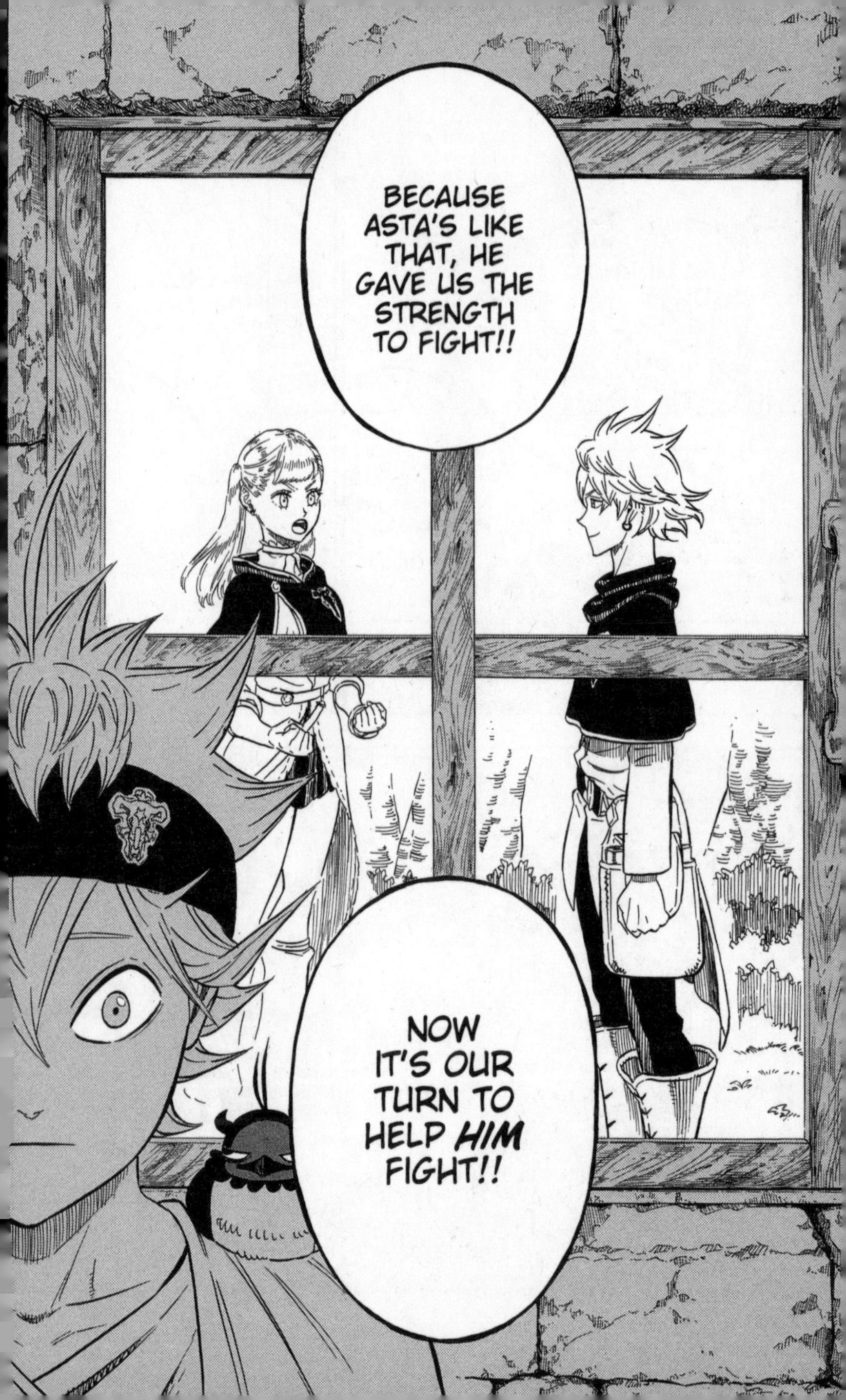
BECAUSE ASTA'S LIKE THAT, HE GAVE US THE STRENGTH TO FIGHT!!
NOW IT'S OUR TURN TO HELP *HIM* FIGHT!!

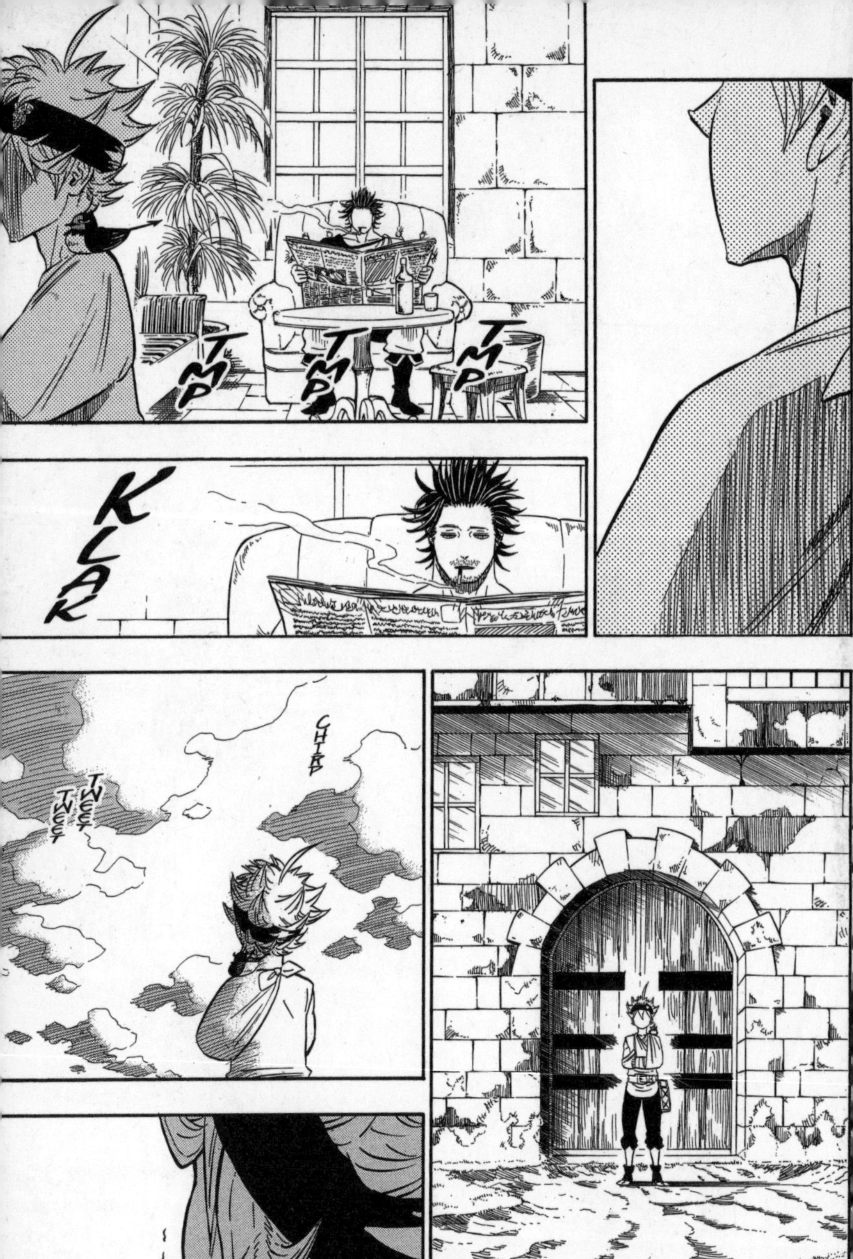
TMP
TMP
TMP
KLAK
CHIRP
TWEET
TWEET

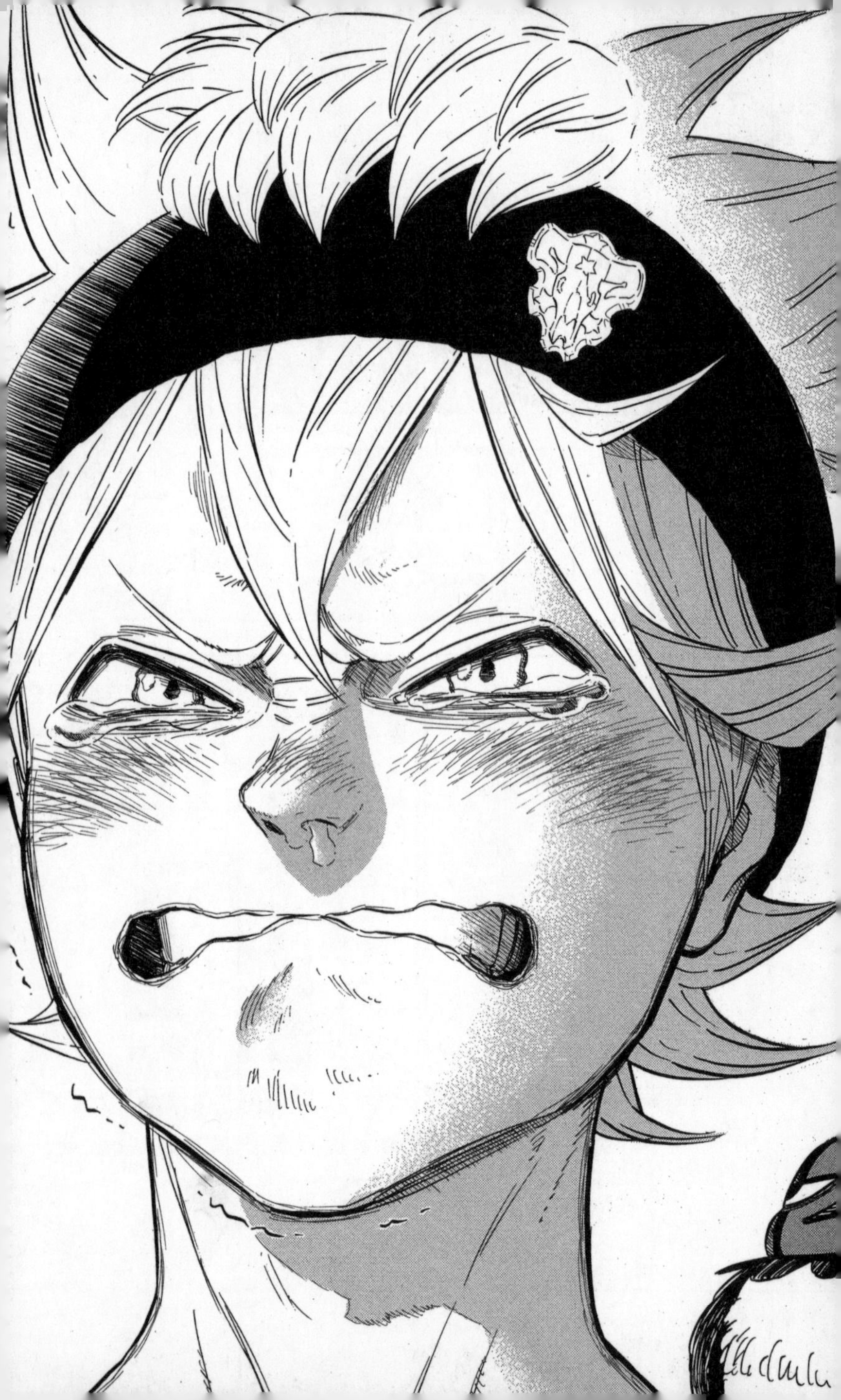

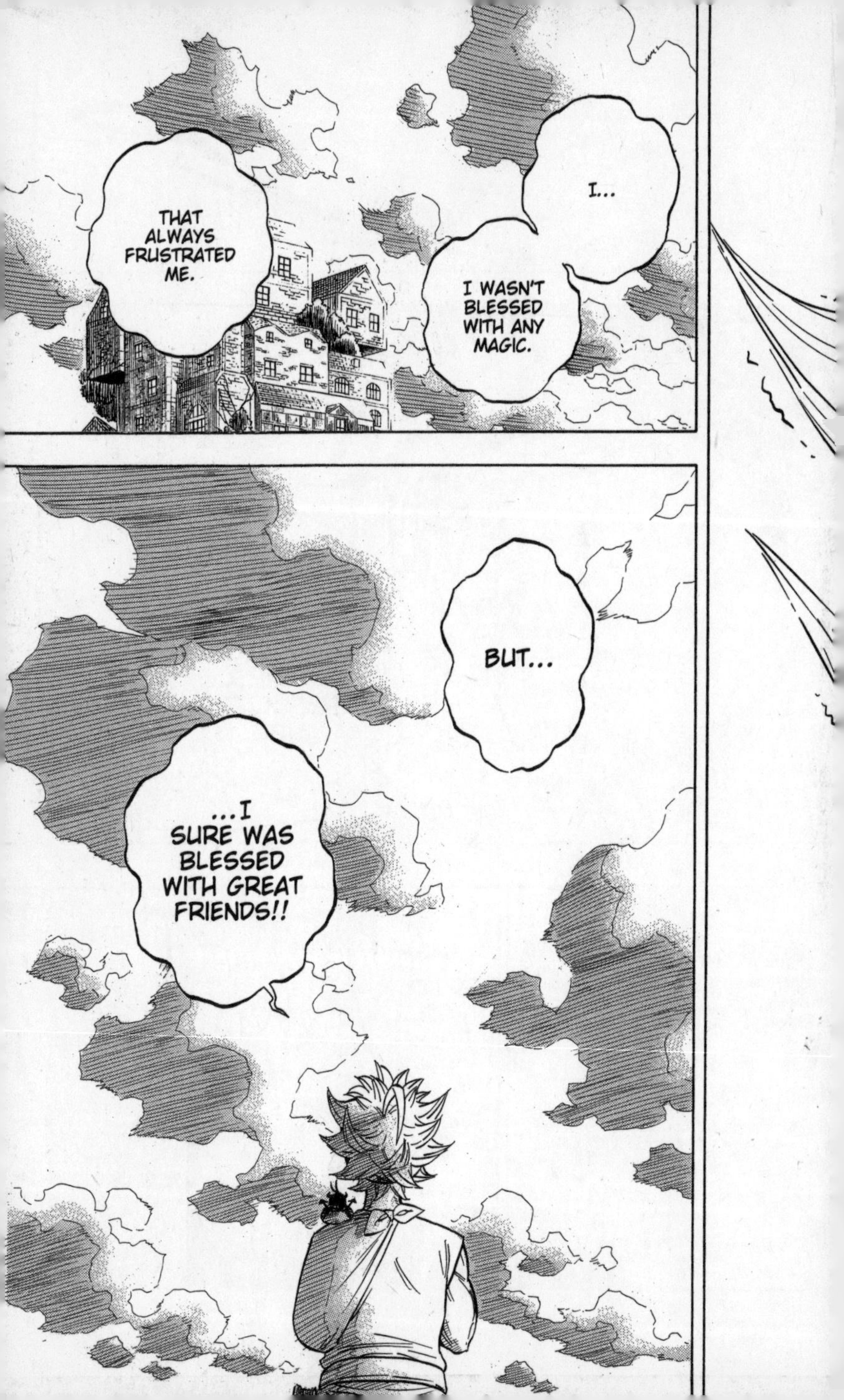
I...
I WASN'T BLESSED WITH ANY MAGIC.
THAT ALWAYS FRUSTRATED ME.
BUT...
...I SURE WAS BLESSED WITH GREAT FRIENDS!!

FOOH♪

HEH. THOSE IDIOTS.

I WISH THEY'D WORK THIS HARD AT THEIR REGULAR JOBS.

HUH?! Where are you going?!

You go anywhere you want, all by yourself.

SORRY, BUT I ALREADY HAVE SOMEWHERE I NEED YOU TO TAKE ME.

CRUNCH

LET'S GO LOOK FOR A PROMISING PLACE TOGETHER!

OKAY, MISS NOELLE!

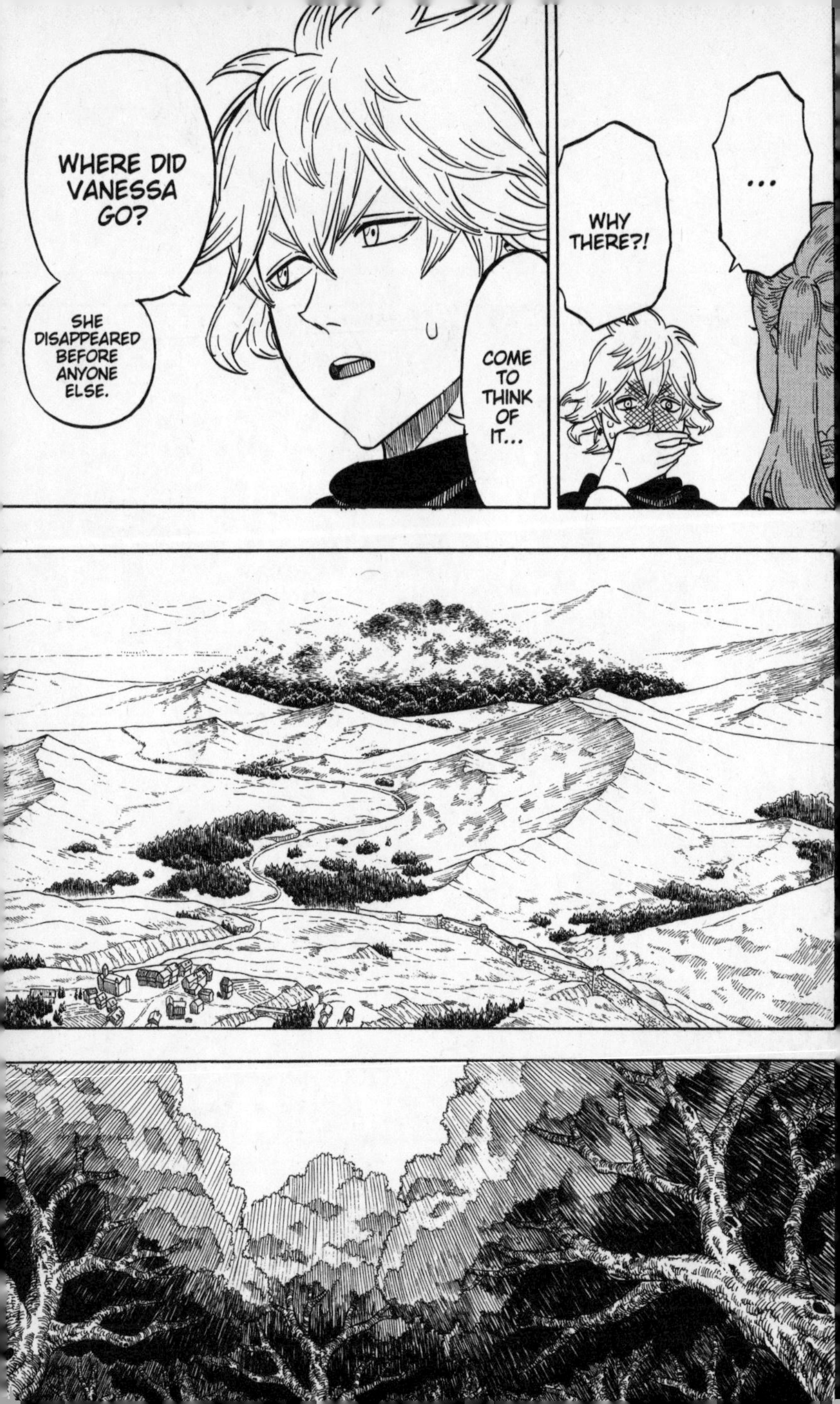
...
WHY THERE?!
COME TO THINK OF IT...
WHERE DID VANESSA GO?
SHE DISAPPEARED BEFORE ANYONE ELSE.

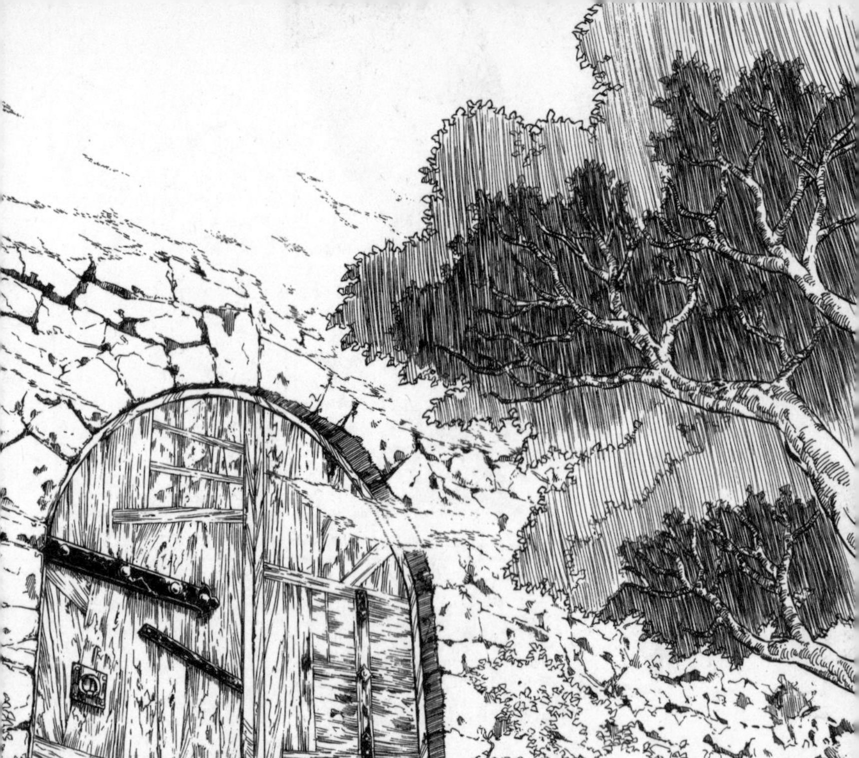

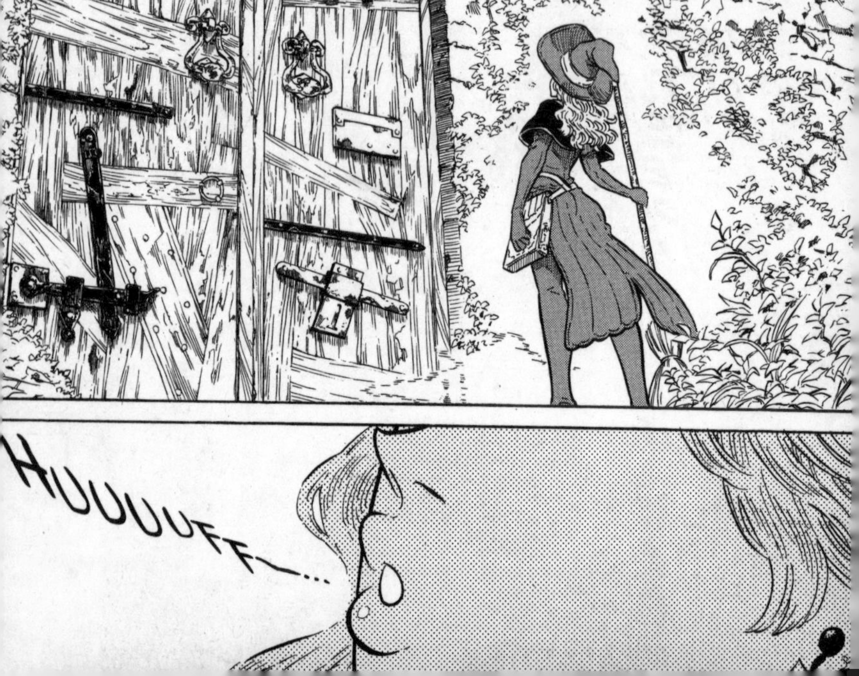
HUUUUFF...

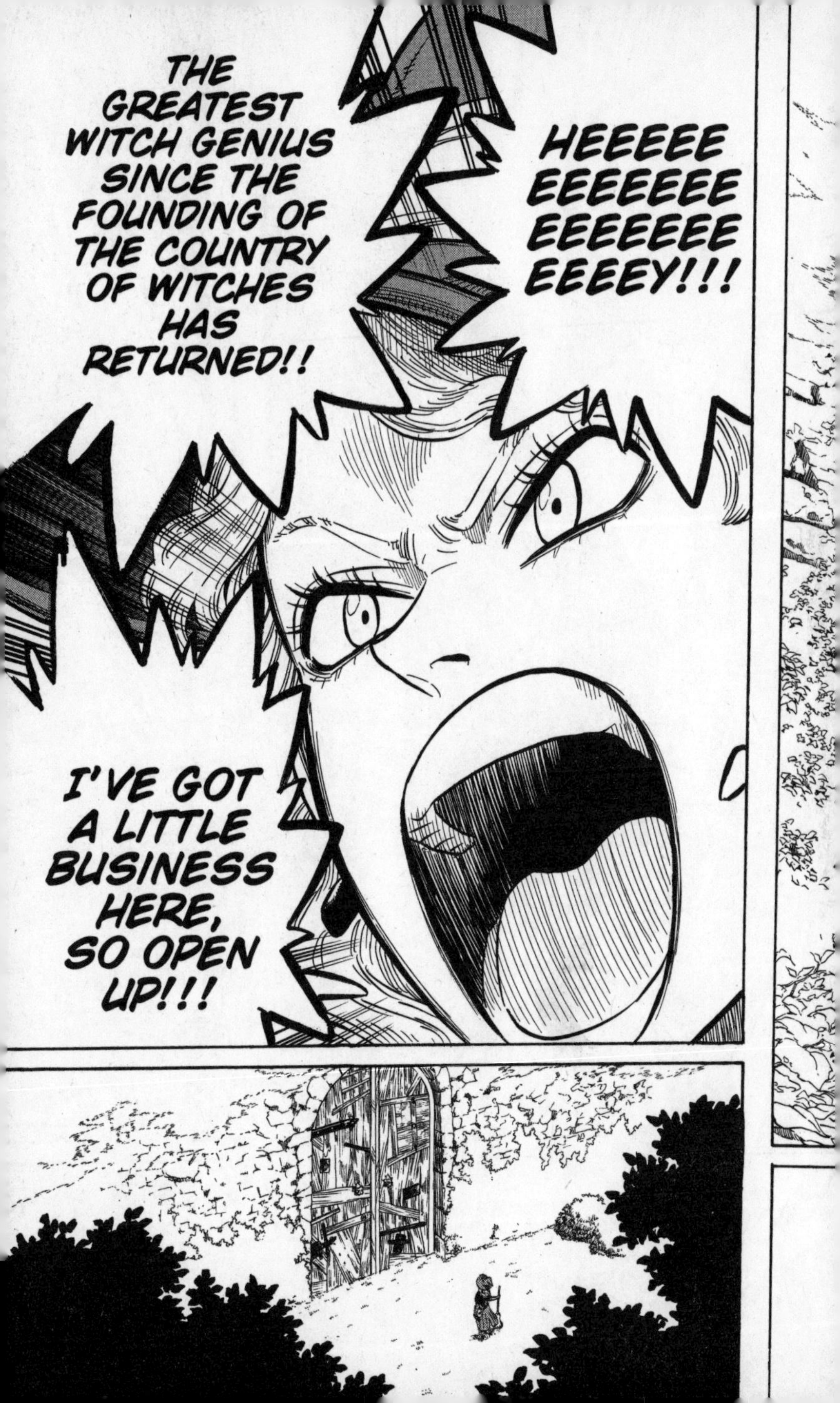
HEEEEEEEEEEEEEEEEEEEEEEEEEY!!!
THE GREATEST WITCH GENIUS SINCE THE FOUNDING OF THE COUNTRY OF WITCHES HAS RETURNED!!
I'VE GOT A LITTLE BUSINESS HERE, SO OPEN UP!!!

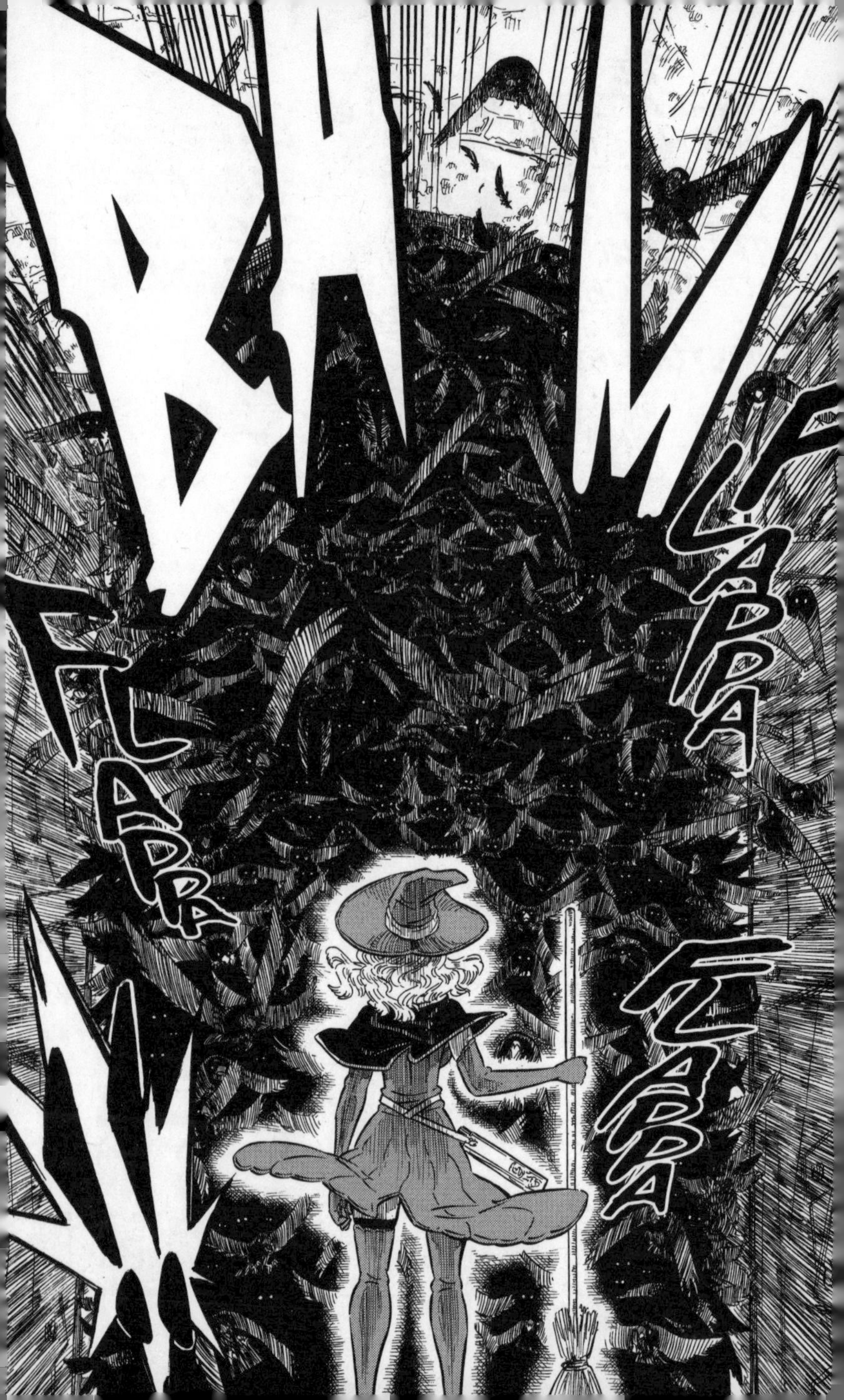
BAM
FLAPPA
FLAPPA
FLAPPA

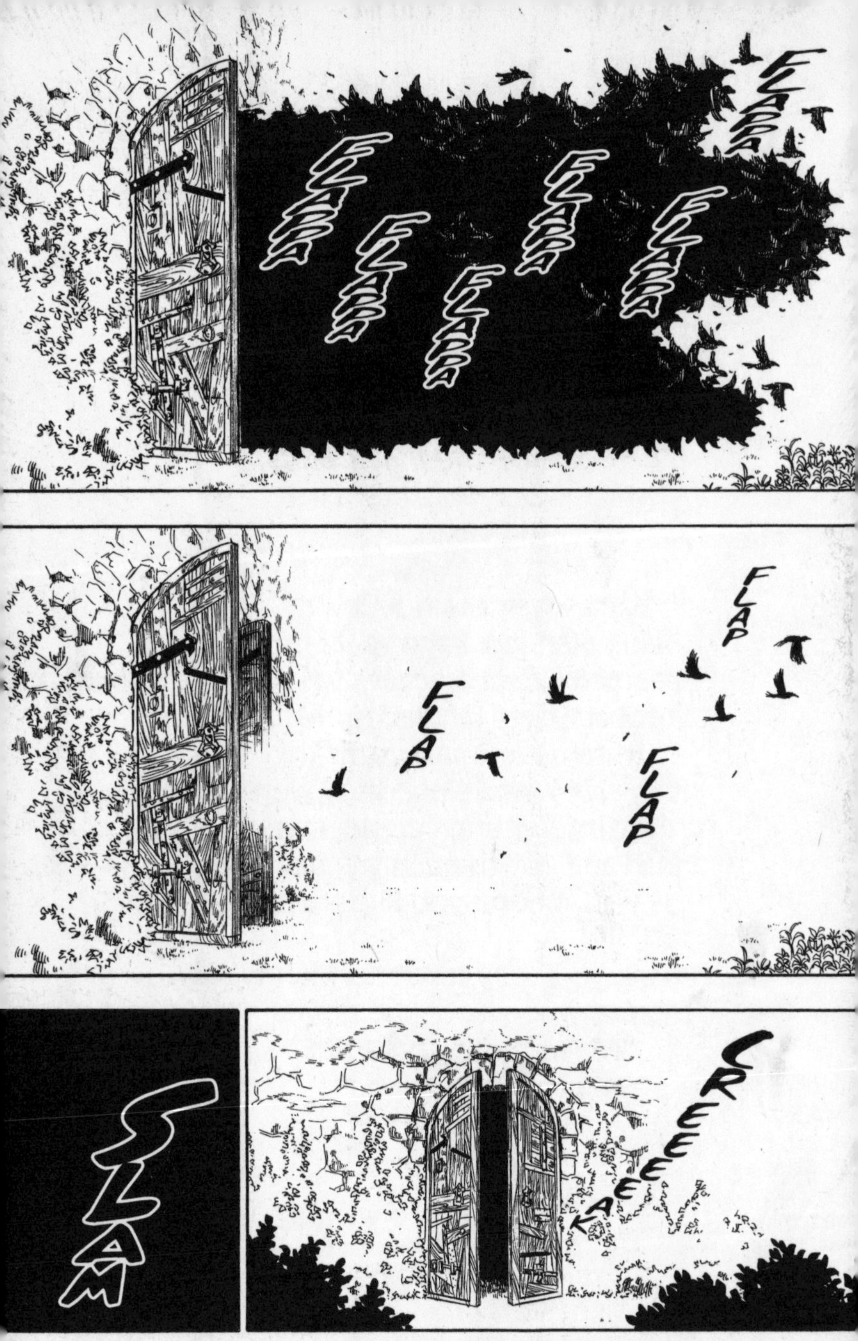
FLAPPA
FLAPPA
FLAPPA
FLAPPA
FLAPPA
FLAPPA
FLAP
FLAP
FLAP
CREEEEAK
SLAM

The three characters who make their appearance in the next chapter are from the novel *The Book of the Black Bulls*, which was released earlier in Japan.

Back when the novel was being planned, I thought they seemed like characters who'd probably get tangled up with future developments in the main story, and since they were pretty interesting people, I went ahead and put them in the manga as well. I hope you like them.

Thank you very much to Johnny Onda, who wrote the novel! (These three have brief introductions on pages 42 and 60!)

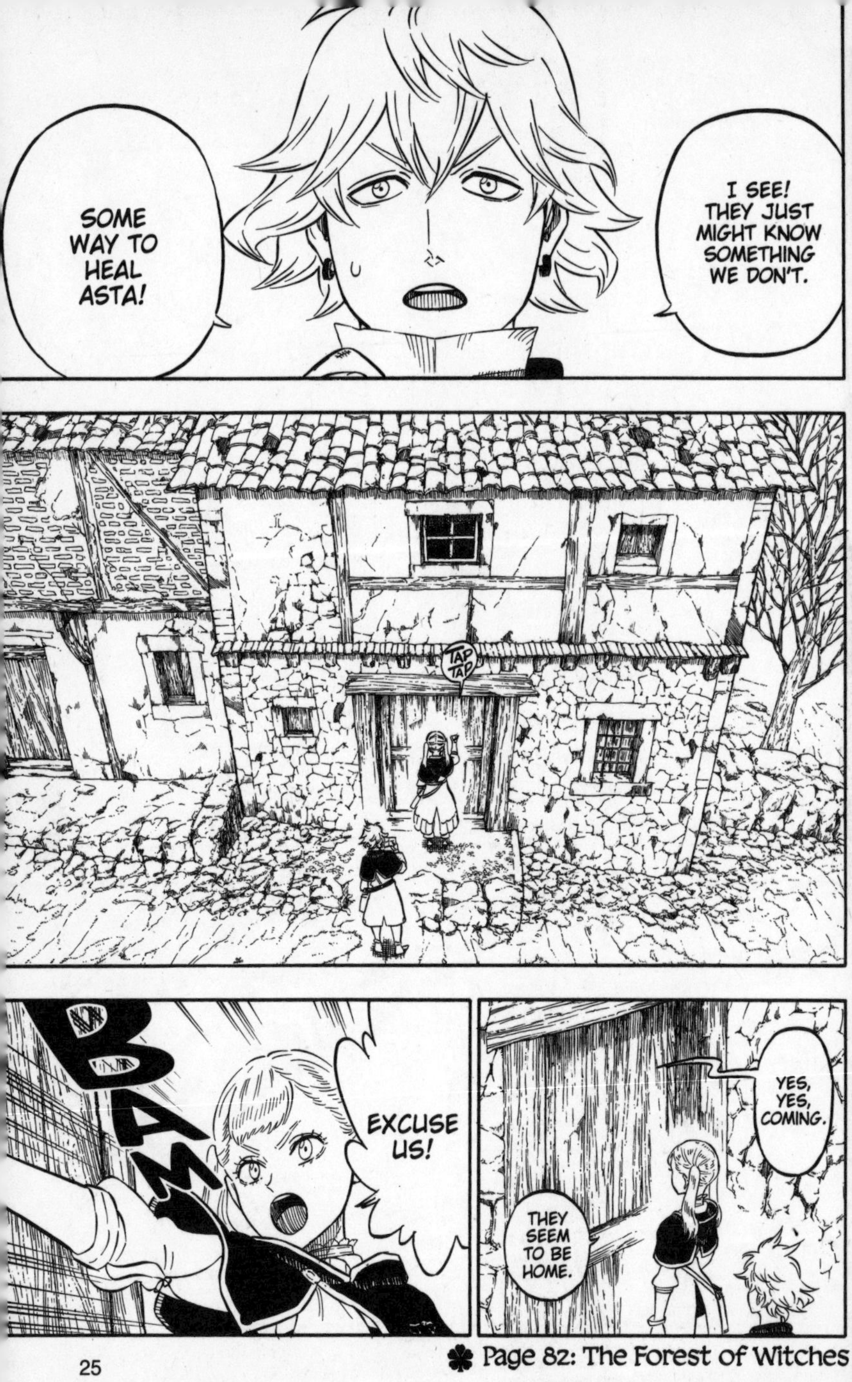
I SEE! THEY JUST MIGHT KNOW SOMETHING WE DON'T.
SOME WAY TO HEAL ASTA!
TAP TAP
YES, YES, COMING.
THEY SEEM TO BE HOME.
BAM
EXCUSE US!

Page 82: The Forest of Witches

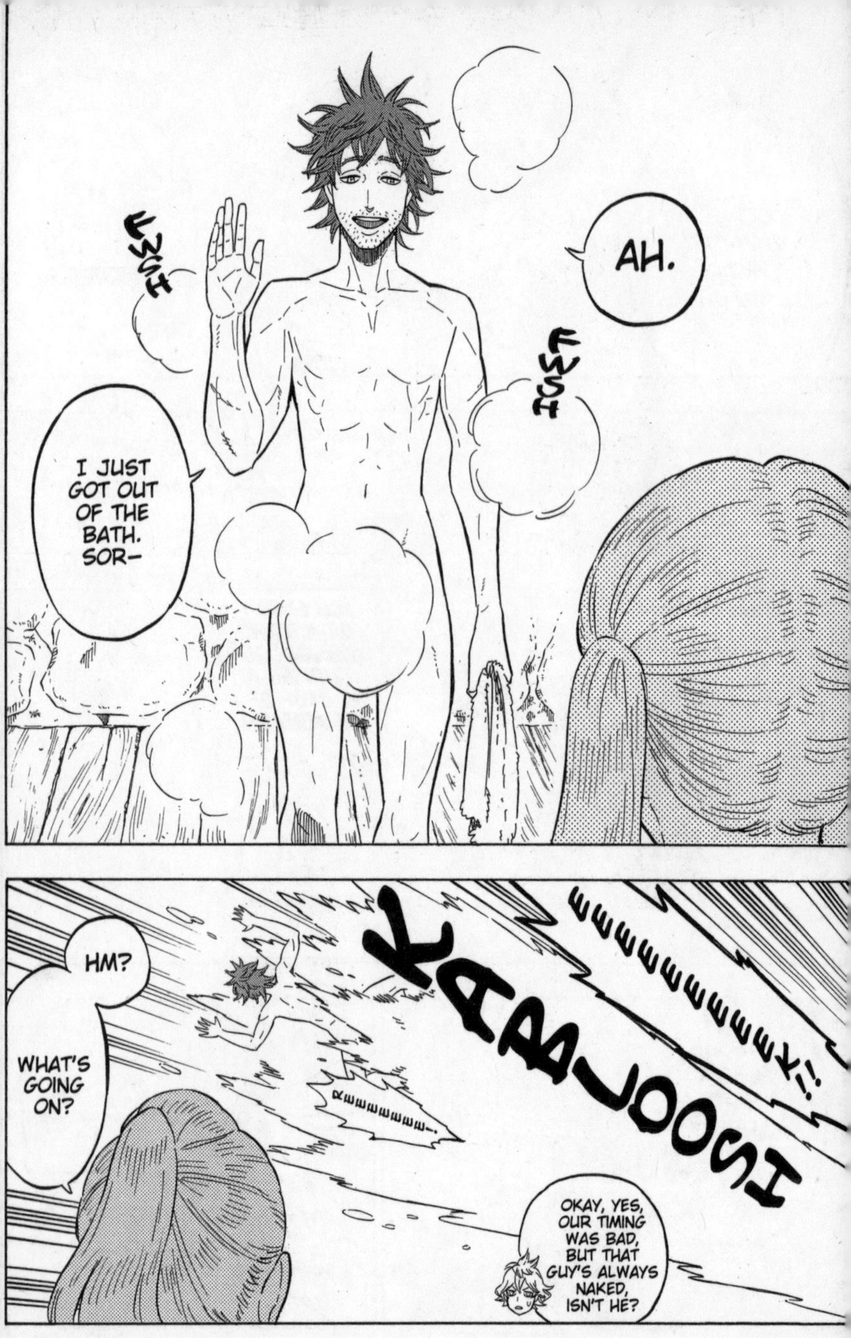
AH.
FWSH
FWSH
I JUST GOT OUT OF THE BATH. SOR-
EEEEEEEEEEEK!!
KAPLOOSH
HM?
WHAT'S GOING ON?
OKAY, YES, OUR TIMING WAS BAD, BUT THAT GUY'S ALWAYS NAKED, ISN'T HE?

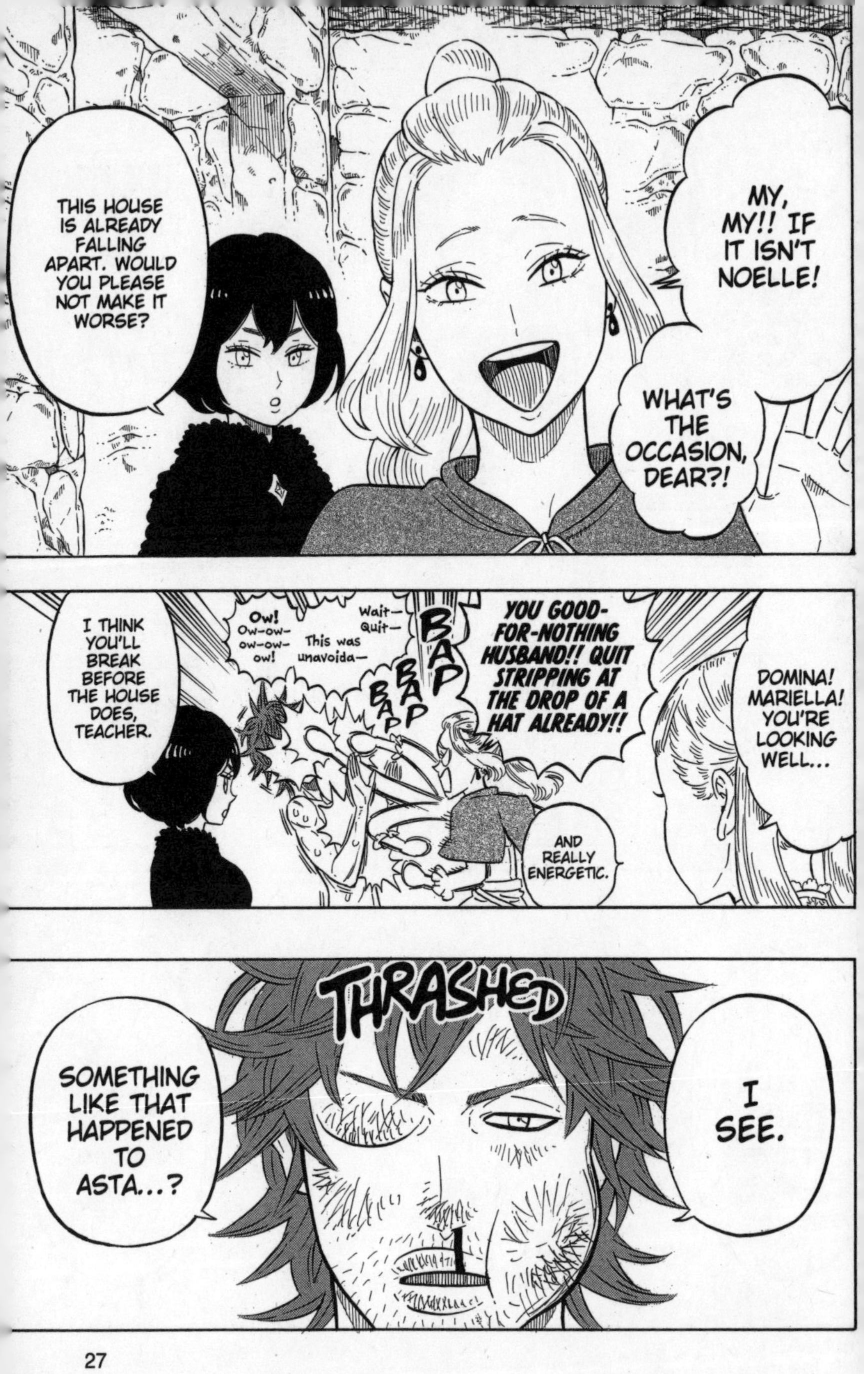
MY, MY!! IF IT ISN'T NOELLE!
WHAT'S THE OCCASION, DEAR?!
THIS HOUSE IS ALREADY FALLING APART. WOULD YOU PLEASE NOT MAKE IT WORSE?
DOMINA! MARIELLA! YOU'RE LOOKING WELL...
AND REALLY ENERGETIC.
YOU GOOD-FOR-NOTHING HUSBAND!! QUIT STRIPPING AT THE DROP OF A HAT ALREADY!!
BAP
BAP
BAP
Wait— Quit— This was unavoida—
Ow! Ow-ow-ow-ow-ow!
I THINK YOU'LL BREAK BEFORE THE HOUSE DOES, TEACHER.
I SEE.
THRASHED
SOMETHING LIKE THAT HAPPENED TO ASTA...?

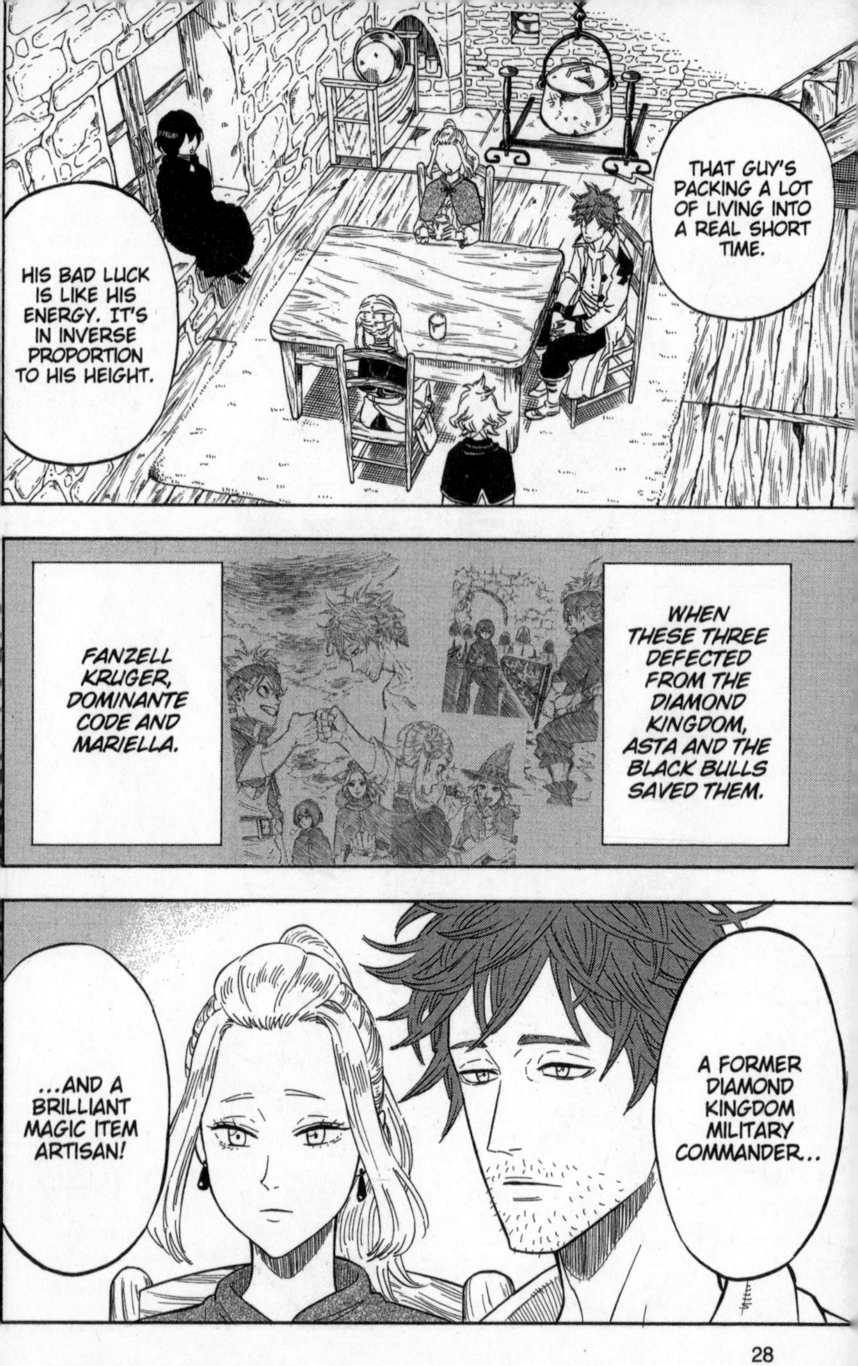
THAT GUY'S PACKING A LOT OF LIVING INTO A REAL SHORT TIME.
HIS BAD LUCK IS LIKE HIS ENERGY. IT'S IN INVERSE PROPORTION TO HIS HEIGHT.
WHEN THESE THREE DEFECTED FROM THE DIAMOND KINGDOM, ASTA AND THE BLACK BULLS SAVED THEM.
FANZELL KRUGER, DOMINANTE CODE AND MARIELLA.
A FORMER DIAMOND KINGDOM MILITARY COMMANDER...
...AND A BRILLIANT MAGIC ITEM ARTISAN!

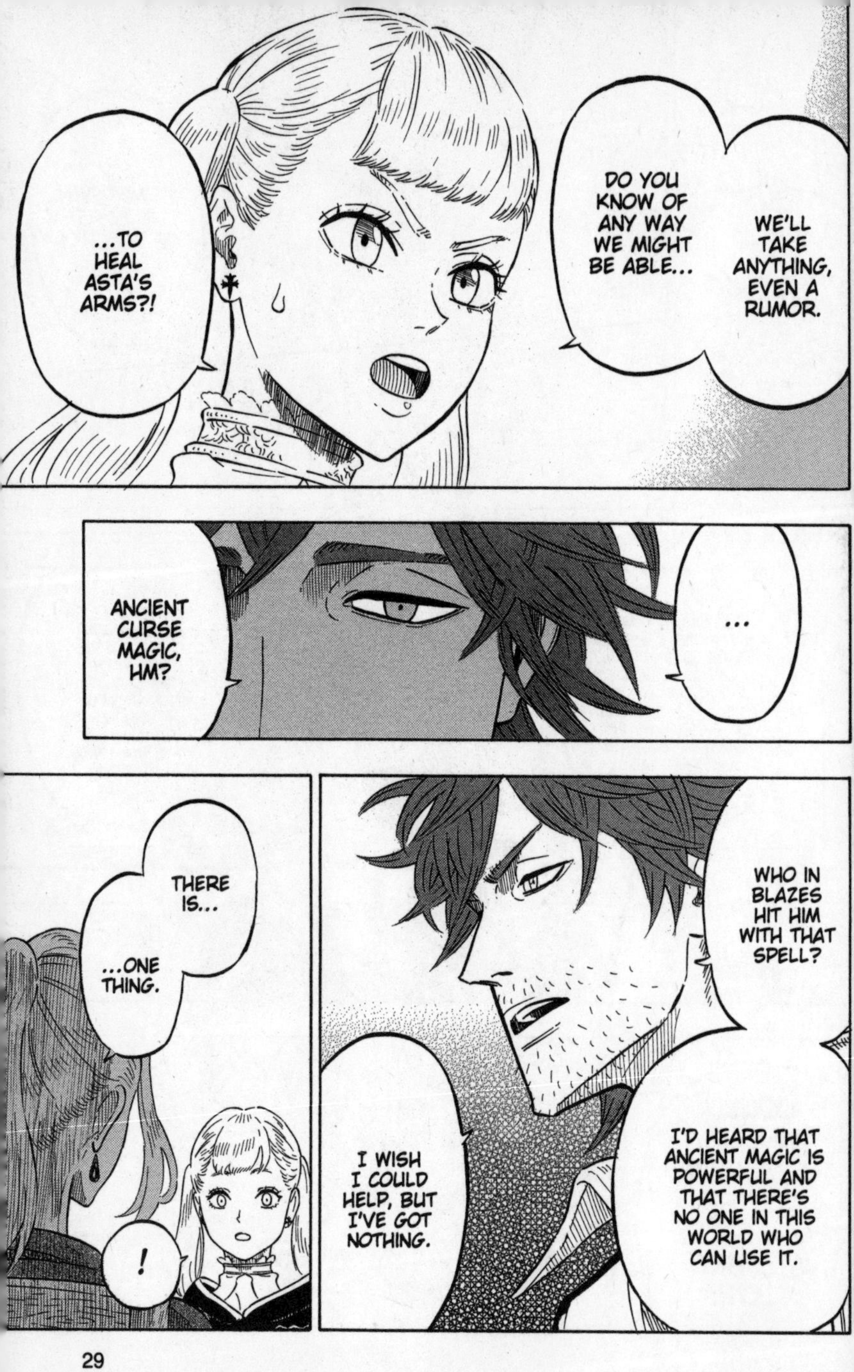

WE'LL TAKE ANYTHING, EVEN A RUMOR.
DO YOU KNOW OF ANY WAY WE MIGHT BE ABLE...
...TO HEAL ASTA'S ARMS?!
...
ANCIENT CURSE MAGIC, HM?
WHO IN BLAZES HIT HIM WITH THAT SPELL?
I'D HEARD THAT ANCIENT MAGIC IS POWERFUL AND THAT THERE'S NO ONE IN THIS WORLD WHO CAN USE IT.
I WISH I COULD HELP, BUT I'VE GOT NOTHING.
THERE IS...
...ONE THING.
!

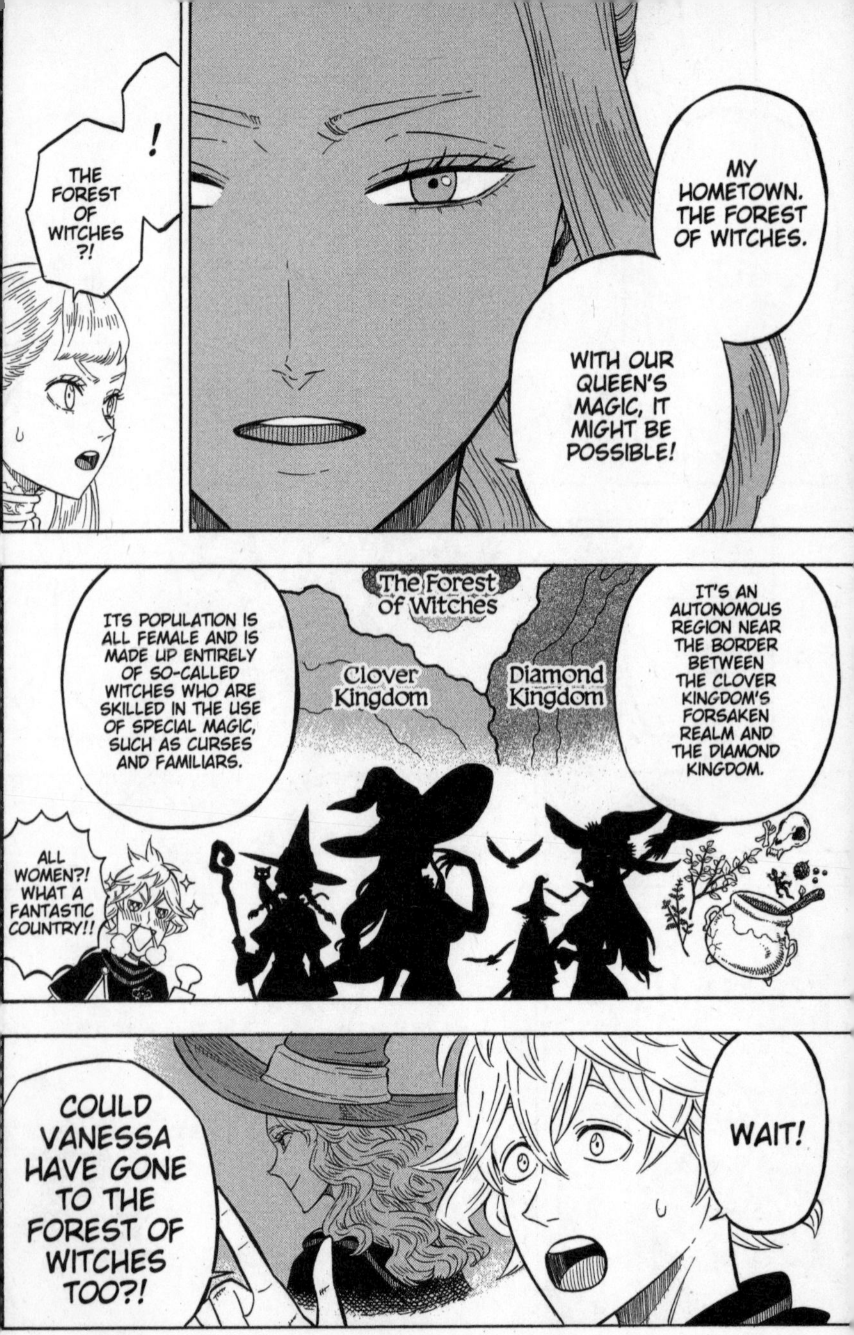
MY HOMETOWN. THE FOREST OF WITCHES.
WITH OUR QUEEN'S MAGIC, IT MIGHT BE POSSIBLE!
!
THE FOREST OF WITCHES ?!
The Forest of Witches
Diamond Kingdom
Clover Kingdom
IT'S AN AUTONOMOUS REGION NEAR THE BORDER BETWEEN THE CLOVER KINGDOM'S FORSAKEN REALM AND THE DIAMOND KINGDOM.
ITS POPULATION IS ALL FEMALE AND IS MADE UP ENTIRELY OF SO-CALLED WITCHES WHO ARE SKILLED IN THE USE OF SPECIAL MAGIC, SUCH AS CURSES AND FAMILIARS.
ALL WOMEN?! WHAT A FANTASTIC COUNTRY!!
WAIT!
COULD VANESSA HAVE GONE TO THE FOREST OF WITCHES TOO?!

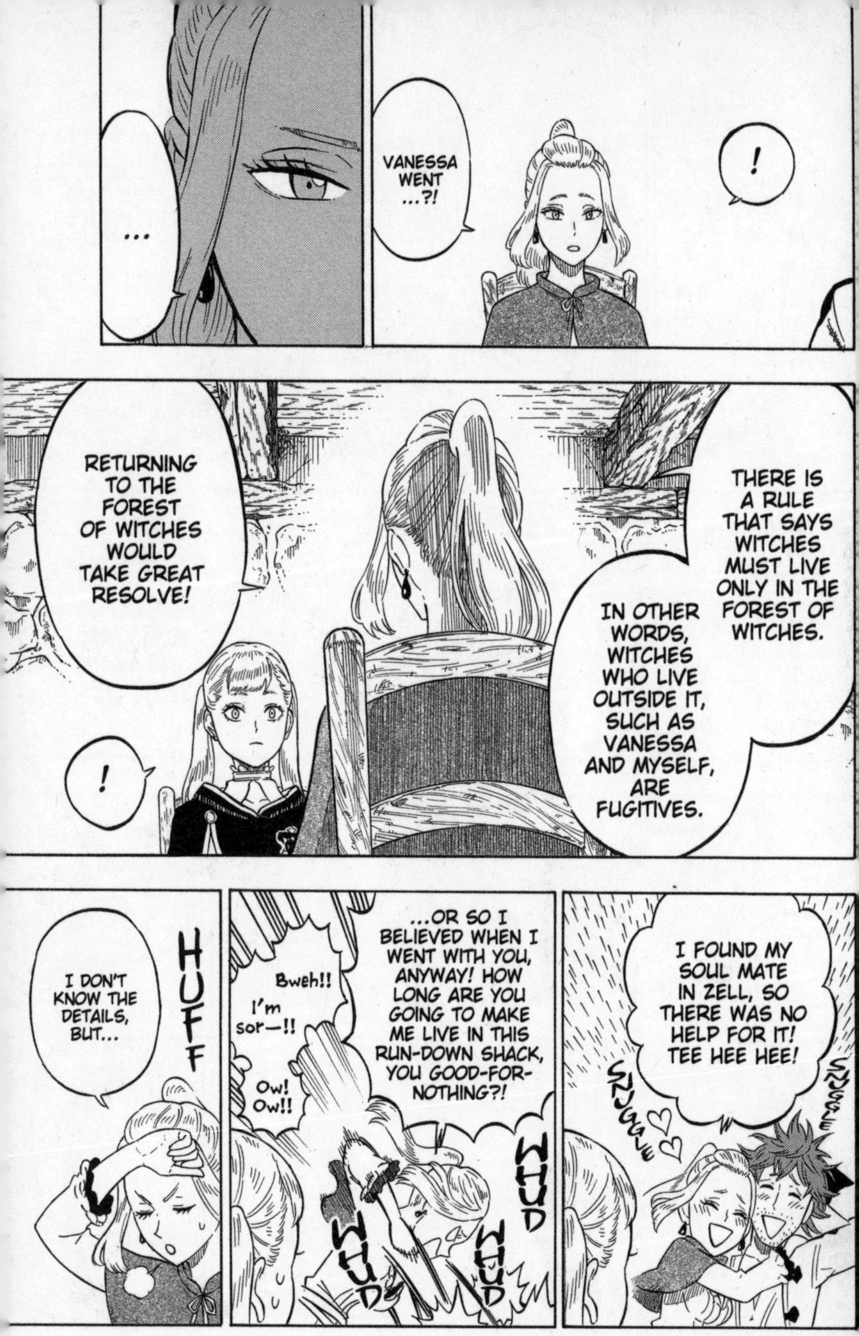
!
VANESSA WENT ...?!
...
THERE IS A RULE THAT SAYS WITCHES MUST LIVE ONLY IN THE FOREST OF WITCHES.
IN OTHER WORDS, WITCHES WHO LIVE OUTSIDE IT, SUCH AS VANESSA AND MYSELF, ARE FUGITIVES.
RETURNING TO THE FOREST OF WITCHES WOULD TAKE GREAT RESOLVE!
!
I FOUND MY SOUL MATE IN ZELL, SO THERE WAS NO HELP FOR IT! TEE HEE HEE!
SNUGGLE
SNUGGLE
...OR SO I BELIEVED WHEN I WENT WITH YOU, ANYWAY! HOW LONG ARE YOU GOING TO MAKE ME LIVE IN THIS RUN-DOWN SHACK, YOU GOOD-FOR-NOTHING?!
WHUD
Bweh!!
I'm sor—!!
Ow! Ow!!
WHUD
WHUD
HUFF
I DON'T KNOW THE DETAILS, BUT...

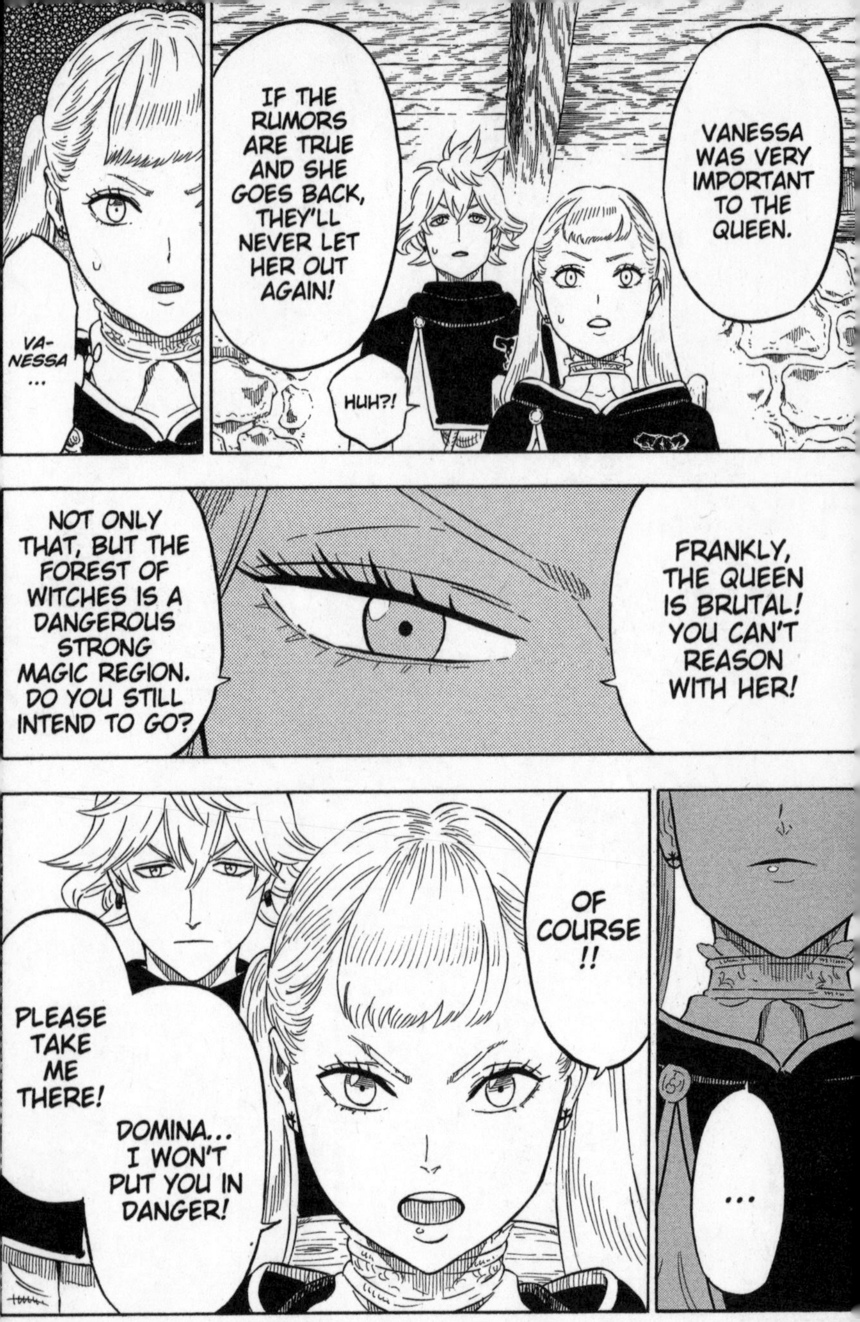
VANESSA WAS VERY IMPORTANT TO THE QUEEN.
IF THE RUMORS ARE TRUE AND SHE GOES BACK, THEY'LL NEVER LET HER OUT AGAIN!
HUH?!
VA-NESSA ...
FRANKLY, THE QUEEN IS BRUTAL! YOU CAN'T REASON WITH HER!
NOT ONLY THAT, BUT THE FOREST OF WITCHES IS A DANGEROUS STRONG MAGIC REGION. DO YOU STILL INTEND TO GO?
...
OF COURSE!!
PLEASE TAKE ME THERE!
DOMINA... I WON'T PUT YOU IN DANGER!

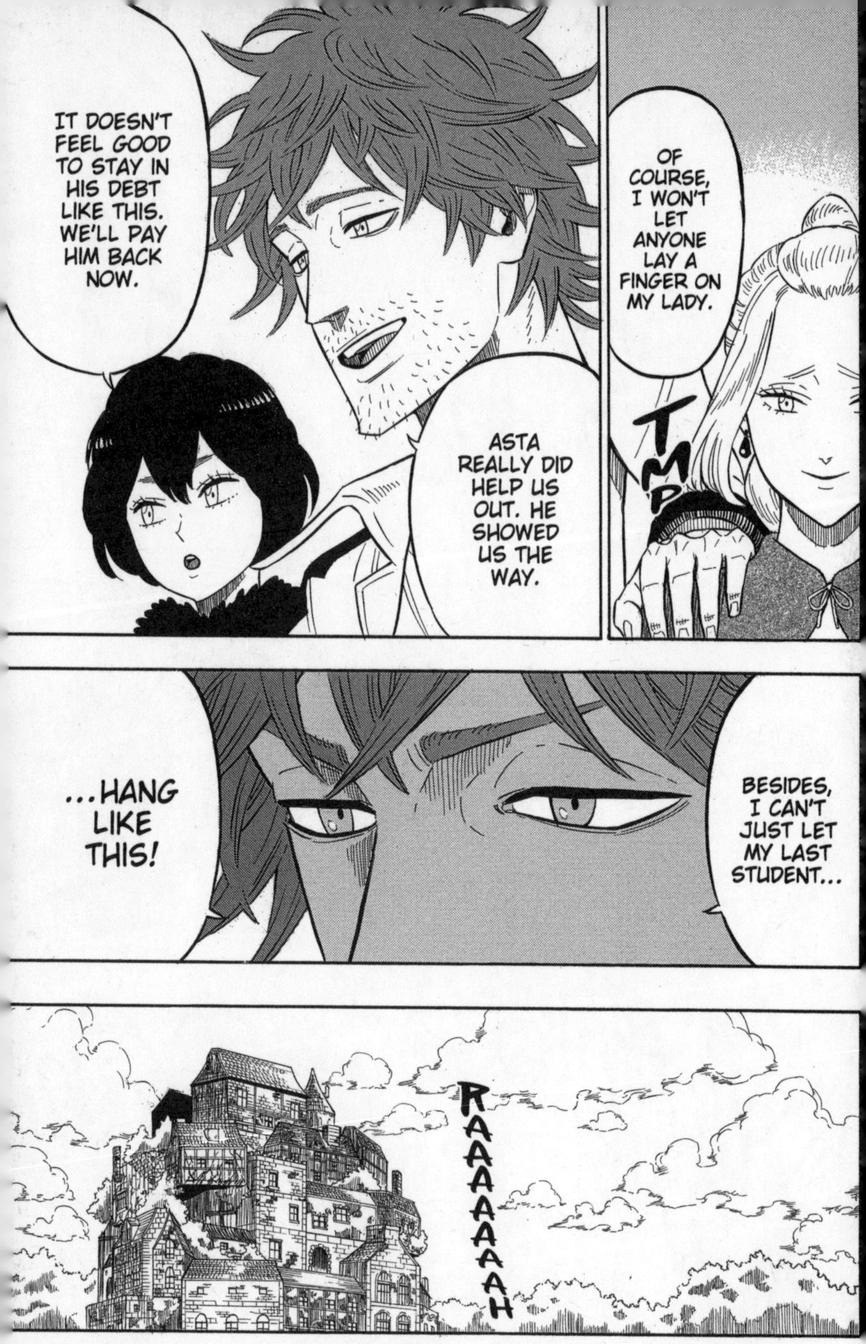
OF COURSE, I WON'T LET ANYONE LAY A FINGER ON MY LADY.
TMP
ASTA REALLY DID HELP US OUT. HE SHOWED US THE WAY.
IT DOESN'T FEEL GOOD TO STAY IN HIS DEBT LIKE THIS. WE'LL PAY HIM BACK NOW.
BESIDES, I CAN'T JUST LET MY LAST STUDENT...
...HANG LIKE THIS!
RAAAAAAAH

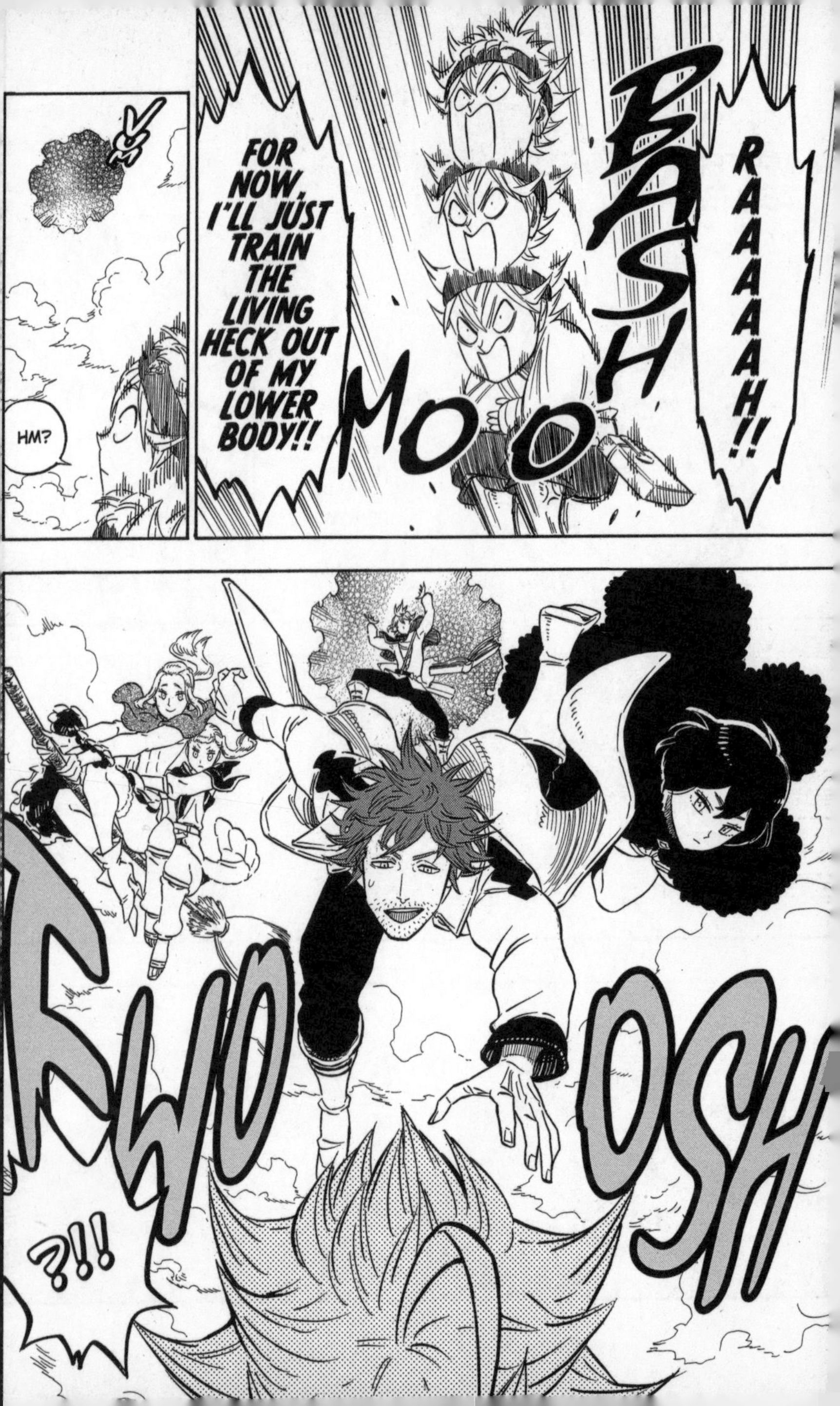
RAAAAAAH!!
BASH
FOR NOW, I'LL JUST TRAIN THE LIVING HECK OUT OF MY LOWER BODY!!
MOO
VM
HM?
FWOOSH
?!!

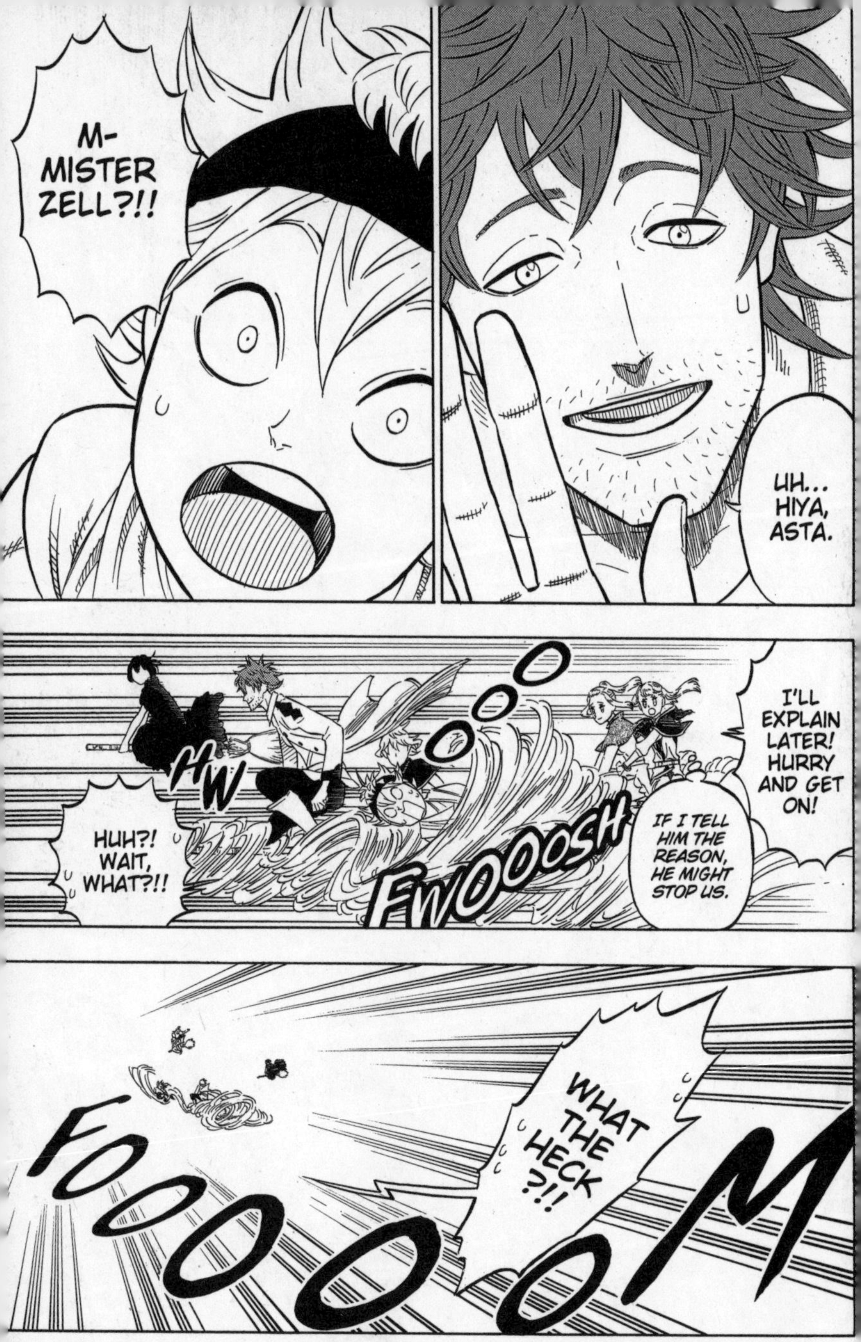
UH... HIYA, ASTA.
M-MISTER ZELL?!!
I'LL EXPLAIN LATER! HURRY AND GET ON!
IF I TELL HIM THE REASON, HE MIGHT STOP US.
FWOOOOSH
HW
HUH?! WAIT, WHAT?!!
WHAT THE HECK ?!!
FOOOOOM

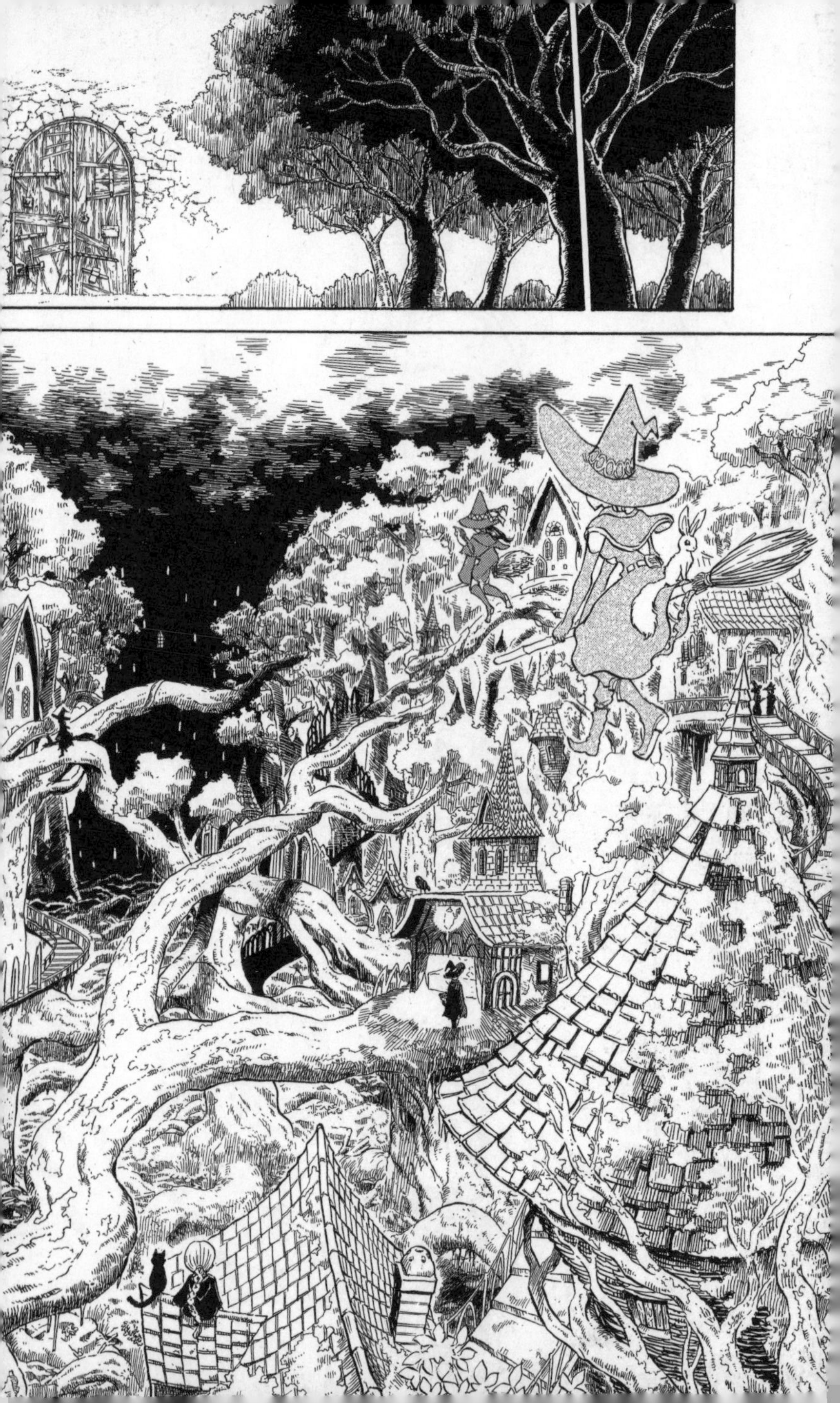

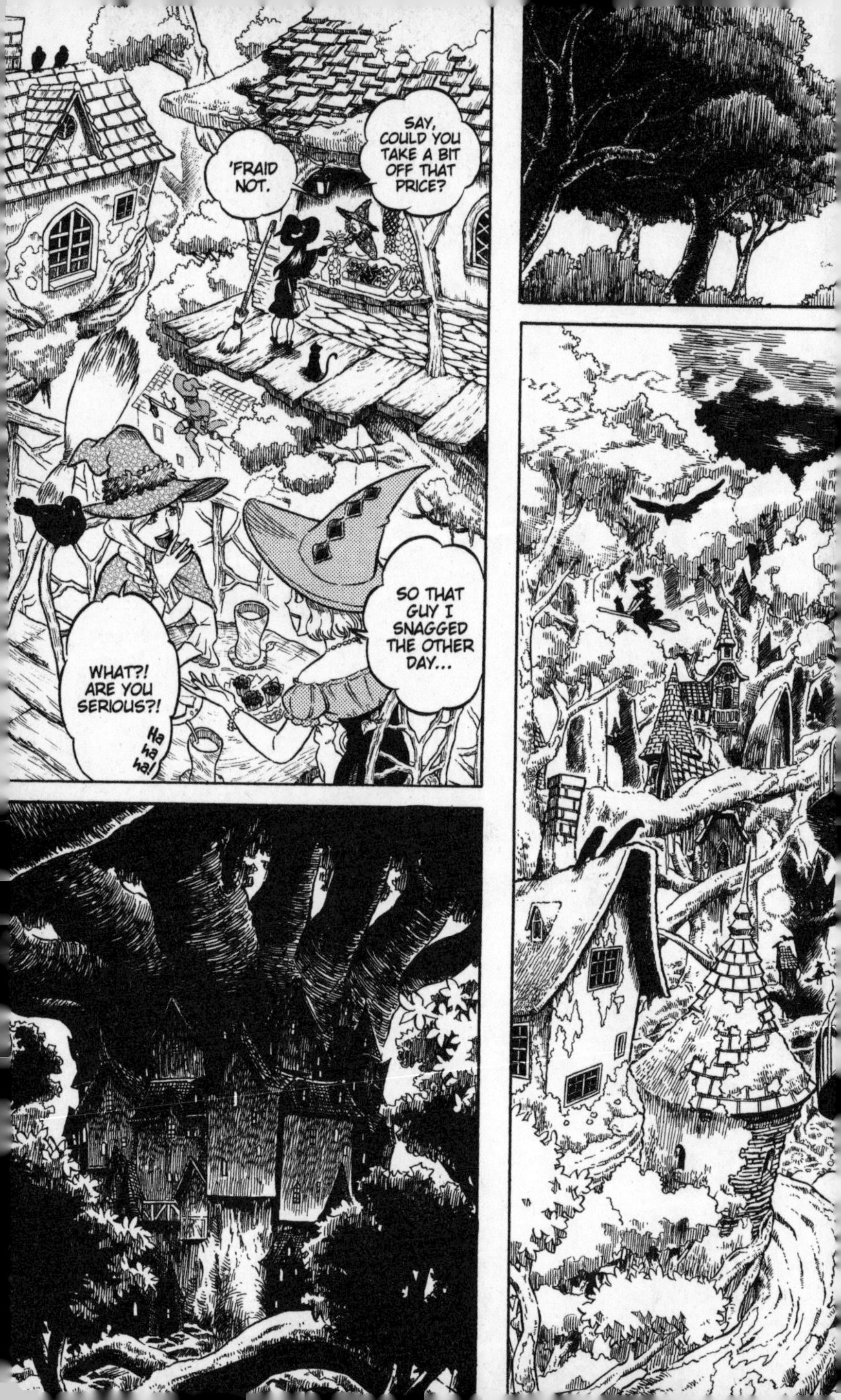
SAY, COULD YOU TAKE A BIT OFF THAT PRICE?
'FRAID NOT.
SO THAT GUY I SNAGGED THE OTHER DAY...
WHAT?! ARE YOU SERIOUS?!
Ha ha ha!

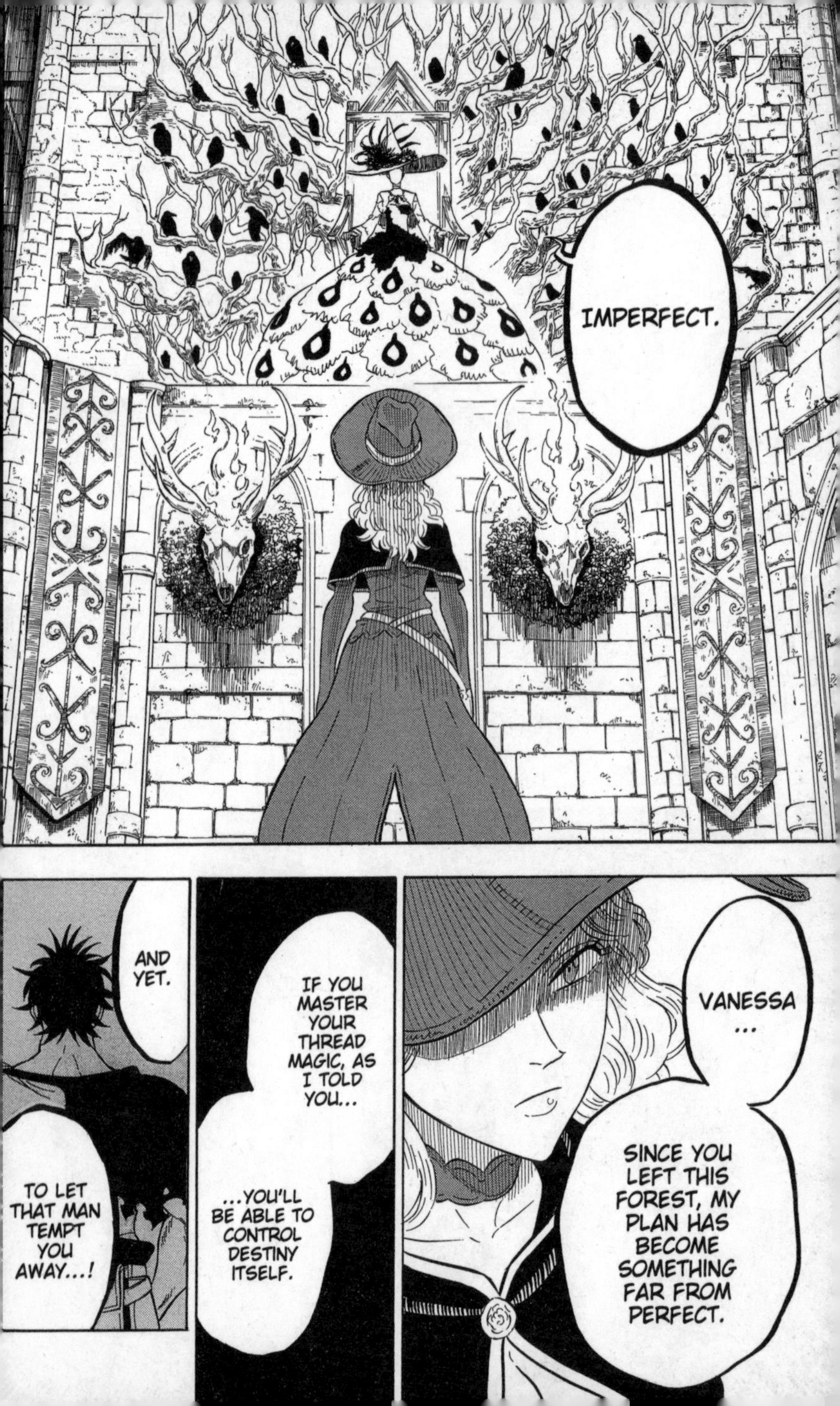
IMPERFECT.
VANESSA ...
SINCE YOU LEFT THIS FOREST, MY PLAN HAS BECOME SOMETHING FAR FROM PERFECT.
IF YOU MASTER YOUR THREAD MAGIC, AS I TOLD YOU...
...YOU'LL BE ABLE TO CONTROL DESTINY ITSELF.
AND YET.
TO LET THAT MAN TEMPT YOU AWAY...!

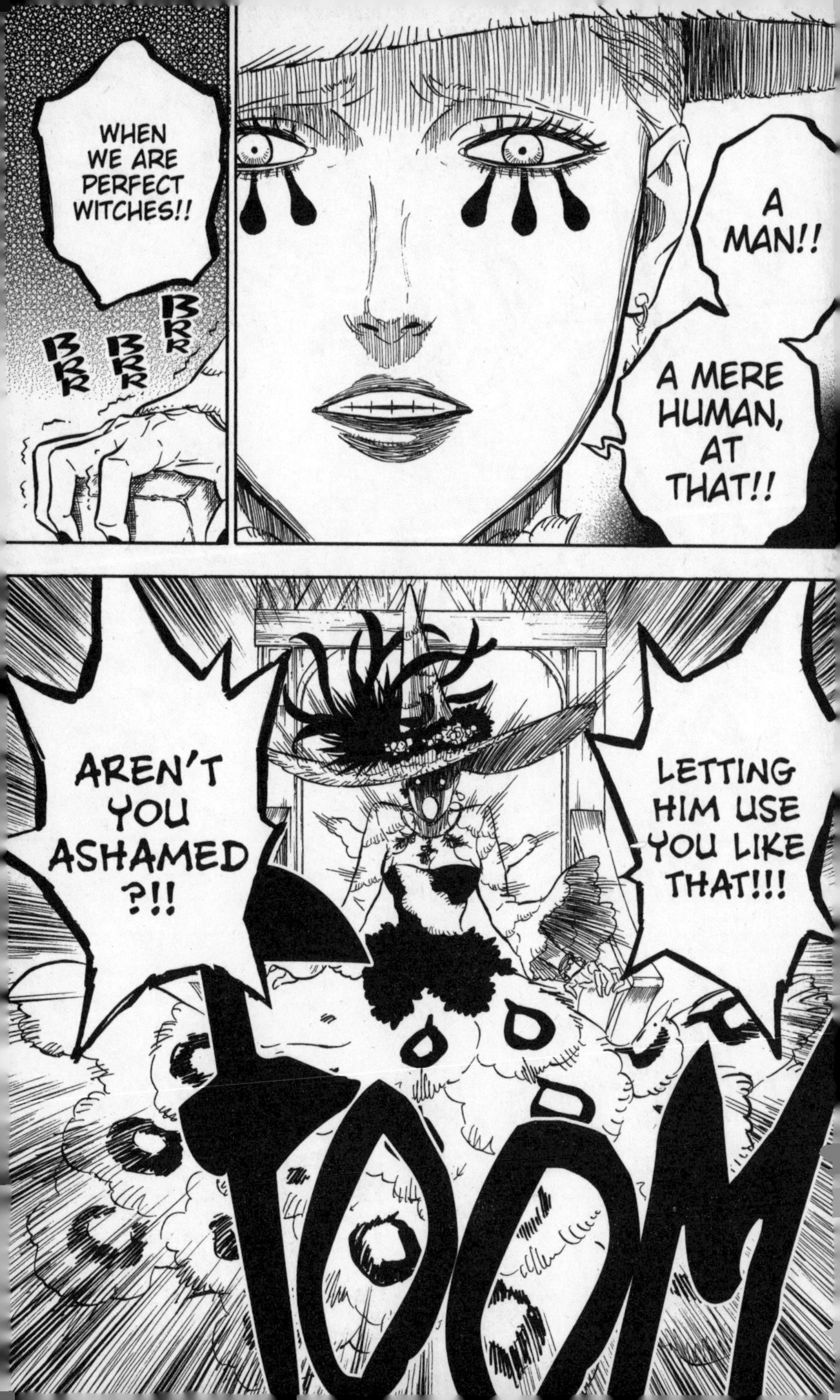
A MAN!!
A MERE HUMAN, AT THAT!!
WHEN WE ARE PERFECT WITCHES!!
BRR
BRR
BRR
LETTING HIM USE YOU LIKE THAT!!!
AREN'T YOU ASHAMED?!!
BOOM

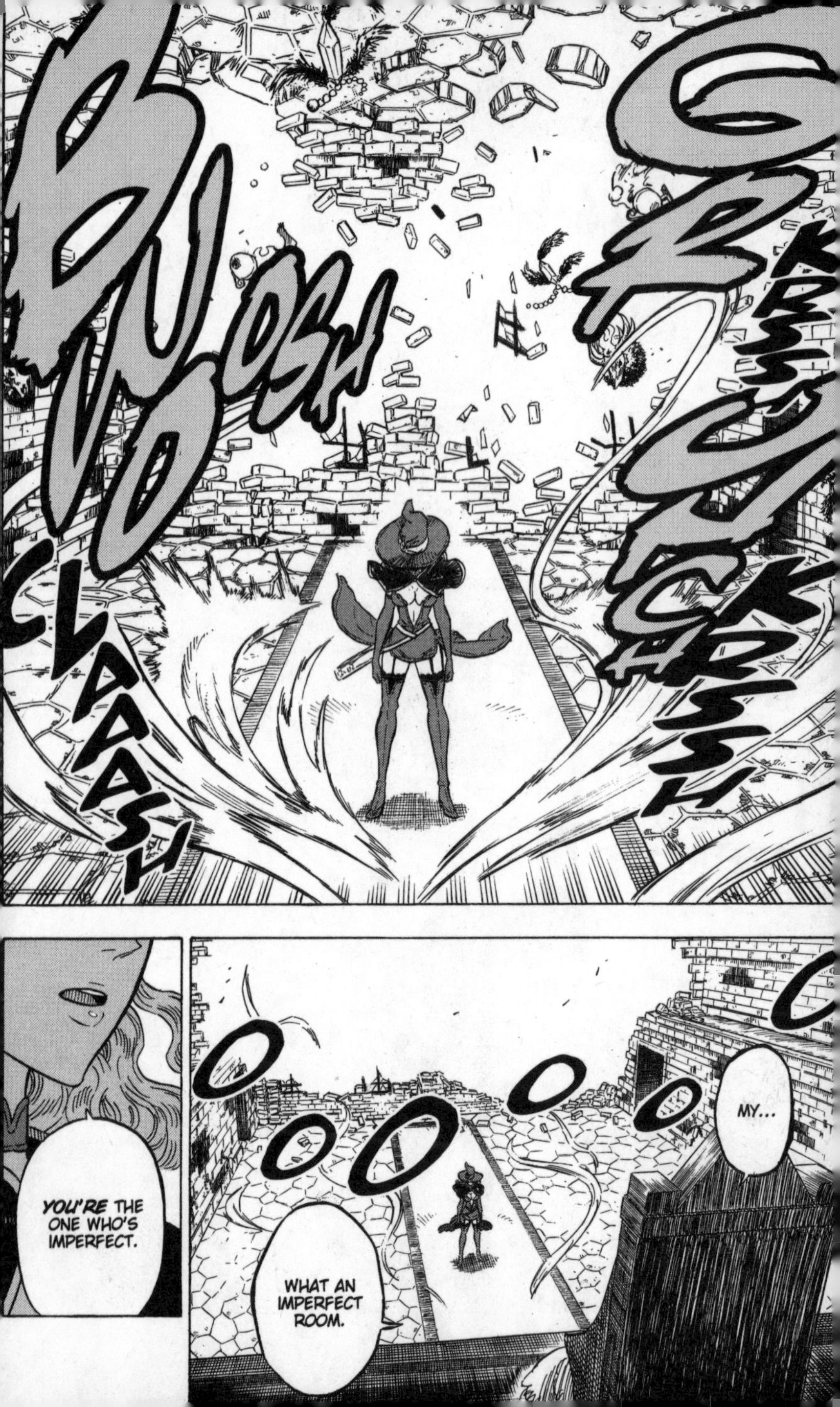
MY...
WHAT AN IMPERFECT ROOM.
YOU'RE THE ONE WHO'S IMPERFECT.

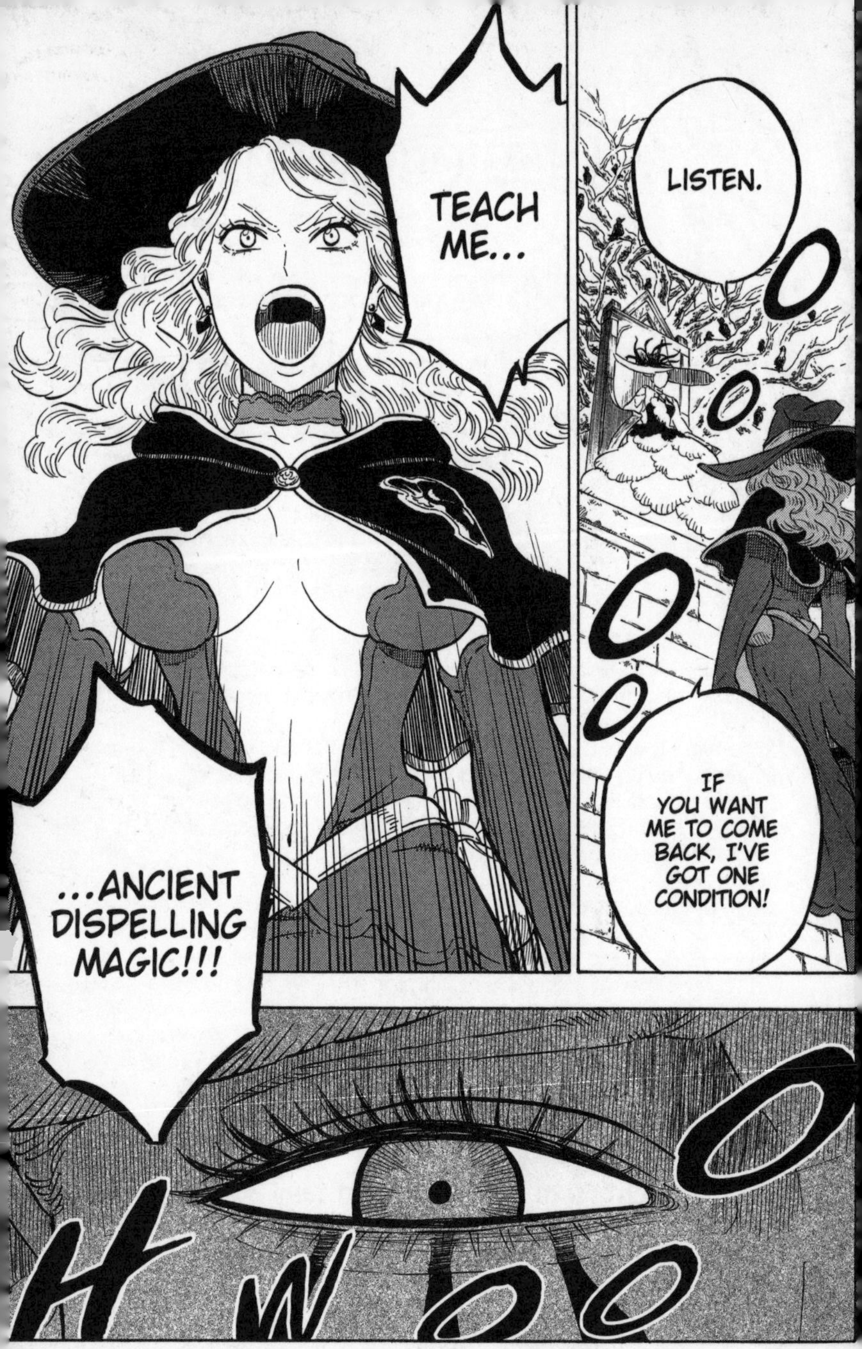
LISTEN.
IF YOU WANT ME TO COME BACK, I'VE GOT ONE CONDITION!
TEACH ME...
...ANCIENT DISPELLING MAGIC!!!
HWOOO

Magic Knight Brigade
The Black Bulls

Mission Report

○ Month × Day

Reporter: Finral Roulacase

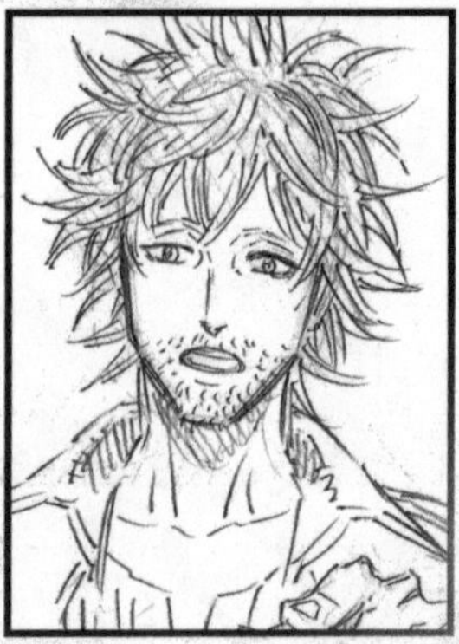

Diamond Kingdom Army Former Adviser

Fanzell Kruger

Former Diamond Kingdom Army adviser.
Age 28.
Male. Wind magic user.
He fights with a physical sword which he cloaks in magic.
For some reason, his clothes frequently come off.

He worked for the military as a mage soldier instructor, but he rejected the army's ideas and fled to the Clover Kingdom.

While lying low in the village of Hage in the Forsaken Realm, he happened to run into Asta, a member of our brigade. He kept his identity hidden, but seems to have taught Asta his own sword skills for a little while. Then Fanzell and Asta fought and defeated a Diamond assassination unit that was after Fanzell.

Later, when they stopped by our brigade's hideout, they were attacked by the assassination unit again. The conflict turned into a large-scale magic battle that pulled in our brigade members as well, but he fought alongside us, and together we routed the enemy.

At present, he is lying low in the Clover Kingdom, living in exile with Domina, his fiancée from the Diamond Kingdom, and his student Mariella.

♣ A comment from brigade captain Yami Sukehiro

I told you that reporting this incident will make things annoyingly complicated, so keep quiet about it.

Write another one and I'll kill you. Burn this report.

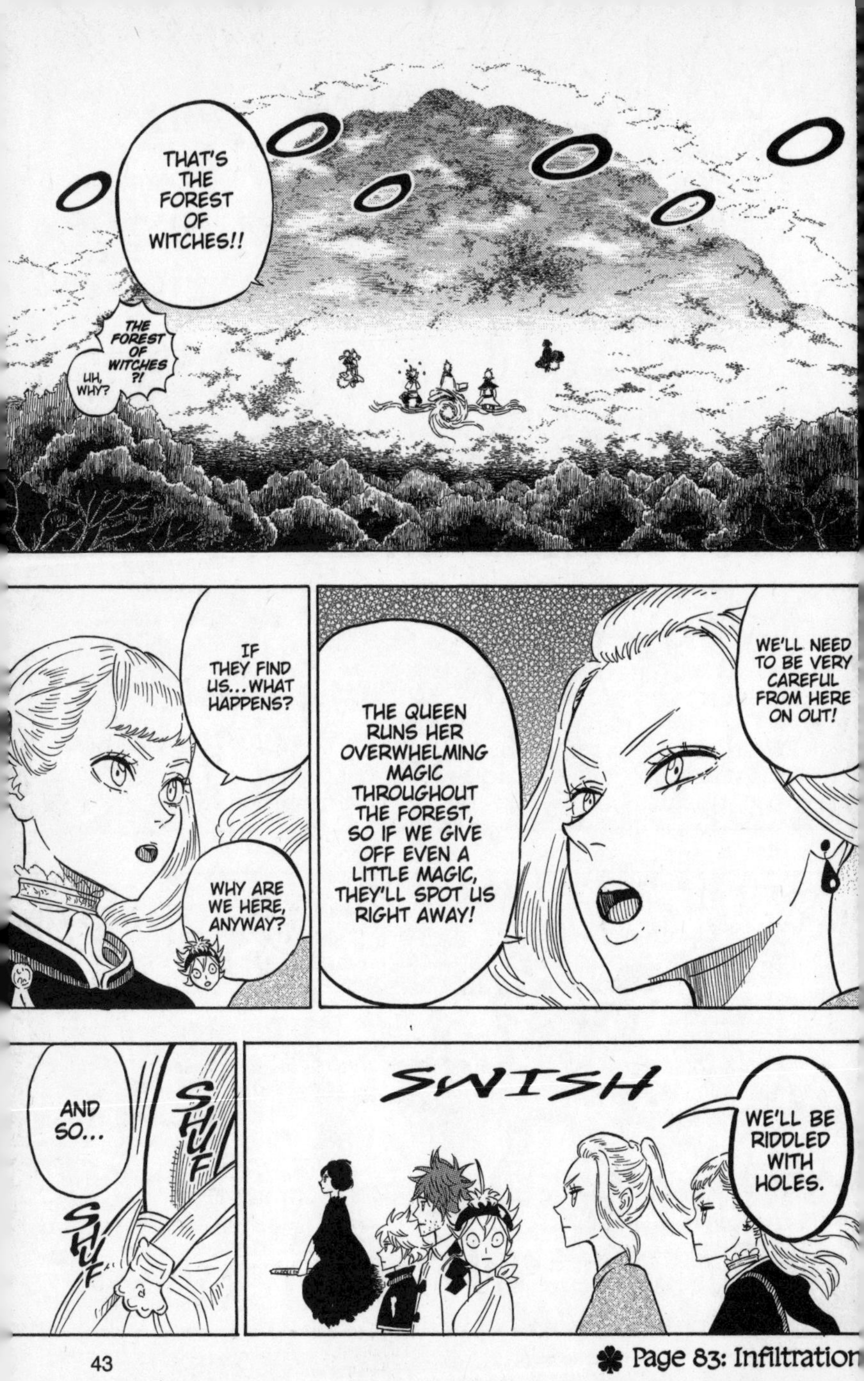

THAT'S THE FOREST OF WITCHES!!
THE FOREST OF WITCHES ?!
UH, WHY?
WE'LL NEED TO BE VERY CAREFUL FROM HERE ON OUT!
THE QUEEN RUNS HER OVERWHELMING MAGIC THROUGHOUT THE FOREST, SO IF WE GIVE OFF EVEN A LITTLE MAGIC, THEY'LL SPOT US RIGHT AWAY!
IF THEY FIND US...WHAT HAPPENS?
WHY ARE WE HERE, ANYWAY?
SWISH
WE'LL BE RIDDLED WITH HOLES.
AND SO...
SHUF
SHUF

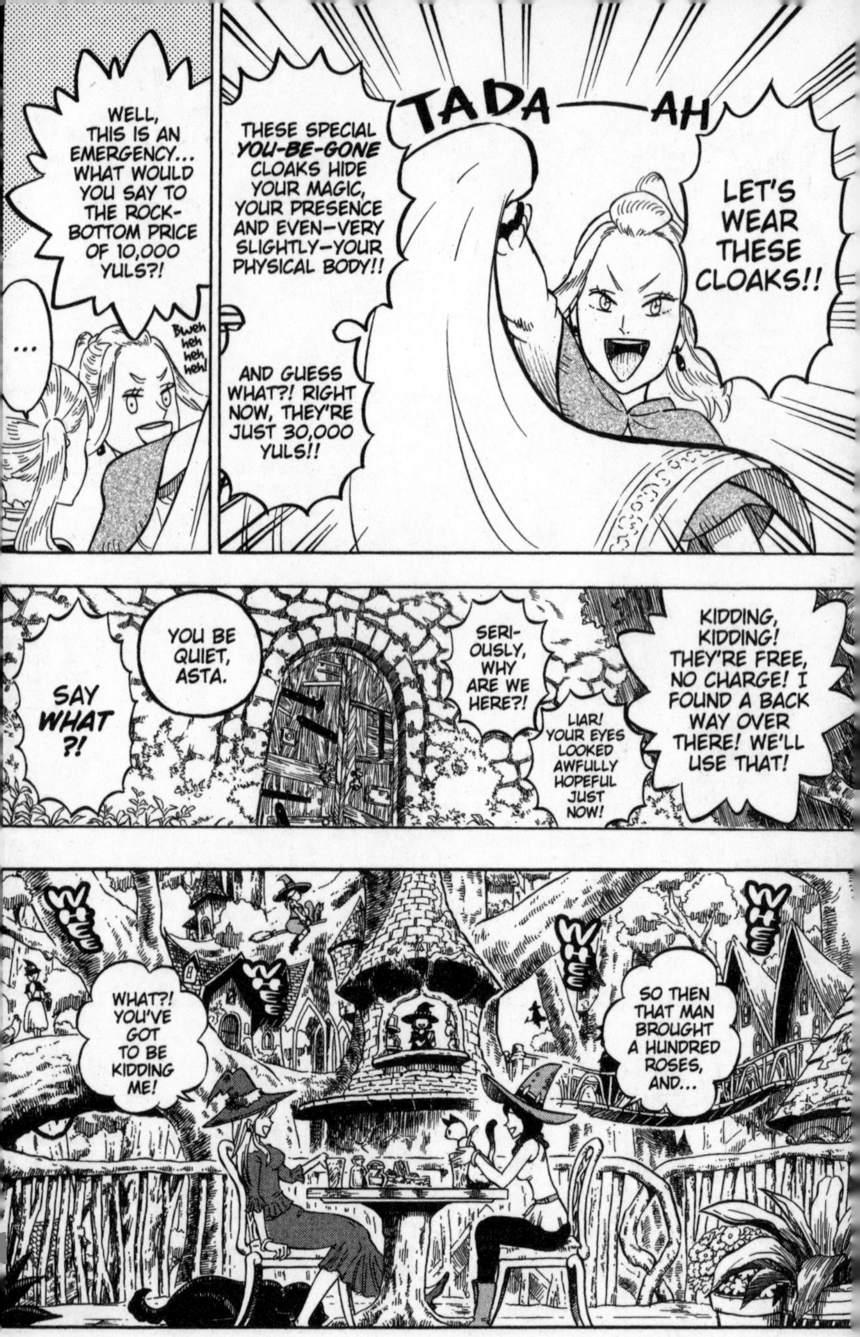
TADA—AH
LET'S WEAR THESE CLOAKS!!
THESE SPECIAL *YOU-BE-GONE* CLOAKS HIDE YOUR MAGIC, YOUR PRESENCE AND EVEN—VERY SLIGHTLY—YOUR PHYSICAL BODY!!
AND GUESS WHAT?! RIGHT NOW, THEY'RE JUST 30,000 YULS!!
WELL, THIS IS AN EMERGENCY... WHAT WOULD YOU SAY TO THE ROCK-BOTTOM PRICE OF 10,000 YULS?!
Bweh heh heh heh!
...
KIDDING, KIDDING! THEY'RE FREE, NO CHARGE! I FOUND A BACK WAY OVER THERE! WE'LL USE THAT!
LIAR! YOUR EYES LOOKED AWFULLY HOPEFUL JUST NOW!
SERI-OUSLY, WHY ARE WE HERE?!
YOU BE QUIET, ASTA.
SAY *WHAT* ?!
WHE
WHE
SO THEN THAT MAN BROUGHT A HUNDRED ROSES, AND...
WHE
WHE
WHAT?! YOU'VE GOT TO BE KIDDING ME!

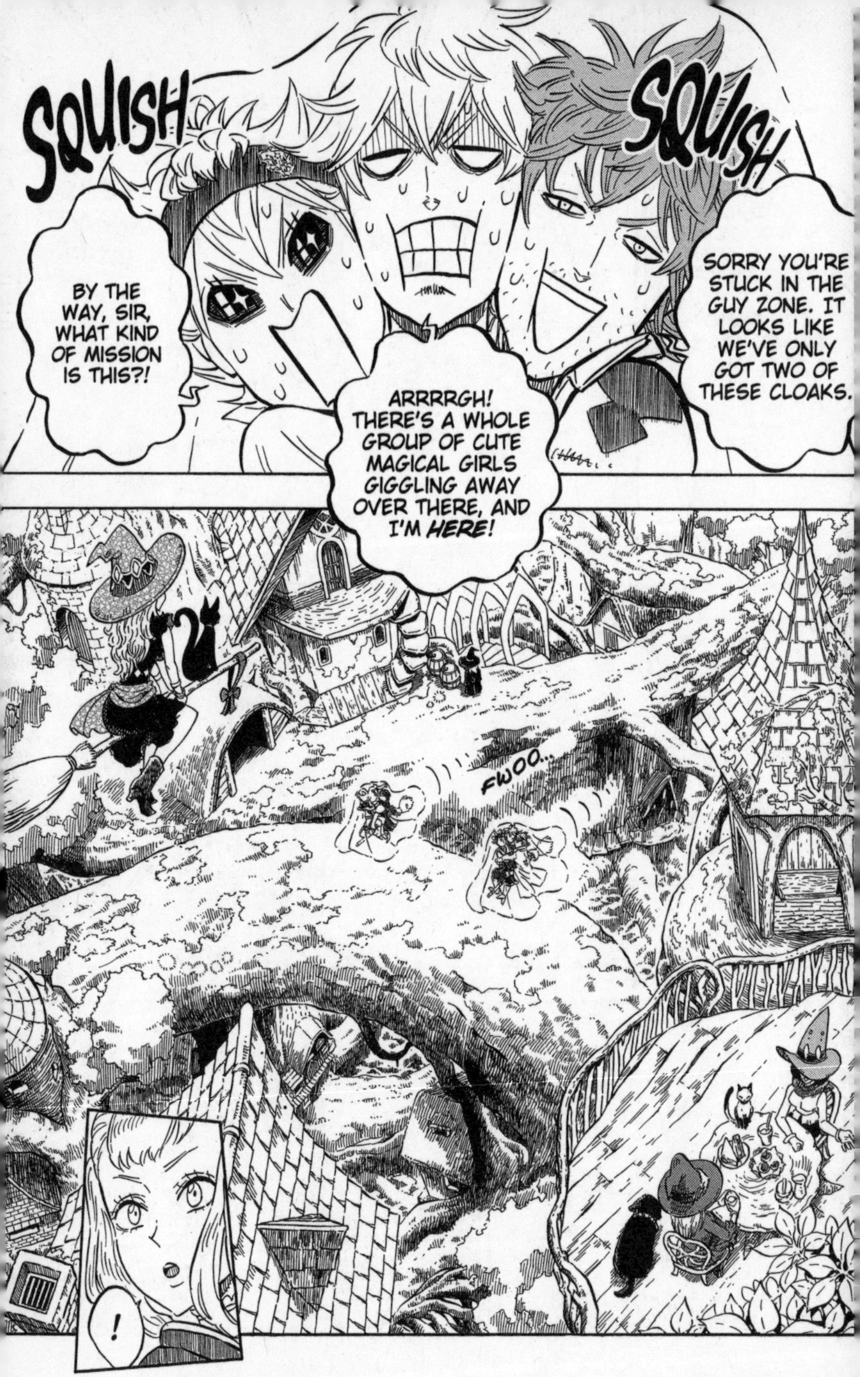
SQUISH
SORRY YOU'RE STUCK IN THE GUY ZONE. IT LOOKS LIKE WE'VE ONLY GOT TWO OF THESE CLOAKS.
SQUISH
BY THE WAY, SIR, WHAT KIND OF MISSION IS THIS?!
ARRRRGH! THERE'S A WHOLE GROUP OF CUTE MAGICAL GIRLS GIGGLING AWAY OVER THERE, AND I'M *HERE*!
FWOO...
!

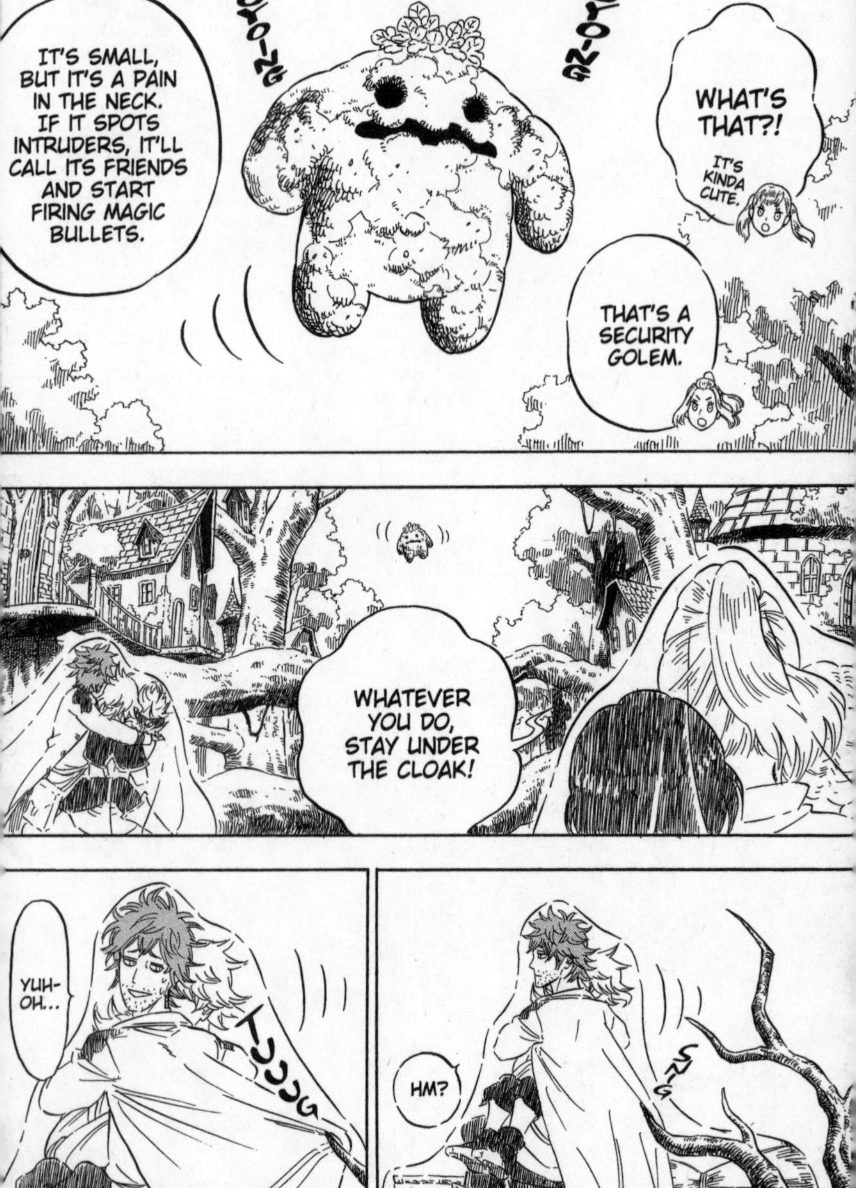
BOYOING
BOYOING
WHAT'S THAT?!
IT'S KINDA CUTE.
THAT'S A SECURITY GOLEM.
IT'S SMALL, BUT IT'S A PAIN IN THE NECK. IF IT SPOTS INTRUDERS, IT'LL CALL ITS FRIENDS AND START FIRING MAGIC BULLETS.
WHATEVER YOU DO, STAY UNDER THE CLOAK!
SNIG
HM?
YUH-OH...
TUUUG

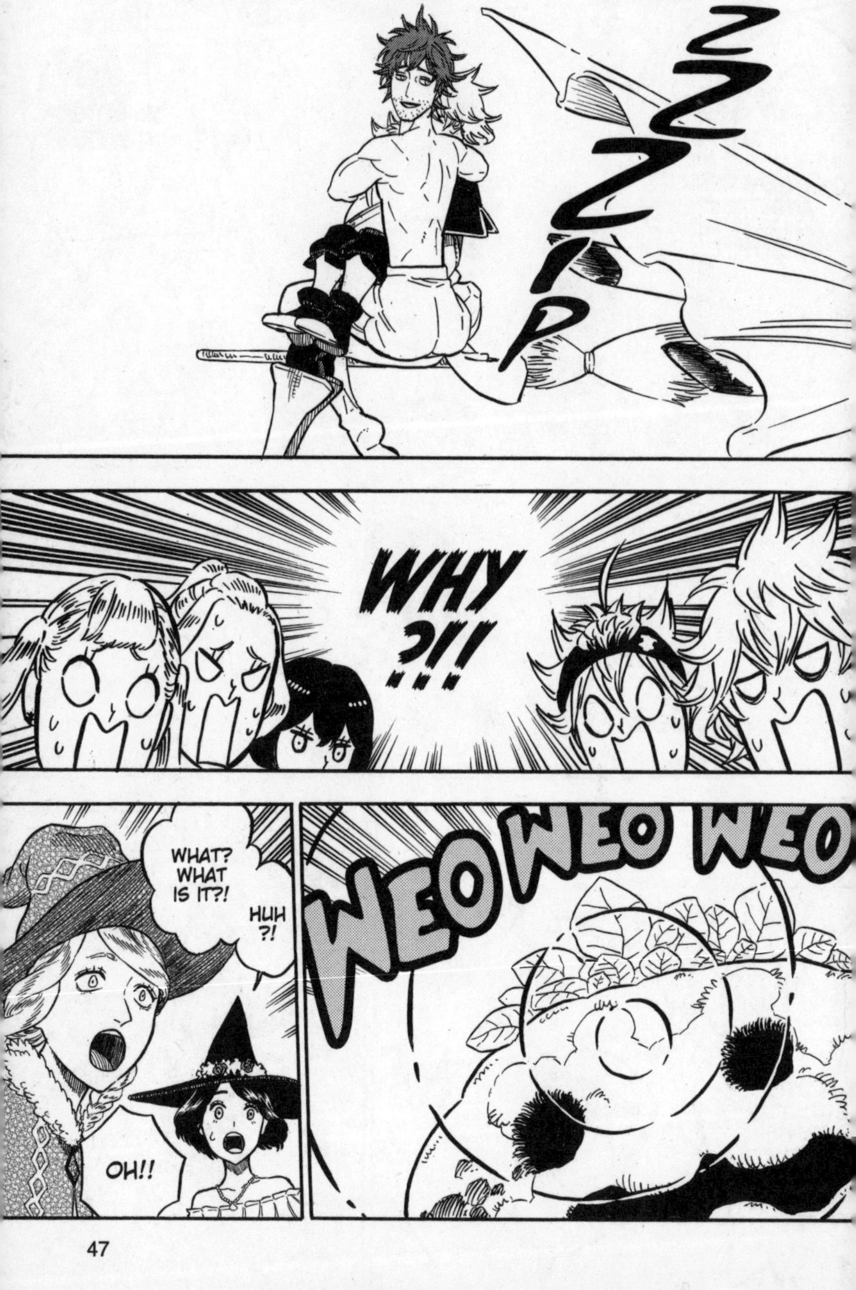
ZZZZIP
WHY ?!!
WEO WEO WEO
WHAT? WHAT IS IT?!
HUH ?!
OH!!

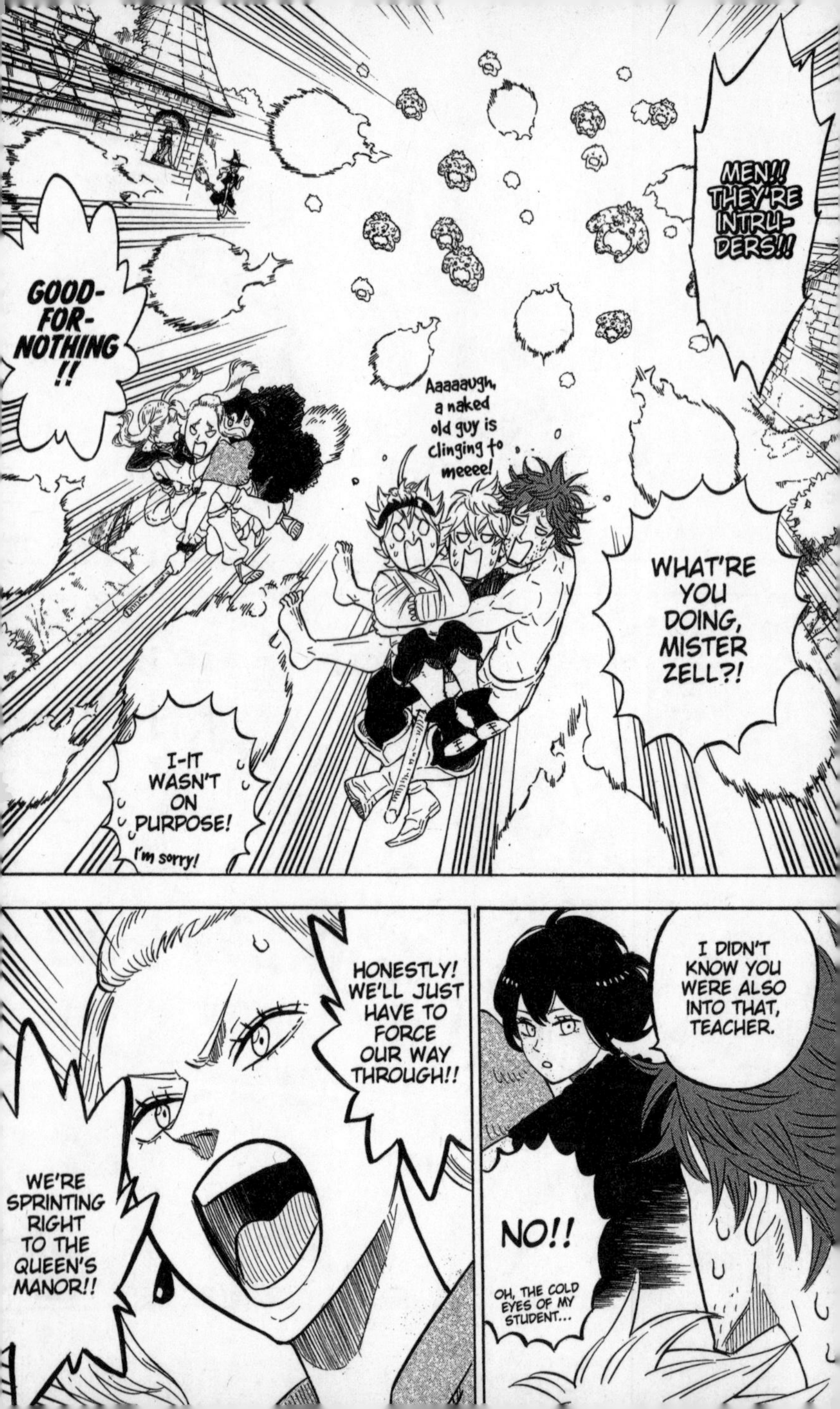
MEN!! THEY'RE INTRU-DERS!!
GOOD-FOR-NOTHING!!
Aaaaaugh, a naked old guy is clinging to meeee!
WHAT'RE YOU DOING, MISTER ZELL?!
I-IT WASN'T ON PURPOSE!
I'm sorry!
I DIDN'T KNOW YOU WERE ALSO INTO THAT, TEACHER.
NO!!
OH, THE COLD EYES OF MY STUDENT...
HONESTLY! WE'LL JUST HAVE TO FORCE OUR WAY THROUGH!!
WE'RE SPRINTING RIGHT TO THE QUEEN'S MANOR!!

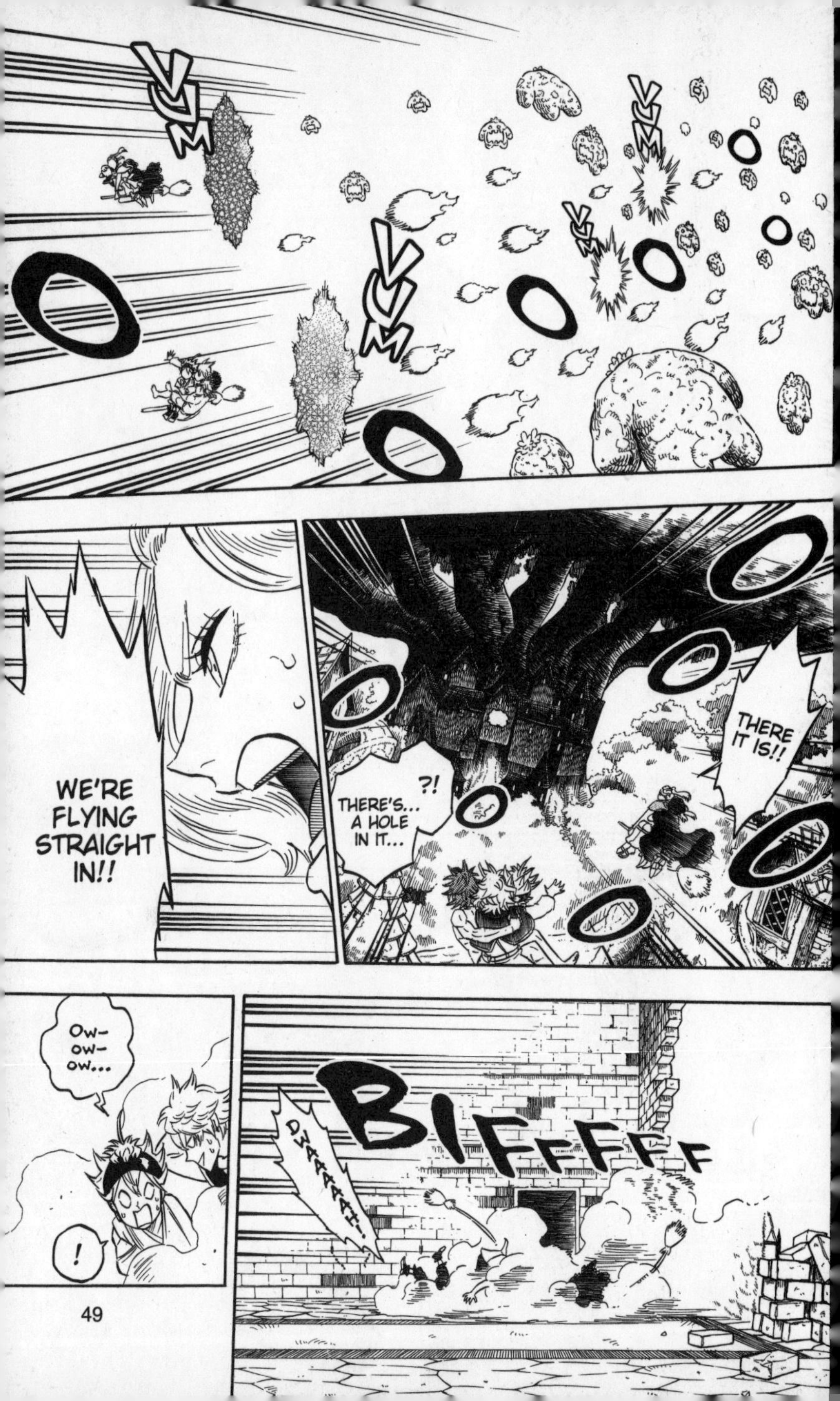

VJM
VJM
VJM
VJM
THERE IT IS!!
?!
THERE'S... A HOLE IN IT...
WE'RE FLYING STRAIGHT IN!!
BIFFFFFF
DWAAAAAH!
Ow-ow-ow...
!

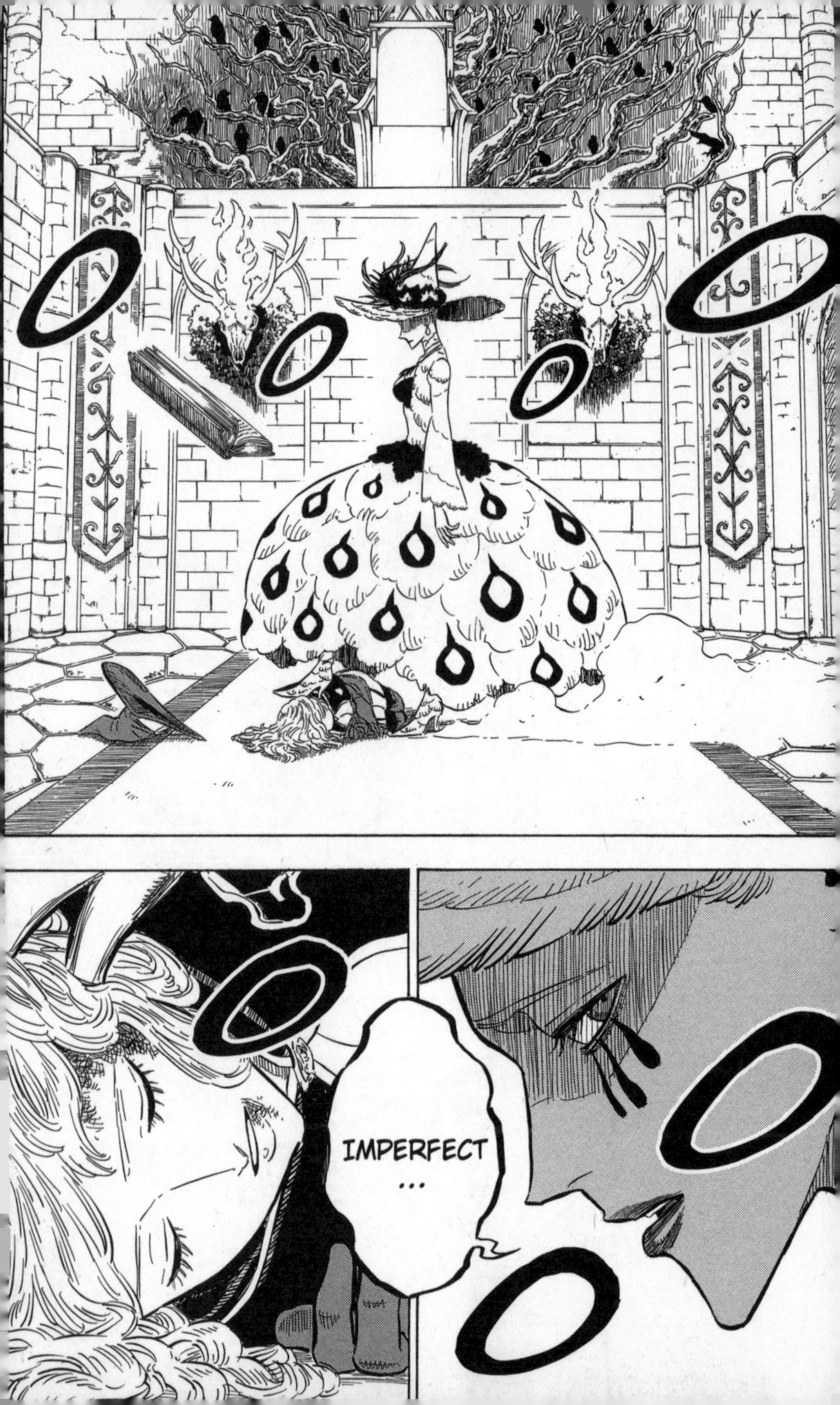
IMPERFECT
...

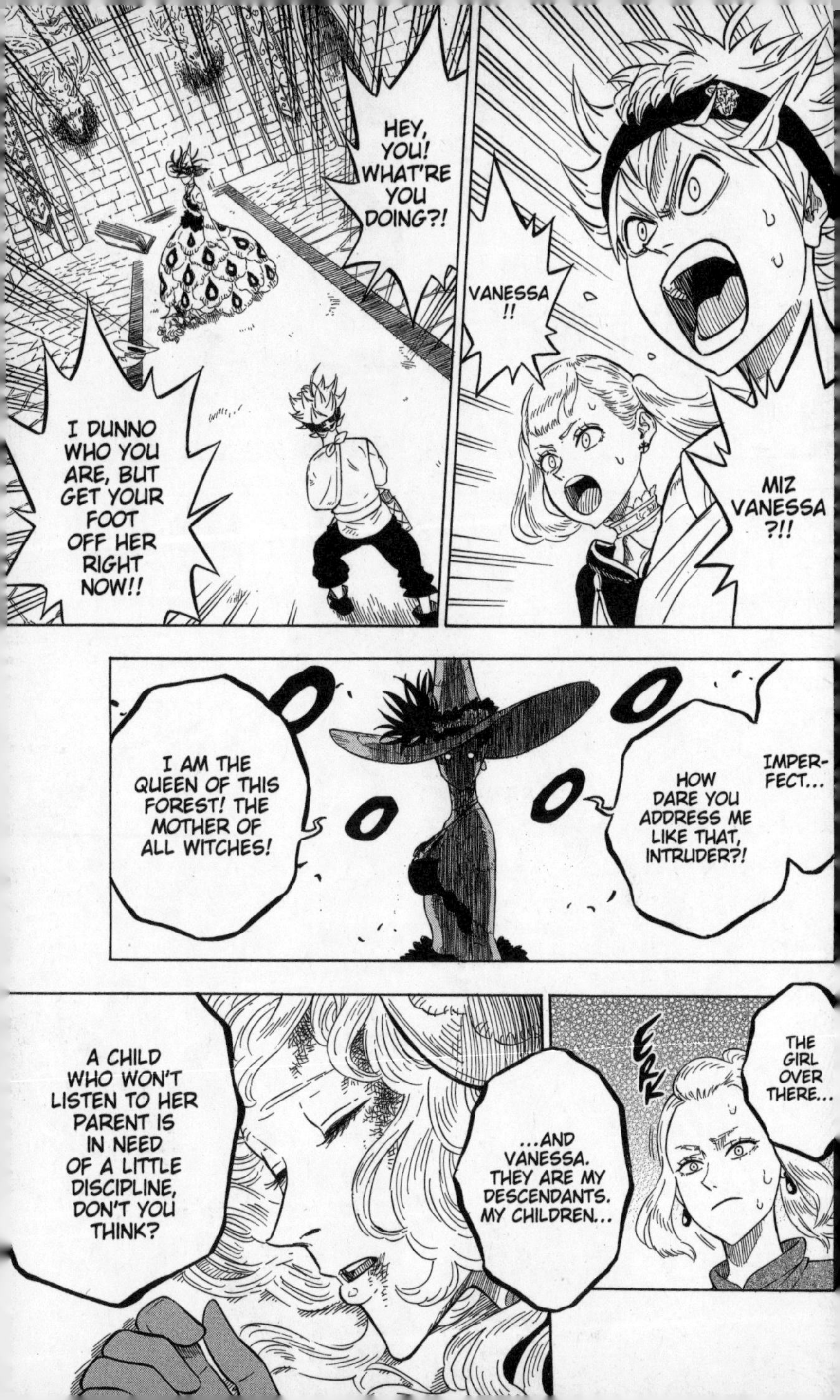
VANESSA!!
MIZ VANESSA?!!
HEY, YOU! WHAT'RE YOU DOING?!
I DUNNO WHO YOU ARE, BUT GET YOUR FOOT OFF HER RIGHT NOW!!
IMPERFECT...
HOW DARE YOU ADDRESS ME LIKE THAT, INTRUDER?!
I AM THE QUEEN OF THIS FOREST! THE MOTHER OF ALL WITCHES!
THE GIRL OVER THERE...
...AND VANESSA. THEY ARE MY DESCENDANTS. MY CHILDREN...
A CHILD WHO WON'T LISTEN TO HER PARENT IS IN NEED OF A LITTLE DISCIPLINE, DON'T YOU THINK?

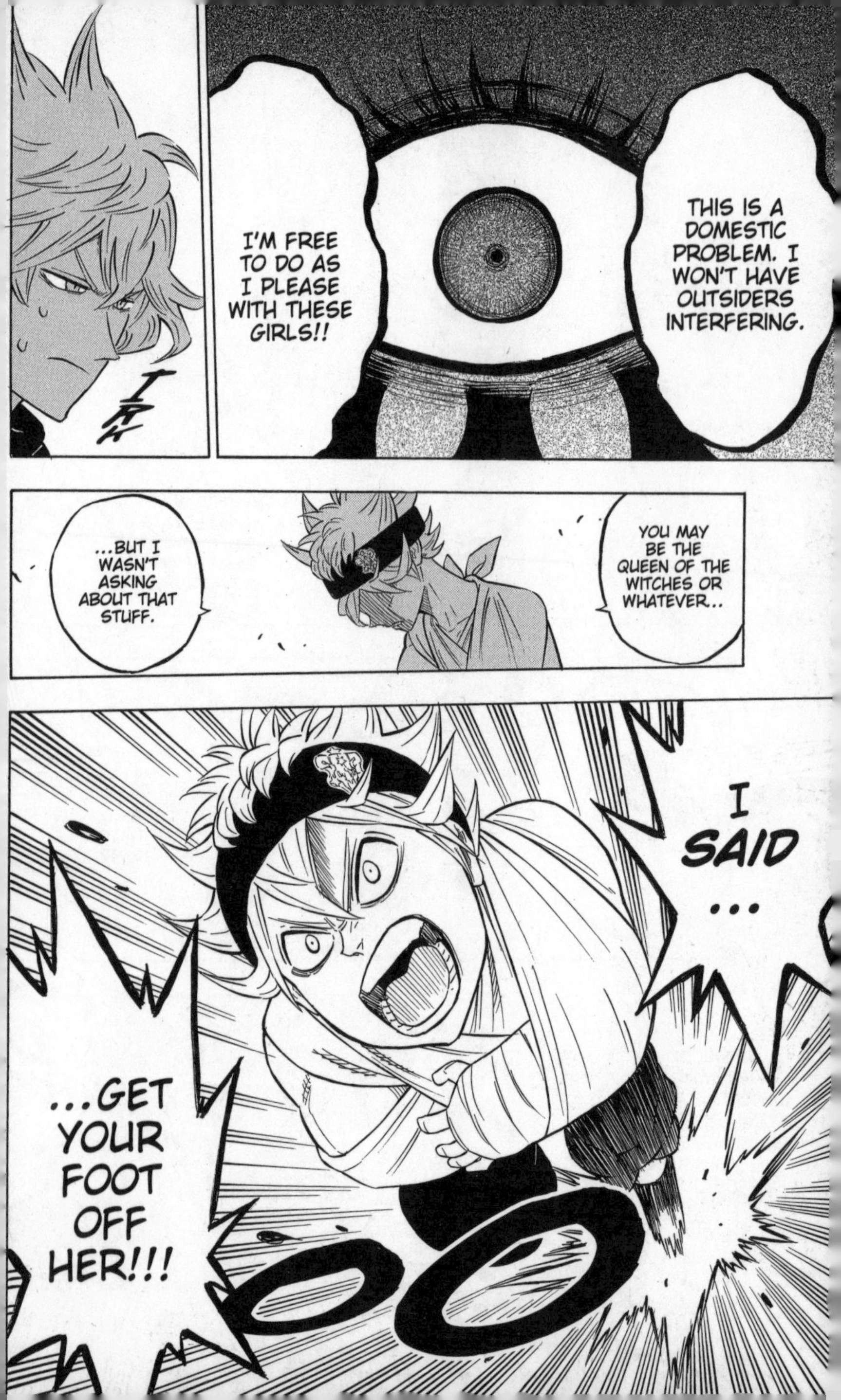
THIS IS A DOMESTIC PROBLEM. I WON'T HAVE OUTSIDERS INTERFERING.
I'M FREE TO DO AS I PLEASE WITH THESE GIRLS!!
YOU MAY BE THE QUEEN OF THE WITCHES OR WHATEVER...
...BUT I WASN'T ASKING ABOUT THAT STUFF.
I SAID ...
...GET YOUR FOOT OFF HER!!!

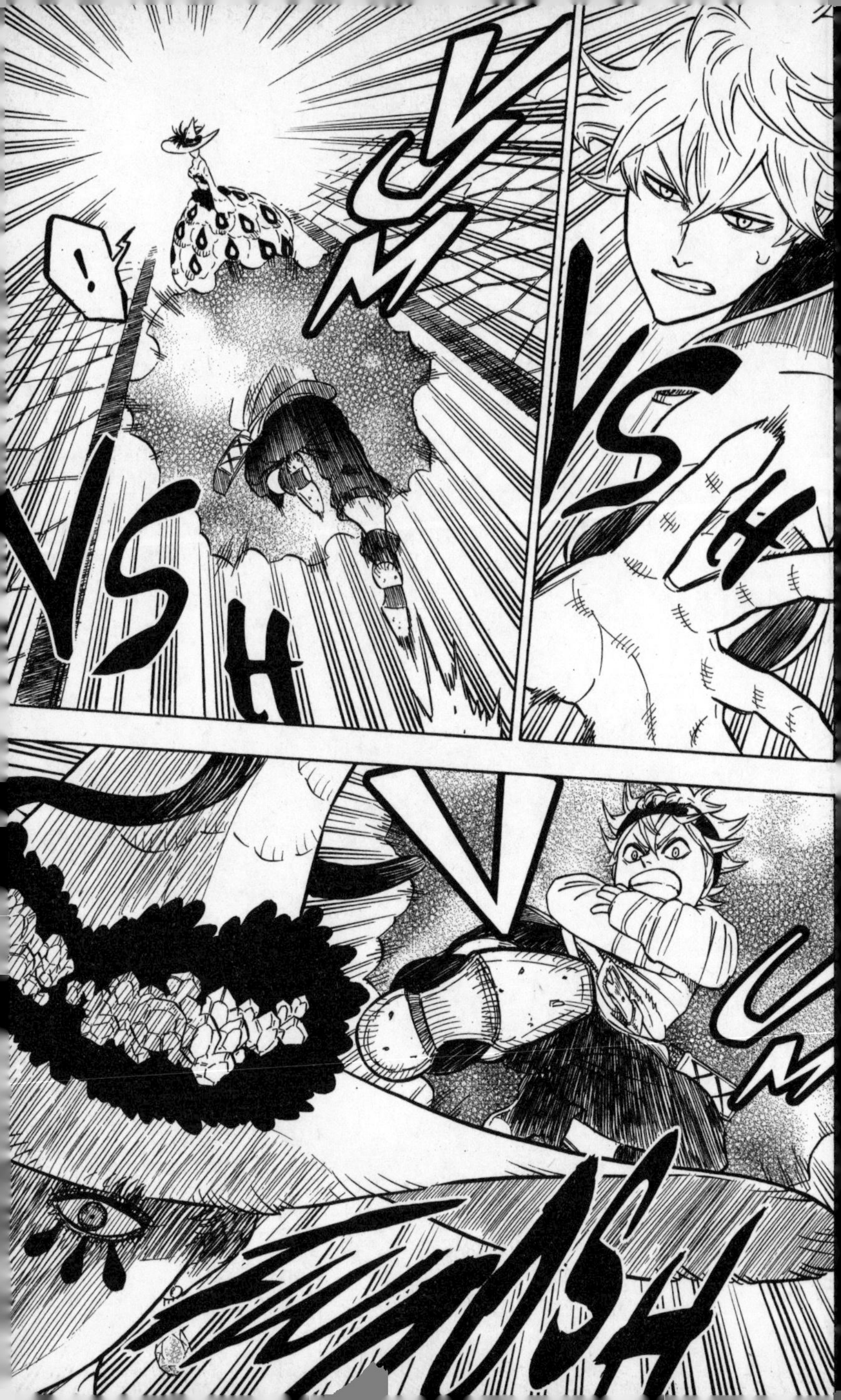
VSH
VUM
!
VSH
VUM

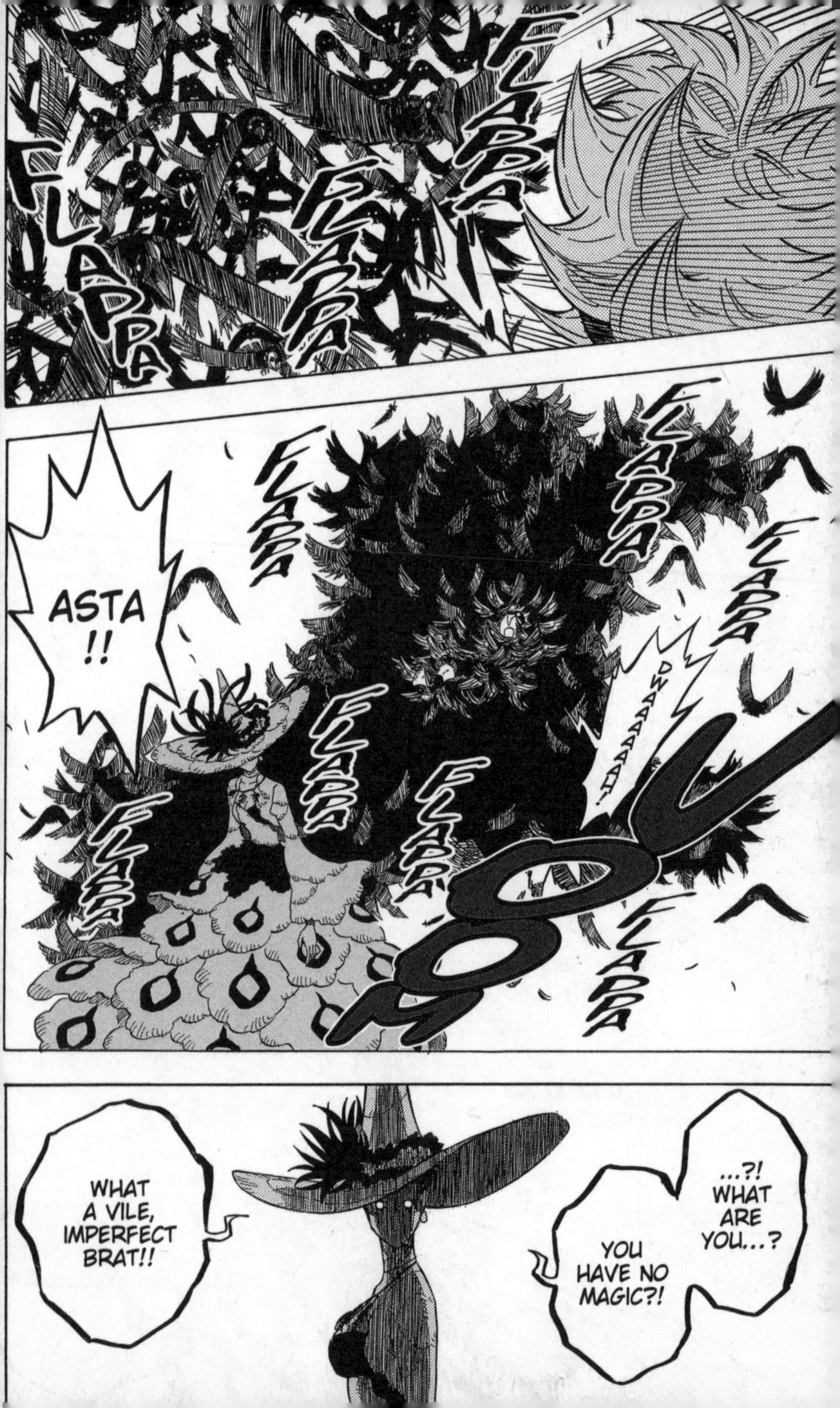
FLAPPA
FLAPPA
FLAPPA
FLAPPA
FLAPPA
FLAPPA
DWAAAAAAH!
SOOM
FLAPPA
FLAPPA
FLAPPA
FLAPPA
ASTA!!
...?! WHAT ARE YOU...?
YOU HAVE NO MAGIC?!
WHAT A VILE, IMPERFECT BRAT!!

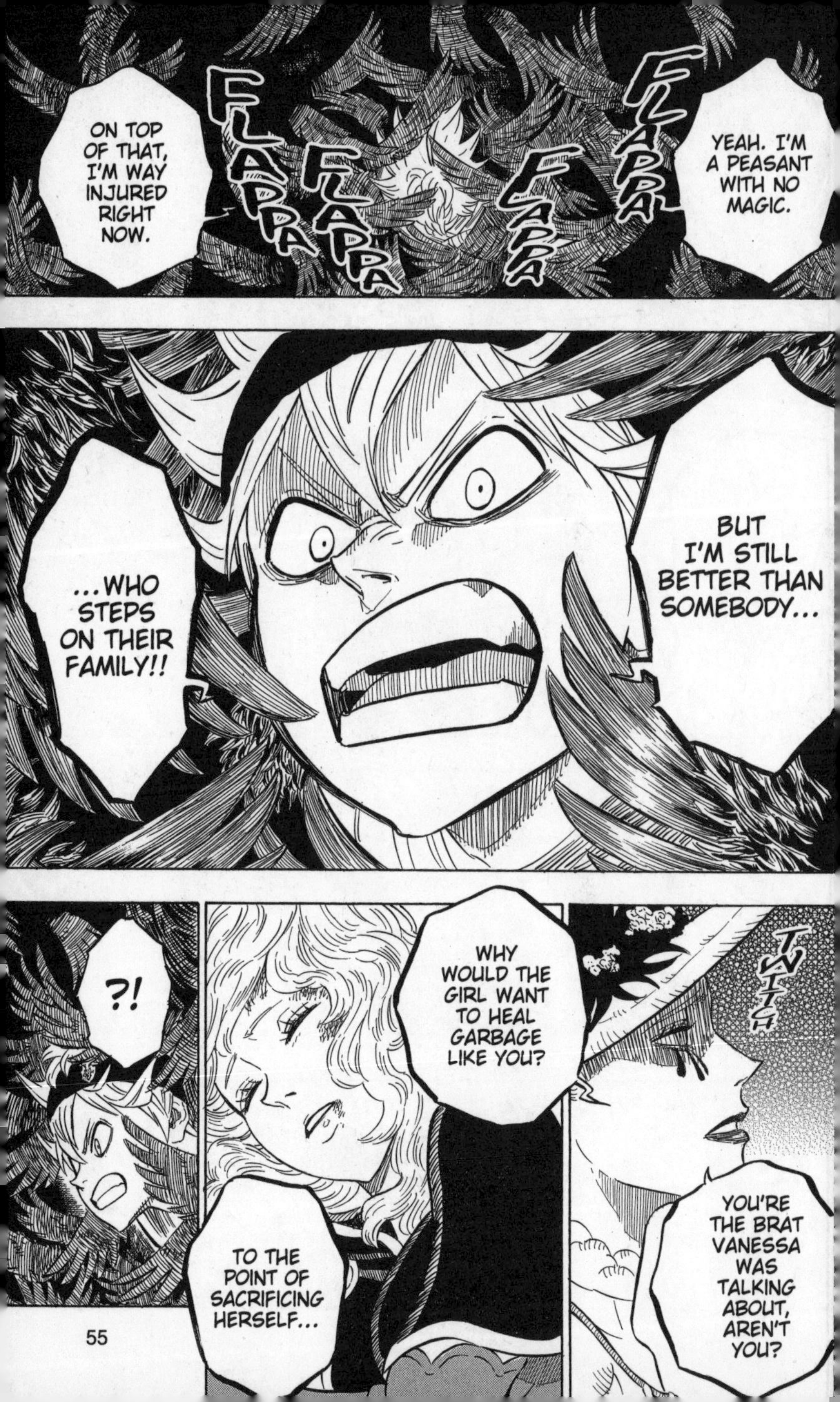
YEAH. I'M A PEASANT WITH NO MAGIC.
FLAPPA
FLAPPA
FLAPPA
FLAPPA
ON TOP OF THAT, I'M WAY INJURED RIGHT NOW.
BUT I'M STILL BETTER THAN SOMEBODY...
...WHO STEPS ON THEIR FAMILY!!
TWITCH
YOU'RE THE BRAT VANESSA WAS TALKING ABOUT, AREN'T YOU?
WHY WOULD THE GIRL WANT TO HEAL GARBAGE LIKE YOU?
TO THE POINT OF SACRIFICING HERSELF...
?!

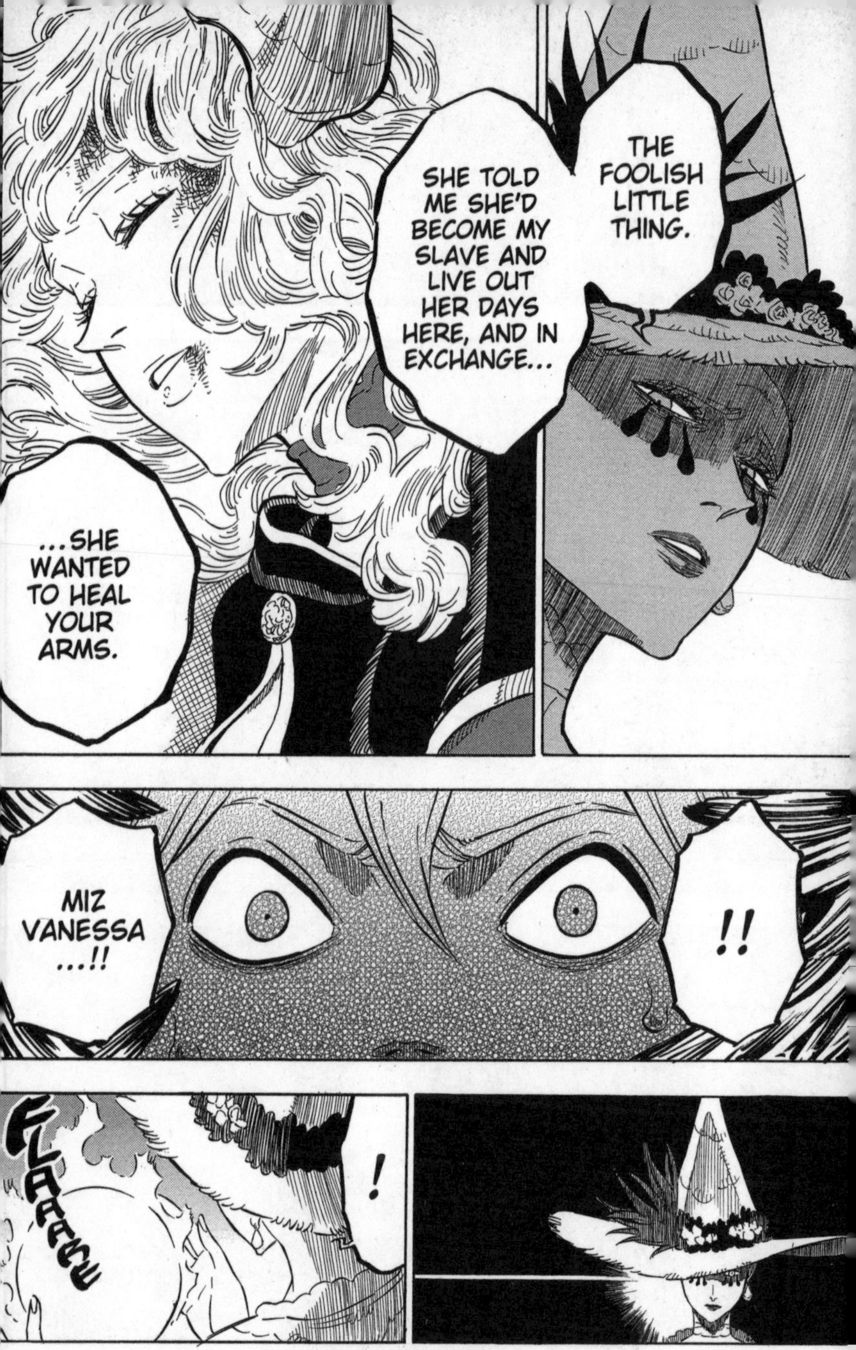
THE FOOLISH LITTLE THING.
SHE TOLD ME SHE'D BECOME MY SLAVE AND LIVE OUT HER DAYS HERE, AND IN EXCHANGE...
...SHE WANTED TO HEAL YOUR ARMS.
!!
MIZ VANESSA ...!!
!
FLAAACE

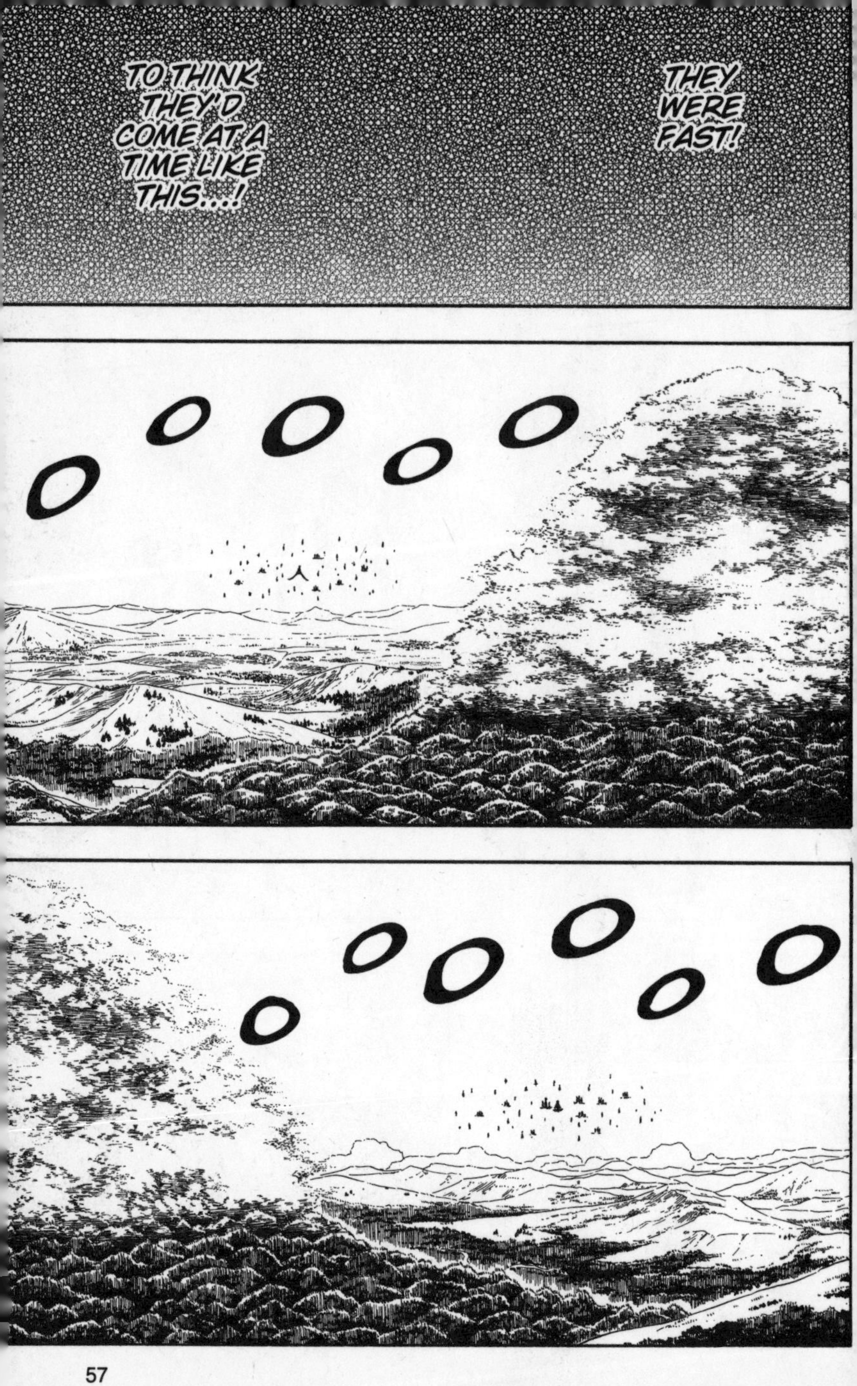
THEY WERE FAST!
TO THINK THEY'D COME AT A TIME LIKE THIS...!

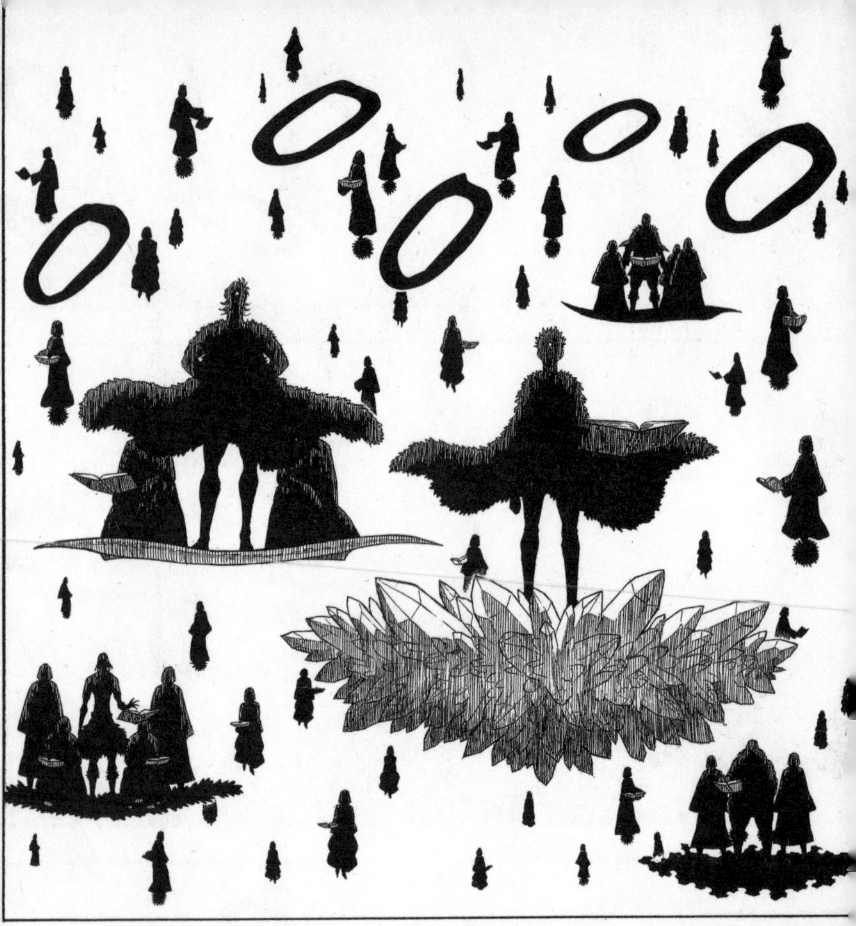

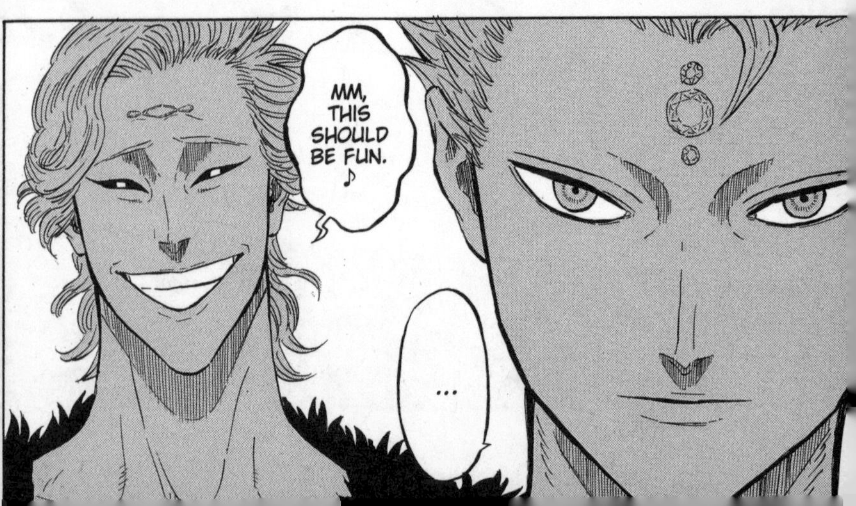
MM, THIS SHOULD BE FUN. ♪
...

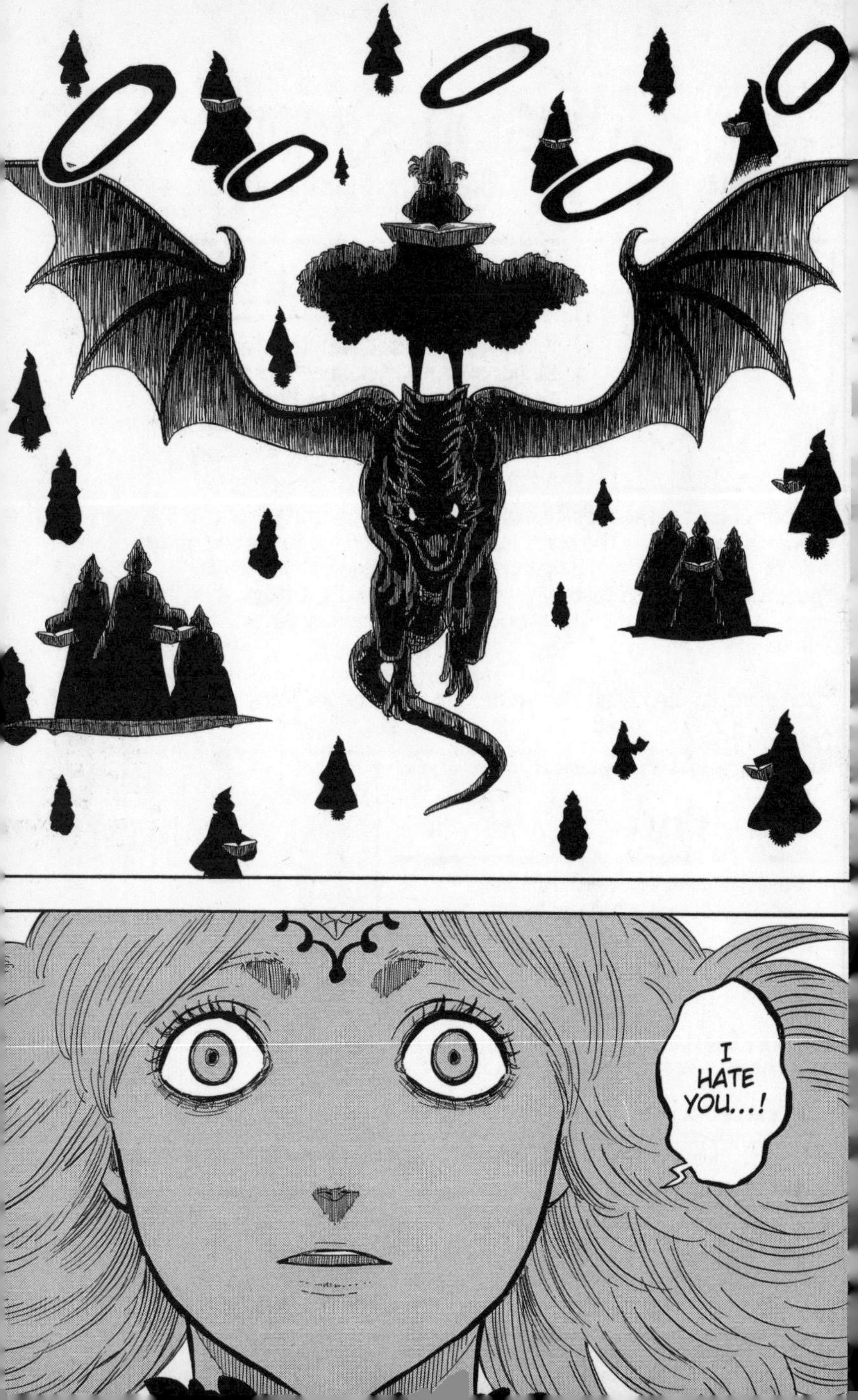
I HATE YOU...!

Magic Knight Brigade The Black Bulls

Mission Report

○ Month × Day

Reporter: Finral Roulacase

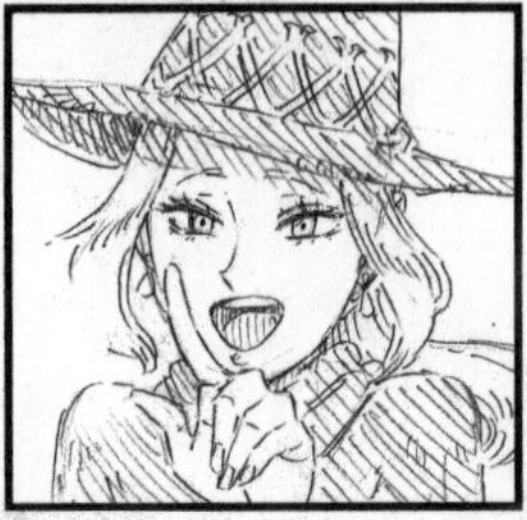

Dominante Code

Formerly affiliated with the Diamond Kingdom army. Nickname "Domina." Female. She's engaged to Fanzell Kruger and fled to the Clover Kingdom with him. She's cheap when it comes to money, but she's gorgeous.

In our country, she mostly makes a living by creating magic items and selling them on the black market. Many of the items she makes are of high quality, and a member of our brigade, Noelle Silva, purchased a brooch that supports magic control. A magical entity named "Bruce" lived in the brooch, and is currently part of the grip of Noelle's wand.

Dominante is also lying low in the Clover Kingdom, living in exile.

Diamond Kingdom Former Assassination Unit Member

Mariella

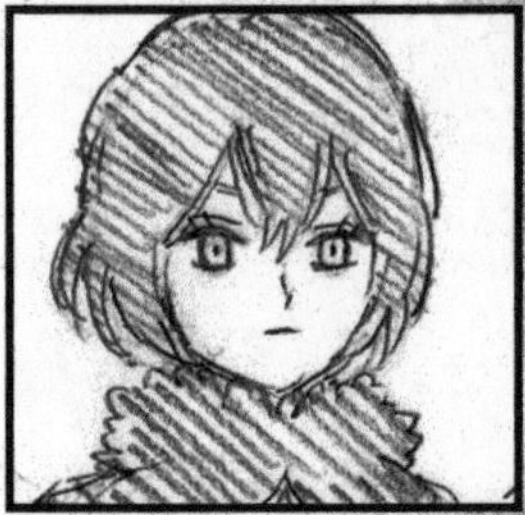

Formerly a member of the Diamond Kingdom Army's Assassination Unit.
Female.
Ice magic user.
Both her words and her magic are sharp.
But she's cute.

Because she was a member of the Diamond Kingdom's assassination unit, she has abundant combat experience and she's resourceful.

On orders from the Diamond Kingdom army, she attempted to kill Fanzell, her former combat instructor, but she broke away from the army. She is currently living in hiding in the Clover Kingdom with Fanzell and Dominante.

♣ A comment from brigade captain Yami Sukehiro

Huh? What is this? I told you to knock it off, so why did you get all diligent on me and write a second report? Are you that scared of not reporting this stuff? Can I burn you along with it later?

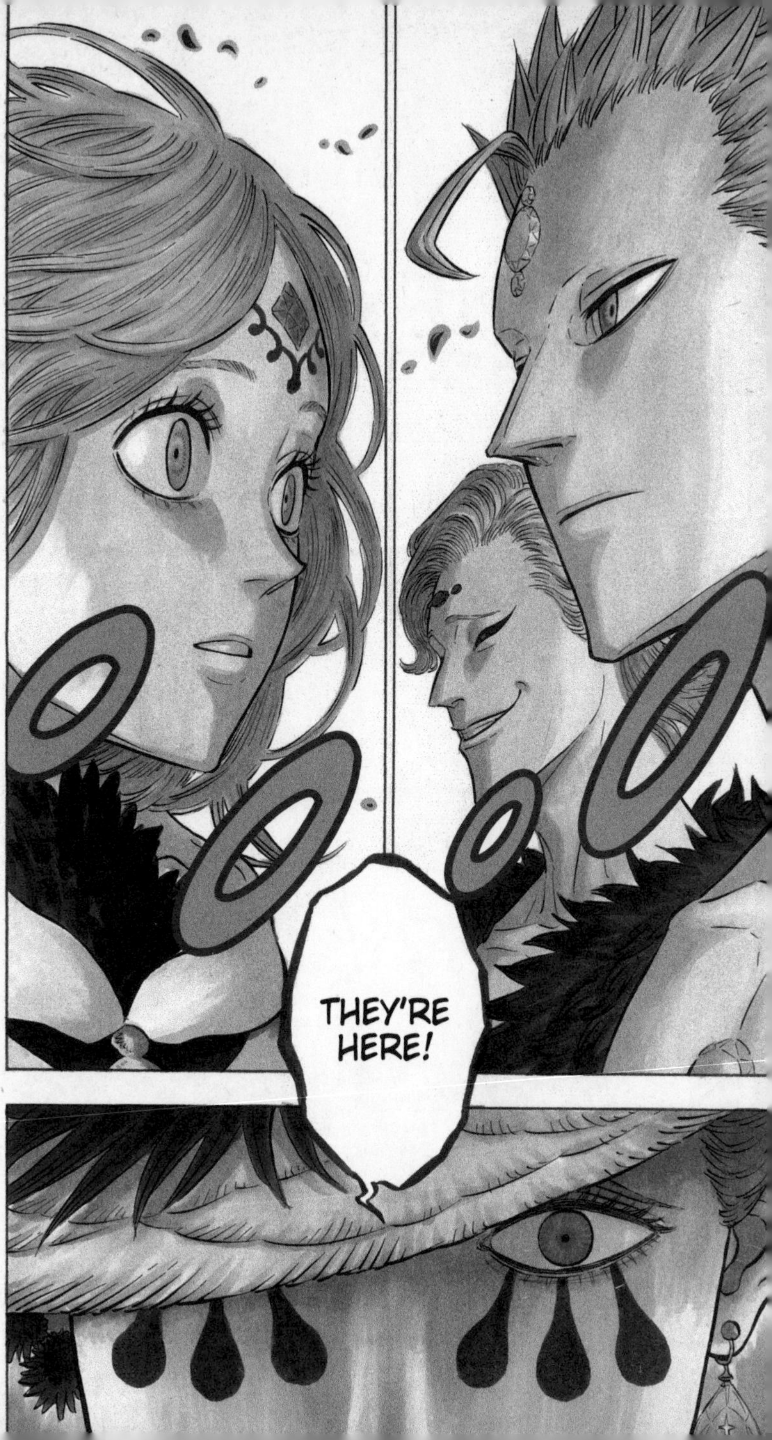
THEY'RE HERE!

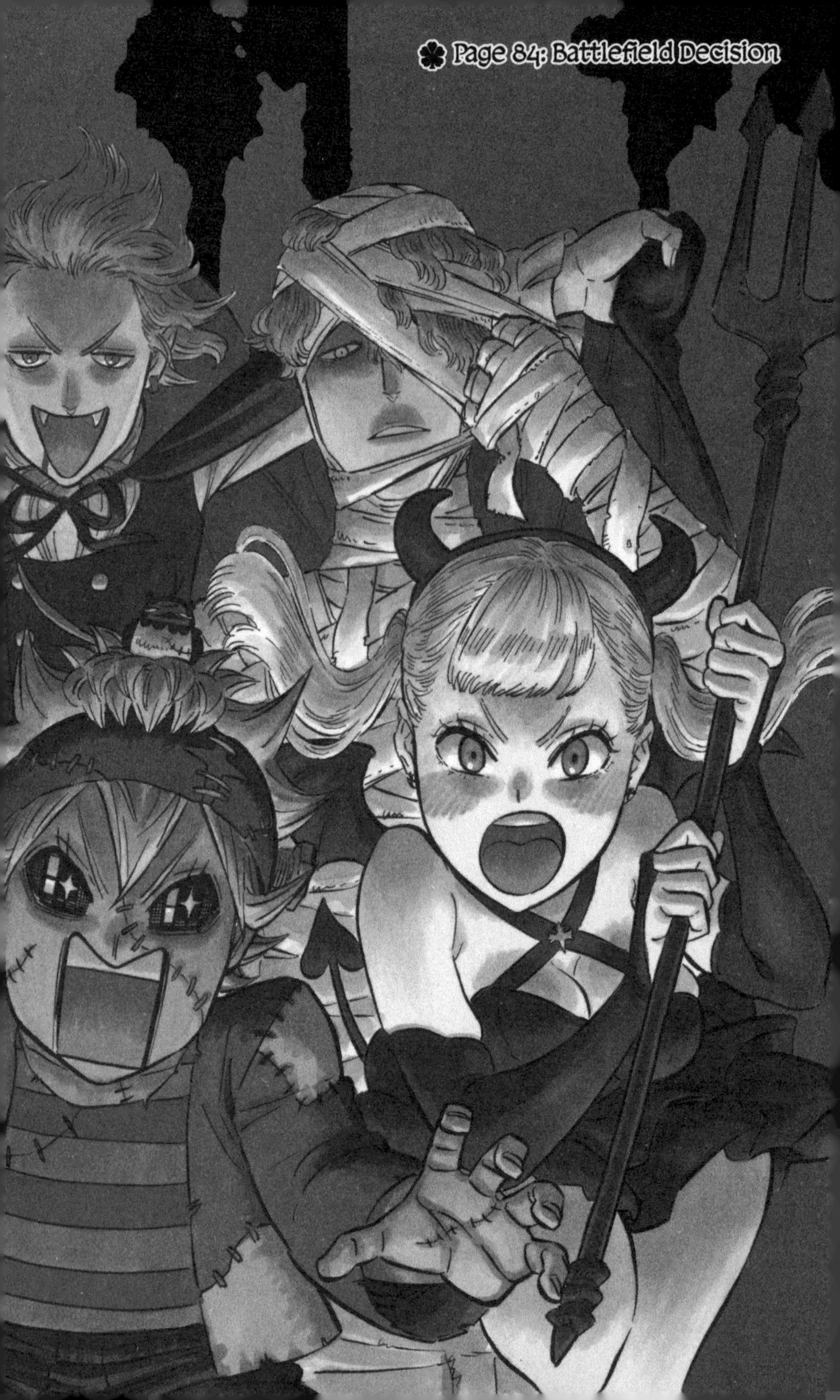
Page 84: Battlefield Decision

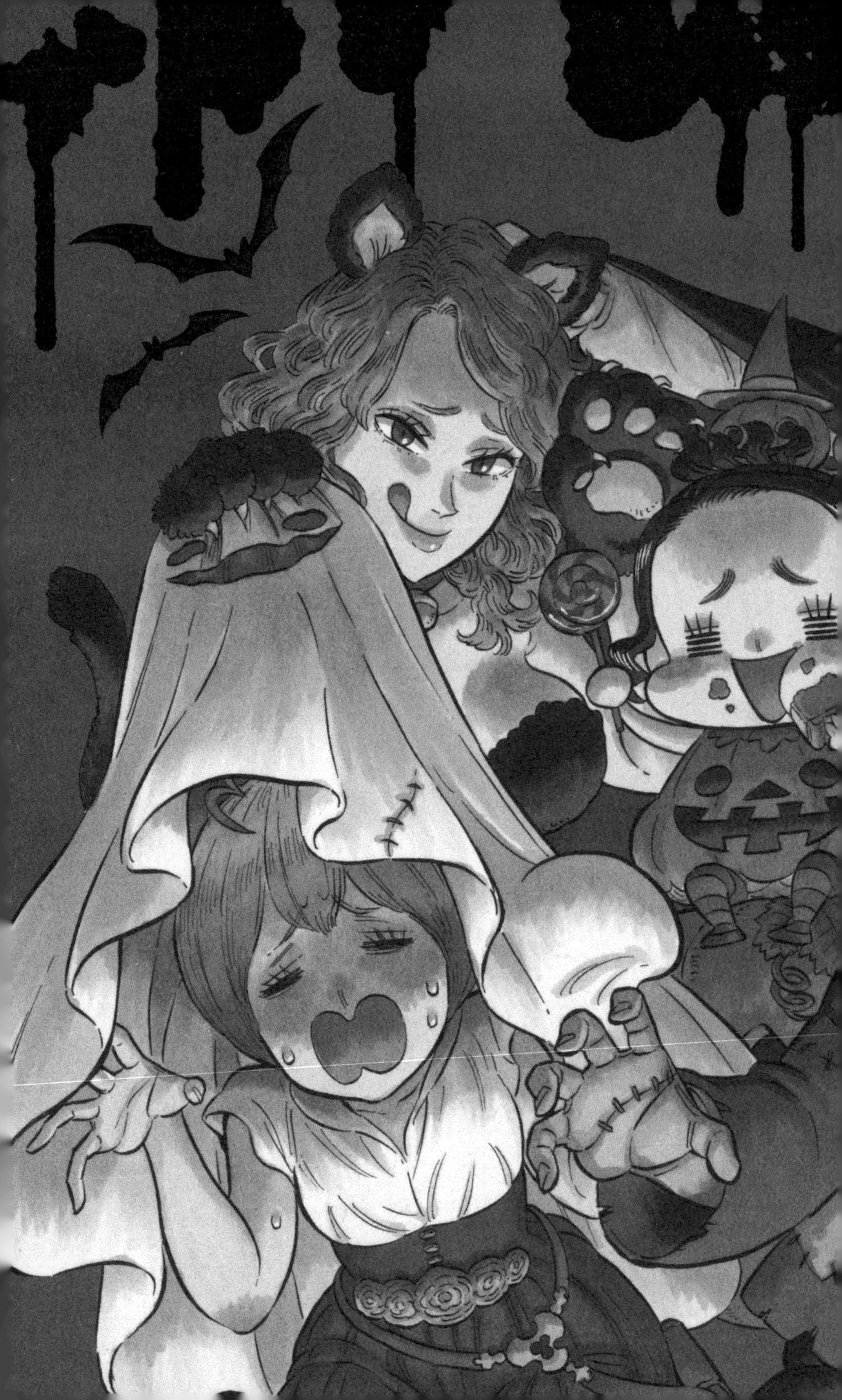

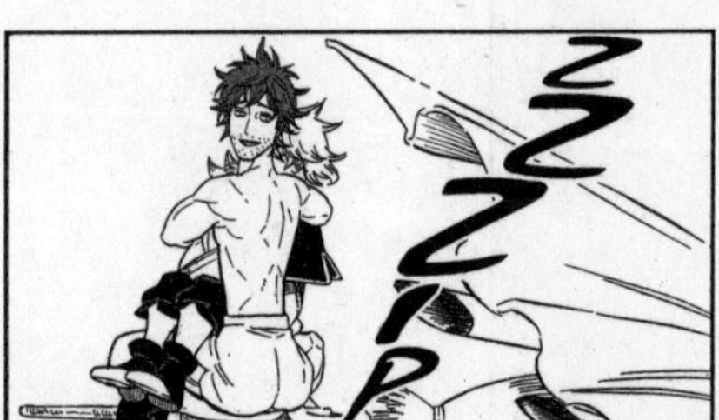
ZZZIP

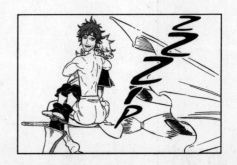

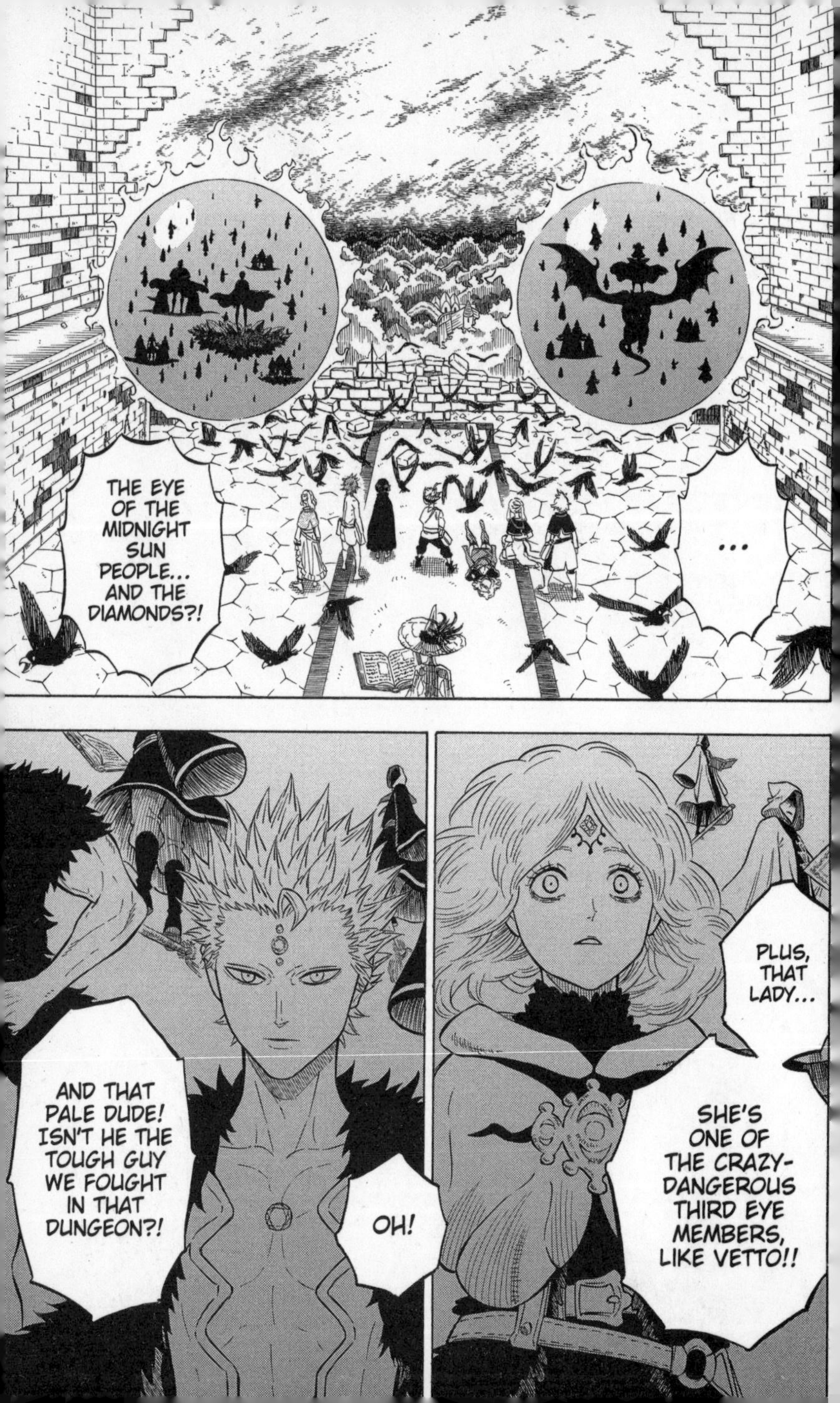
...
THE EYE OF THE MIDNIGHT SUN PEOPLE... AND THE DIAMONDS?!
PLUS, THAT LADY...
SHE'S ONE OF THE CRAZY-DANGEROUS THIRD EYE MEMBERS, LIKE VETTO!!
OH!
AND THAT PALE DUDE! ISN'T HE THE TOUGH GUY WE FOUGHT IN THAT DUNGEON?!

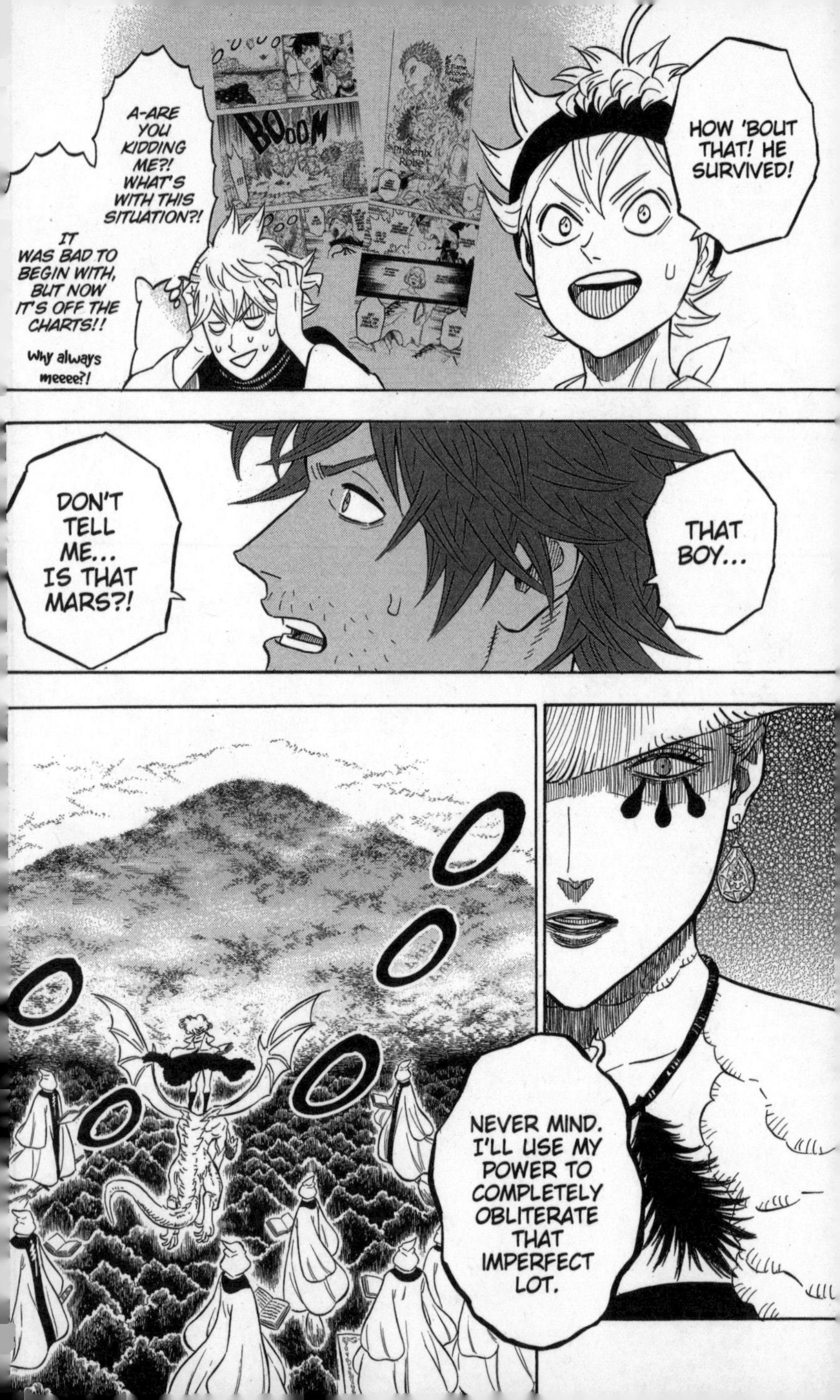
HOW 'BOUT THAT! HE SURVIVED!
BOOOM
Phoenix Robe
A-ARE YOU KIDDING ME?! WHAT'S WITH THIS SITUATION?!
IT WAS BAD TO BEGIN WITH, BUT NOW IT'S OFF THE CHARTS!!
Why always meeee?!
THAT BOY...
DON'T TELL ME... IS THAT MARS?!
NEVER MIND. I'LL USE MY POWER TO COMPLETELY OBLITERATE THAT IMPERFECT LOT.

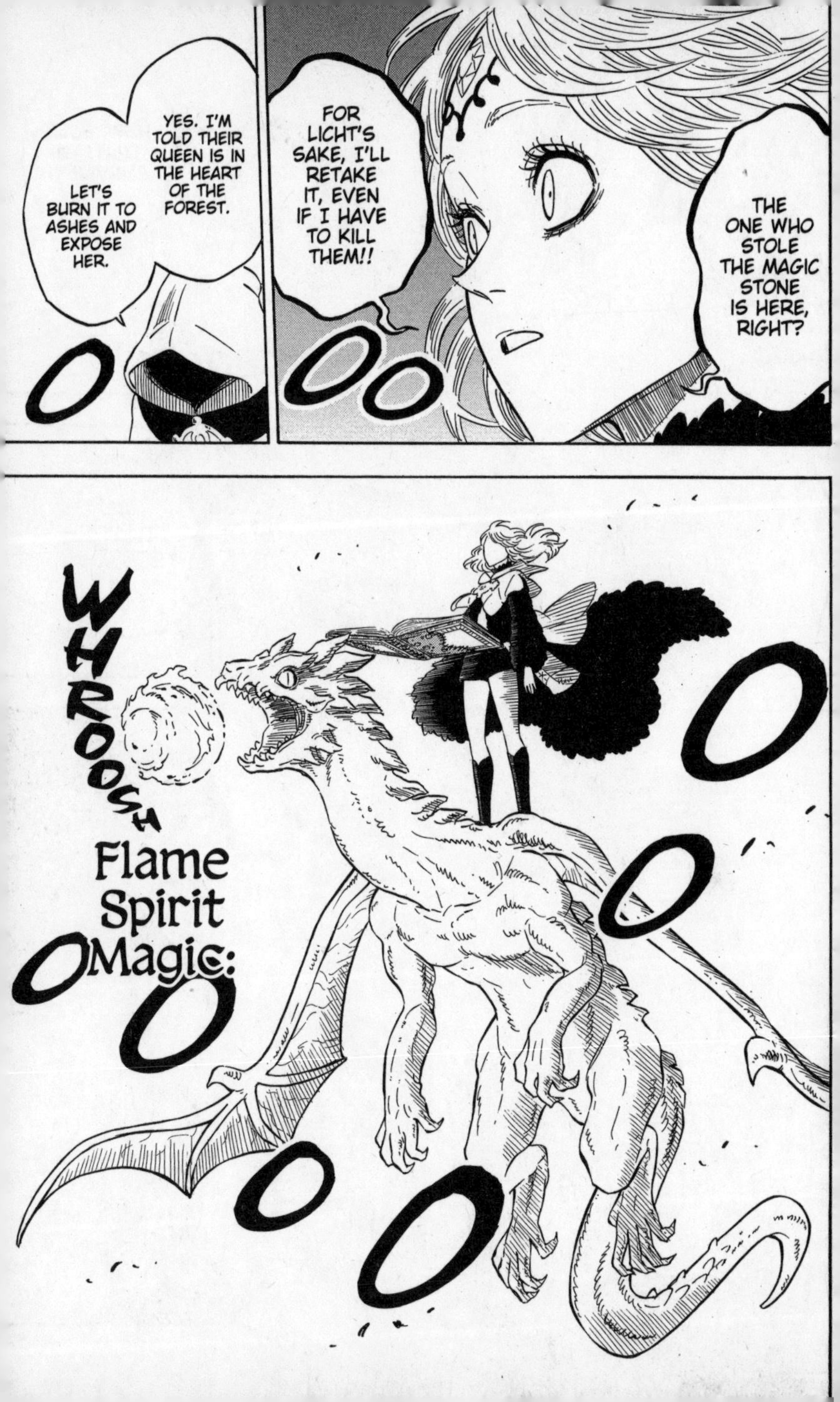
THE ONE WHO STOLE THE MAGIC STONE IS HERE, RIGHT?
FOR LICHT'S SAKE, I'LL RETAKE IT, EVEN IF I HAVE TO KILL THEM!!
YES. I'M TOLD THEIR QUEEN IS IN THE HEART OF THE FOREST.
LET'S BURN IT TO ASHES AND EXPOSE HER.
WHROOSH
Flame Spirit Magic:

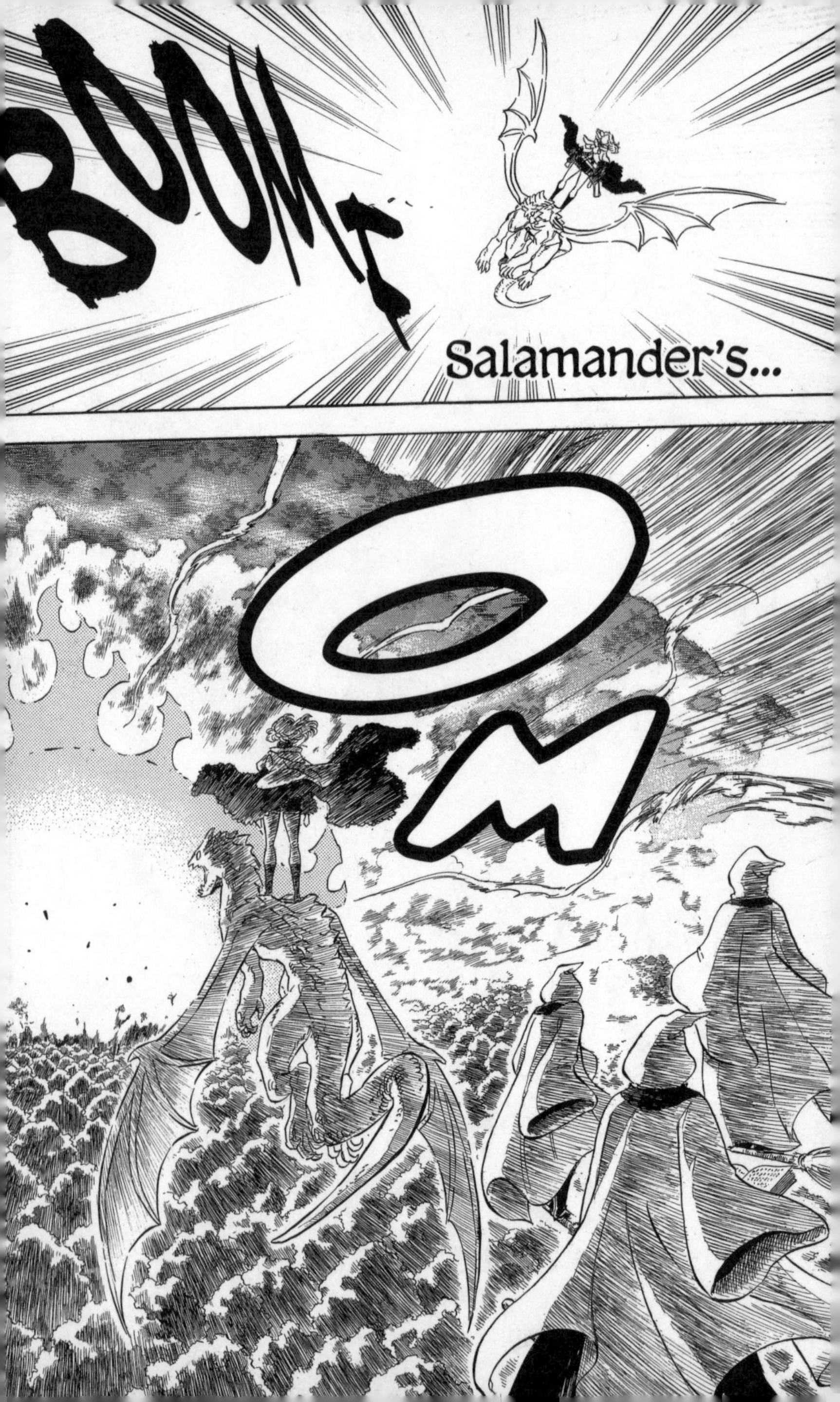
BOOM
Salamander's...
OM

...Breath!!

CHDOOM

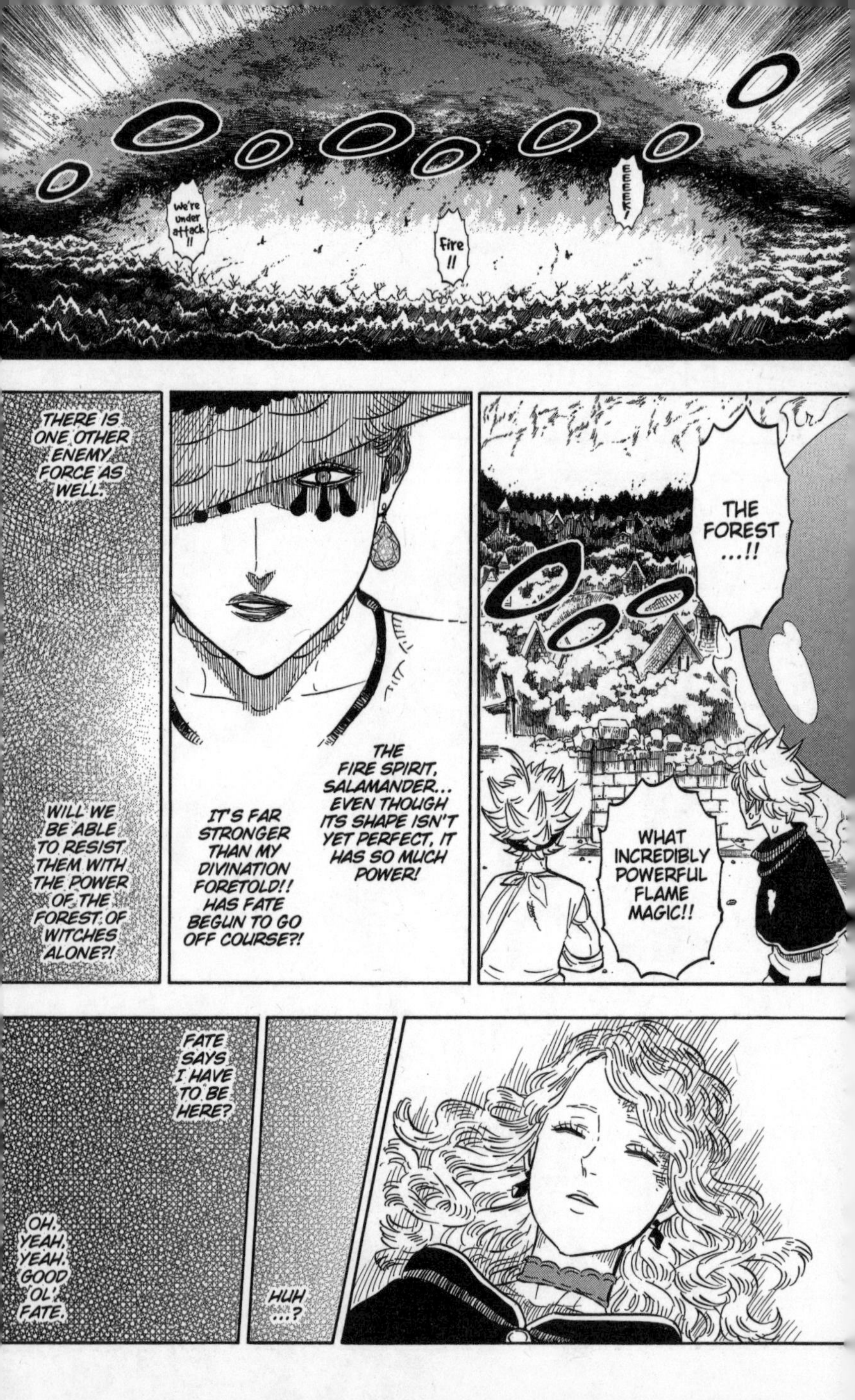
EEEEK!
Fire!!
We're under attack!!
THE FOREST...!!
WHAT INCREDIBLY POWERFUL FLAME MAGIC!!
THE FIRE SPIRIT, SALAMANDER... EVEN THOUGH ITS SHAPE ISN'T YET PERFECT, IT HAS SO MUCH POWER!
IT'S FAR STRONGER THAN MY DIVINATION FORETOLD!! HAS FATE BEGUN TO GO OFF COURSE?!
THERE IS ONE OTHER ENEMY FORCE AS WELL.
WILL WE BE ABLE TO RESIST THEM WITH THE POWER OF THE FOREST OF WITCHES ALONE?!
HUH...?
FATE SAYS I HAVE TO BE HERE?
OH. YEAH, YEAH. GOOD OL' FATE.

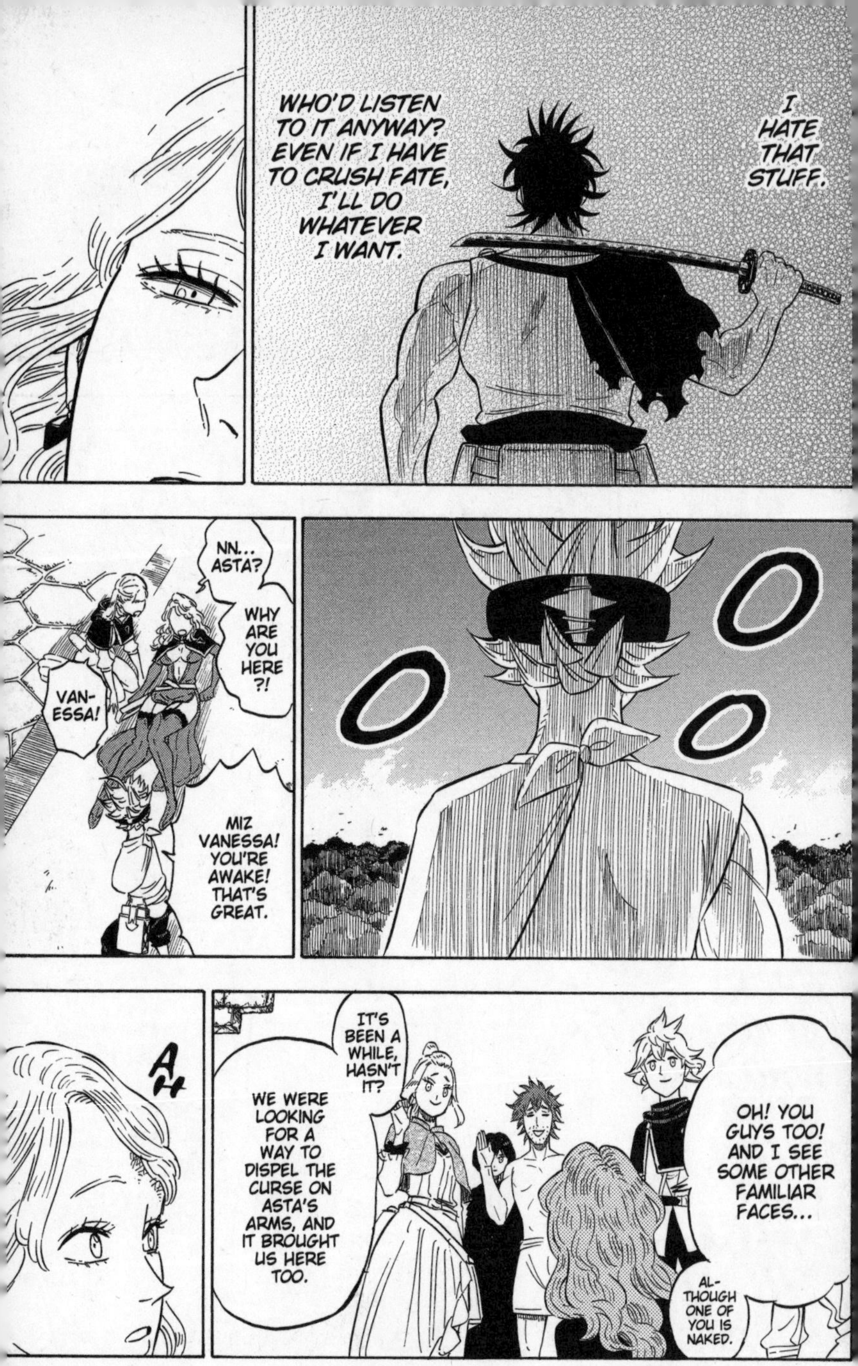
I HATE THAT STUFF.
WHO'D LISTEN TO IT ANYWAY? EVEN IF I HAVE TO CRUSH FATE, I'LL DO WHATEVER I WANT.
NN... ASTA?
WHY ARE YOU HERE?!
VAN-ESSA!
MIZ VANESSA! YOU'RE AWAKE! THAT'S GREAT.
OH! YOU GUYS TOO! AND I SEE SOME OTHER FAMILIAR FACES...
AL-THOUGH ONE OF YOU IS NAKED.
IT'S BEEN A WHILE, HASN'T IT?
WE WERE LOOKING FOR A WAY TO DISPEL THE CURSE ON ASTA'S ARMS, AND IT BROUGHT US HERE TOO.
AH

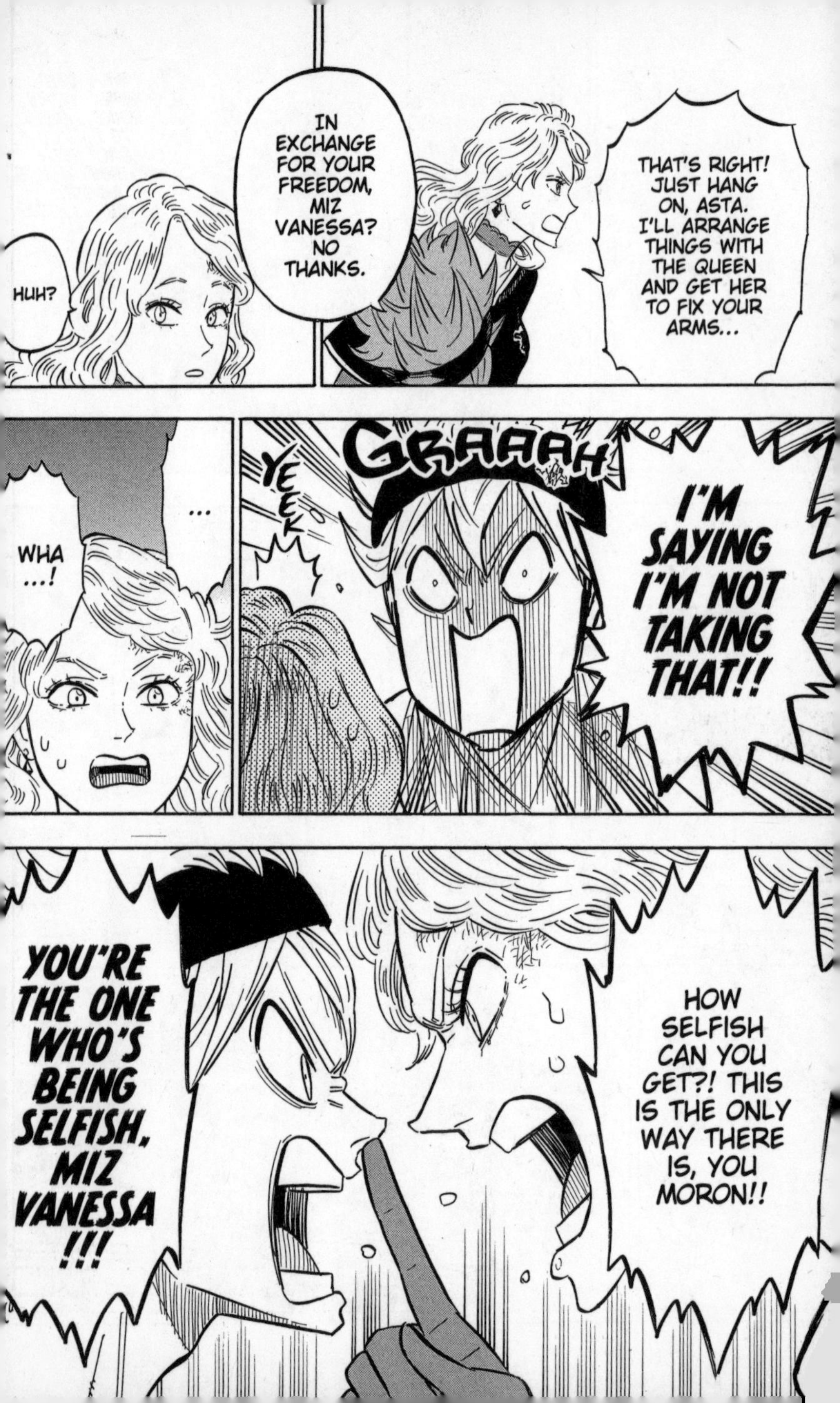
THAT'S RIGHT! JUST HANG ON, ASTA. I'LL ARRANGE THINGS WITH THE QUEEN AND GET HER TO FIX YOUR ARMS...
IN EXCHANGE FOR YOUR FREEDOM, MIZ VANESSA? NO THANKS.
HUH?
GRAAAH
YEEEK
I'M SAYING I'M NOT TAKING THAT!!
...
WHA...!
HOW SELFISH CAN YOU GET?! THIS IS THE ONLY WAY THERE IS, YOU MORON!!
YOU'RE THE ONE WHO'S BEING SELFISH, MIZ VANESSA!!!

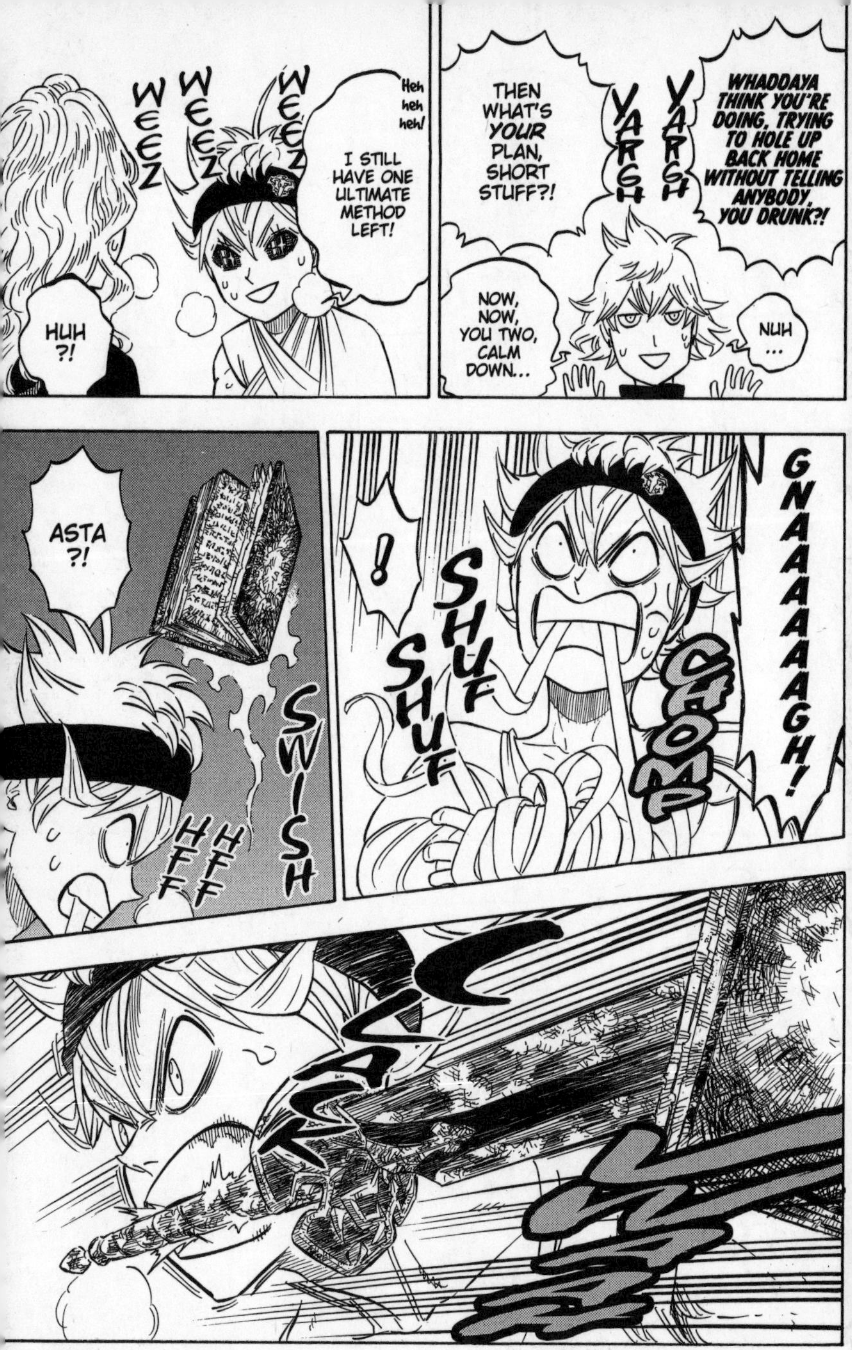

WHADDAYA THINK YOU'RE DOING, TRYING TO HOLE UP BACK HOME WITHOUT TELLING ANYBODY, YOU DRUNK?!
YARGH
YARGH
THEN WHAT'S YOUR PLAN, SHORT STUFF?!
NUH...
NOW, NOW, YOU TWO, CALM DOWN...
Heh heh heh!
I STILL HAVE ONE ULTIMATE METHOD LEFT!
WEEZ
WEEZ
WEEZ
HUH?!
GNAAAAAAAGH!
CHOMP
SHUF
SHUF
!
ASTA?!
SWISH
HFF
HFF
CLACK

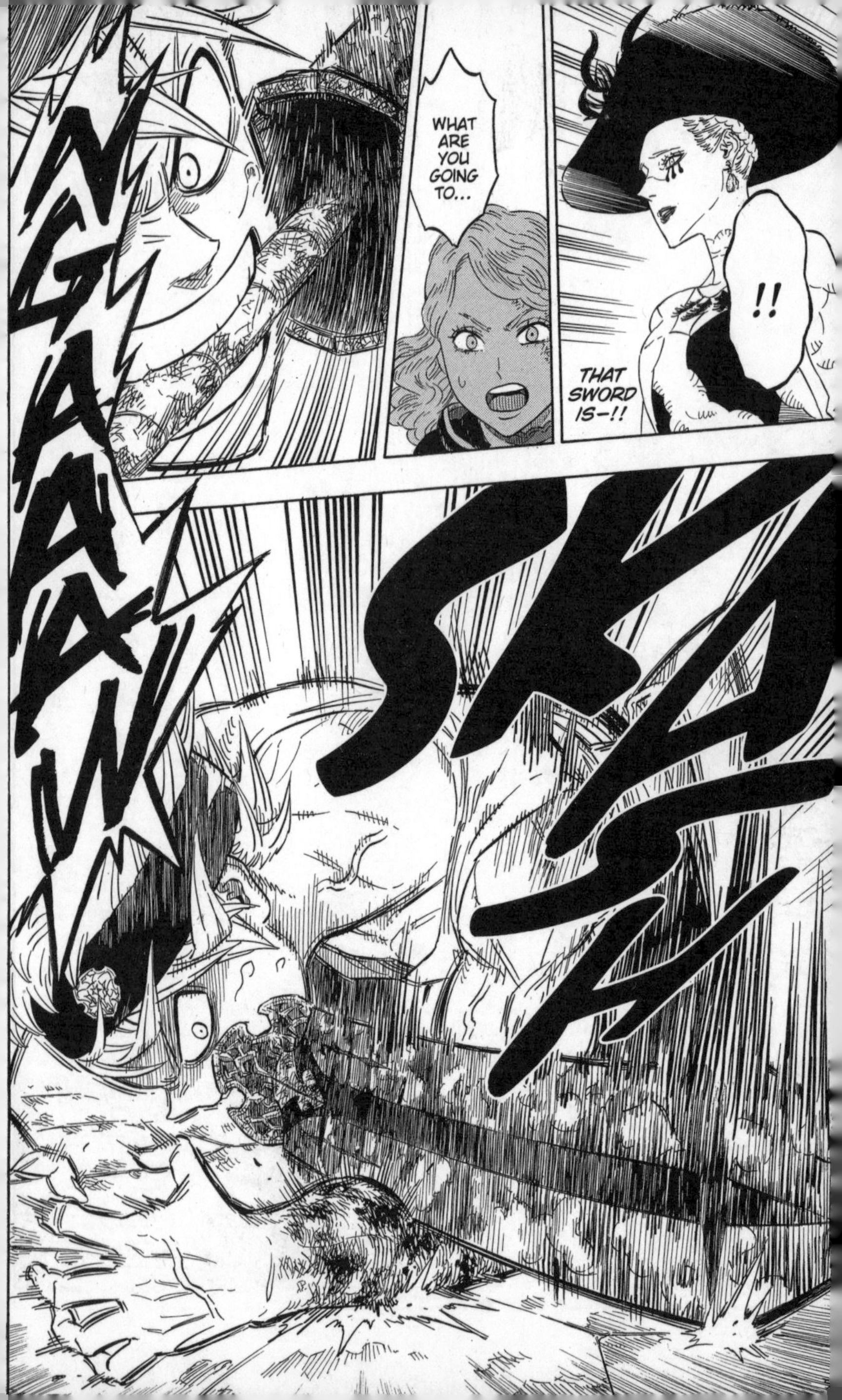
!!
THAT SWORD IS–!!
WHAT ARE YOU GOING TO...

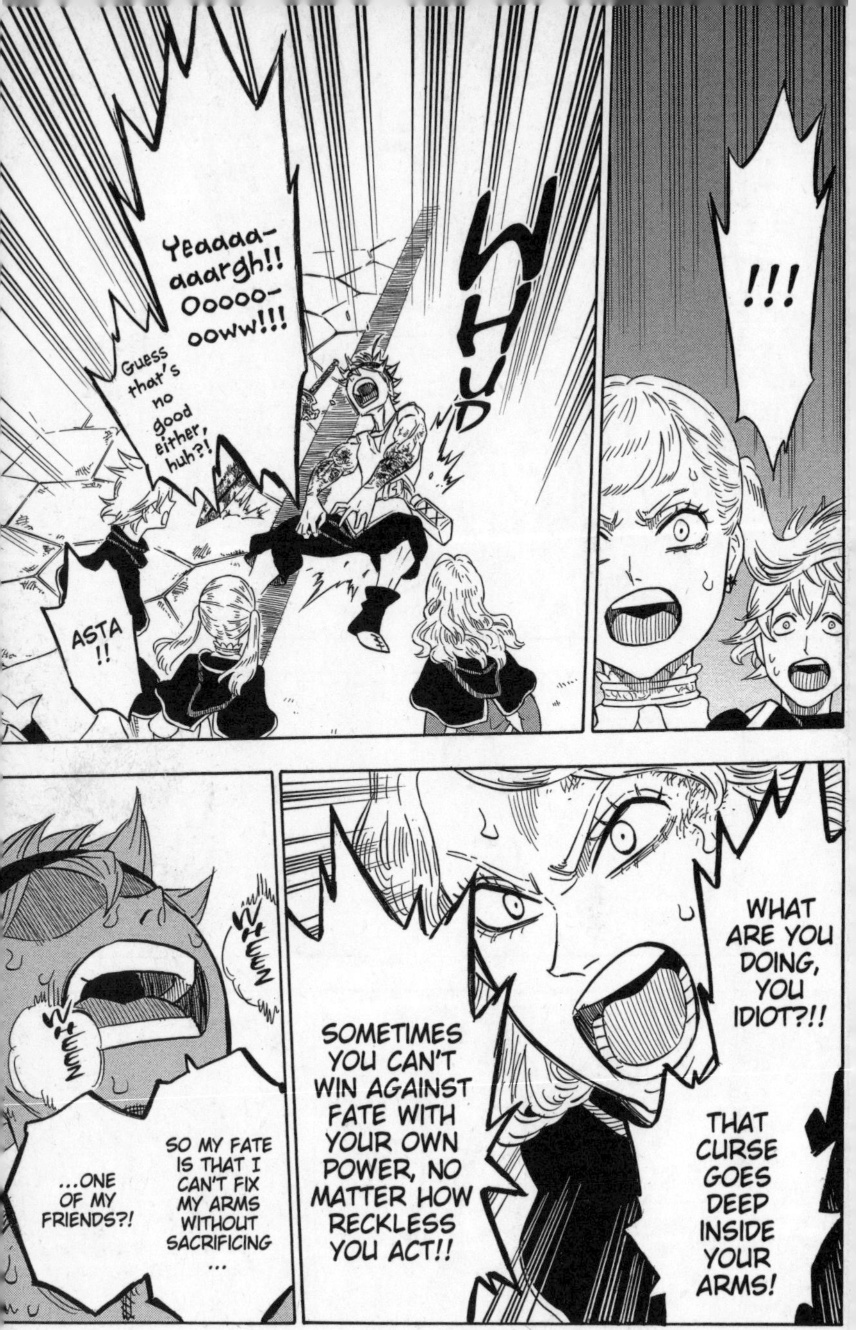
!!!
SHUD
Yeaaaa-aaargh!! Ooooo-ooww!!!
Guess that's no good either, huh?!
ASTA!!
WHAT ARE YOU DOING, YOU IDIOT?!!
THAT CURSE GOES DEEP INSIDE YOUR ARMS!
SOMETIMES YOU CAN'T WIN AGAINST FATE WITH YOUR OWN POWER, NO MATTER HOW RECKLESS YOU ACT!!
WHEEZ
WHEEZ
SO MY FATE IS THAT I CAN'T FIX MY ARMS WITHOUT SACRIFICING...
...ONE OF MY FRIENDS?!

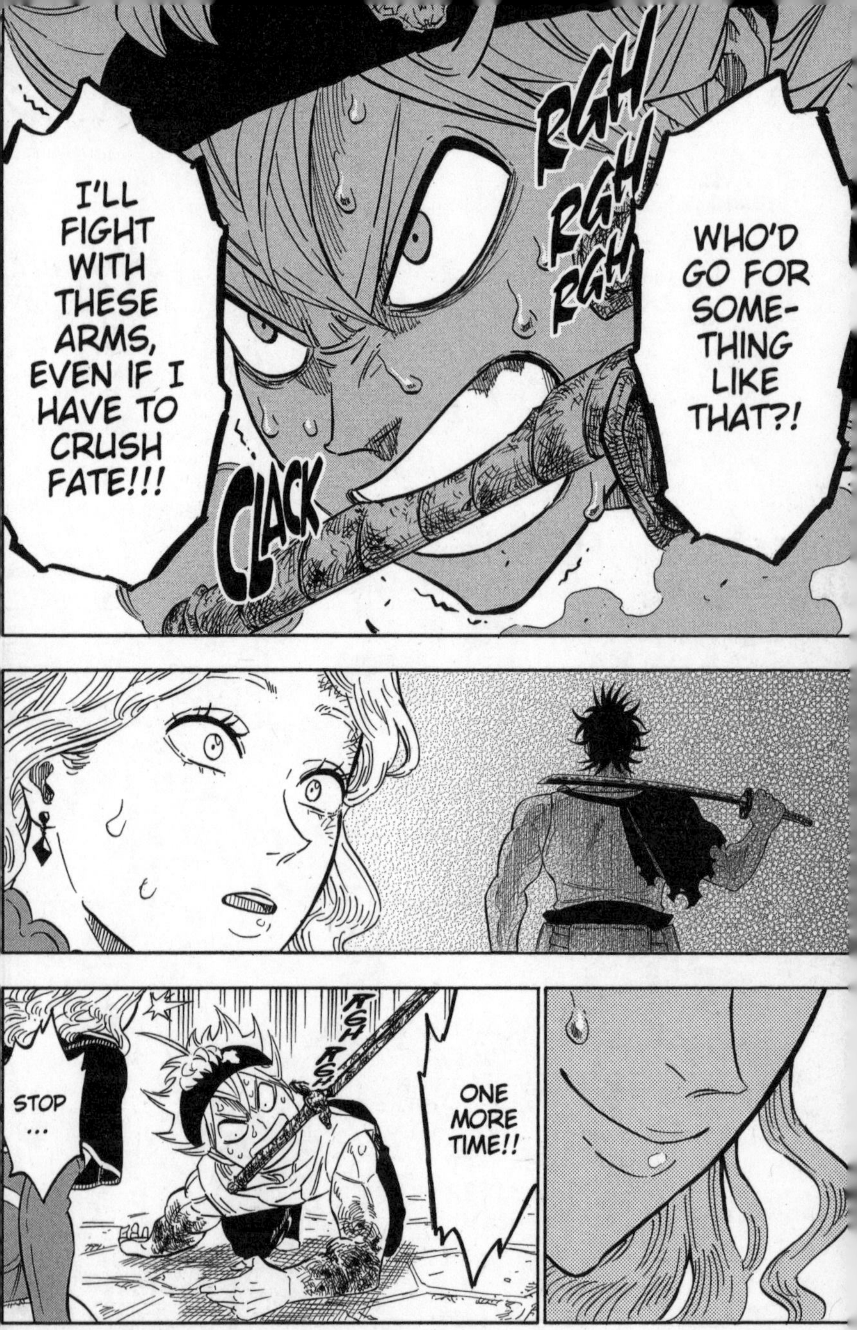
WHO'D GO FOR SOME-THING LIKE THAT?!
RGH RGH RGH
I'LL FIGHT WITH THESE ARMS, EVEN IF I HAVE TO CRUSH FATE!!!
CLACK
ONE MORE TIME!!
RGH RGH
STOP ...

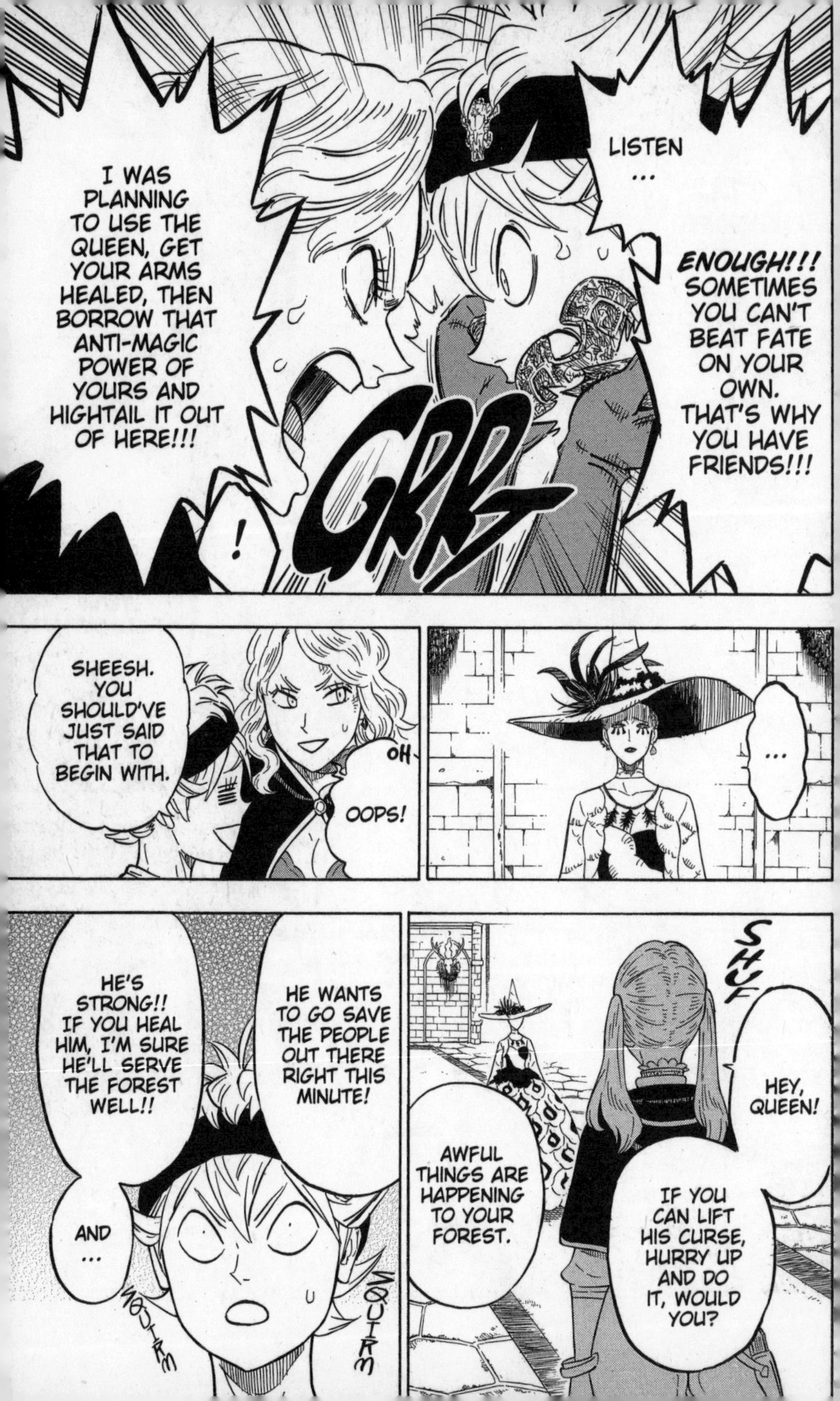

LISTEN ...
ENOUGH!!! SOMETIMES YOU CAN'T BEAT FATE ON YOUR OWN. THAT'S WHY YOU HAVE FRIENDS!!!
I WAS PLANNING TO USE THE QUEEN, GET YOUR ARMS HEALED, THEN BORROW THAT ANTI-MAGIC POWER OF YOURS AND HIGHTAIL IT OUT OF HERE!!!
GRR
!
...
SHEESH. YOU SHOULD'VE JUST SAID THAT TO BEGIN WITH.
OH-
OOPS!
SHUF
HEY, QUEEN!
IF YOU CAN LIFT HIS CURSE, HURRY UP AND DO IT, WOULD YOU?
AWFUL THINGS ARE HAPPENING TO YOUR FOREST.
HE WANTS TO GO SAVE THE PEOPLE OUT THERE RIGHT THIS MINUTE!
HE'S STRONG!! IF YOU HEAL HIM, I'M SURE HE'LL SERVE THE FOREST WELL!!
AND ...
SQUIRM
SQUIRM

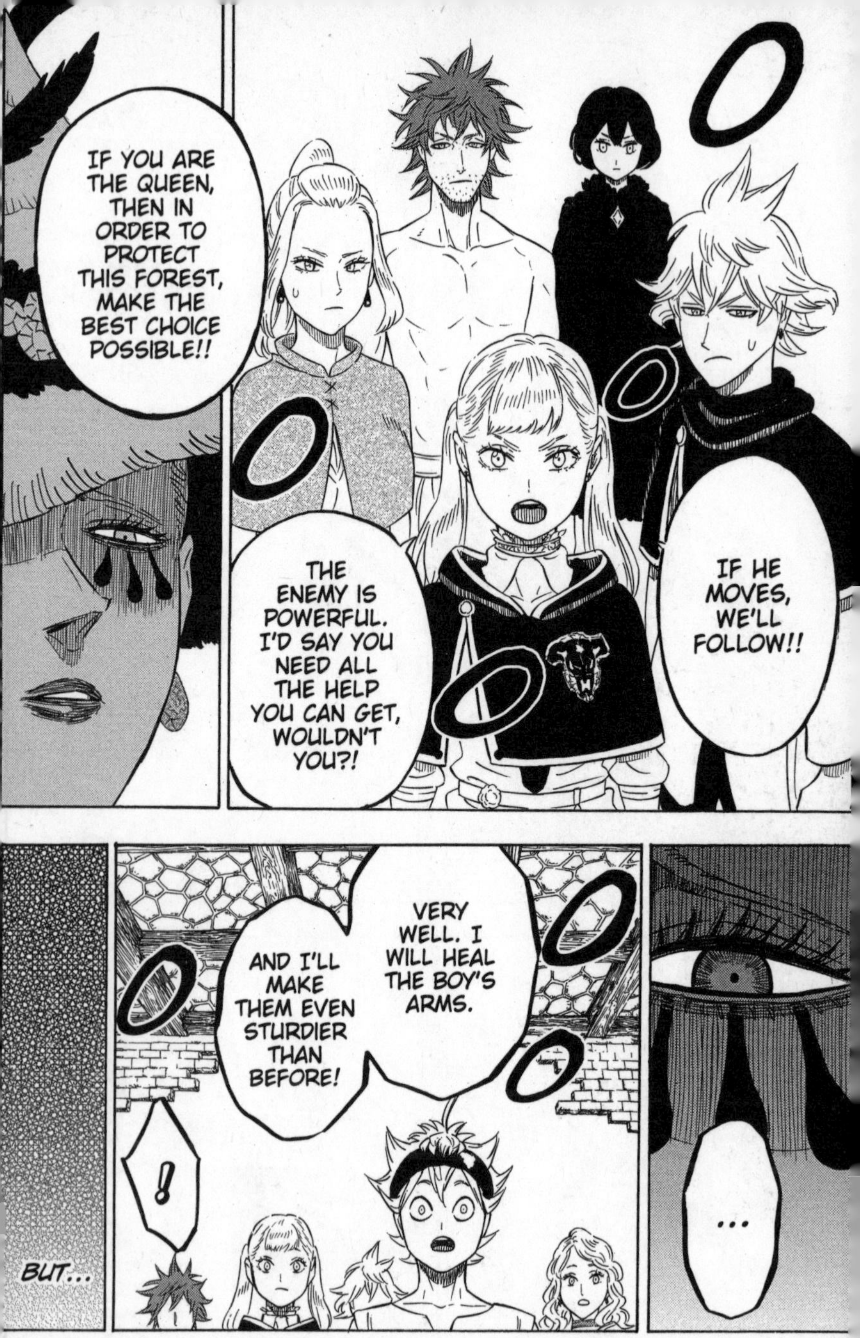
IF HE MOVES, WE'LL FOLLOW!!
THE ENEMY IS POWERFUL. I'D SAY YOU NEED ALL THE HELP YOU CAN GET, WOULDN'T YOU?!
IF YOU ARE THE QUEEN, THEN IN ORDER TO PROTECT THIS FOREST, MAKE THE BEST CHOICE POSSIBLE!!
...
VERY WELL. I WILL HEAL THE BOY'S ARMS.
AND I'LL MAKE THEM EVEN STURDIER THAN BEFORE!
!
BUT...

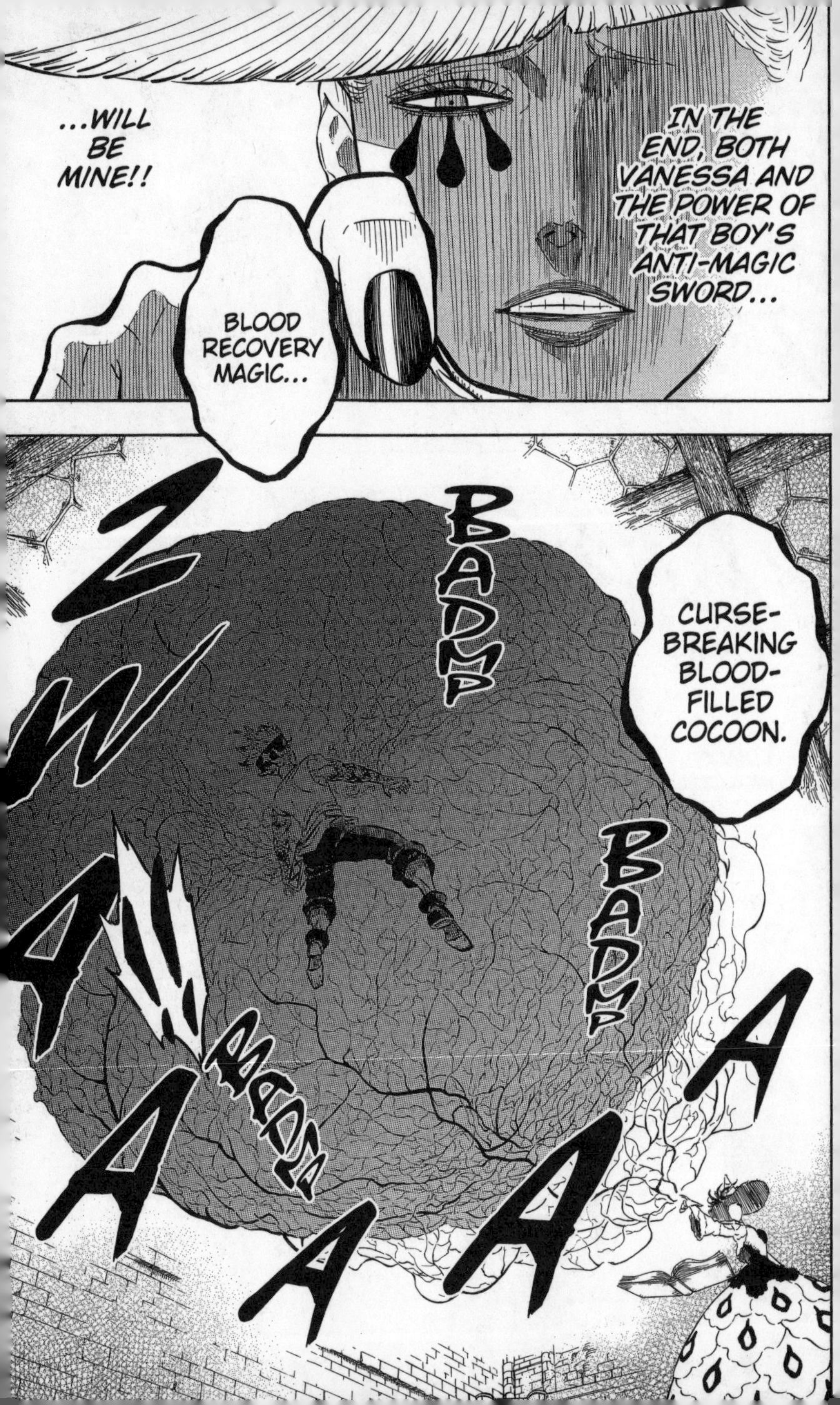
IN THE END, BOTH VANESSA AND THE POWER OF THAT BOY'S ANTI-MAGIC SWORD...
...WILL BE MINE!!
BLOOD RECOVERY MAGIC...
CURSE-BREAKING BLOOD-FILLED COCOON.
BADMP
BADMP
BADMP
ZWAA!!
AAAA

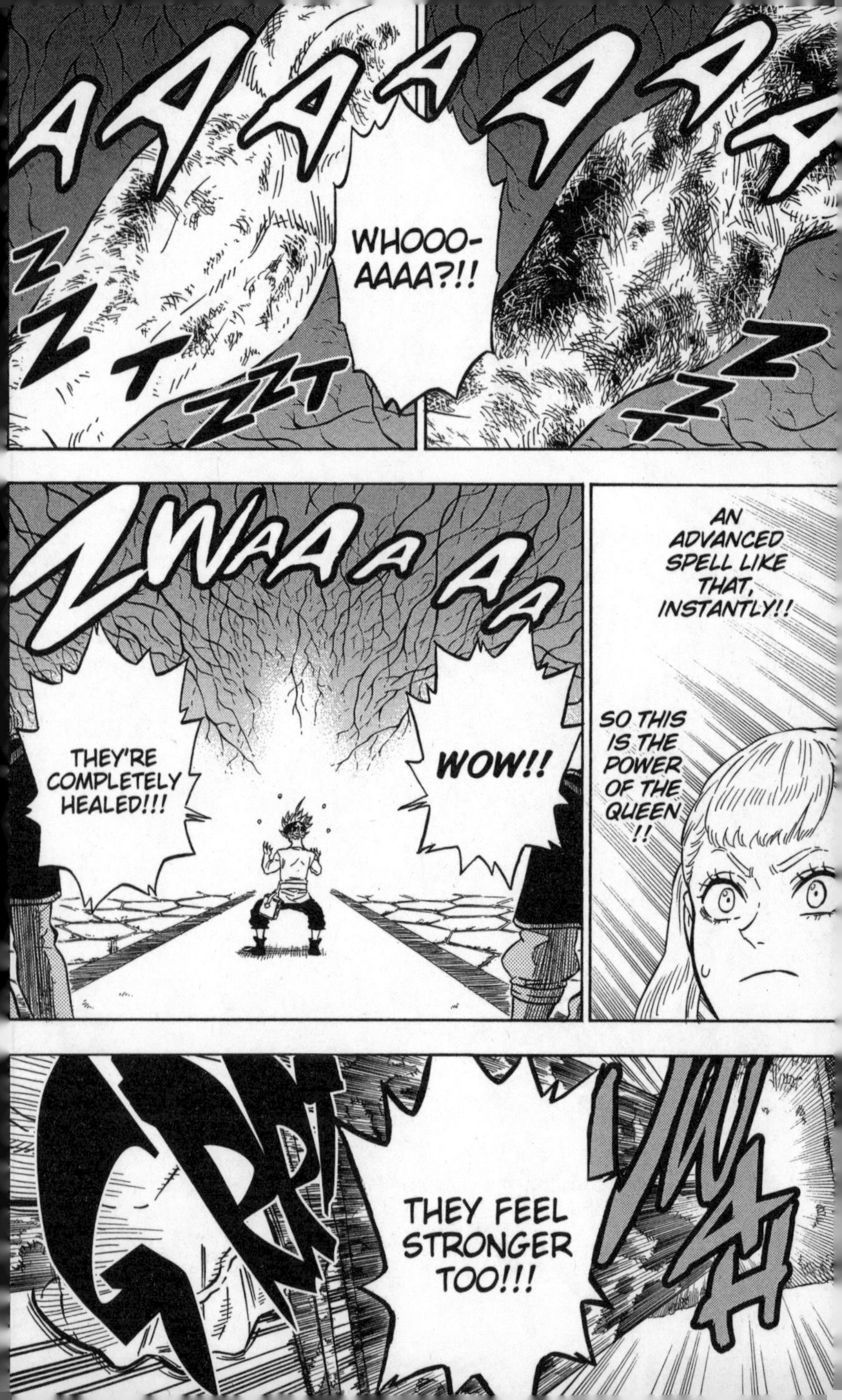
WHOOOO-AAAA?!!
AN ADVANCED SPELL LIKE THAT, INSTANTLY!!
SO THIS IS THE POWER OF THE QUEEN!!
ZWAAAAAA
WOW!!
THEY'RE COMPLETELY HEALED!!!
THEY FEEL STRONGER TOO!!!

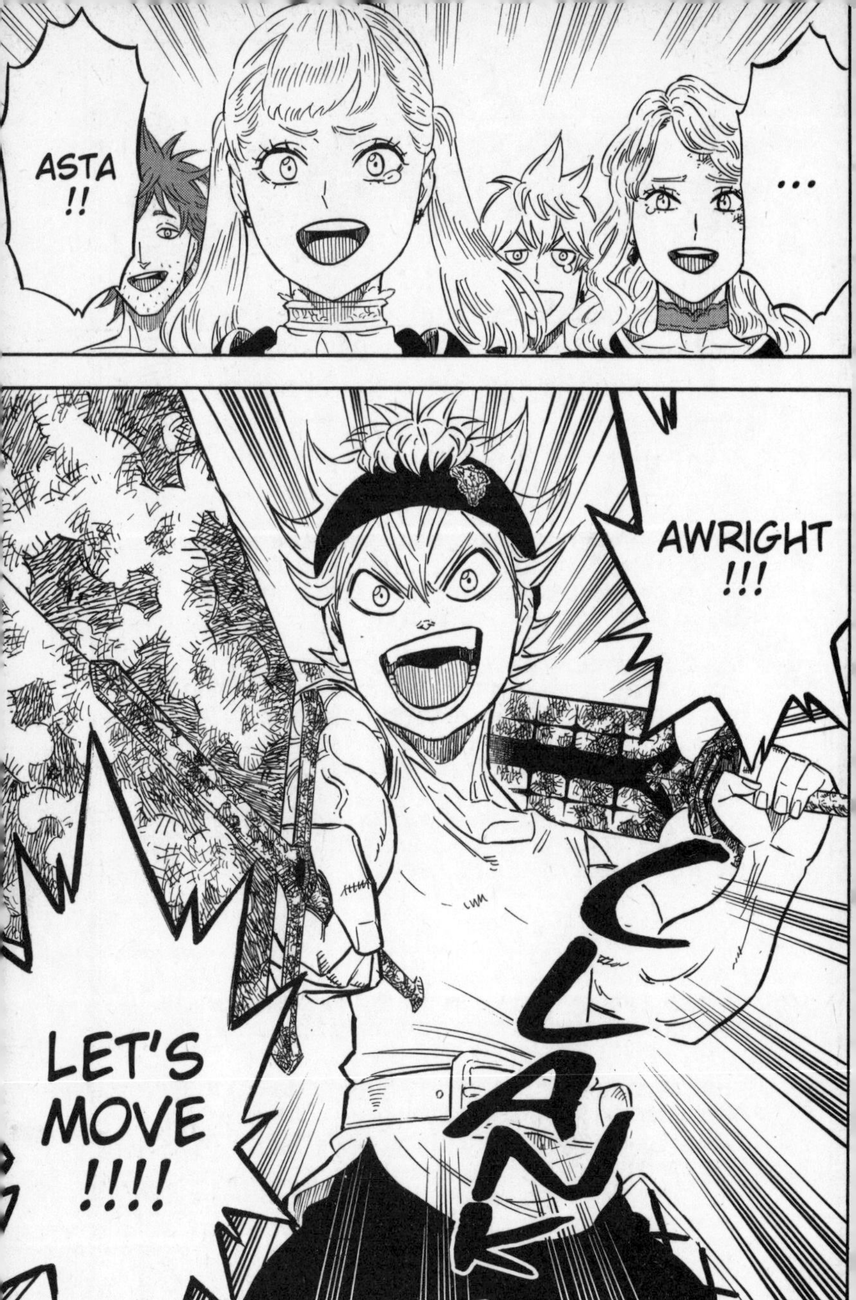
...
ASTA!!
AWRIGHT!!!
LET'S MOVE!!!!
CLANK

The Assorted Questions Brigade No. 1

Good day! Good evening! Good morning!
It's time for the letters corner. This time,
I'll tackle the mysteries surrounding
grimoires, and maybe publicize the results
of that one ranking!! Don't miss it!!

Q: Captain Yami, Yuno as a kid, and Mars used magic without their grimoires. How much magic, and what kind of magic, can you use without a grimoire? (Good Dog, Shizuoka Prefecture)

A: You can use simple spells that don't have a special shape. That means firing magic bullets, charging magic items and simply emitting and controlling magic. If you have a fire attribute, you can produce fire; if it's a water attribute, you can produce water. The more magic power you have, the greater the amount of fire you can produce. How well you can control it determines your amount of control over the movement of the flames.

Q: Whose grimoire is used in the cover design on the comics?! (Niigata Prefecture, Candy Magician)

A: The grimoire in the cover design belongs to the character on the spine of the next volume. The flow may change one of these days, but for now, that's what it is.

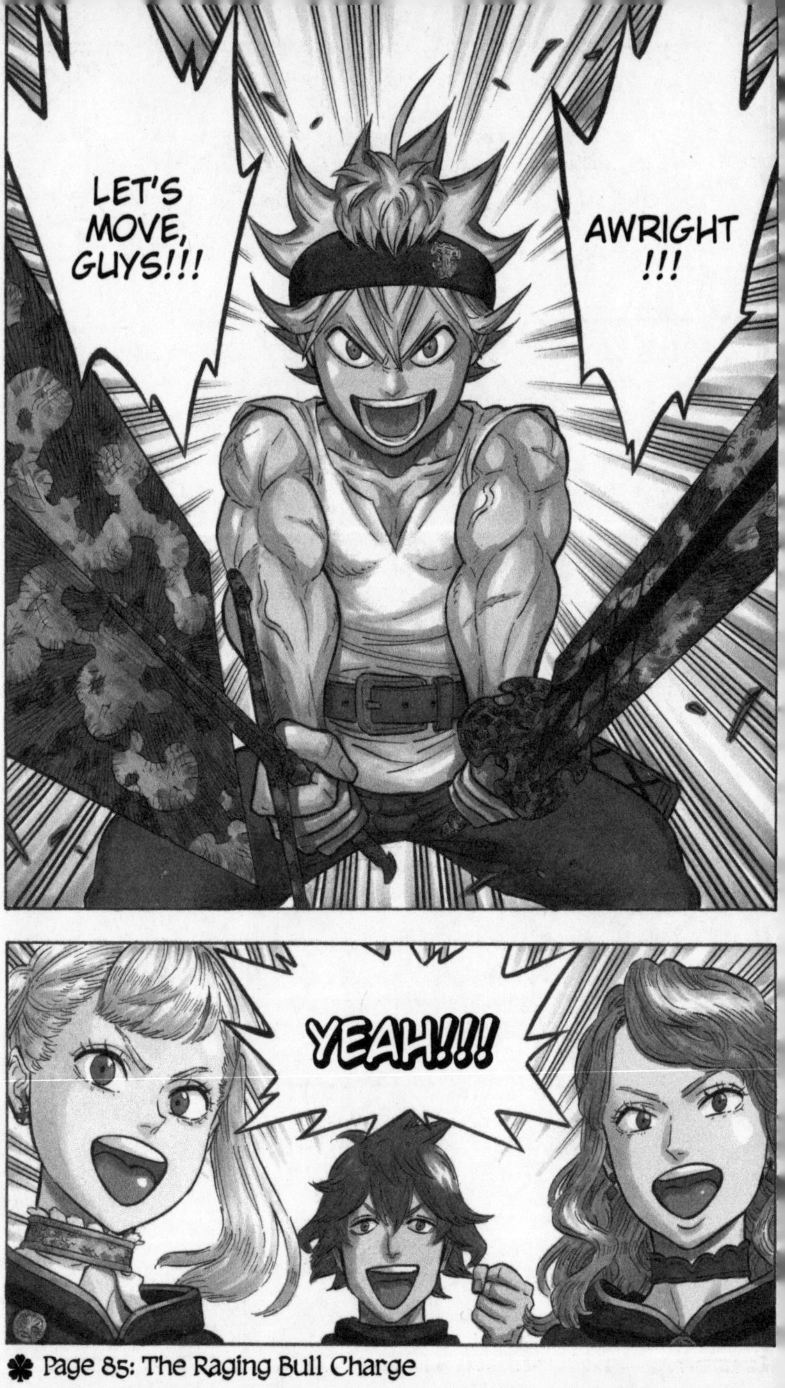
LET'S MOVE, GUYS!!!
AWRIGHT !!!
YEAH!!!

Page 85: The Raging Bull Charge

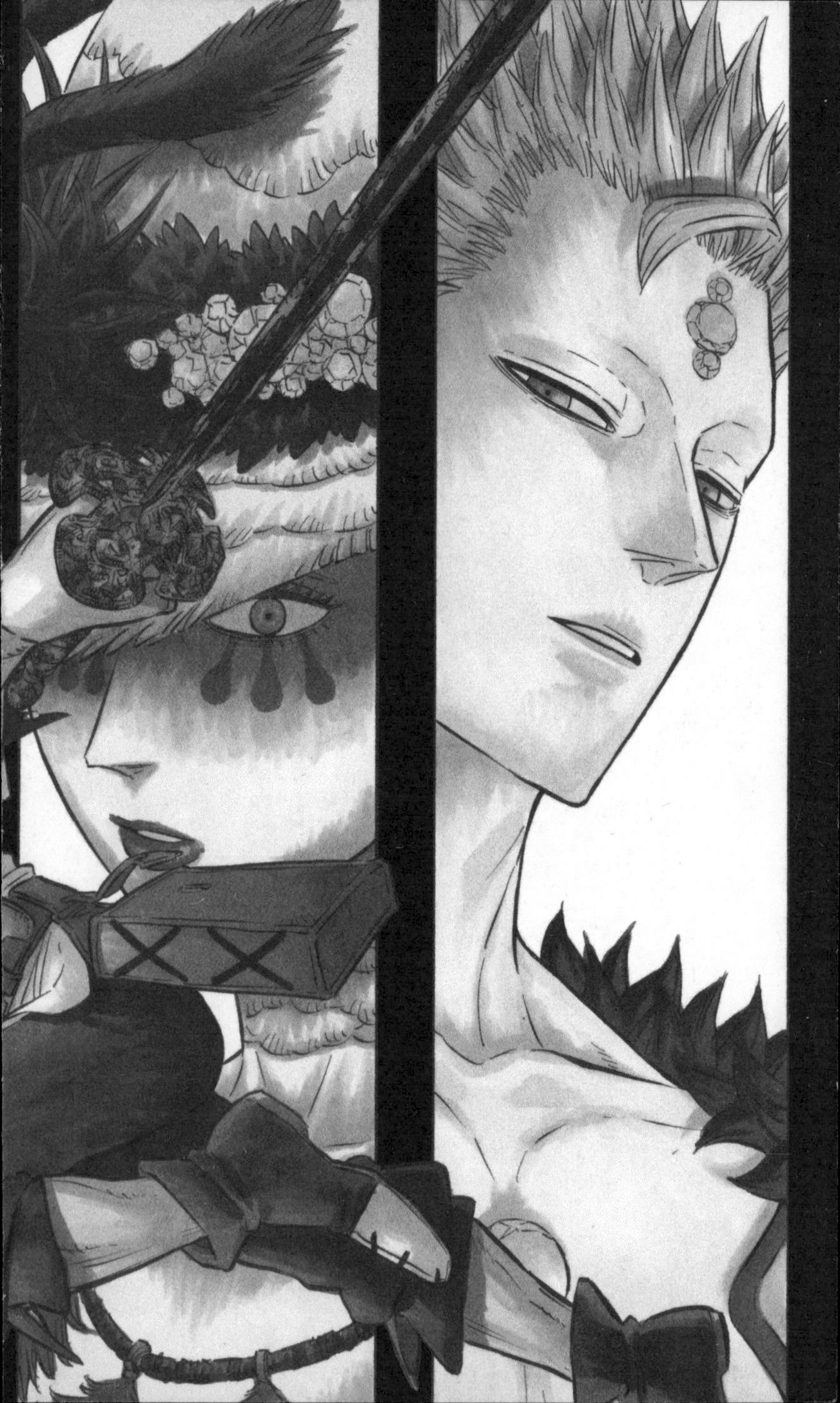

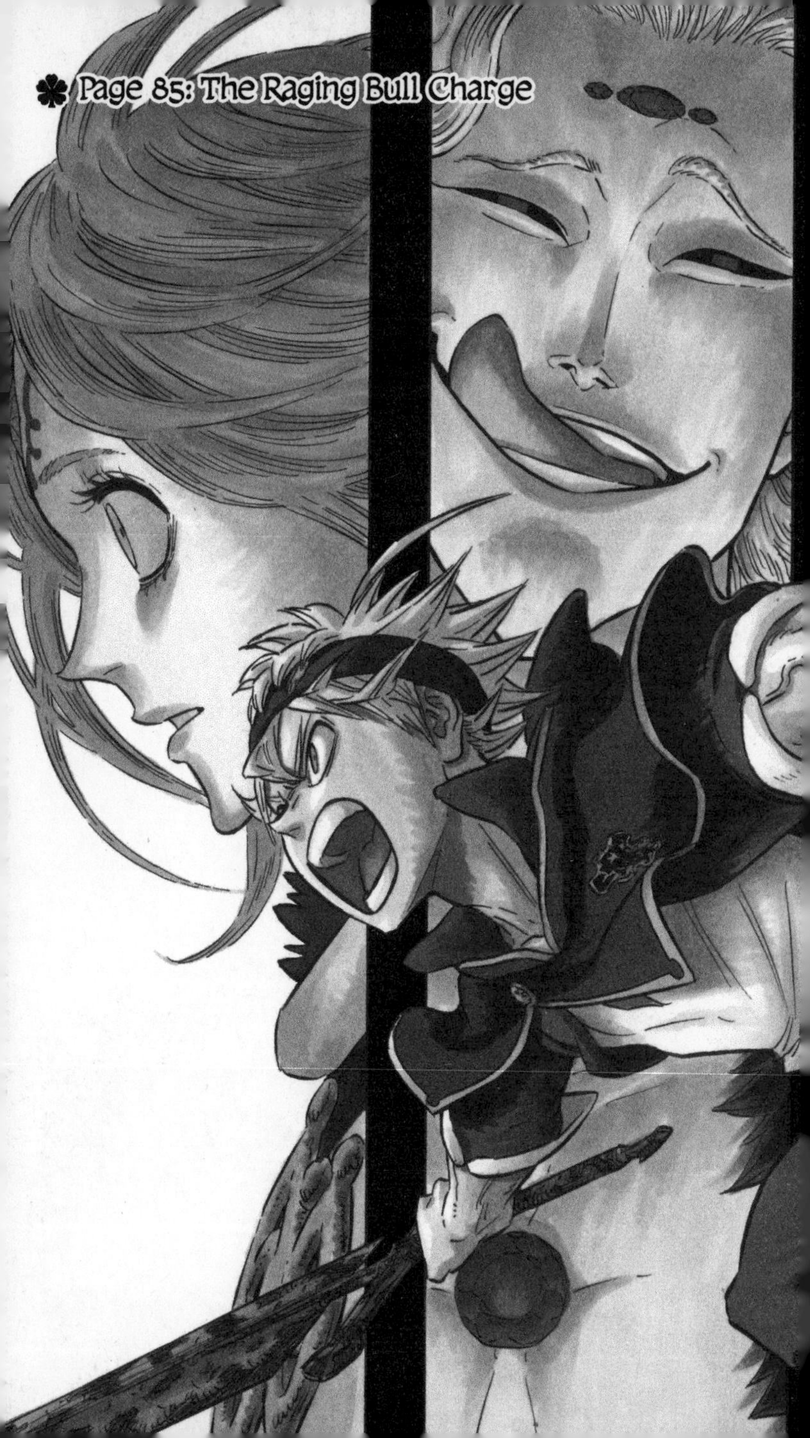
Page 85: The Raging Bull Charge

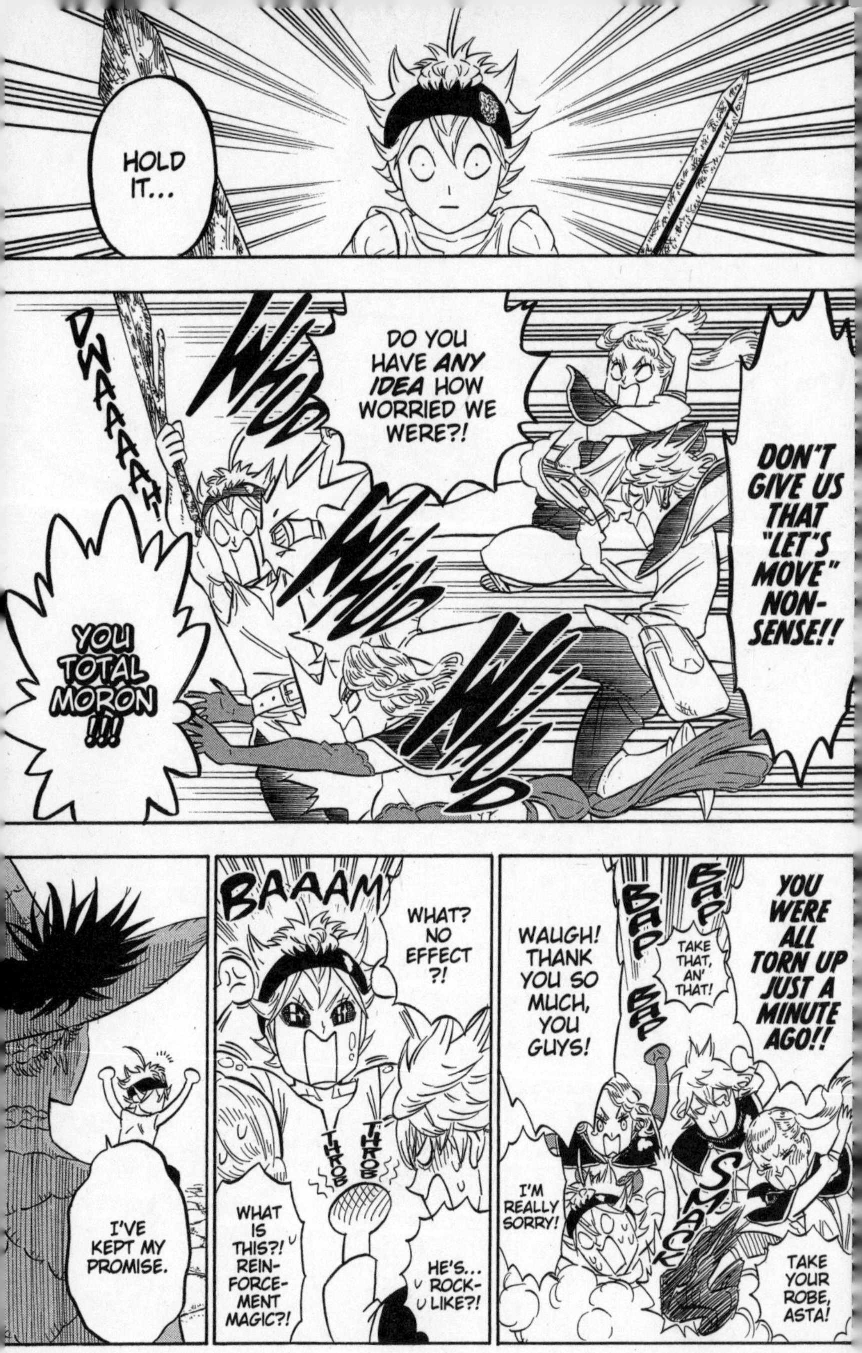

HOLD IT...
DON'T GIVE US THAT "LET'S MOVE" NON-SENSE!!
DO YOU HAVE ANY IDEA HOW WORRIED WE WERE?!
DWAAAAAH!
YOU TOTAL MORON!!!
YOU WERE ALL TORN UP JUST A MINUTE AGO!!
BAP
TAKE THAT, AN' THAT!
BAP
BAP
WAUGH! THANK YOU SO MUCH, YOU GUYS!
SMACK
I'M REALLY SORRY!
TAKE YOUR ROBE, ASTA!
BAAAM
WHAT? NO EFFECT?!
THROB
THROB
HE'S... ROCK-LIKE?!
WHAT IS THIS?! REIN-FORCEMENT MAGIC?!
I'VE KEPT MY PROMISE.

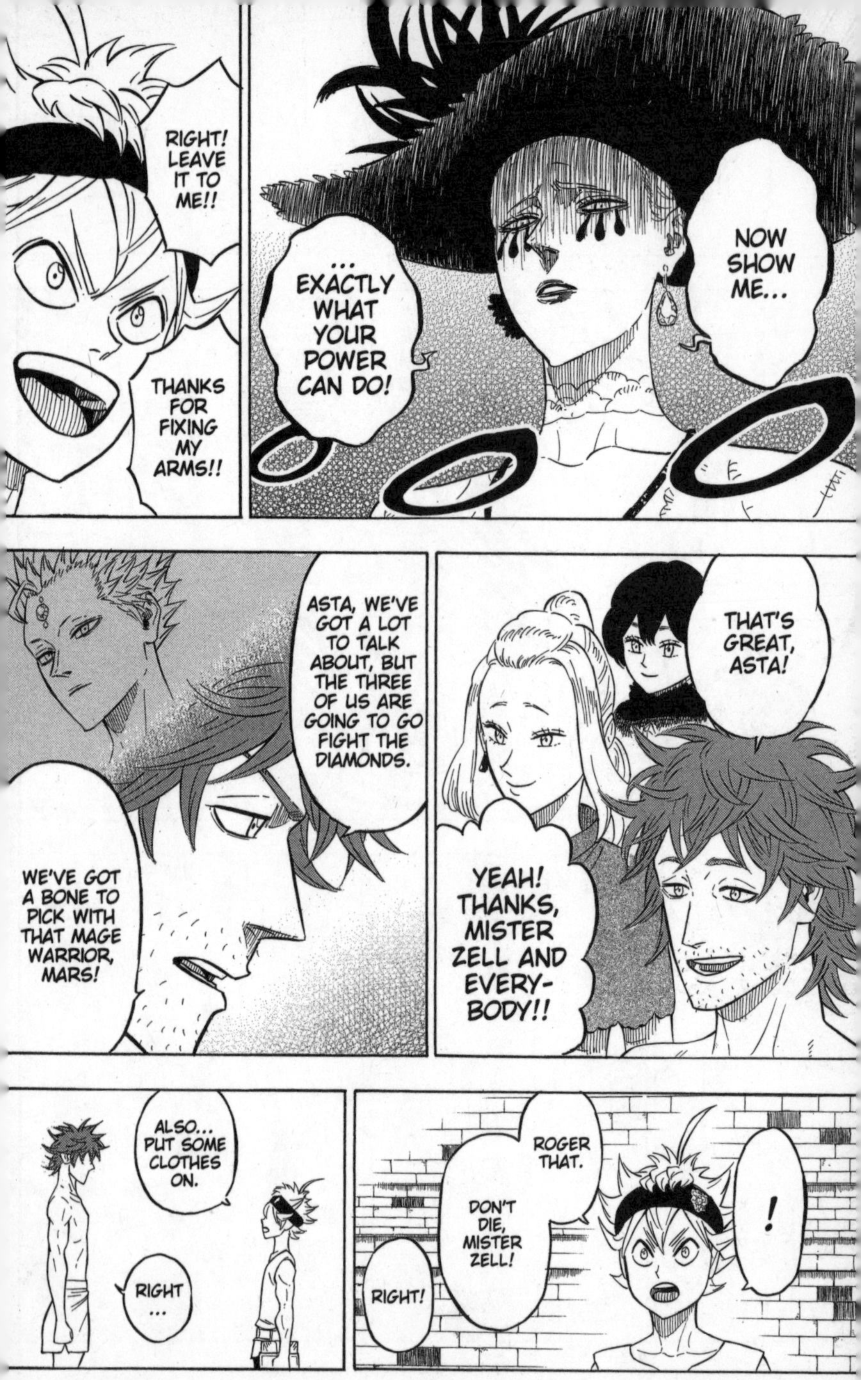
NOW SHOW ME...
...EXACTLY WHAT YOUR POWER CAN DO!
RIGHT! LEAVE IT TO ME!!
THANKS FOR FIXING MY ARMS!!
THAT'S GREAT, ASTA!
YEAH! THANKS, MISTER ZELL AND EVERY-BODY!!
ASTA, WE'VE GOT A LOT TO TALK ABOUT, BUT THE THREE OF US ARE GOING TO GO FIGHT THE DIAMONDS.
WE'VE GOT A BONE TO PICK WITH THAT MAGE WARRIOR, MARS!
!
ROGER THAT.
DON'T DIE, MISTER ZELL!
RIGHT!
ALSO... PUT SOME CLOTHES ON.
RIGHT ...

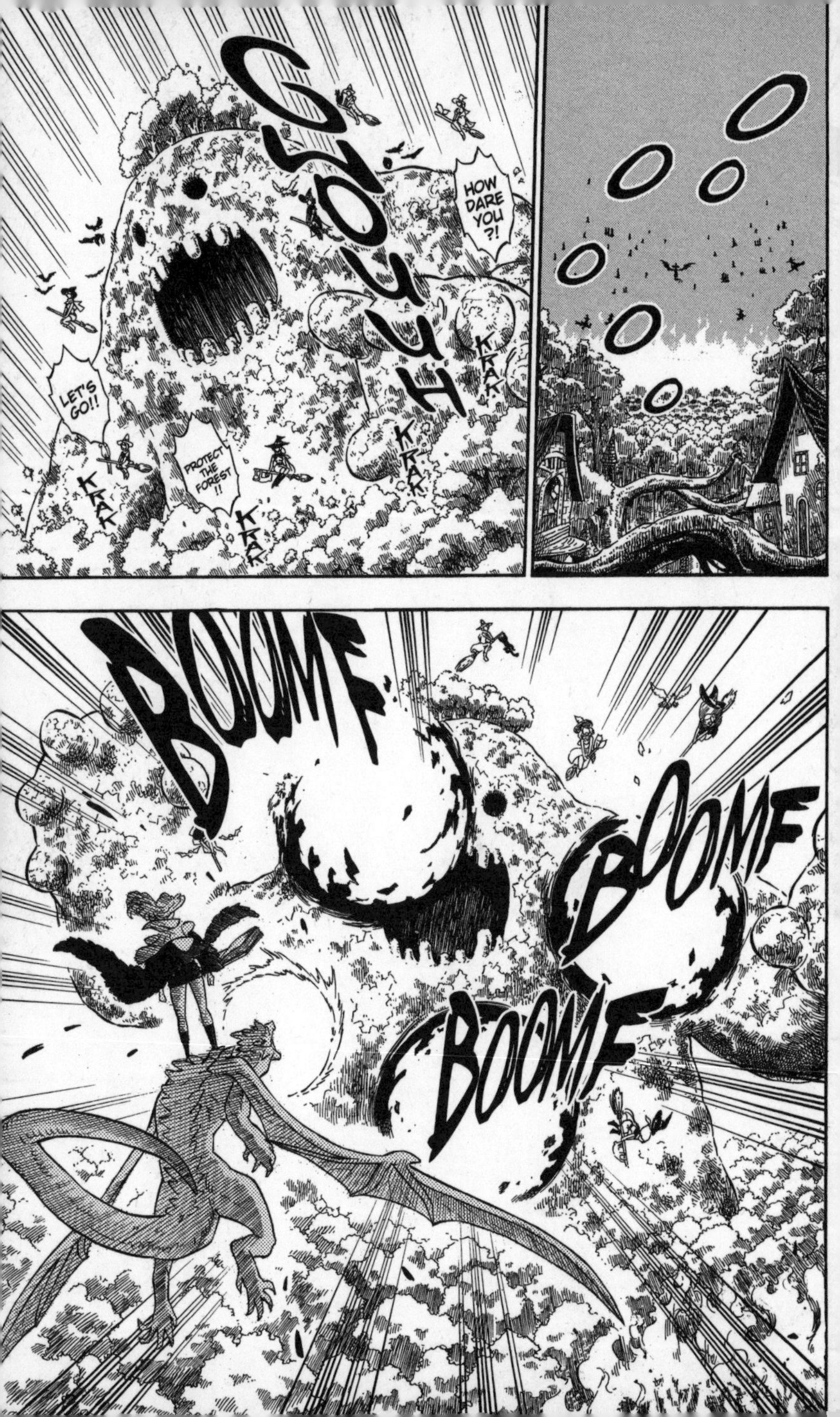
OOOOOO
GOUUUH
HOW DARE YOU ?!
KRAK
KRAK
LET'S GO!!
PROTECT THE FOREST !!
KRAK
KRAK
BOOMF
BOOMF
BOOMF

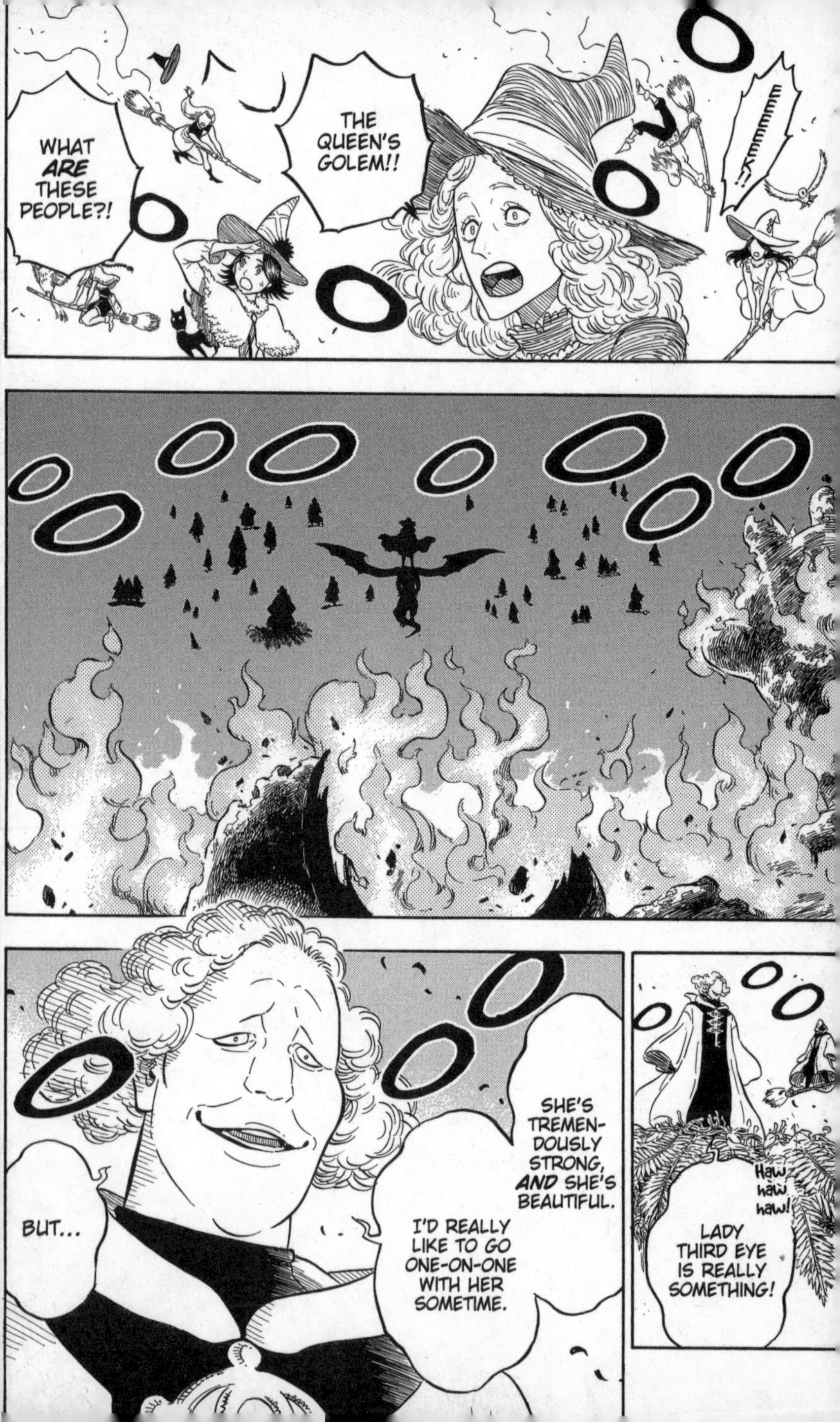
EEEEEEEEEEK!!
THE QUEEN'S GOLEM!!
WHAT ***ARE*** THESE PEOPLE?!
Haw haw haw!
LADY THIRD EYE IS REALLY SOMETHING!
SHE'S TREMENDOUSLY STRONG, ***AND*** SHE'S BEAUTIFUL.
I'D REALLY LIKE TO GO ONE-ON-ONE WITH HER SOMETIME.
BUT...

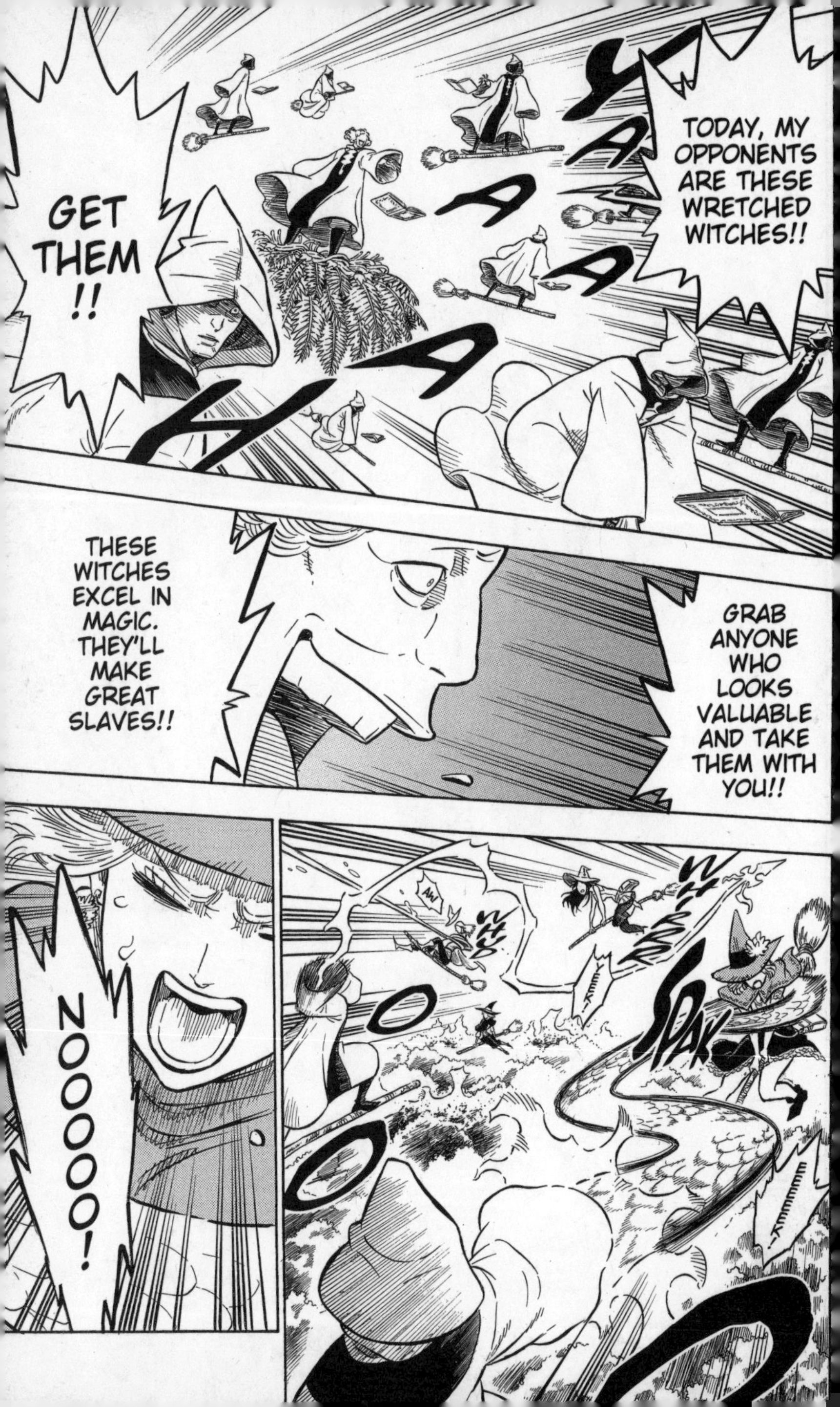
TODAY, MY OPPONENTS ARE THESE WRETCHED WITCHES!!
YAAAAH
GET THEM!!
GRAB ANYONE WHO LOOKS VALUABLE AND TAKE THEM WITH YOU!!
THESE WITCHES EXCEL IN MAGIC. THEY'LL MAKE GREAT SLAVES!!
SPAK
YEEK!
AW
NOOOOOO!

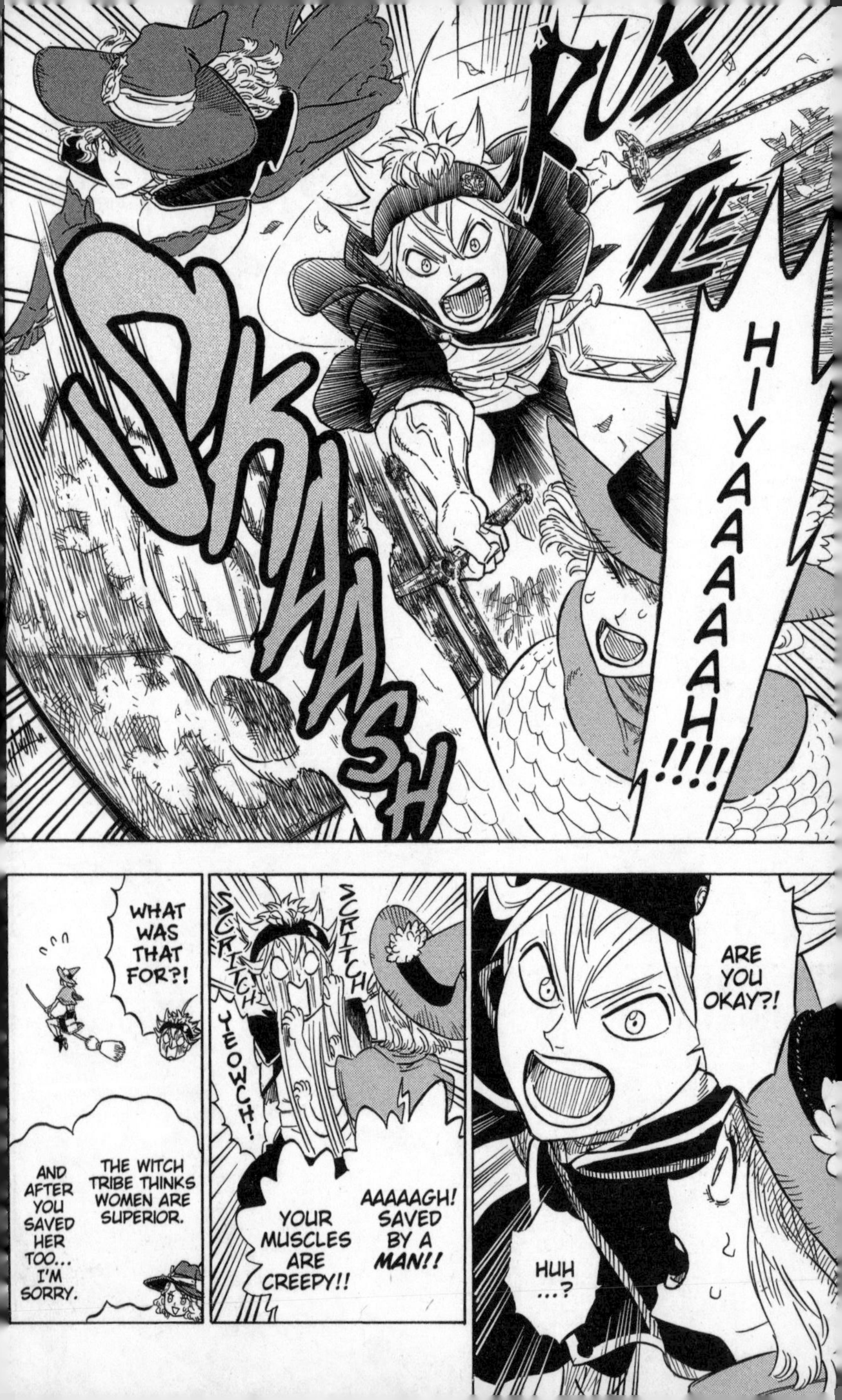
RUSTLE
HIYAAAAAAH!!!!
ARE YOU OKAY?!
HUH ...?
AAAAAGH! SAVED BY A MAN!!
YOUR MUSCLES ARE CREEPY!!
SCRITCH
SCRITCH
YEOWCH!
WHAT WAS THAT FOR?!
THE WITCH TRIBE THINKS WOMEN ARE SUPERIOR.
AND AFTER YOU SAVED HER TOO... I'M SORRY.

YOU THINK YOU CAN JUST DO WHATEVER YOU WANT?!

THIS HAPPENS TO BE MY HOMETOWN, AND I *WILL* PROTECT IT!!

SPLOOSH

LET'S PUT THAT FIRE OUT FIRST!!

THANK YOU, NOELLE!!

THAT TAKES CARE OF TONIGHT'S ENTERTAINMENT!!

LET ME GOOOO!!

THIS PLACE HAS ALL SORTS OF FINE SLAVE GIRLS!!

HAW HAW HAW!

NOOOOO!

HUH?! IF I SHOOT YOU THAT FAR, I WON'T BE ABLE TO STEER YOU!!

MIZ VANESSA! USE YOUR THREAD AND BLAST ME OVER TO THEM!

IT'S FINE!

THAT SCUMBAG!! WHAT IS HE DOING TO THOSE CUTIES?!

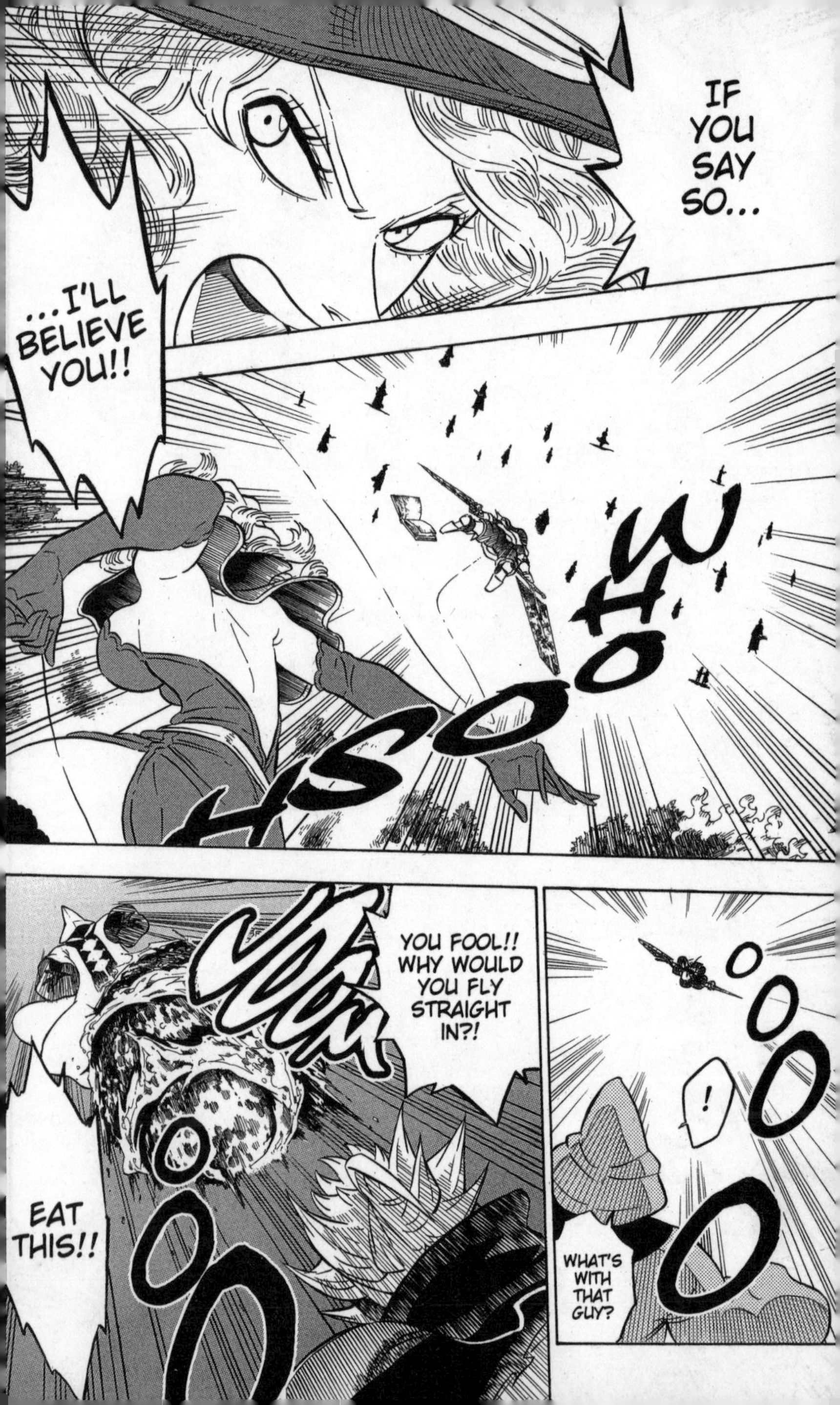
IF YOU SAY SO...
...I'LL BELIEVE YOU!!
WHOOSH
!
WHAT'S WITH THAT GUY?
YOU FOOL!! WHY WOULD YOU FLY STRAIGHT IN?!
EAT THIS!!

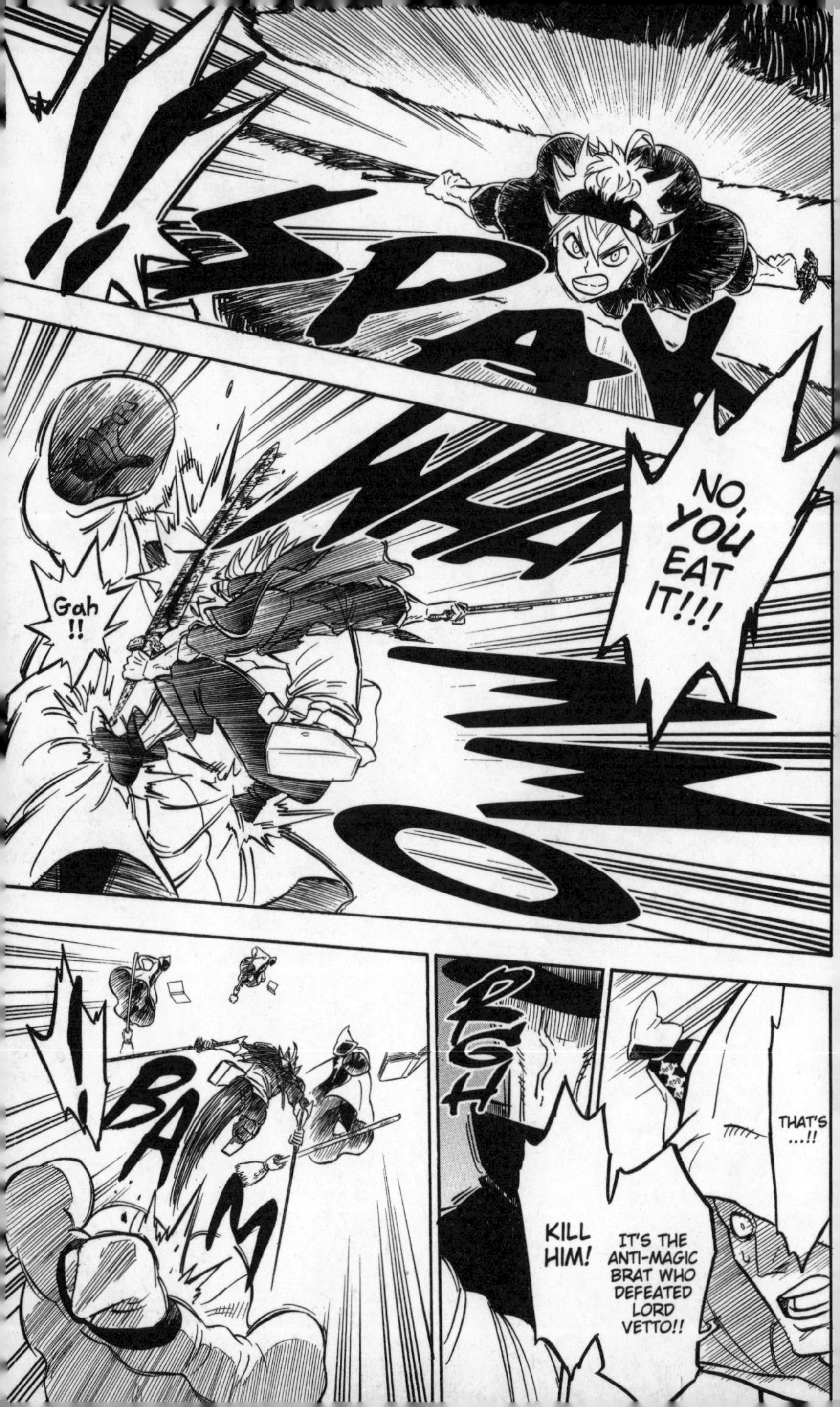
NO, YOU EAT IT!!!
Gah !!
THAT'S ...!!
IT'S THE ANTI-MAGIC BRAT WHO DEFEATED LORD VETTO!!
KILL HIM!
BAM

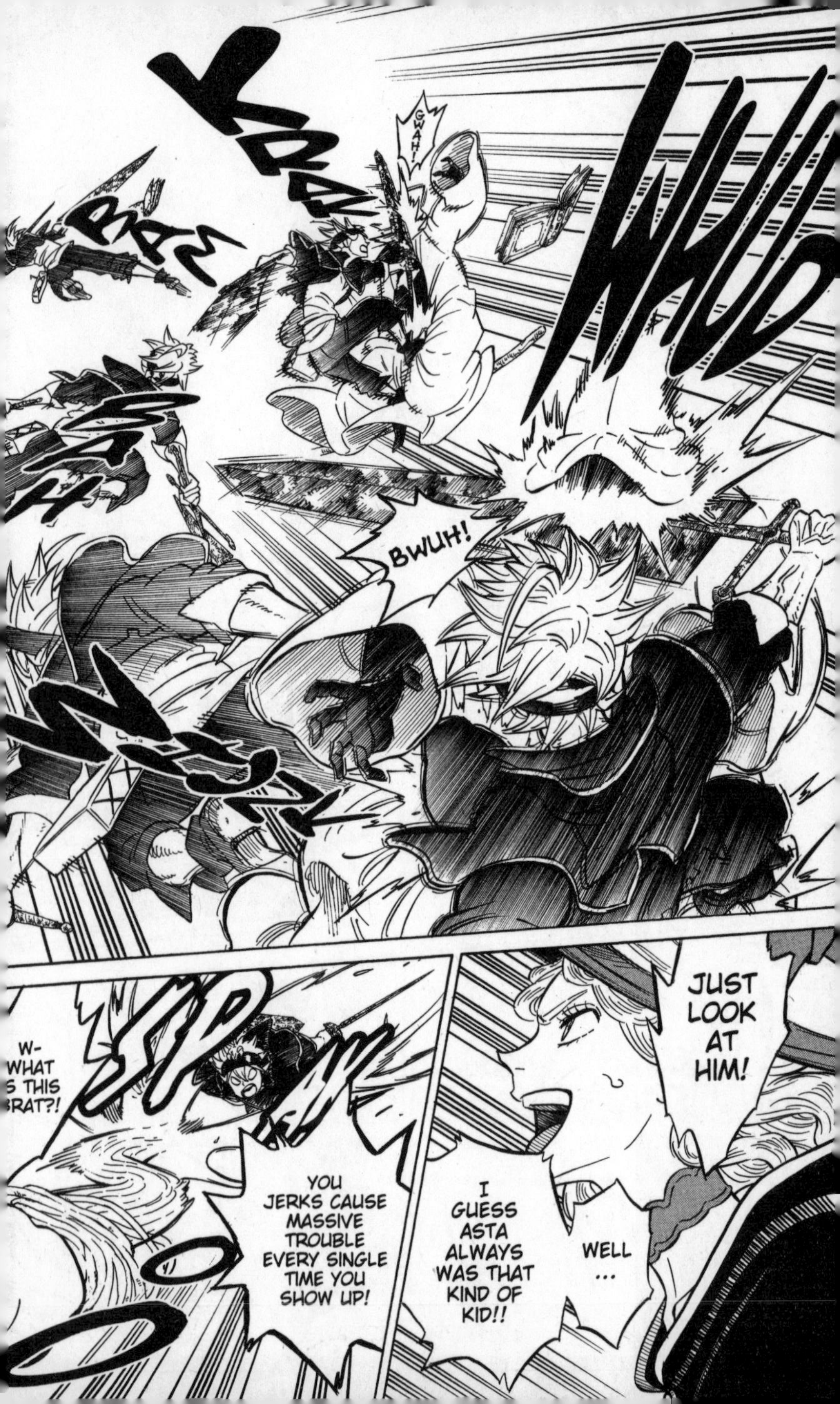
WHUD
GWAH!
BWUH!
JUST LOOK AT HIM!
WELL...
I GUESS ASTA ALWAYS WAS THAT KIND OF KID!!
YOU JERKS CAUSE MASSIVE TROUBLE EVERY SINGLE TIME YOU SHOW UP!
W-WHAT S THIS RAT?!

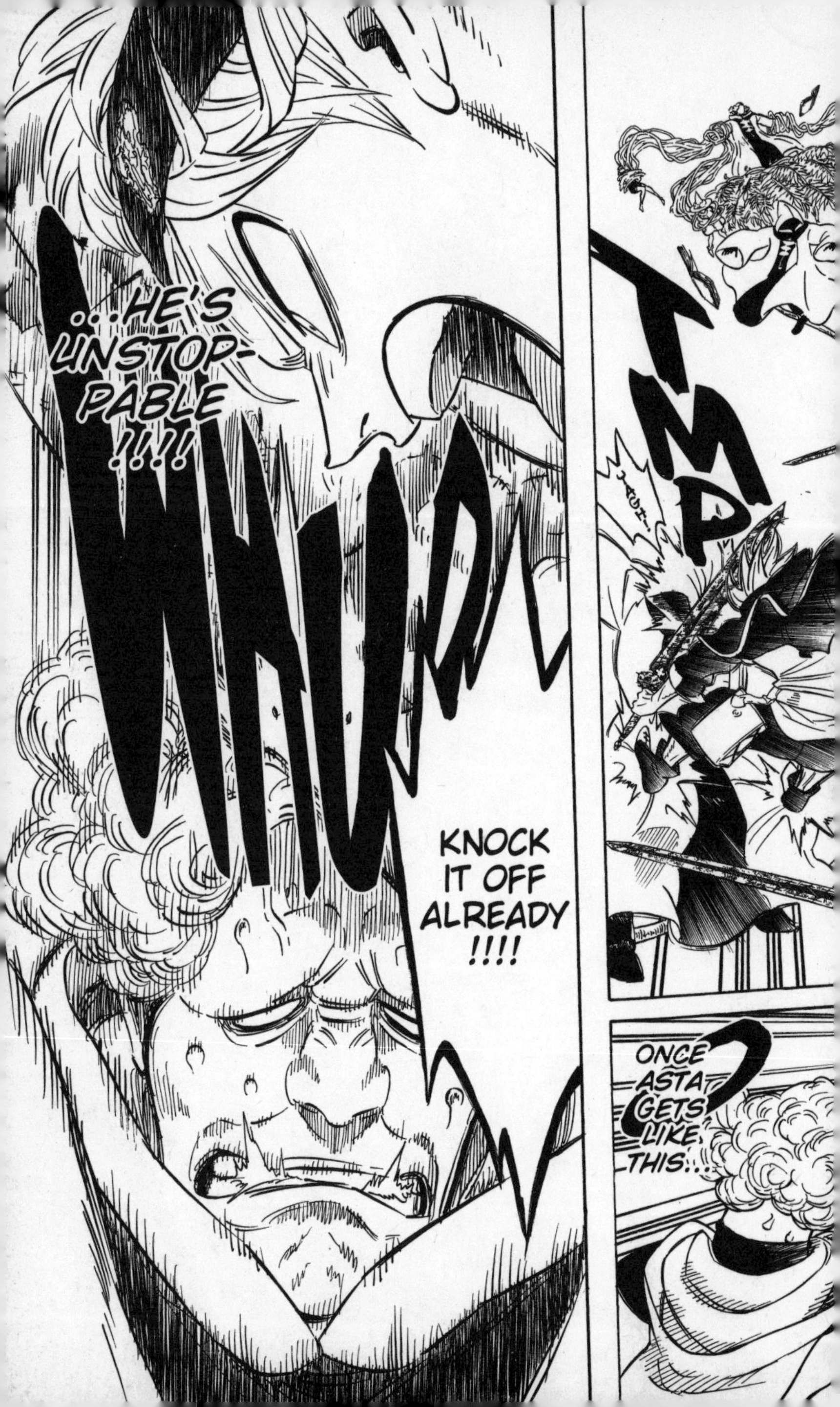
TMP
JAGH!
ONCE ASTA GETS LIKE THIS...
...HE'S UNSTOP-PABLE!!!!
WHUD
KNOCK IT OFF ALREADY!!!!

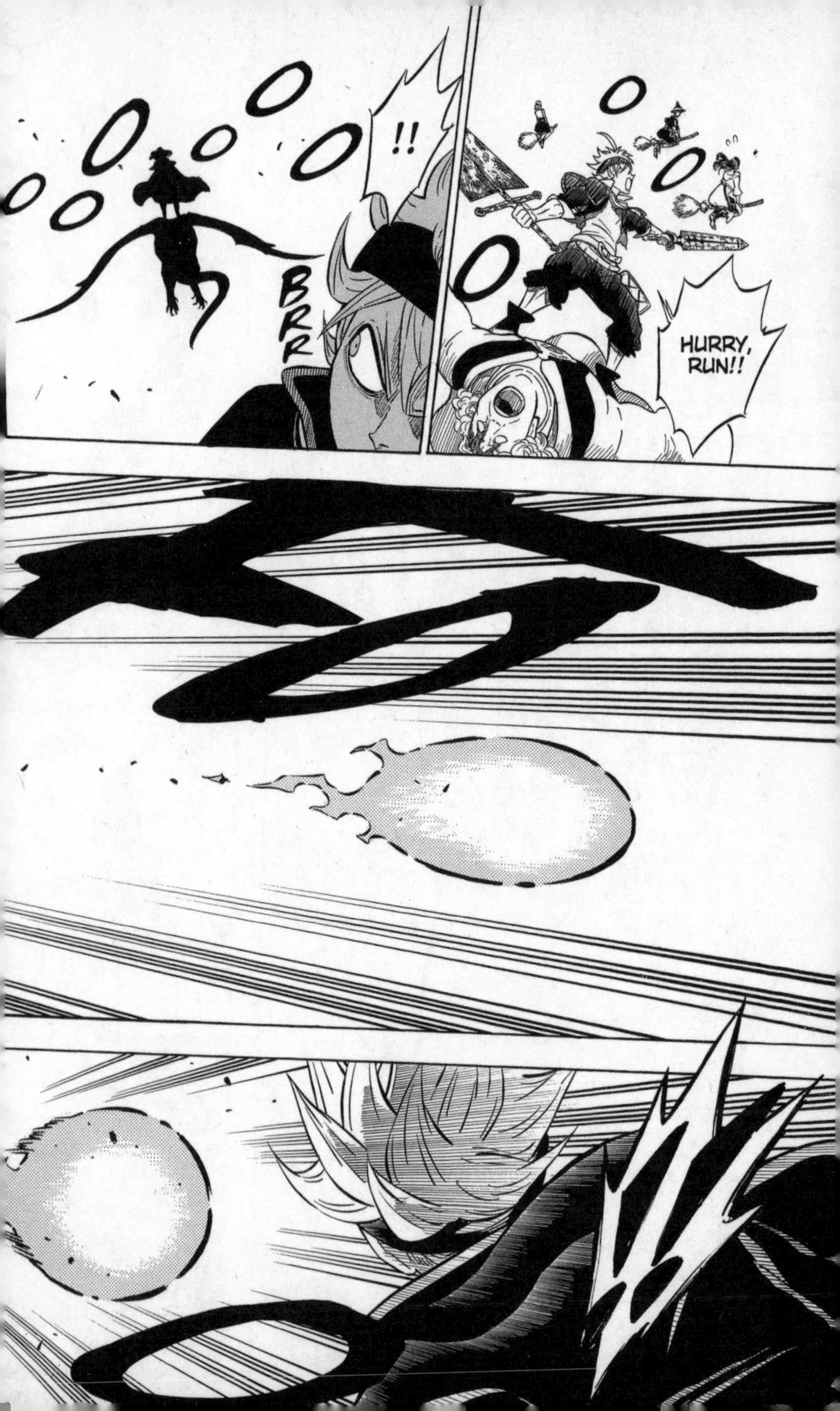
HURRY, RUN!!
!!
BRRR

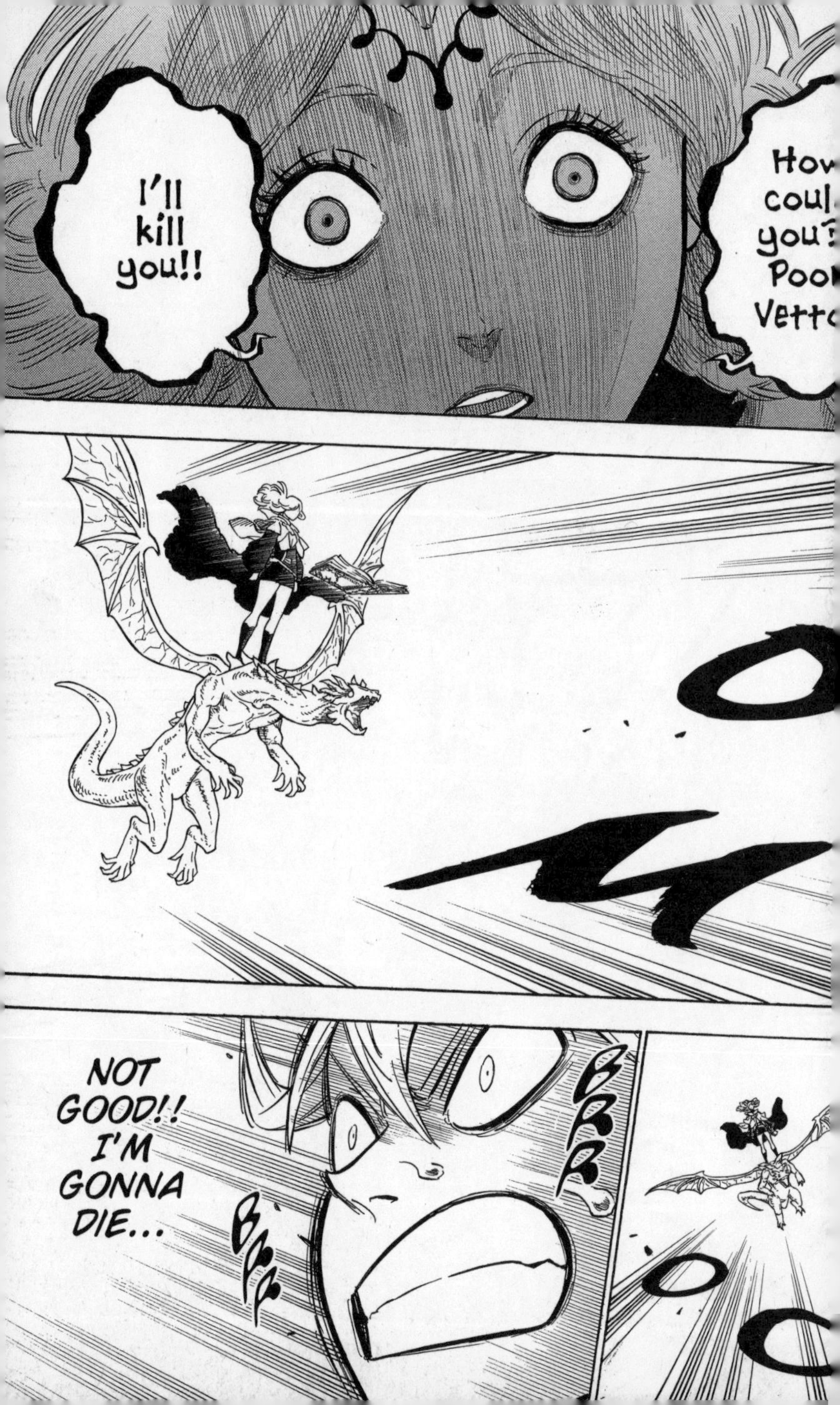
How coul you?! Poo Vett
I'll kill you!!
NOT GOOD!! I'M GONNA DIE...

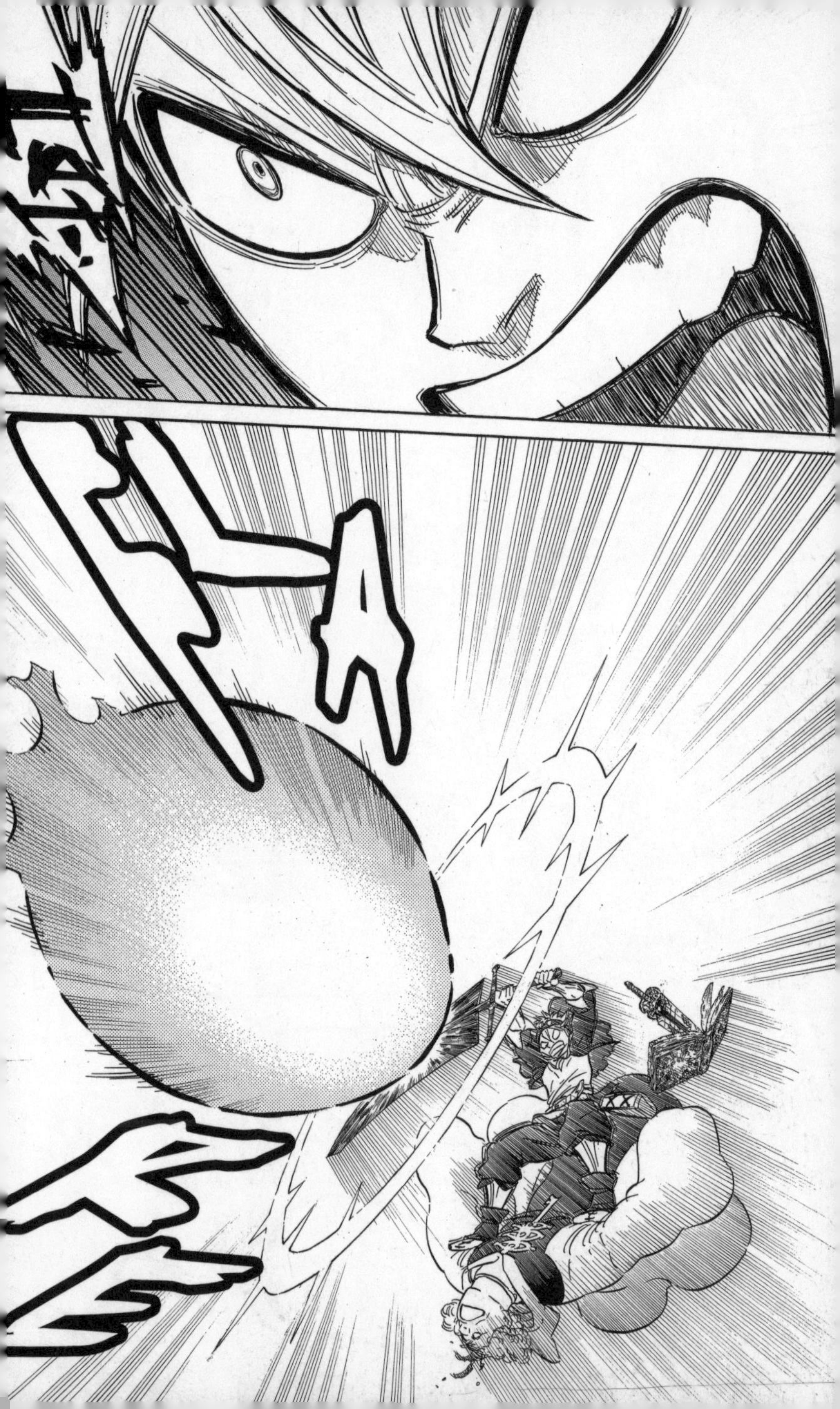

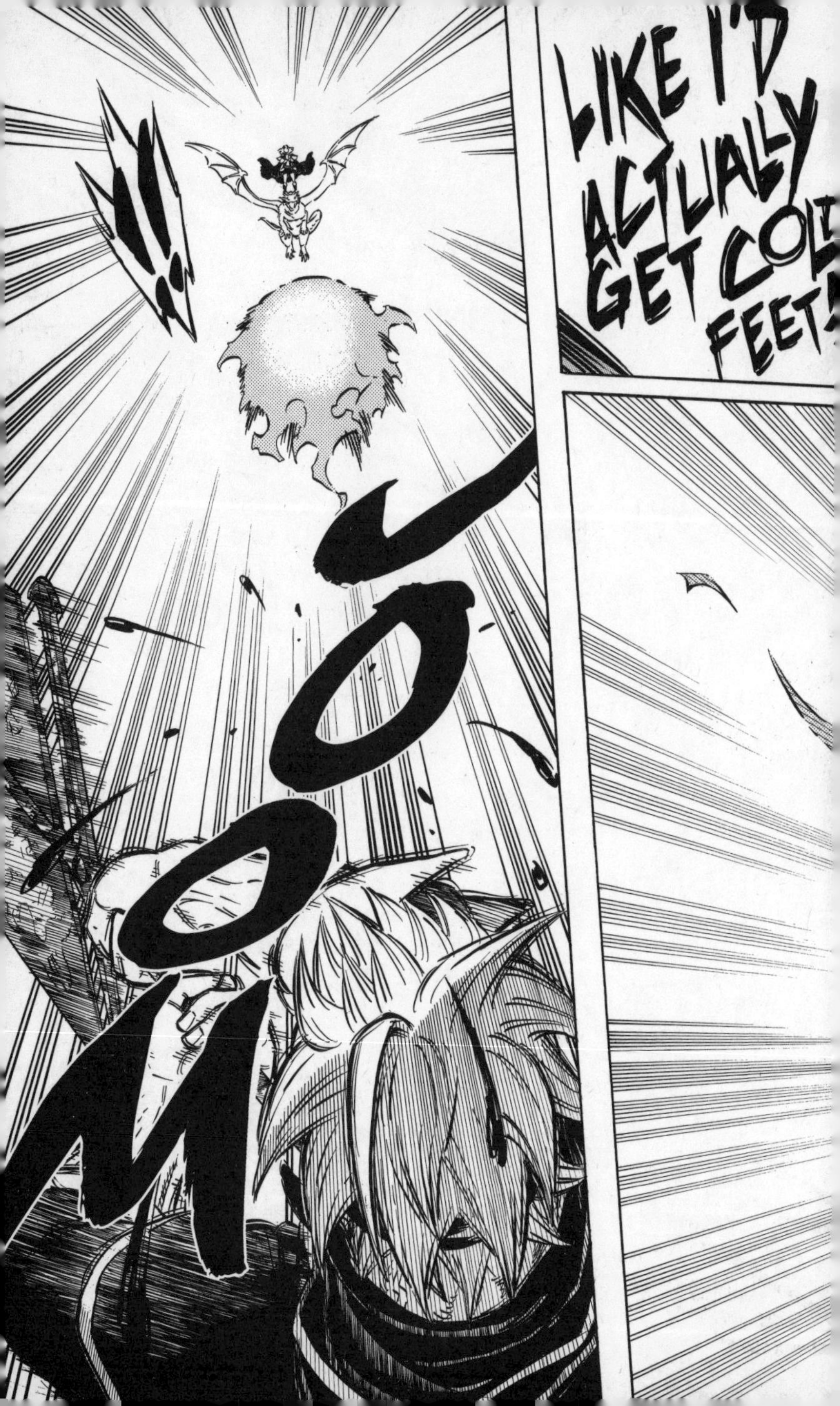
LIKE I'D ACTUALLY GET COL FEET!
!!

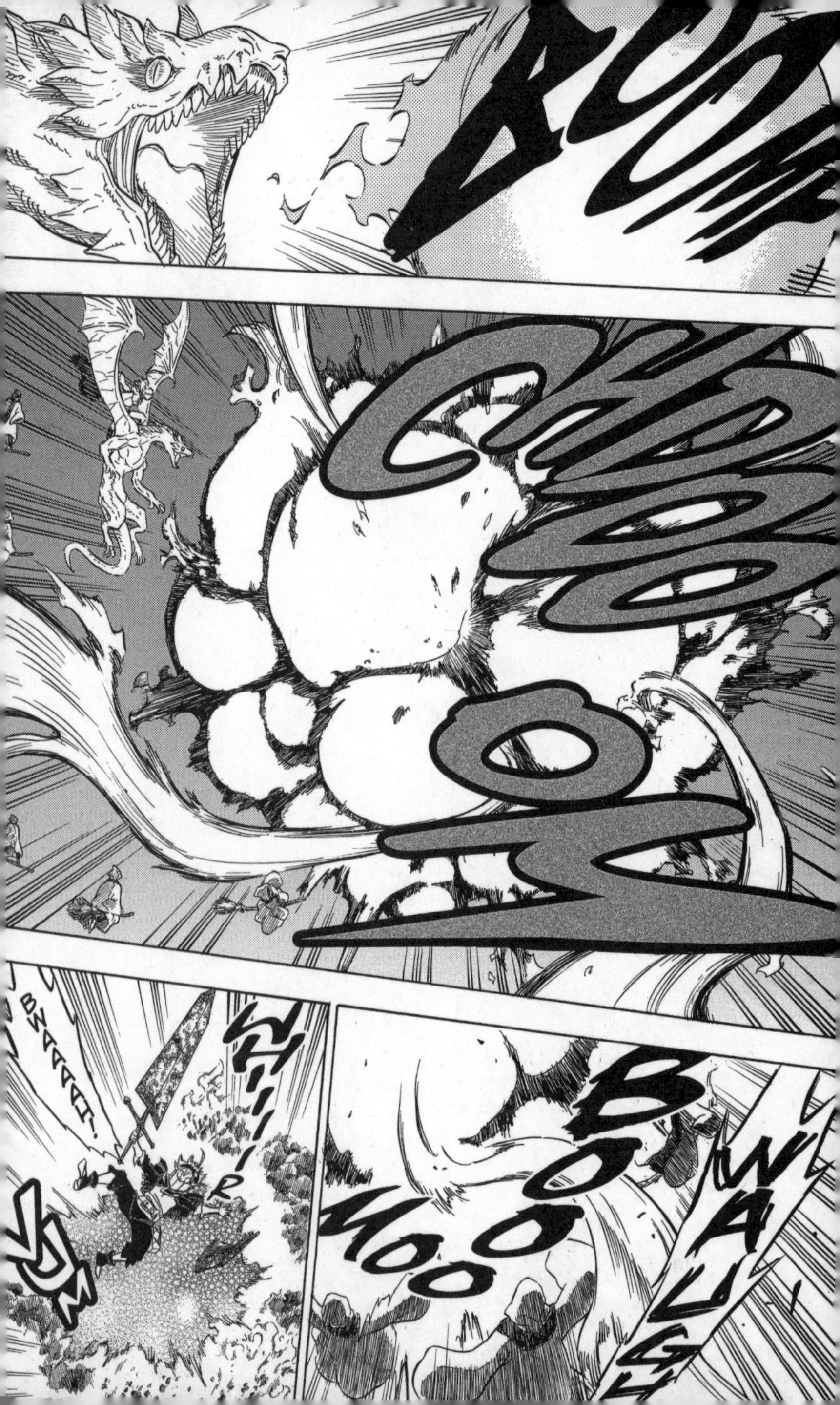
BOOM
BWAAAAH!
WHIIIIR
WAUGH

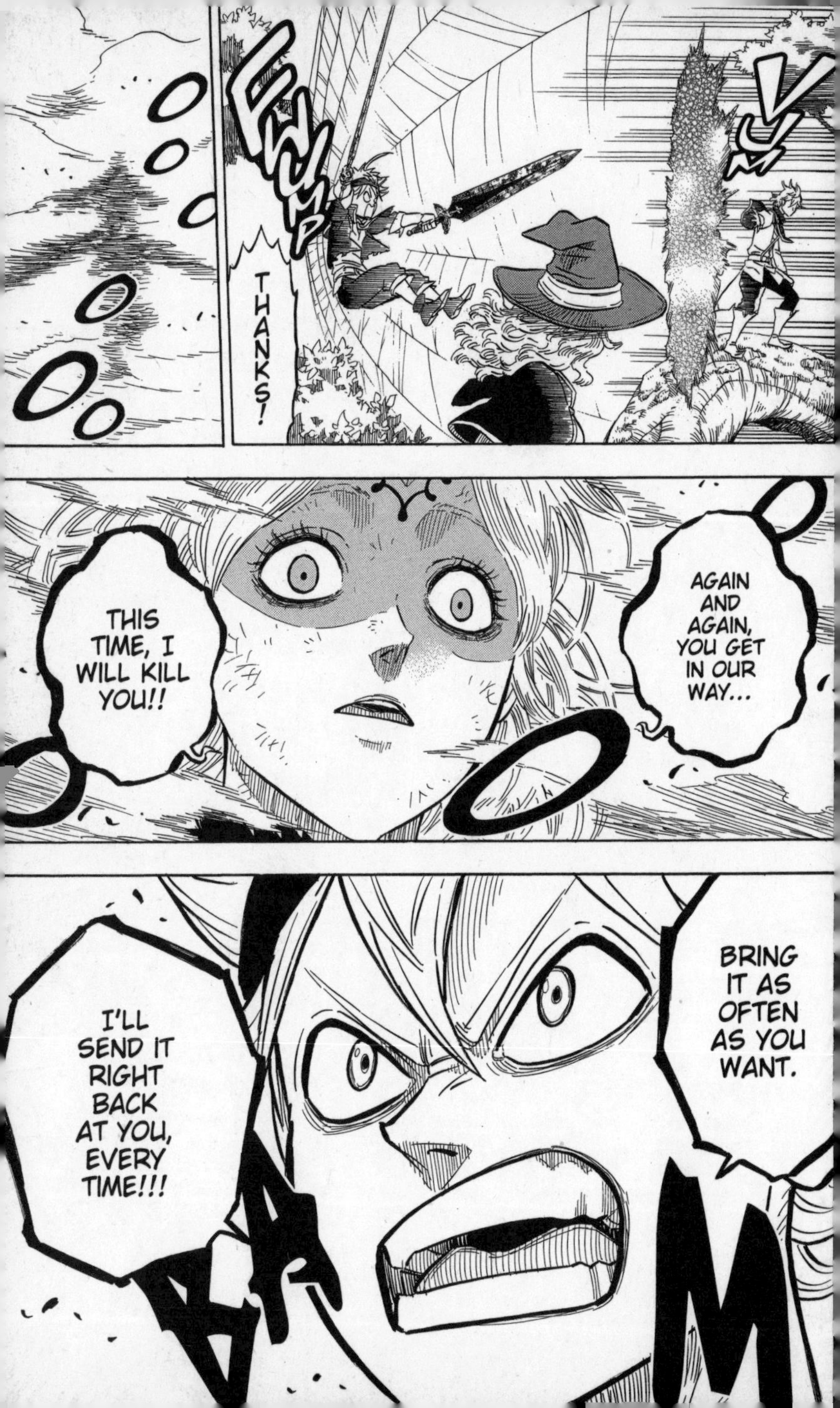
VUM
FWUMP
THANKS!
AGAIN AND AGAIN, YOU GET IN OUR WAY...
THIS TIME, I WILL KILL YOU!!
BRING IT AS OFTEN AS YOU WANT.
I'LL SEND IT RIGHT BACK AT YOU, EVERY TIME!!!

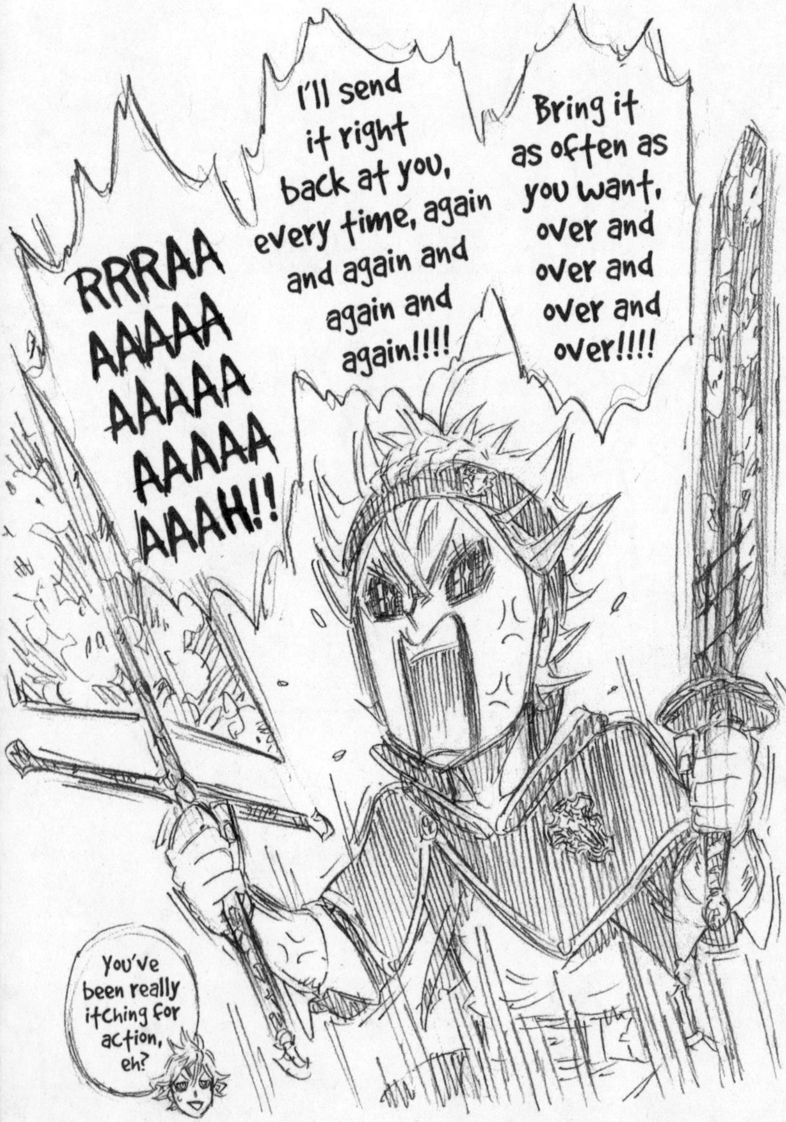
Bring it as often as you want, over and over and over and over!!!!
I'll send it right back at you, every time, again and again and again and again!!!!
RRRAAAAAAAAAAAAAAAAAAAAAAH!!
You've been really itching for action, eh?

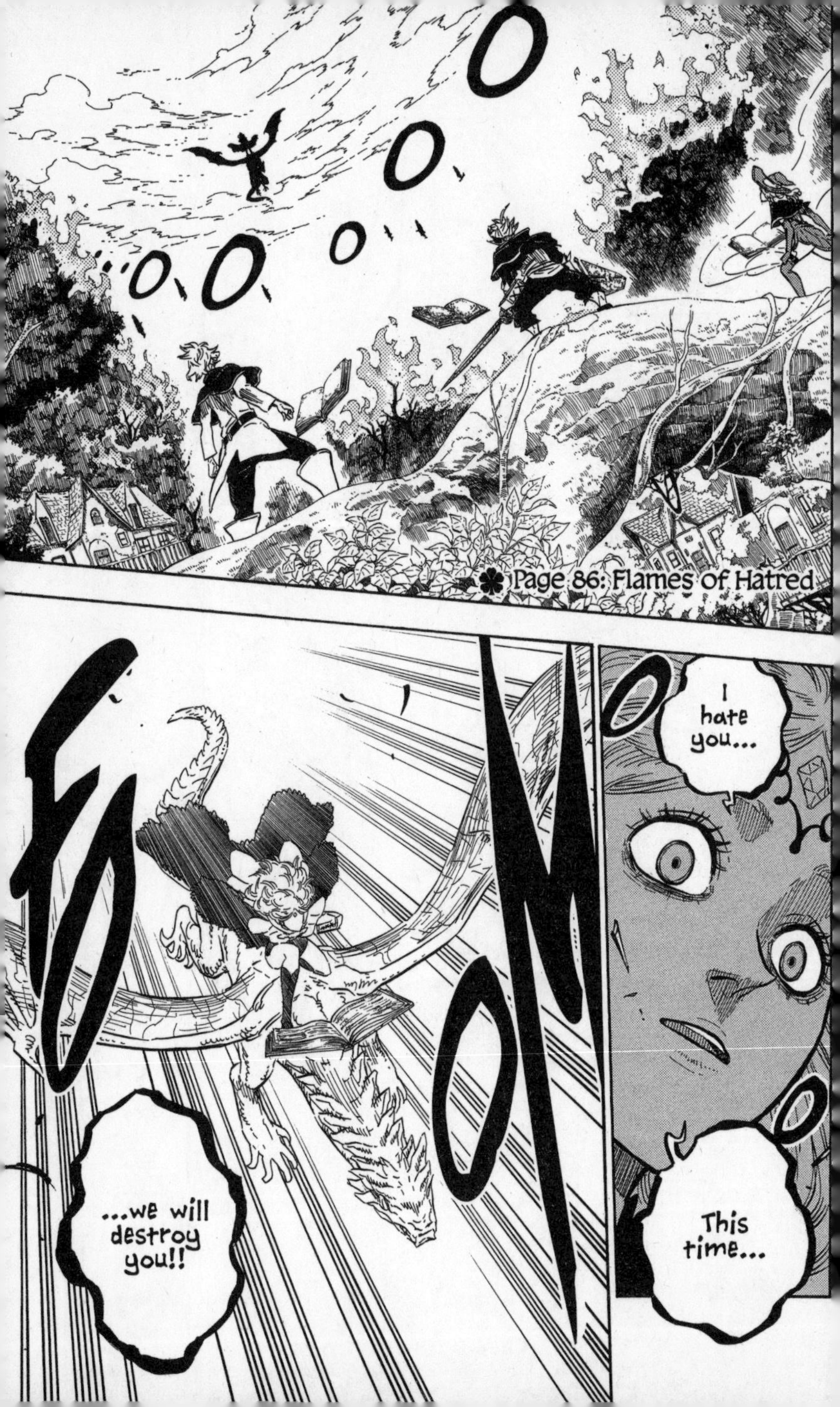
Page 86: Flames of Hatred
I hate you...
This time...
...we will destroy you!!

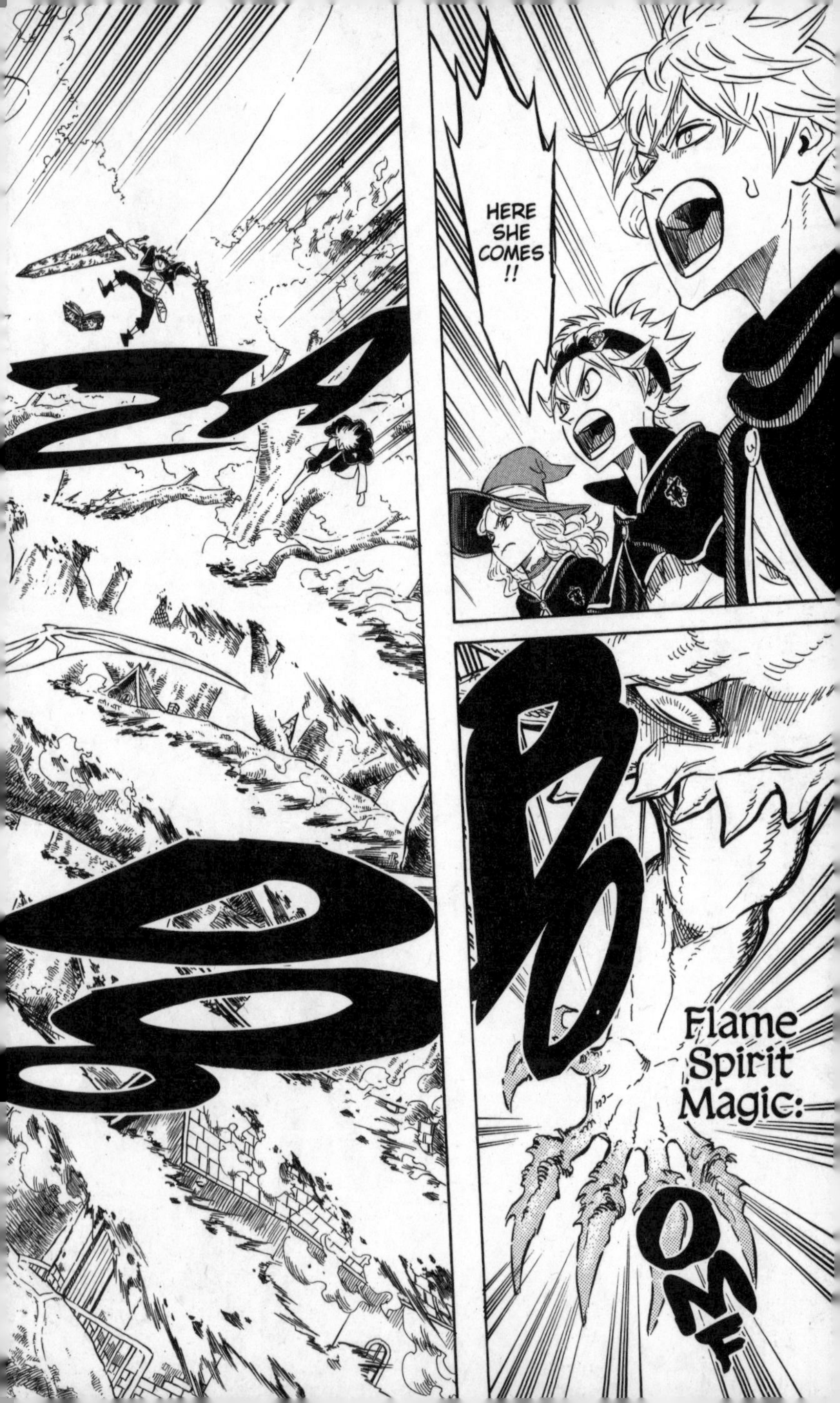
HERE SHE COMES!!
Flame Spirit Magic:
OMF

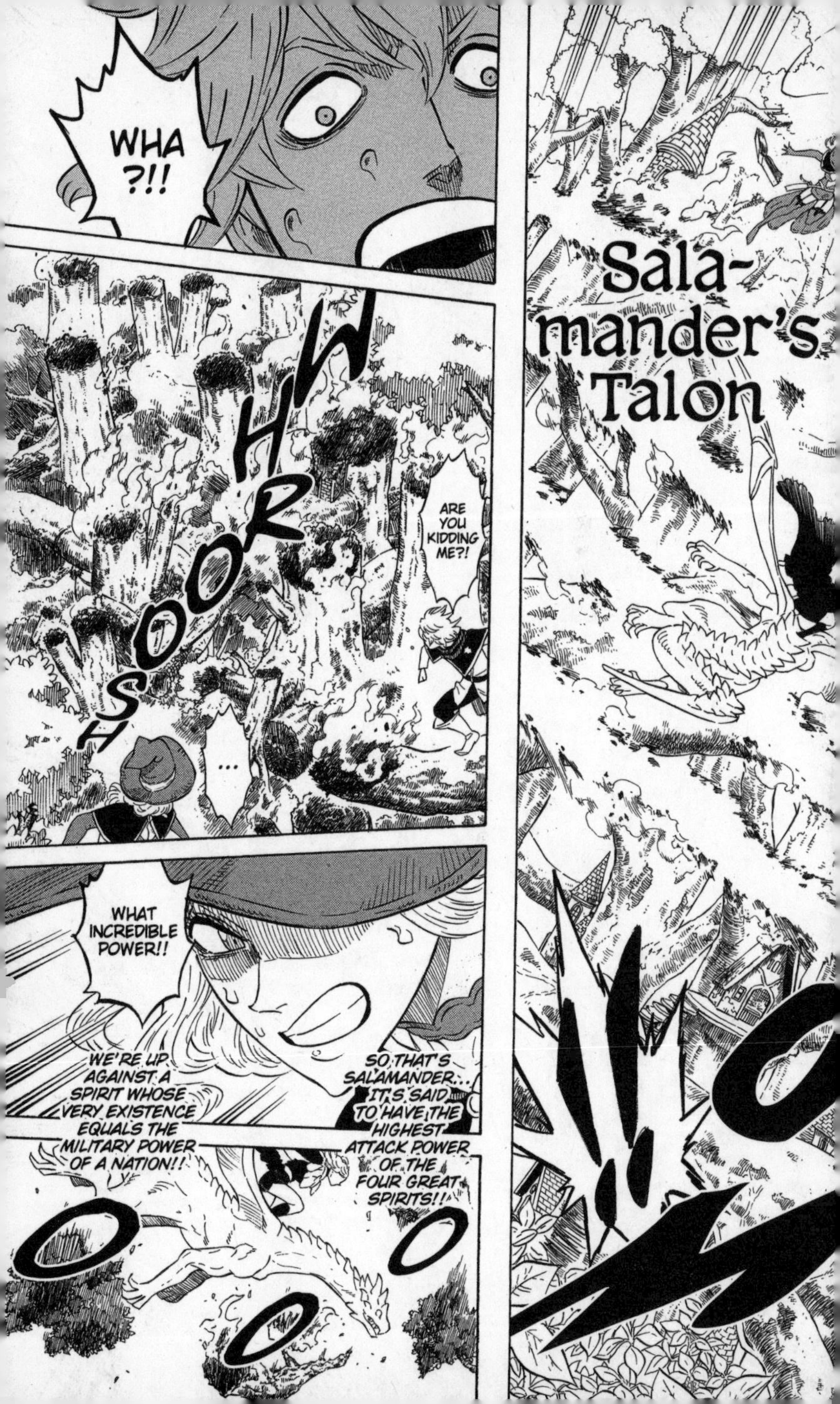

Sala-mander's Talon
WHA ?!!
WHROOOSH
ARE YOU KIDDING ME?!
...
WHAT INCREDIBLE POWER!!
SO THAT'S SALAMANDER... IT'S SAID TO HAVE THE HIGHEST ATTACK POWER OF THE FOUR GREAT SPIRITS!!
WE'RE UP AGAINST A SPIRIT WHOSE VERY EXISTENCE EQUALS THE MILITARY POWER OF A NATION!!

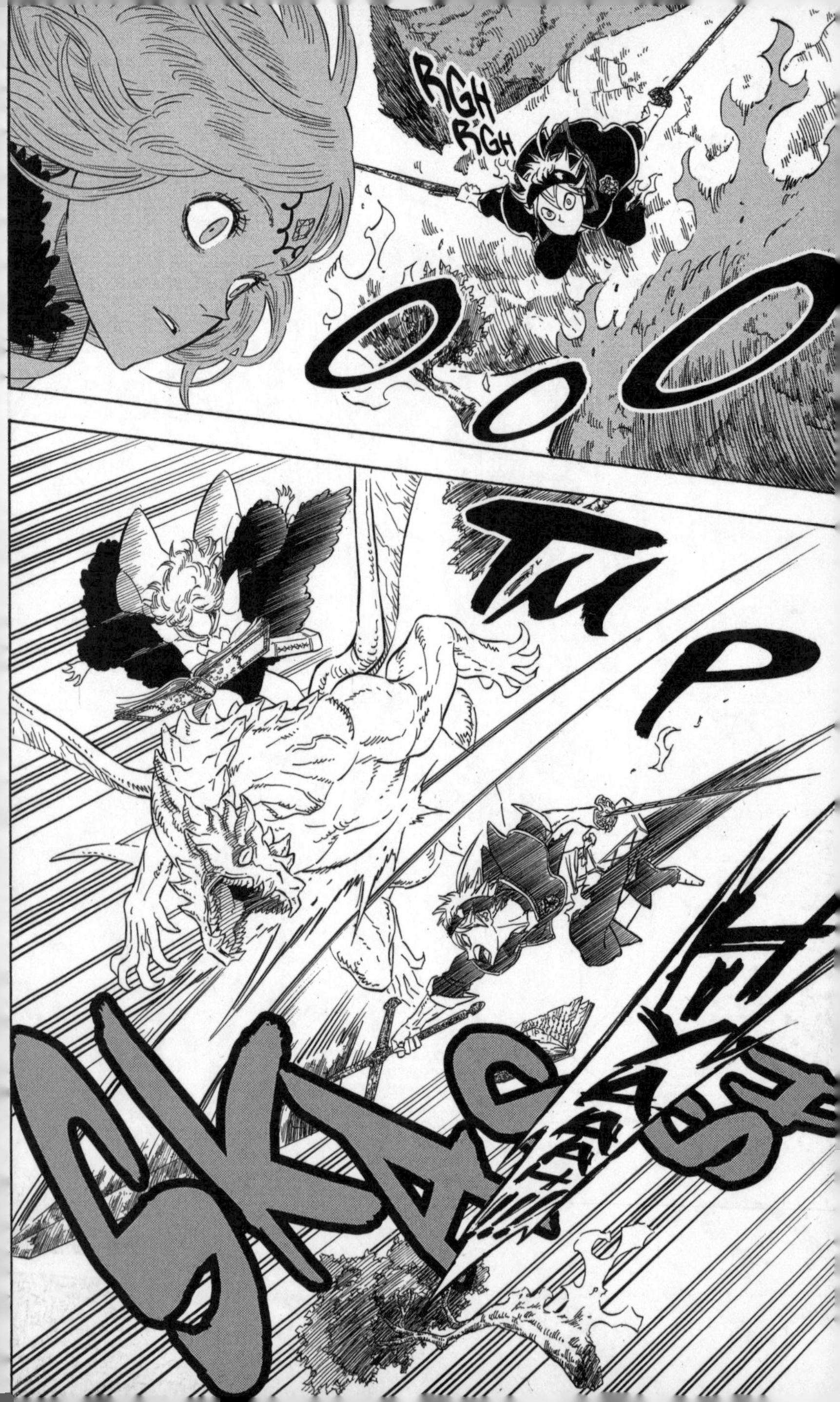
RGH RGH
OOO
TUP
SKASH!!

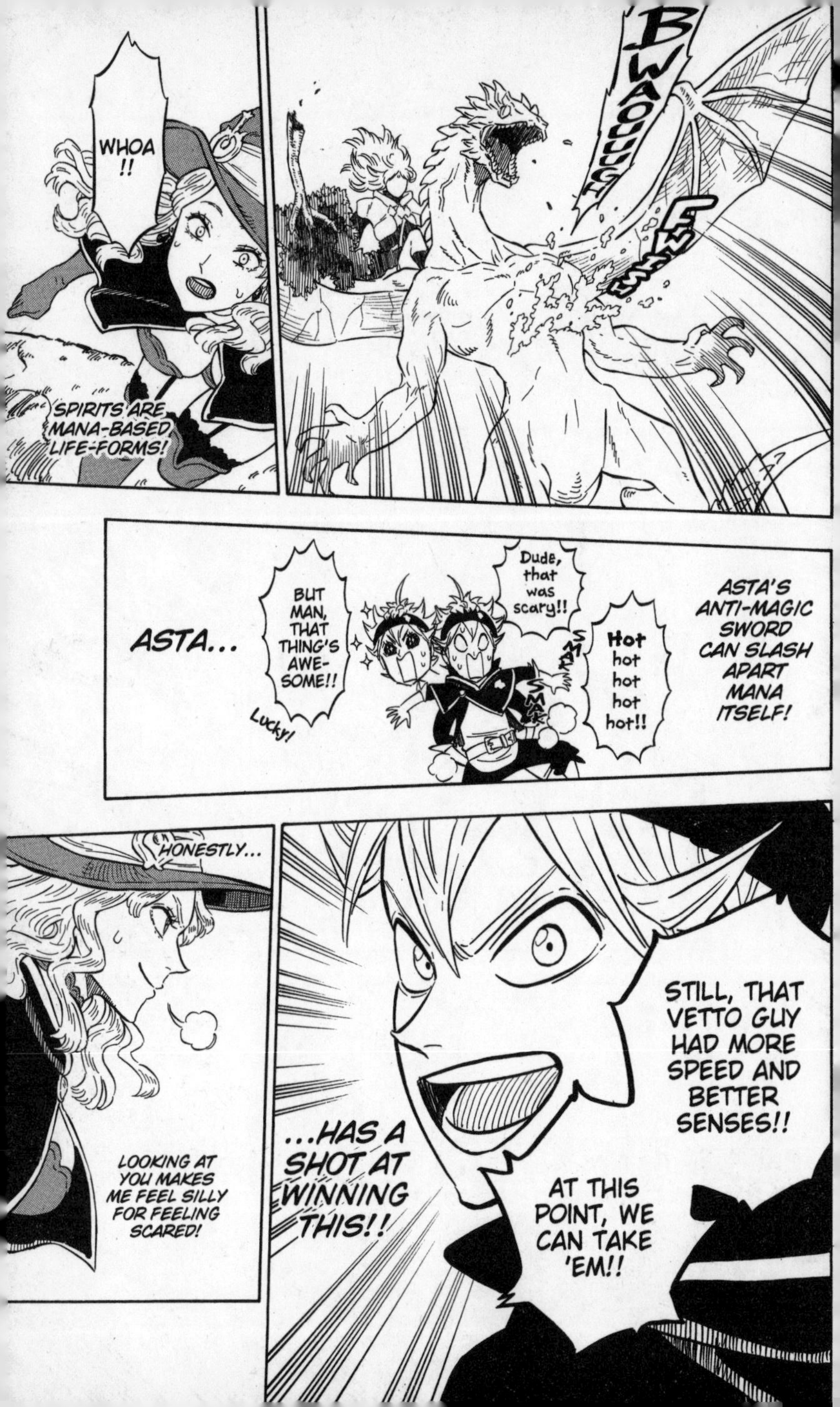
BWAOUUUGH
FWISH
WHOA!!
SPIRITS ARE MANA-BASED LIFE-FORMS!
ASTA'S ANTI-MAGIC SWORD CAN SLASH APART MANA ITSELF!
Hot hot hot hot hot!!
SMAK
SMAK
Dude, that was scary!!
BUT MAN, THAT THING'S AWESOME!!
Lucky!
ASTA...
STILL, THAT VETTO GUY HAD MORE SPEED AND BETTER SENSES!!
AT THIS POINT, WE CAN TAKE 'EM!!
...HAS A SHOT AT WINNING THIS!!
HONESTLY...
LOOKING AT YOU MAKES ME FEEL SILLY FOR FEELING SCARED!

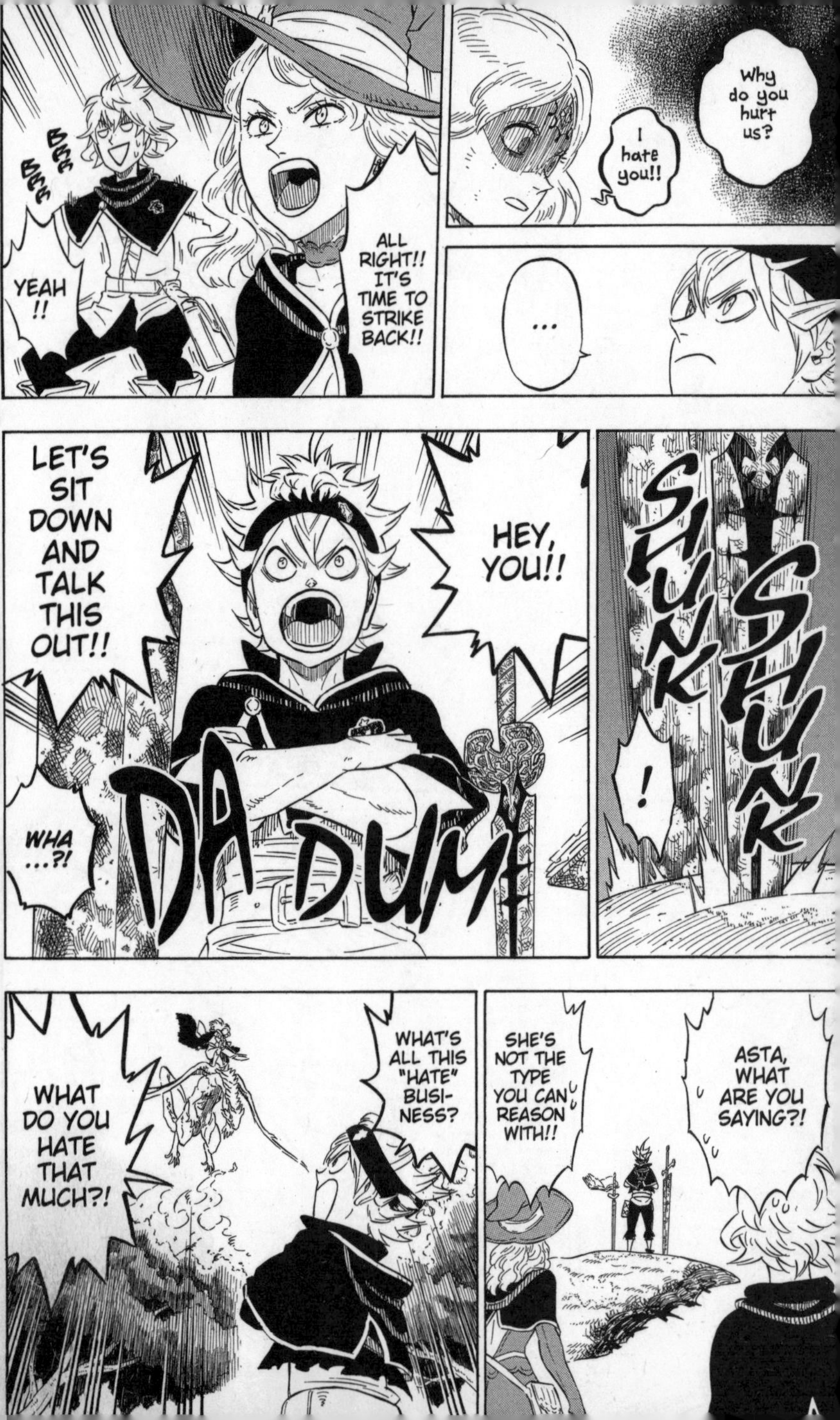
Why do you hurt us?
I hate you!!
...
ALL RIGHT!! IT'S TIME TO STRIKE BACK!!
BAA BAA
YEAH!!
SHUNK SHUNK
!
HEY, YOU!!
LET'S SIT DOWN AND TALK THIS OUT!!
DA DUM
WHA...?!
ASTA, WHAT ARE YOU SAYING?!
SHE'S NOT THE TYPE YOU CAN REASON WITH!!
WHAT'S ALL THIS "HATE" BUSINESS?
WHAT DO YOU HATE THAT MUCH?!

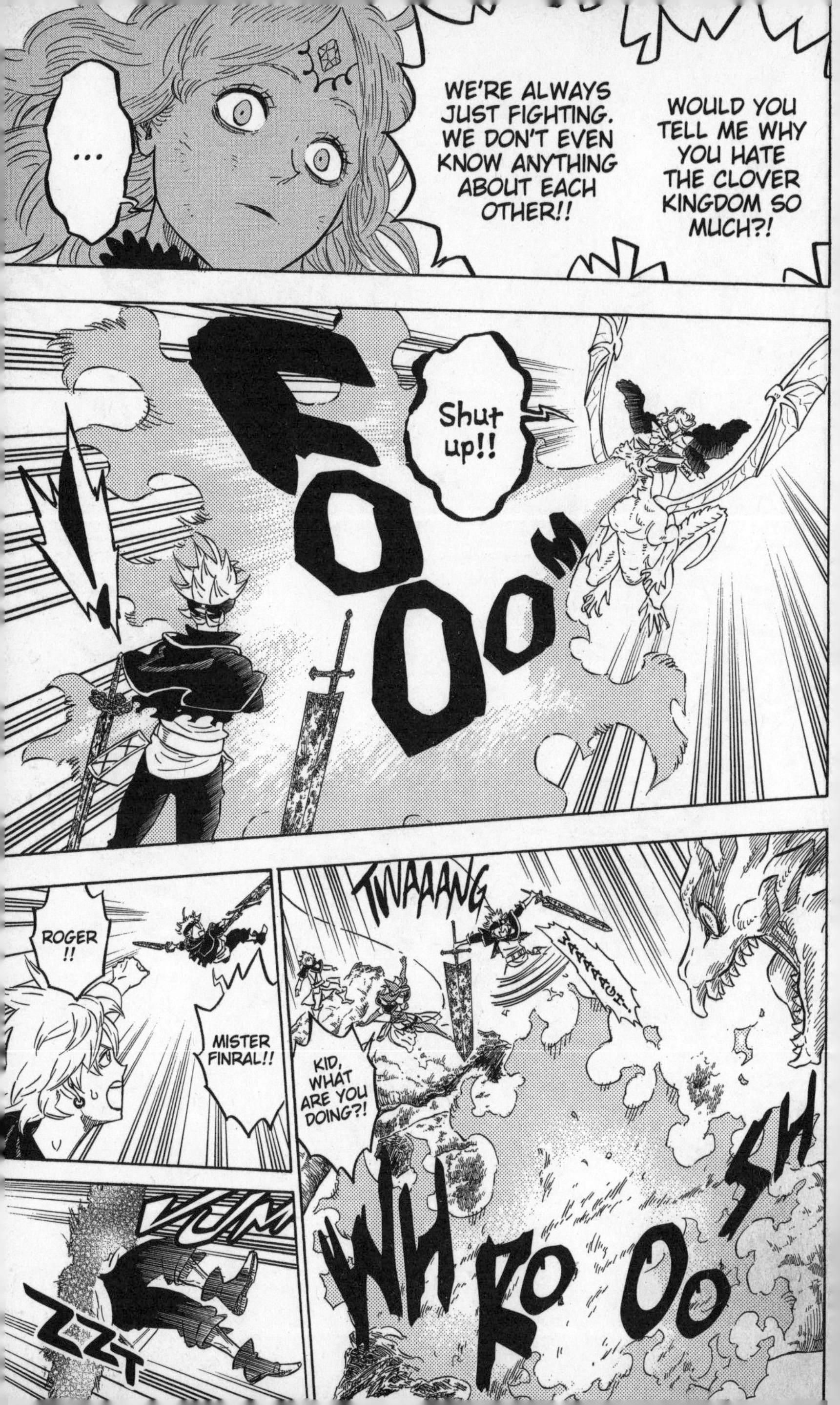
WOULD YOU TELL ME WHY YOU HATE THE CLOVER KINGDOM SO MUCH?!
WE'RE ALWAYS JUST FIGHTING. WE DON'T EVEN KNOW ANYTHING ABOUT EACH OTHER!!
...
Shut up!!
FOOOOM
TWAAANG
KID, WHAT ARE YOU DOING?!
WHROOOSH
ROGER!!
MISTER FINRAL!!
VUM
ZZZT

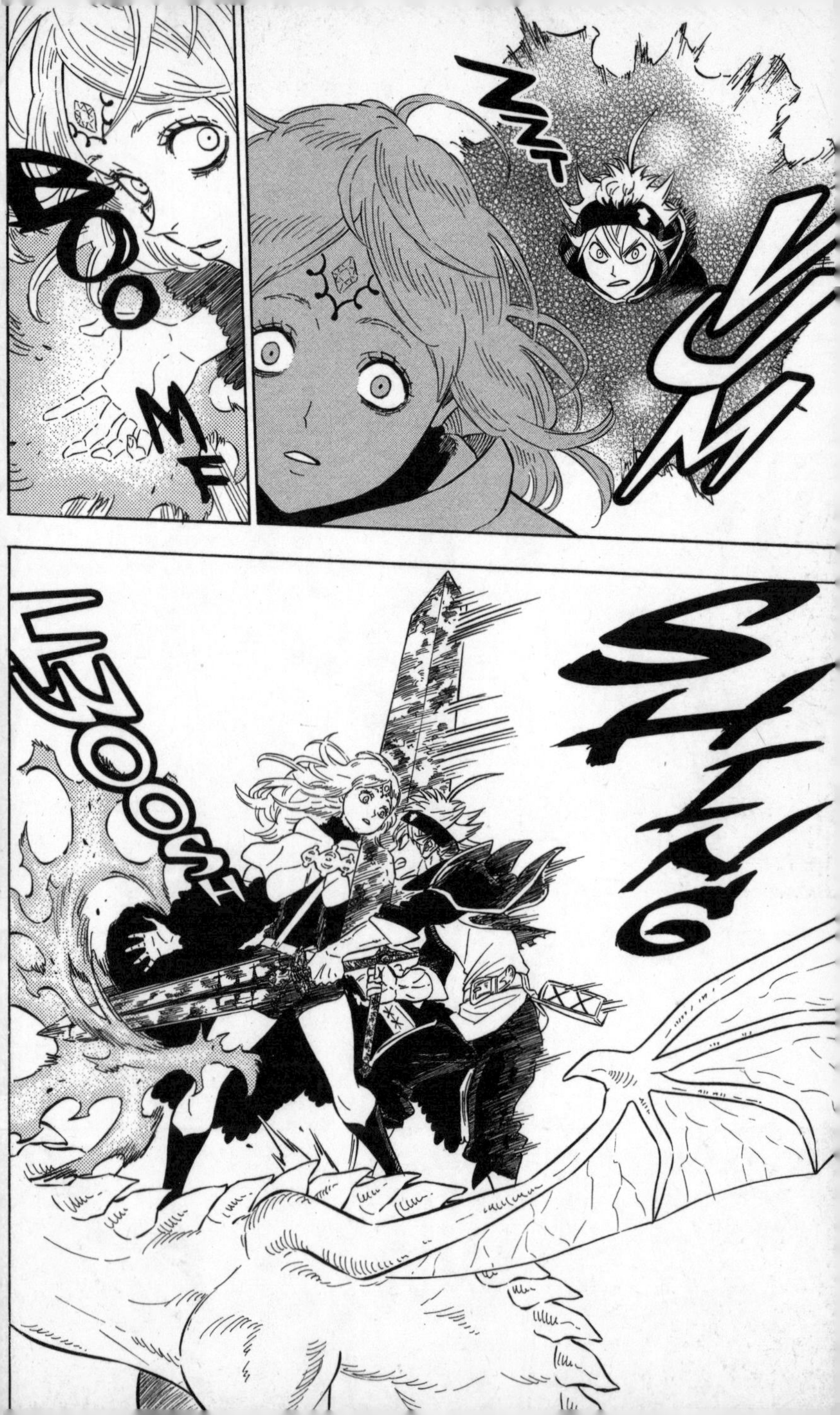
ZZZT
VUM
BOOOMF
SHIING
WOOOSH

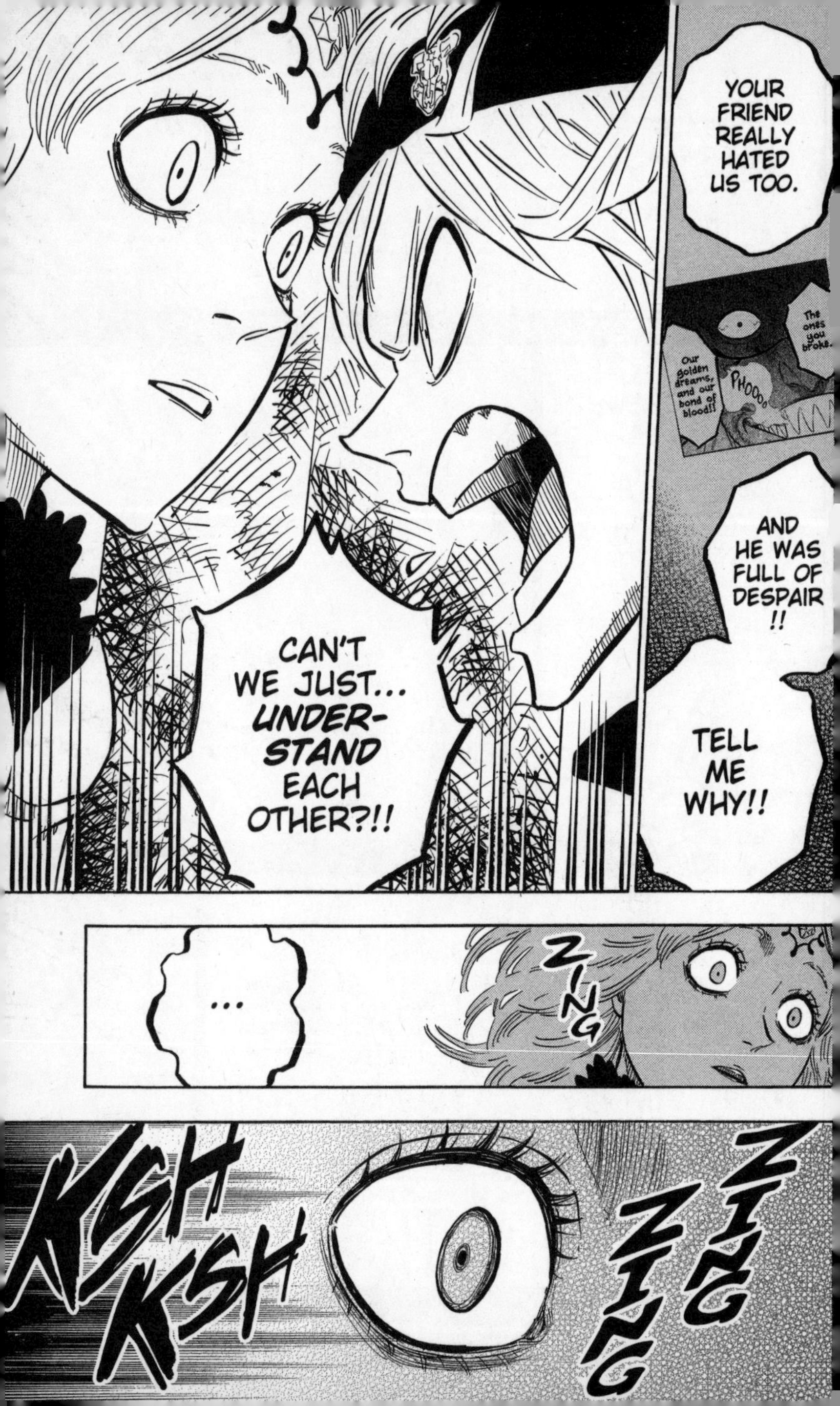
YOUR FRIEND REALLY HATED US TOO.
The ones you broke.
Our golden dreams, and our bond of blood!!
PHOOOO
AND HE WAS FULL OF DESPAIR!!
TELL ME WHY!!
CAN'T WE JUST... UNDER-STAND EACH OTHER?!!
ZING
...
ZING ZING
KSH KSH

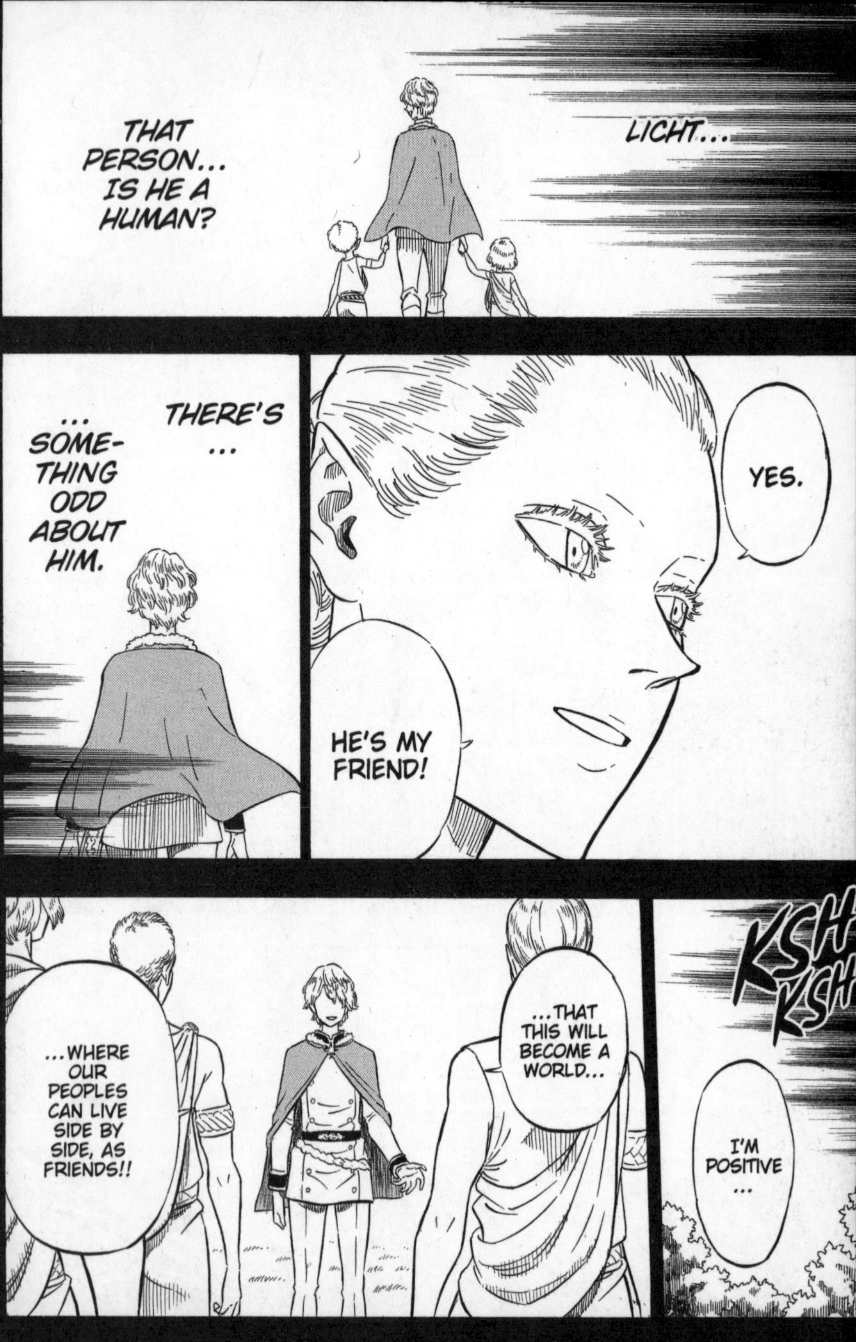
LICHT...
THAT PERSON... IS HE A HUMAN?
YES.
HE'S MY FRIEND!
THERE'S ...
... SOME-THING ODD ABOUT HIM.
KSH KSH
I'M POSITIVE ...
...THAT THIS WILL BECOME A WORLD...
...WHERE OUR PEOPLES CAN LIVE SIDE BY SIDE, AS FRIENDS!!

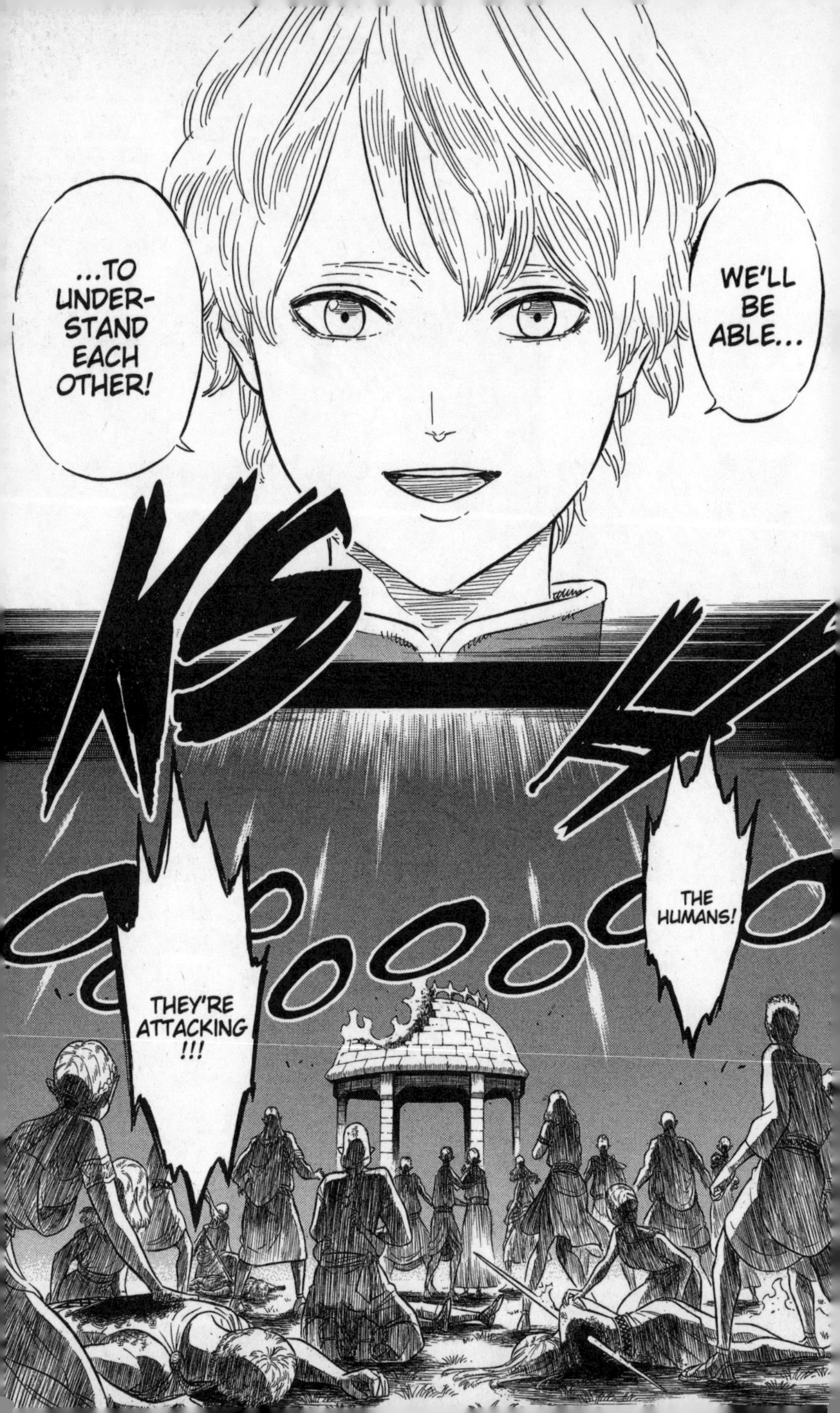
WE'LL BE ABLE...
...TO UNDER-STAND EACH OTHER!
KSHOOOOOOOO
THE HUMANS!
THEY'RE ATTACKING!!!

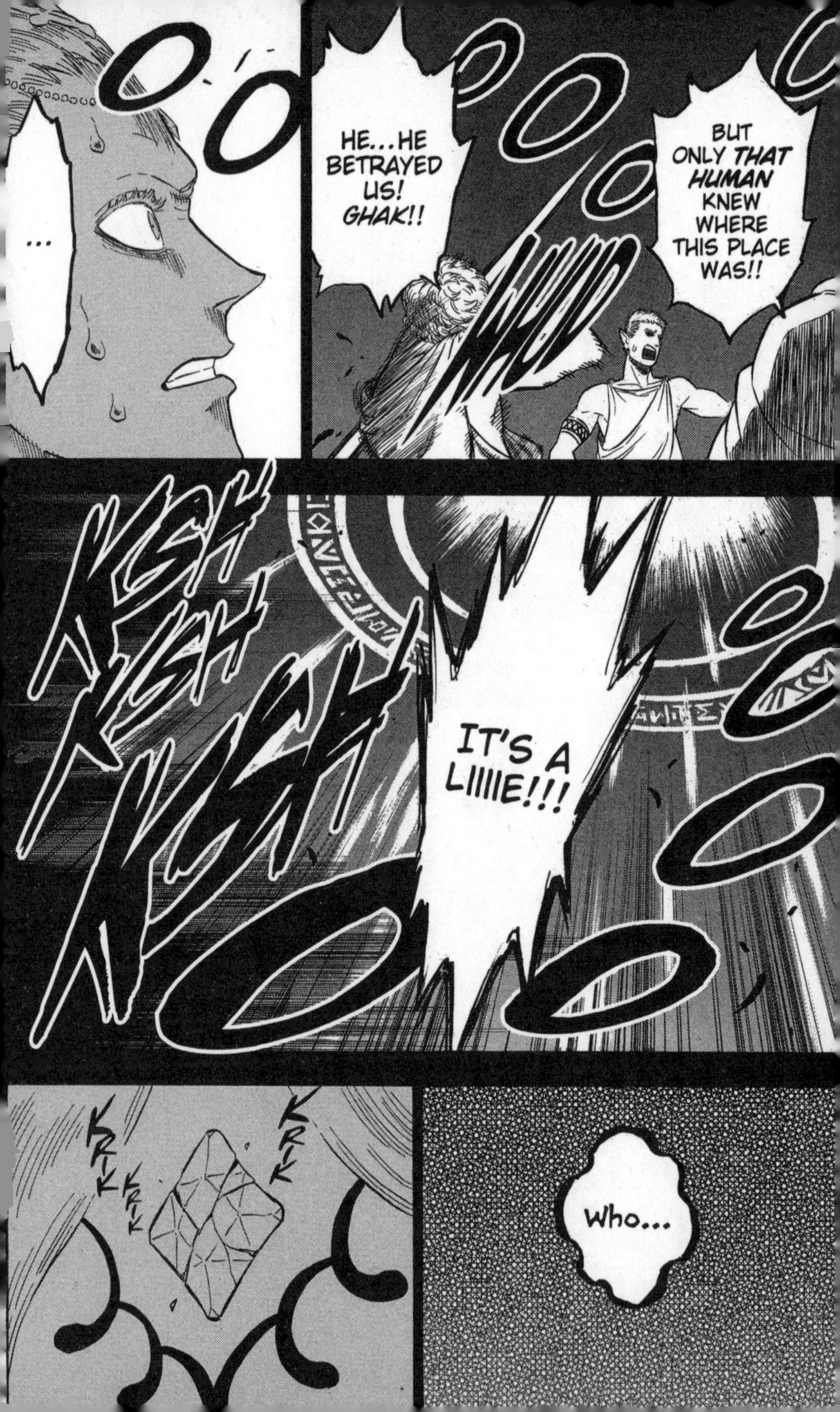
BUT ONLY *THAT HUMAN* KNEW WHERE THIS PLACE WAS!!
HE...HE BETRAYED US! *GHAK!!*
...
IT'S A LIIIIE!!!
Who...
KRIK
KRIK
KRIK

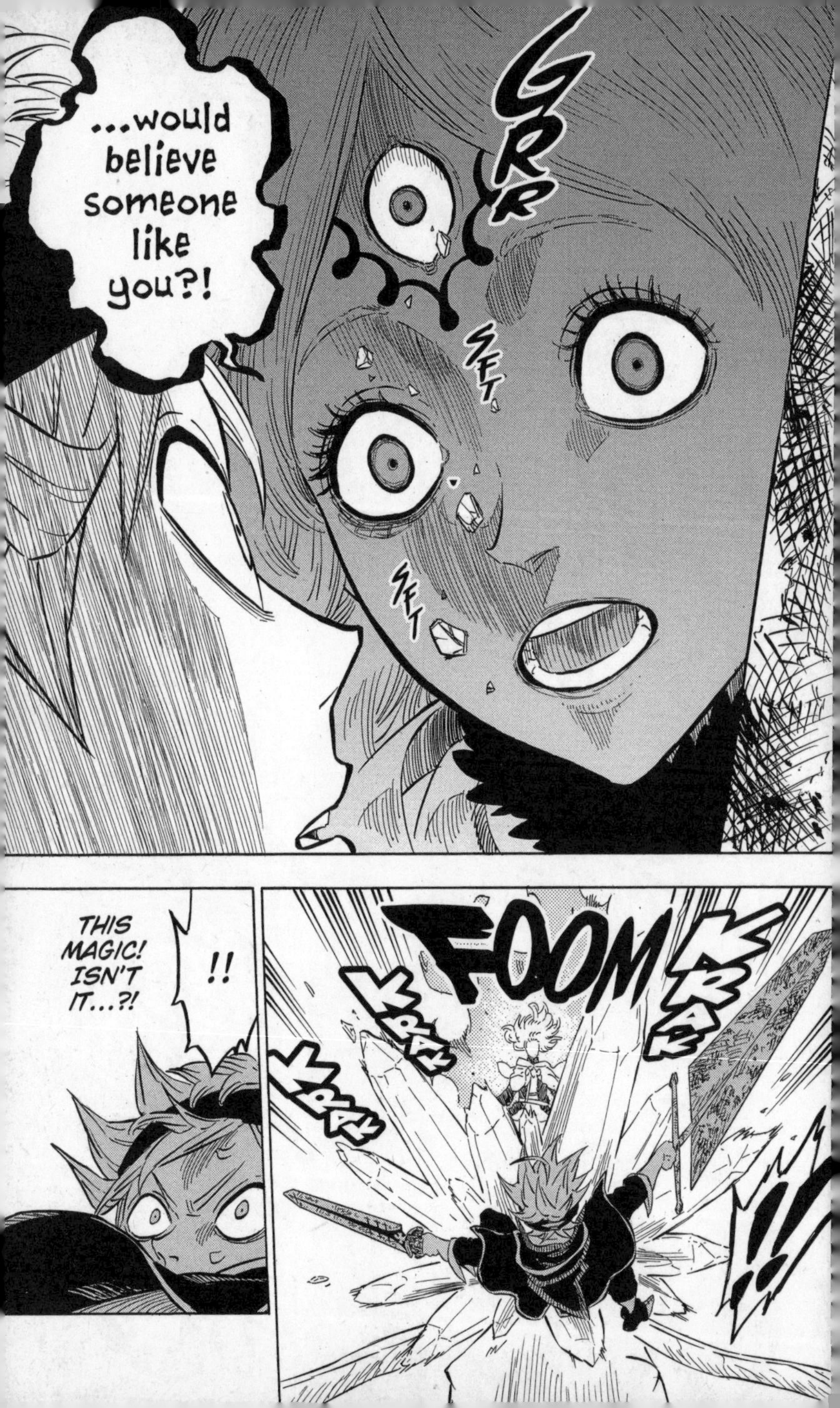
...would believe someone like you?!
GRR
SFT
SFT
FOOM
KRAK
KRAK
KRAK
!!!
THIS MAGIC! ISN'T IT...?!
!!

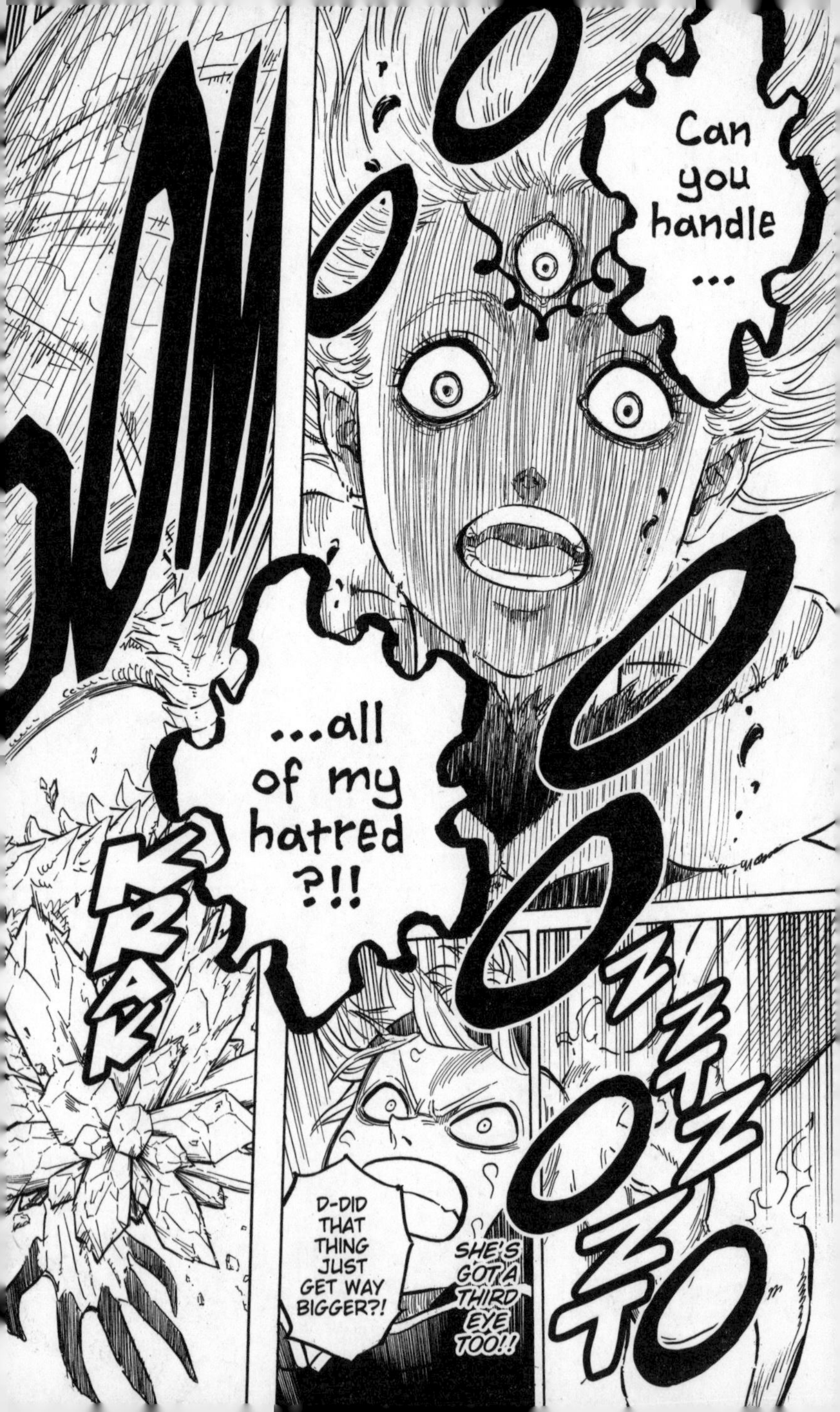
Can you handle ...
...all of my hatred ?!!
KRAK
SHE'S GOT A THIRD EYE TOO!!
D-DID THAT THING JUST GET WAY BIGGER?!

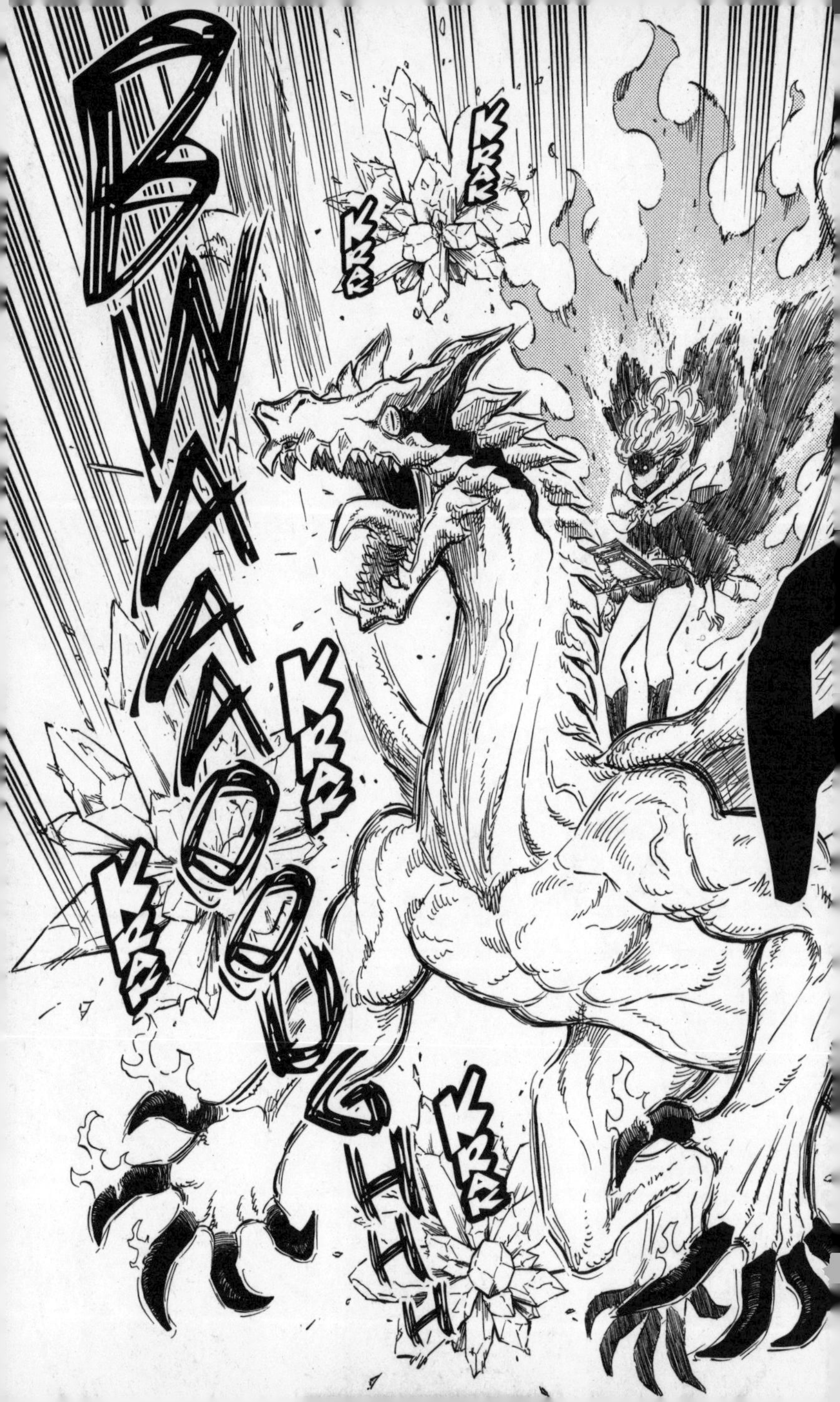
KRAK
KRAK
BWAAAOOOUGHHH
KRAK
KRAK
KRAK

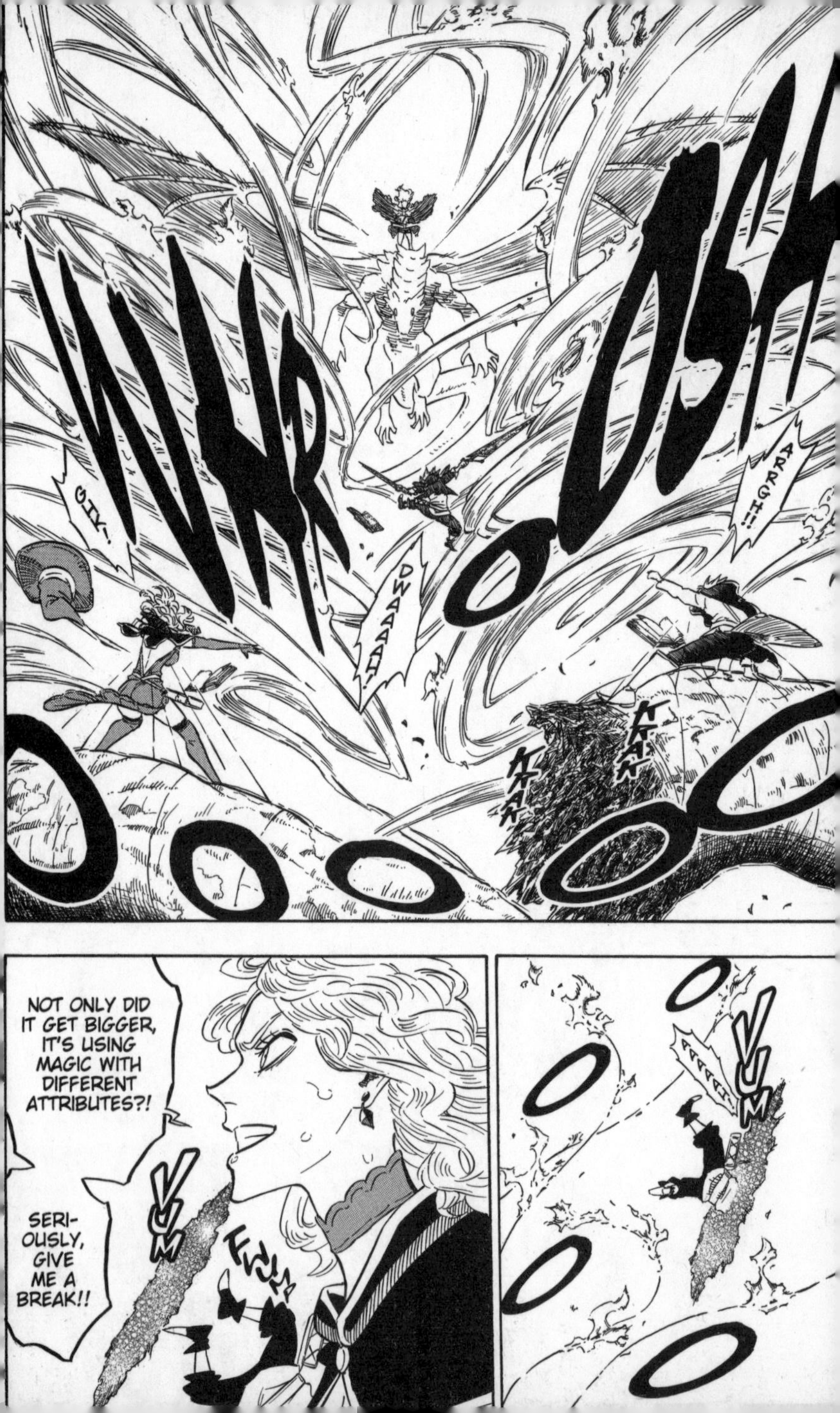
ARRGH!!
DWAAAAAH!
GIK!
KRAK
KRAK
AAAAAH!
VUM
NOT ONLY DID IT GET BIGGER, IT'S USING MAGIC WITH DIFFERENT ATTRIBUTES?!
SERI-OUSLY, GIVE ME A BREAK!!
VUM
FWUM

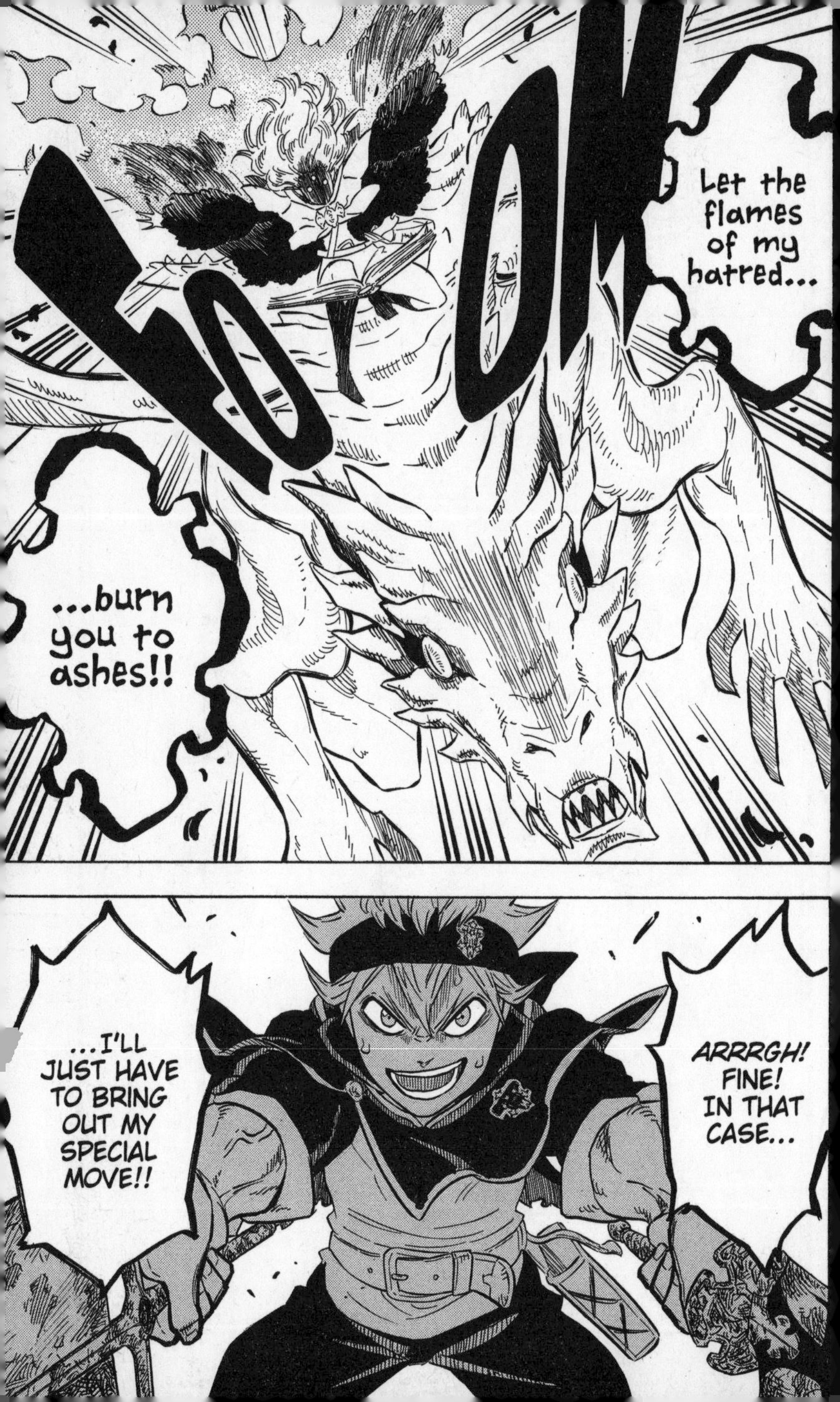
BOOOM
Let the flames of my hatred...
...burn you to ashes!!
ARRRGH! FINE! IN THAT CASE...
...I'LL JUST HAVE TO BRING OUT MY SPECIAL MOVE!!

The Assorted Questions Brigade No. 2

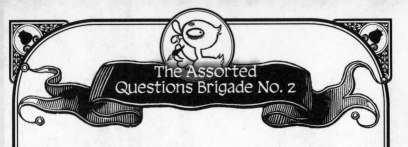

Q: I'd like to know the physical strength rankings for the *Black Clover* characters. (Want To Remain Anonymous)

A:

1 Yami

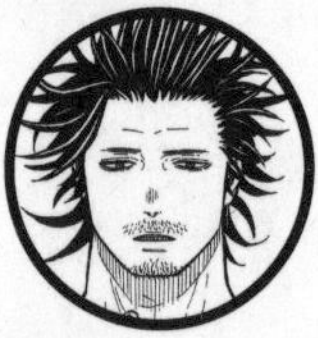

2 Asta

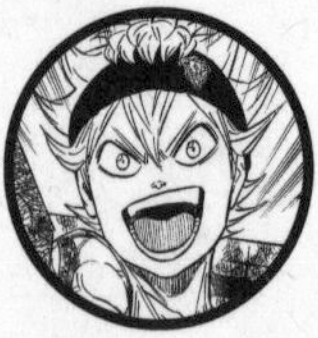

3 Vetto

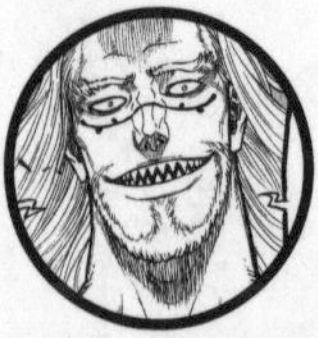

4 Brocks

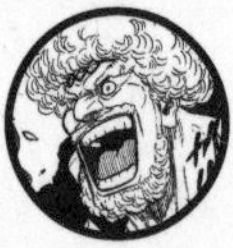

5 Ladros

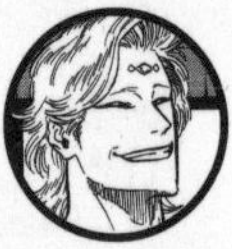

6 Mars

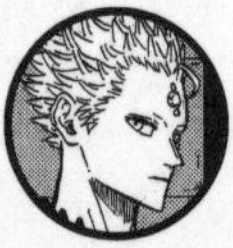

7 Fuegoleon

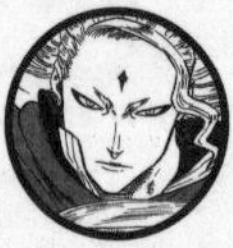

8 Leopold

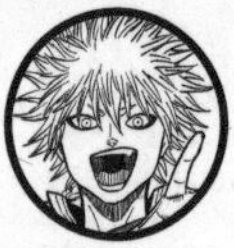

9 Kiato

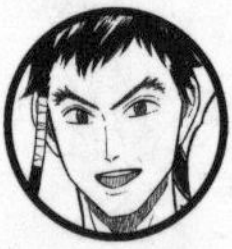

10 Yuno

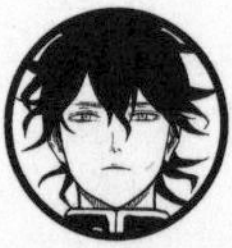

11 Magna

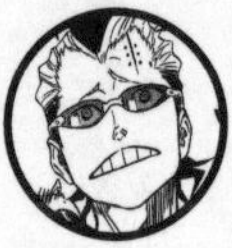

Most other characters don't have much in the way of muscle, since they can reinforce their physical capabilities with magic.

Page 87: Not a Failure

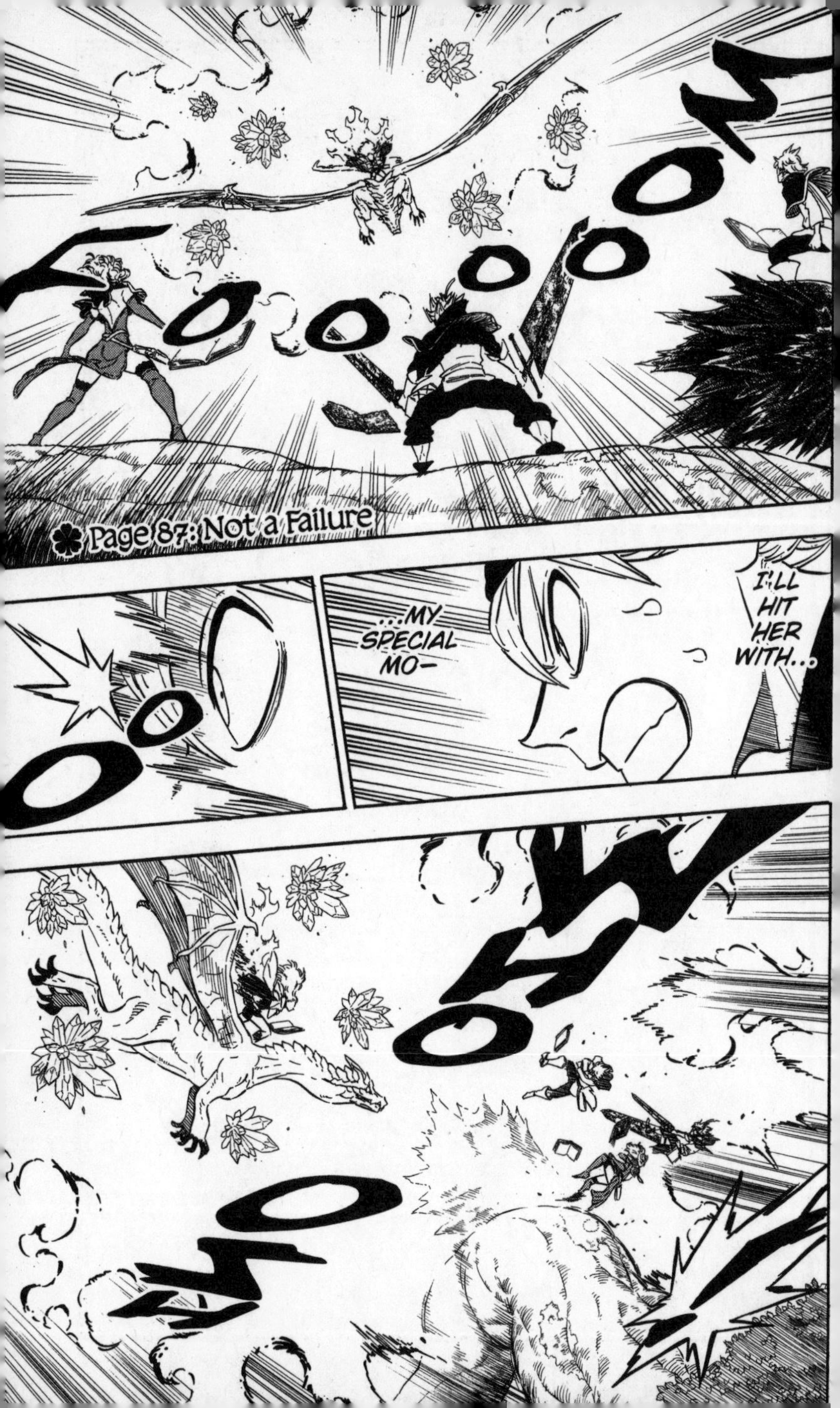
FOOOOOM
I'LL HIT HER WITH...
...MY SPECIAL MO-

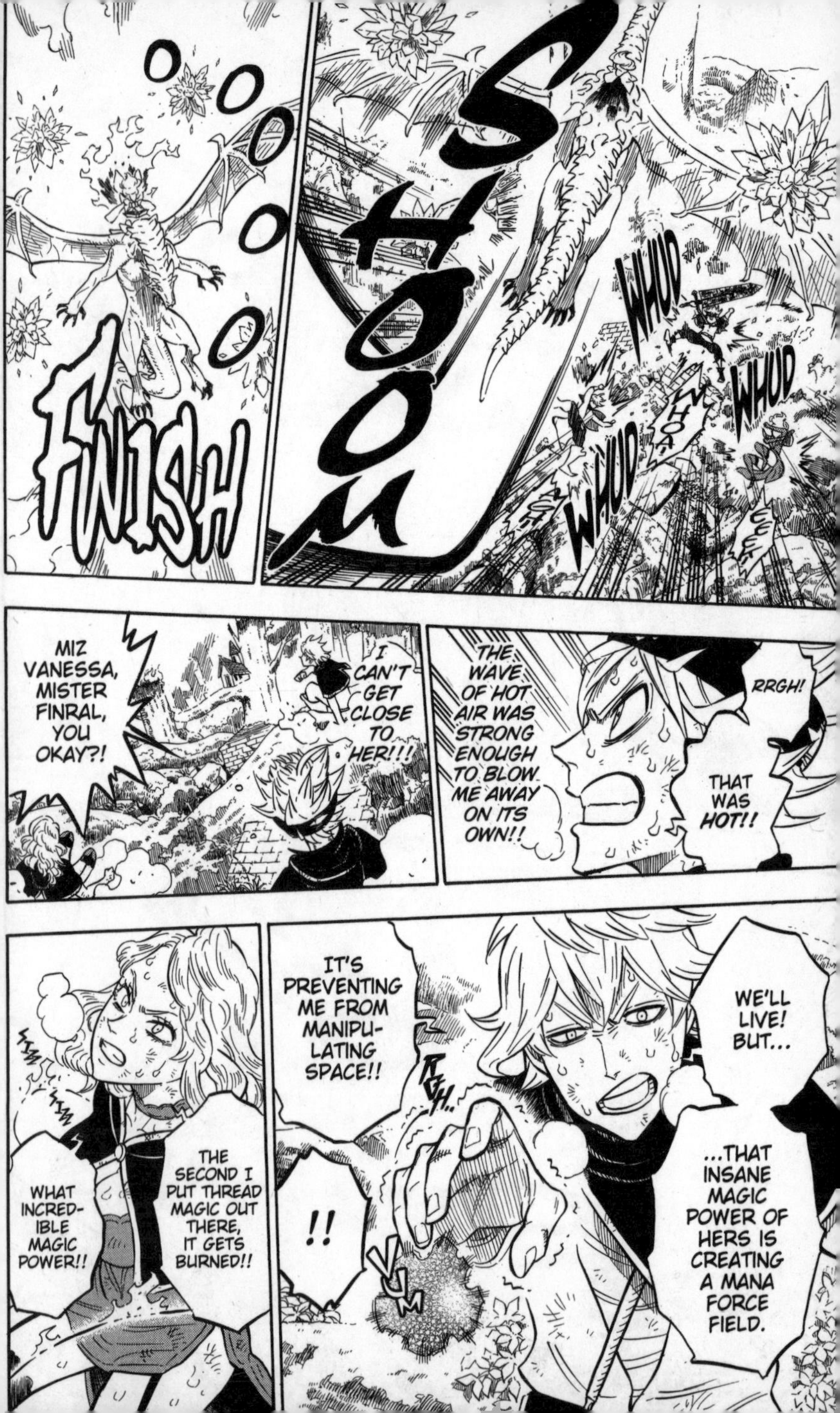
SHOOOM
WHUD
WHUD
WHOA!
WHUD
WHUD
OOOOOO
FINISH
THE WAVE OF HOT AIR WAS STRONG ENOUGH TO BLOW ME AWAY ON ITS OWN!!
RRGH!
THAT WAS HOT!!
I CAN'T GET CLOSE TO HER!!!
MIZ VANESSA, MISTER FINRAL, YOU OKAY?!
WE'LL LIVE! BUT...
IT'S PREVENTING ME FROM MANIPU-LATING SPACE!!
...THAT INSANE MAGIC POWER OF HERS IS CREATING A MANA FORCE FIELD.
!!
THE SECOND I PUT THREAD MAGIC OUT THERE, IT GETS BURNED!!
WHAT INCRED-IBLE MAGIC POWER!!

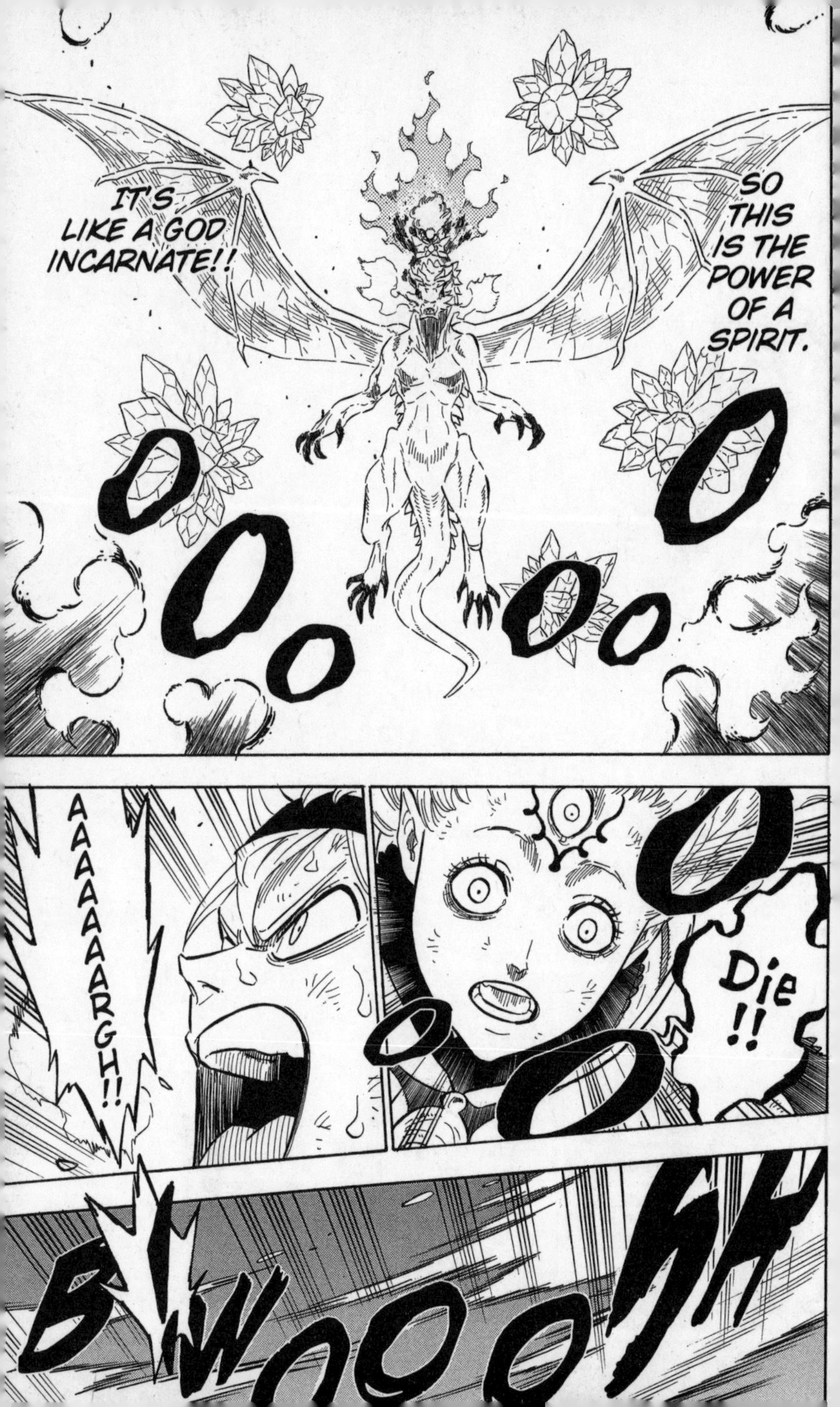
SO THIS IS THE POWER OF A SPIRIT.
IT'S LIKE A GOD INCARNATE!!
Die!!
AAAAAAAARGH!!
BWOOOOHH

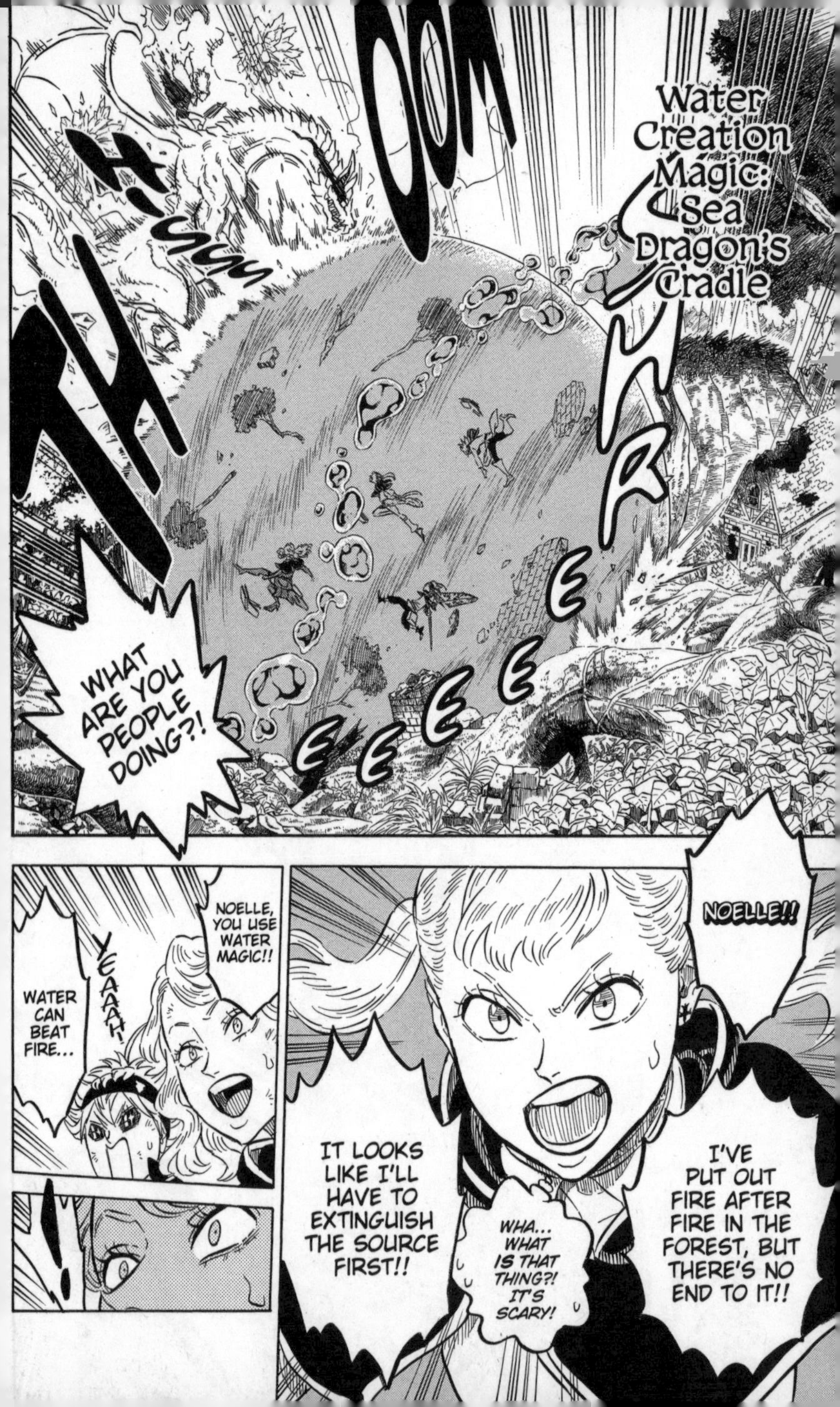

Water Creation Magic: Sea Dragon's Cradle
WHAT ARE YOU PEOPLE DOING?!
NOELLE!!
I'VE PUT OUT FIRE AFTER FIRE IN THE FOREST, BUT THERE'S NO END TO IT!!
WHA... WHAT IS THAT THING?! IT'S SCARY!
IT LOOKS LIKE I'LL HAVE TO EXTINGUISH THE SOURCE FIRST!!
NOELLE, YOU USE WATER MAGIC!!
YEAAAAH!
WATER CAN BEAT FIRE...
!

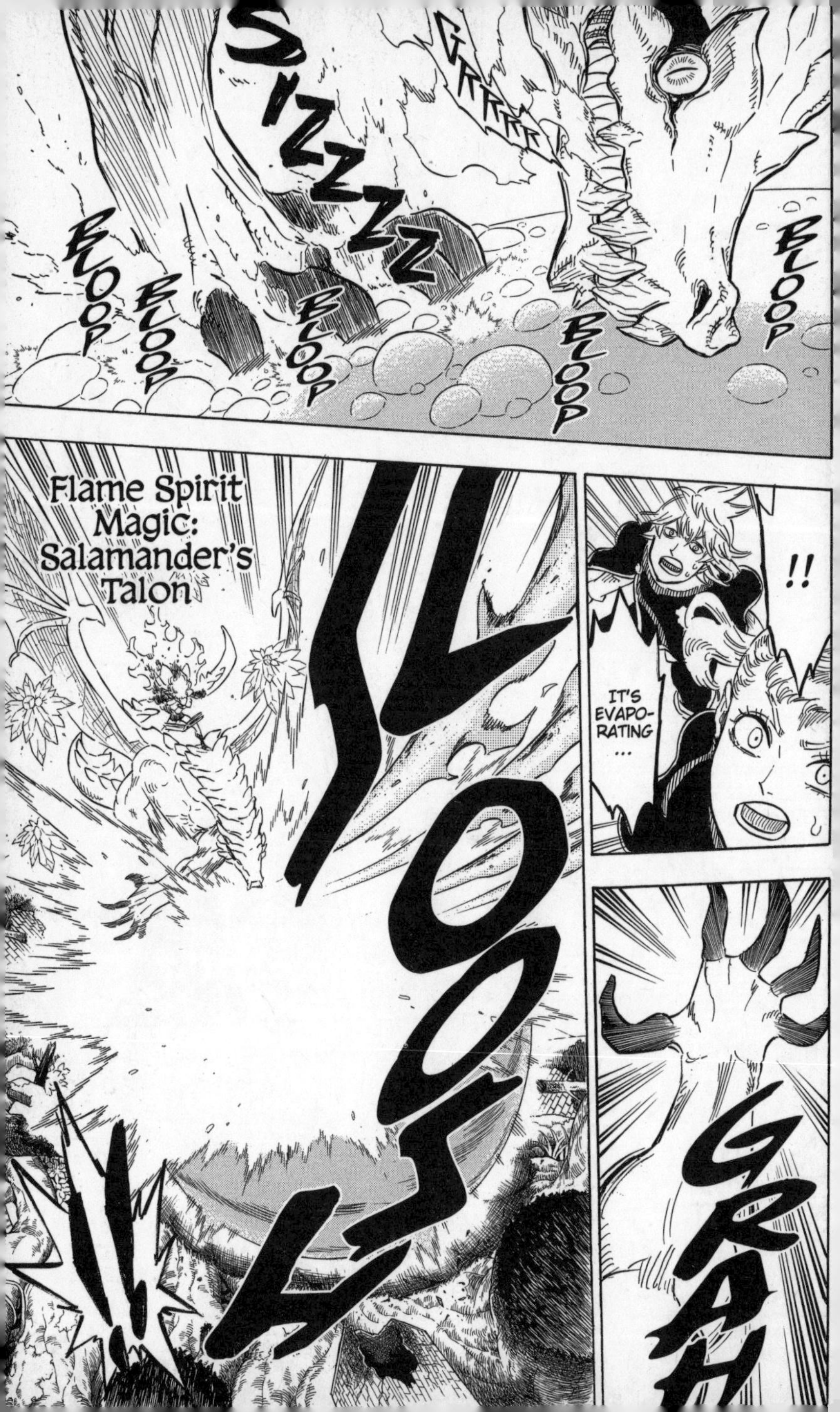
GRRRRR
SIZZZZZ
BLOOP
BLOOP
BLOOP
BLOOP
BLOOP
!!
IT'S EVAPORATING...
GRAB
Flame Spirit Magic: Salamander's Talon
WOOSH
!!

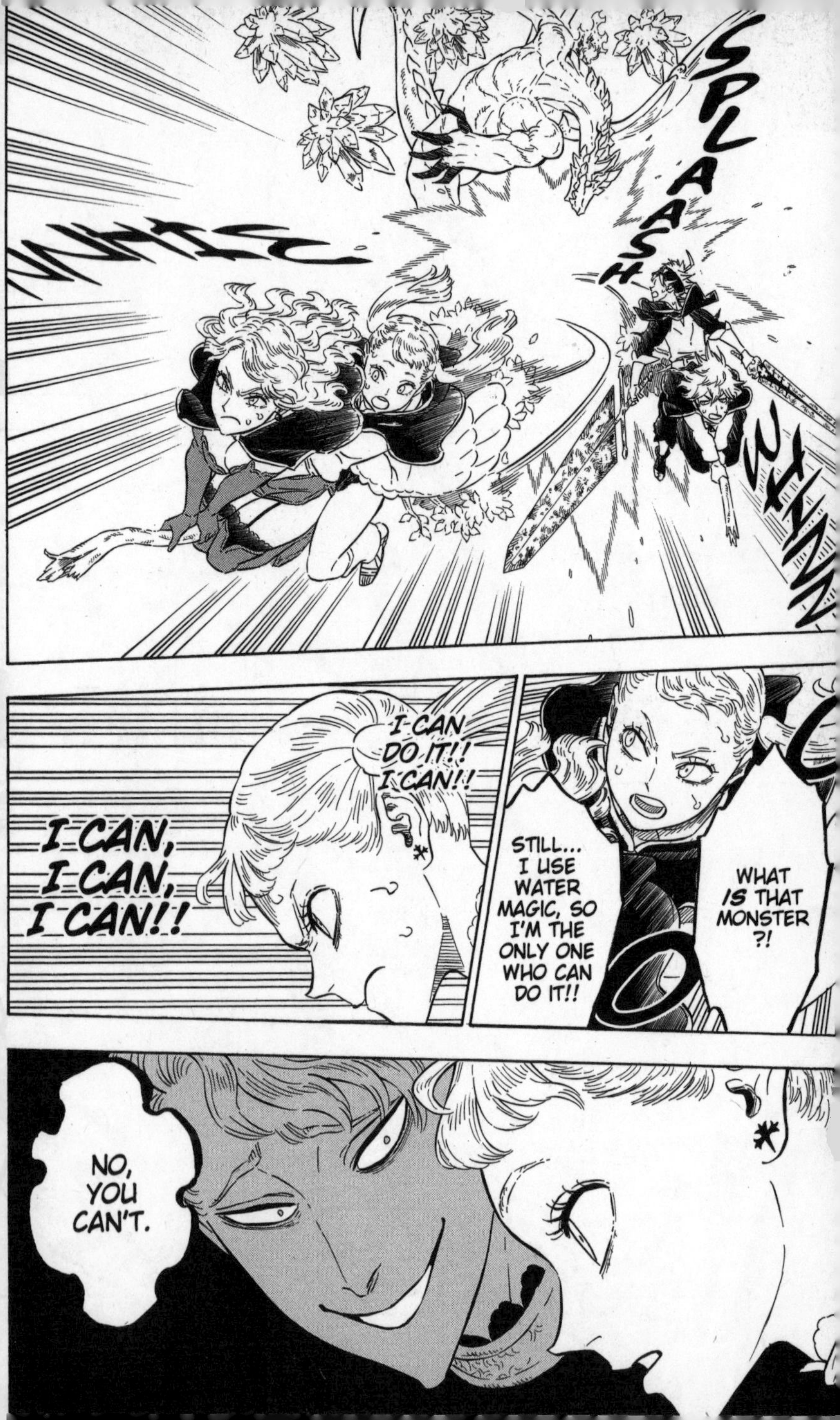
SPLAASH
WHAT IS THAT MONSTER?!
STILL... I USE WATER MAGIC, SO I'M THE ONLY ONE WHO CAN DO IT!!
I CAN DO IT!! I CAN!!
I CAN, I CAN, I CAN!!
NO, YOU CAN'T.

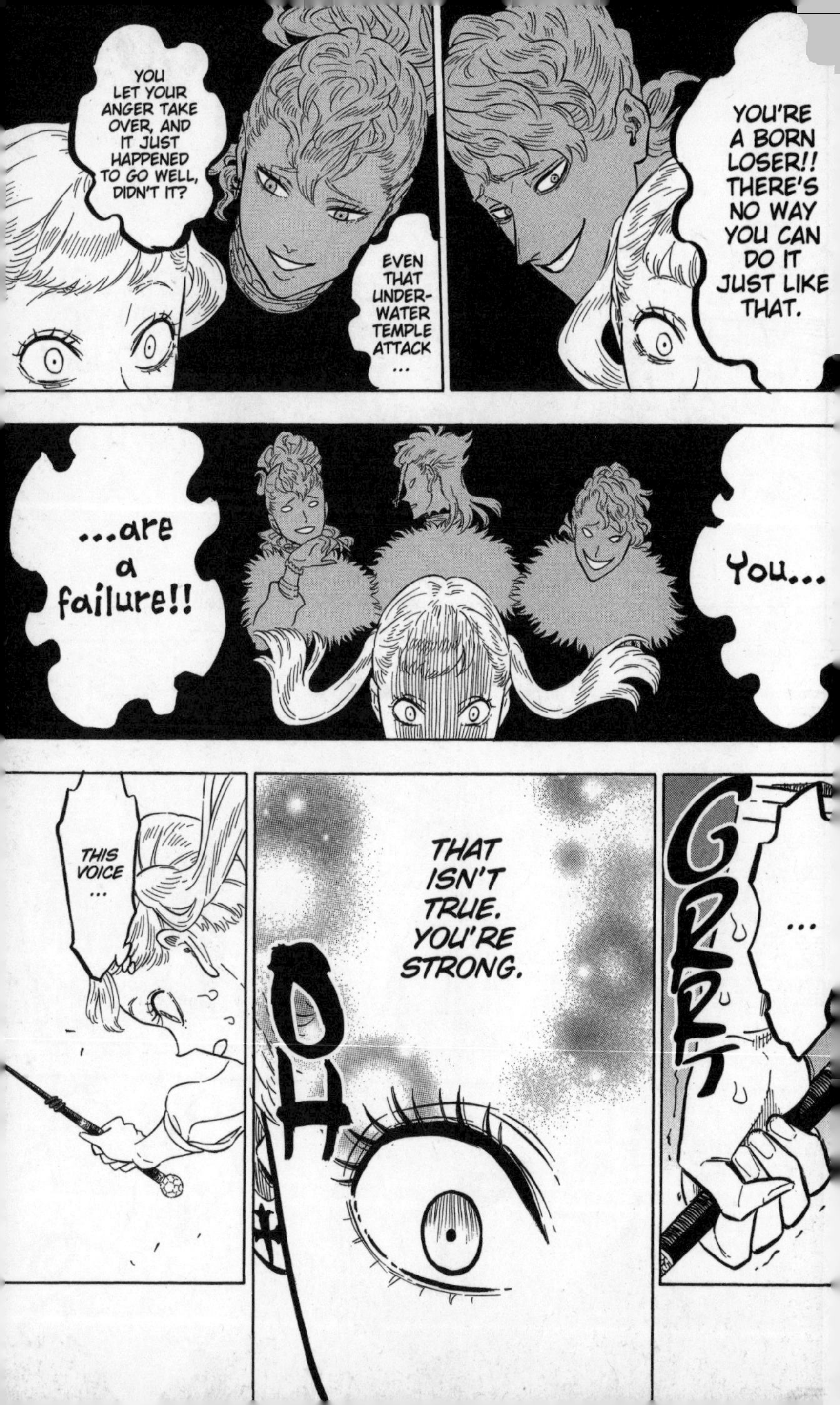
YOU'RE A BORN LOSER!! THERE'S NO WAY YOU CAN DO IT JUST LIKE THAT.
EVEN THAT UNDER-WATER TEMPLE ATTACK...
YOU LET YOUR ANGER TAKE OVER, AND IT JUST HAPPENED TO GO WELL, DIDN'T IT?
You...
...are a failure!!
GRRR
...
THAT ISN'T TRUE. YOU'RE STRONG.
THIS VOICE...

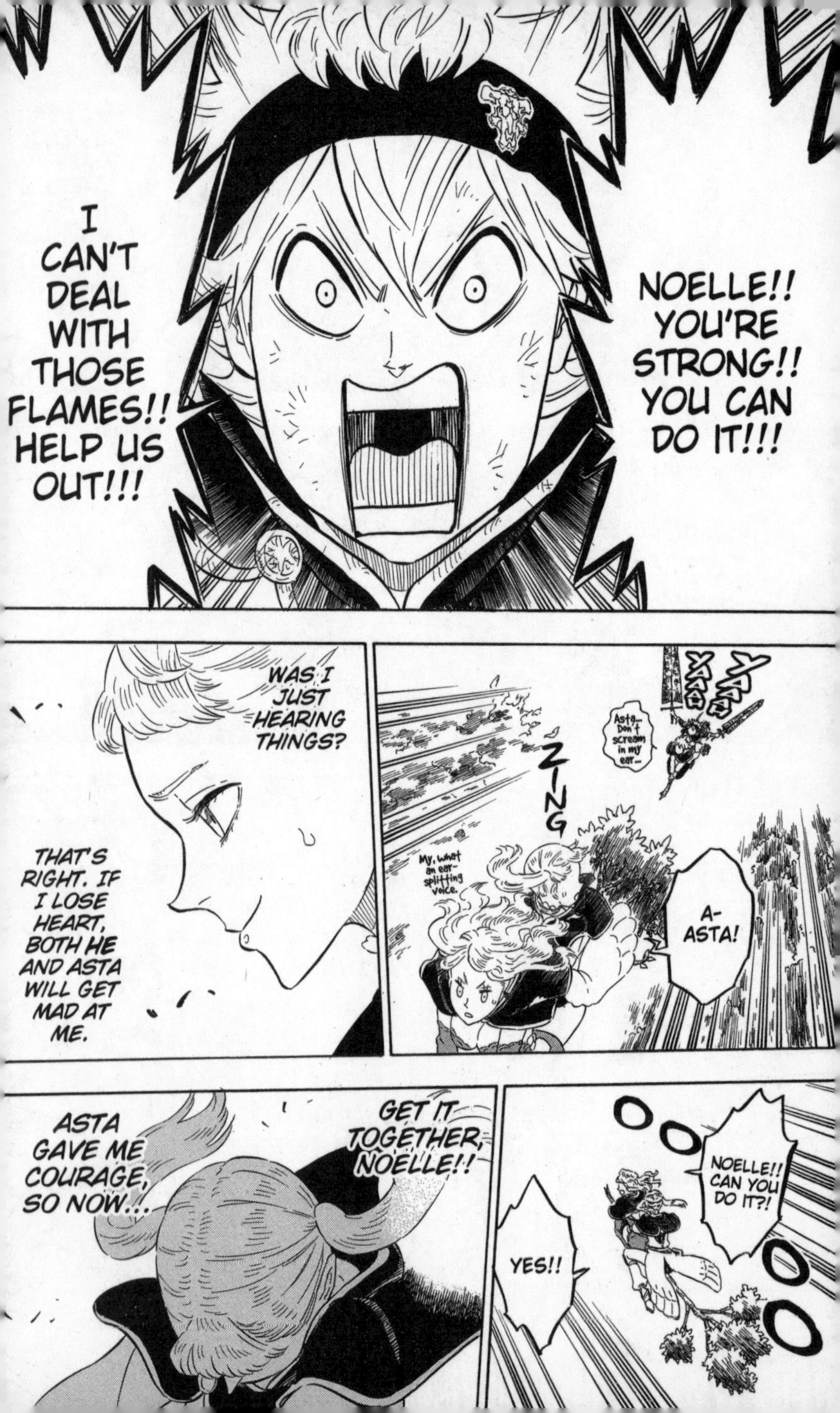
NOELLE!! YOU'RE STRONG!! YOU CAN DO IT!!!
I CAN'T DEAL WITH THOSE FLAMES!! HELP US OUT!!!
YAAA YAAA
Asta... Don't scream in my ear...
ZING
A-ASTA!
My, what an ear-splitting voice.
WAS I JUST HEARING THINGS?
THAT'S RIGHT. IF I LOSE HEART, BOTH HE AND ASTA WILL GET MAD AT ME.
NOELLE!! CAN YOU DO IT?!
OOOOO
YES!!
GET IT TOGETHER, NOELLE!!
ASTA GAVE ME COURAGE, SO NOW...

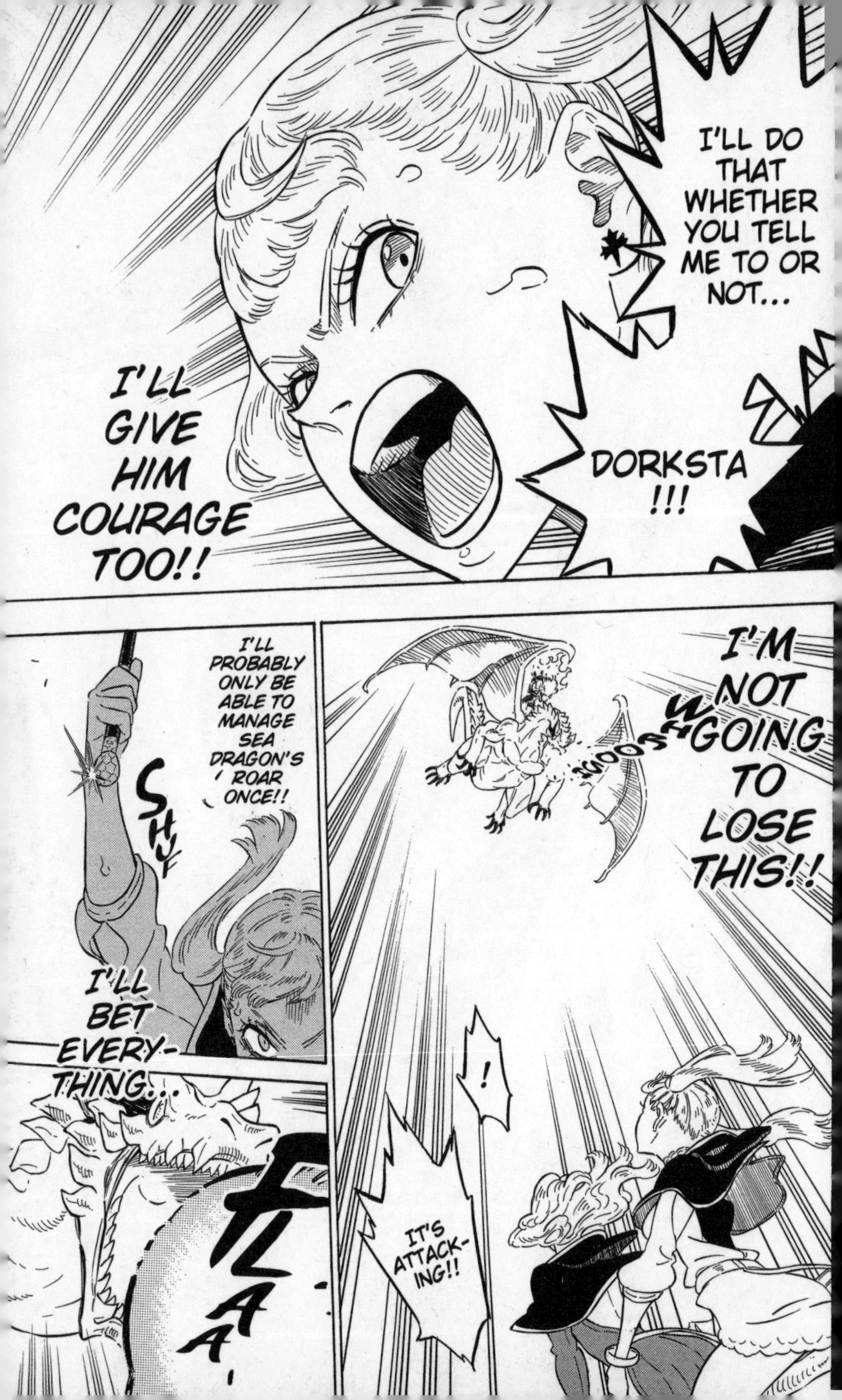
I'LL DO THAT WHETHER YOU TELL ME TO OR NOT...
DORKSTA!!!
I'LL GIVE HIM COURAGE TOO!!
I'M NOT GOING TO LOSE THIS!!
I'LL PROBABLY ONLY BE ABLE TO MANAGE SEA DRAGON'S ROAR ONCE!!
I'LL BET EVERYTHING...
!
IT'S ATTACKING!!

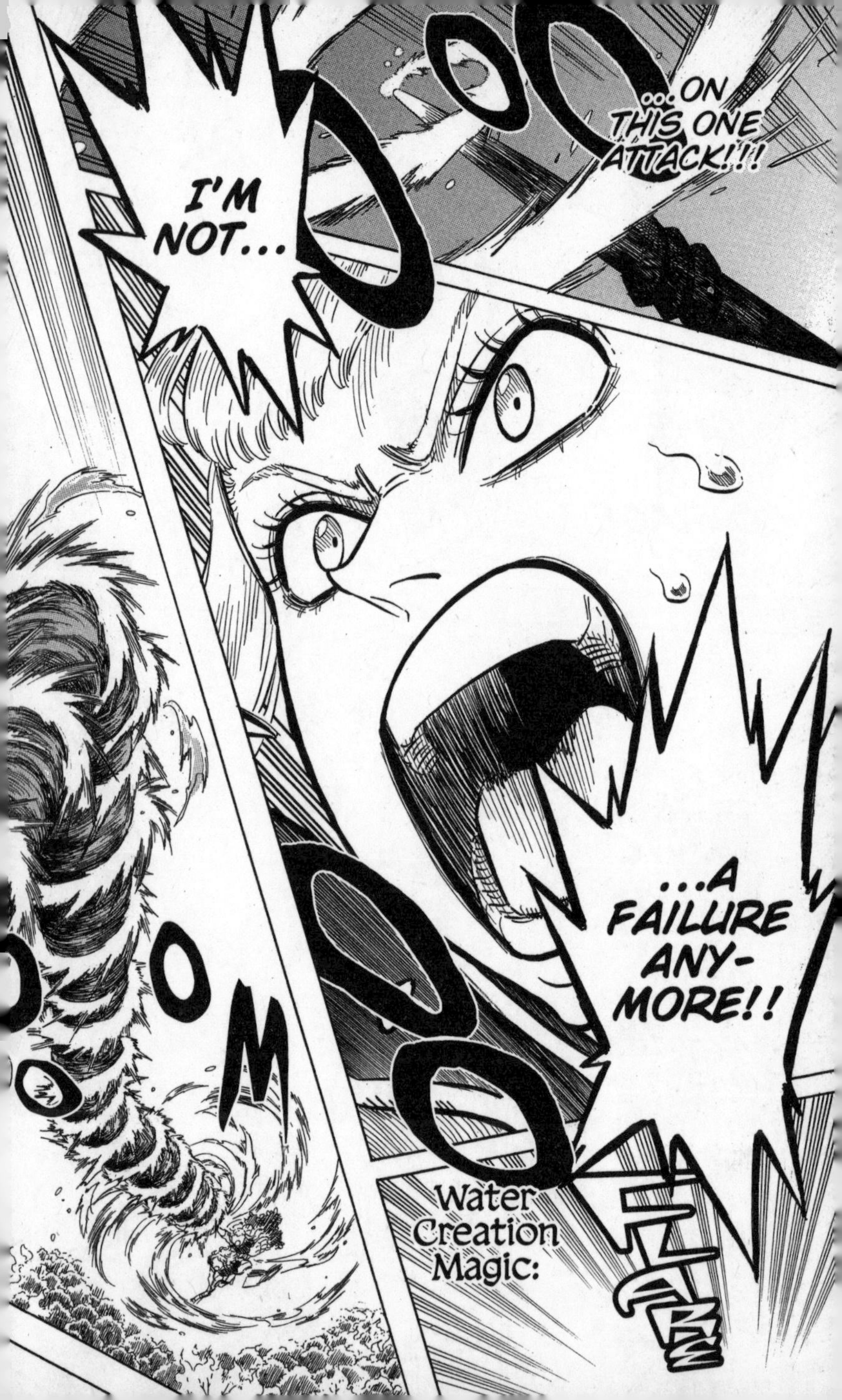
...ON THIS ONE ATTACK!!!
I'M NOT...
...A FAILURE ANYMORE!!
Water Creation Magic:

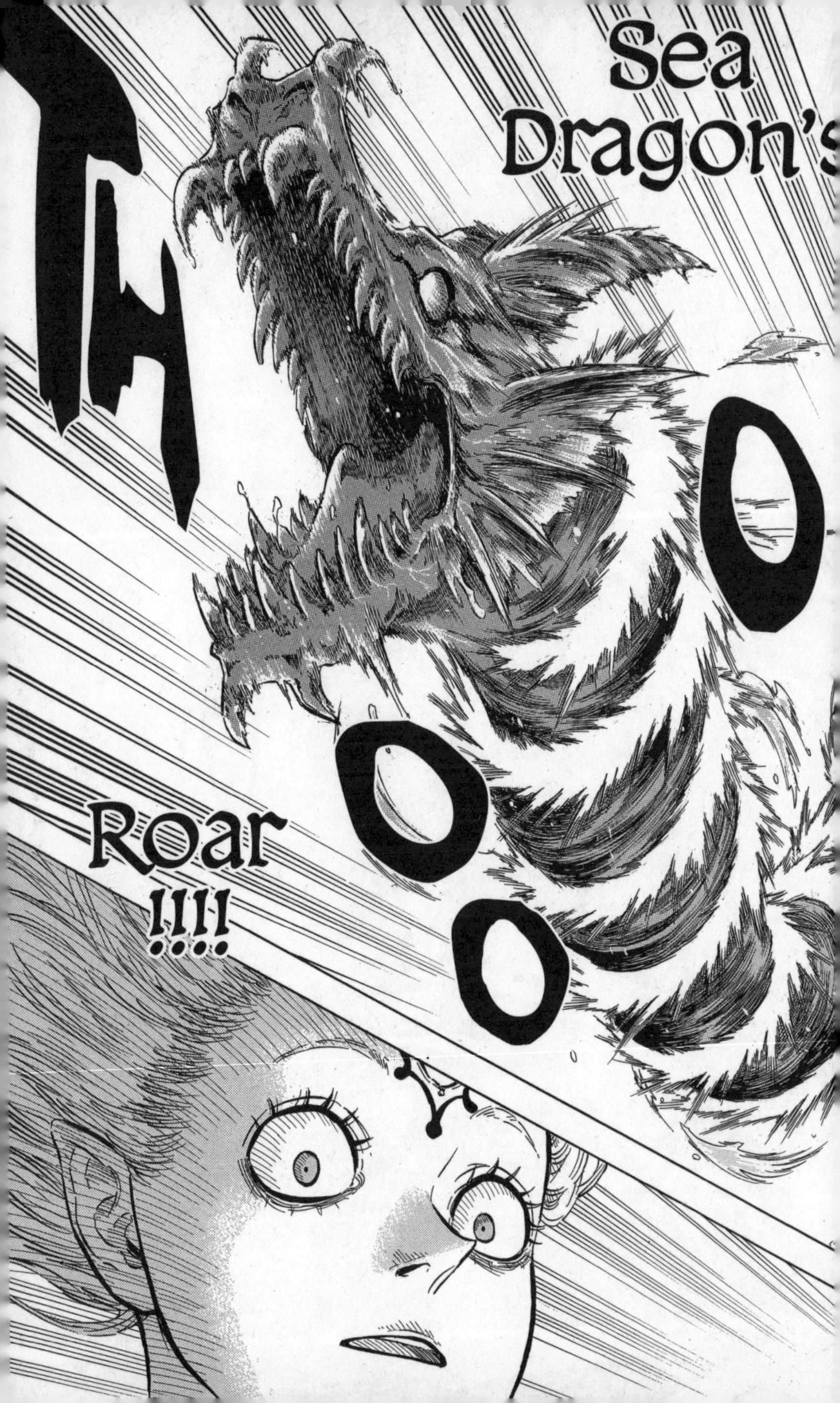
Sea Dragon's
Roar!!!!

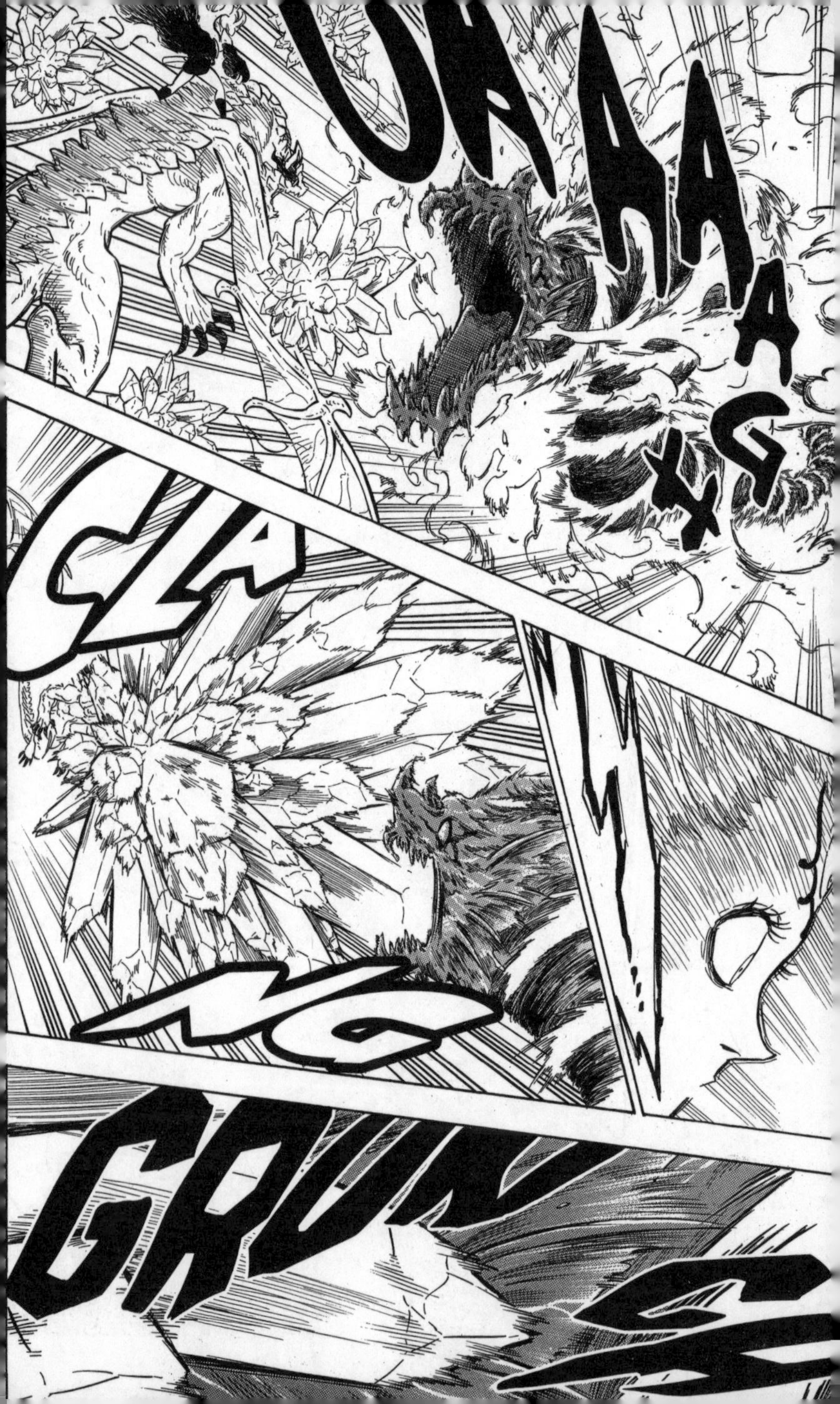
CLANG

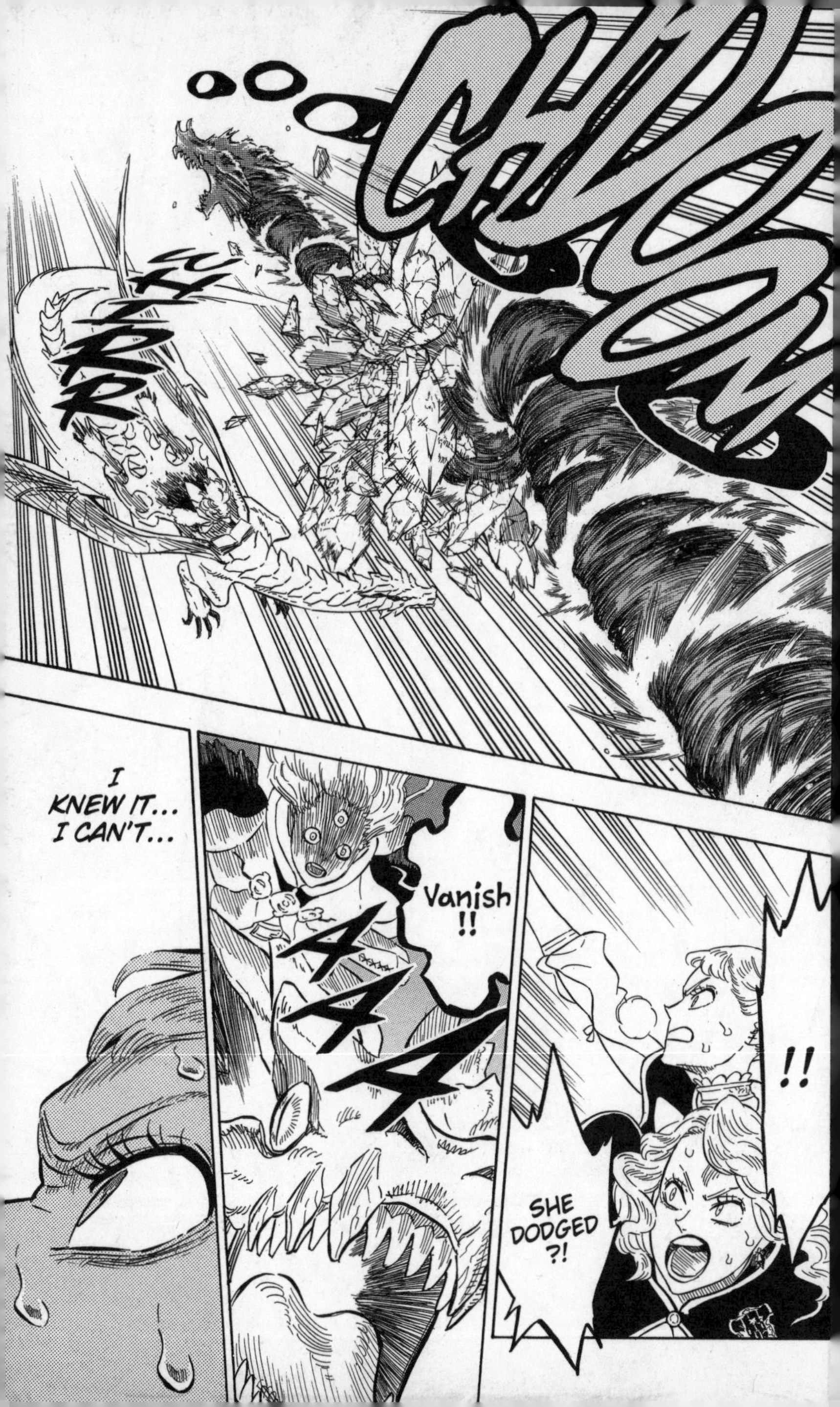
SHIRR
!!
SHE DODGED ?!
Vanish !!
AAA
I KNEW IT... I CAN'T...

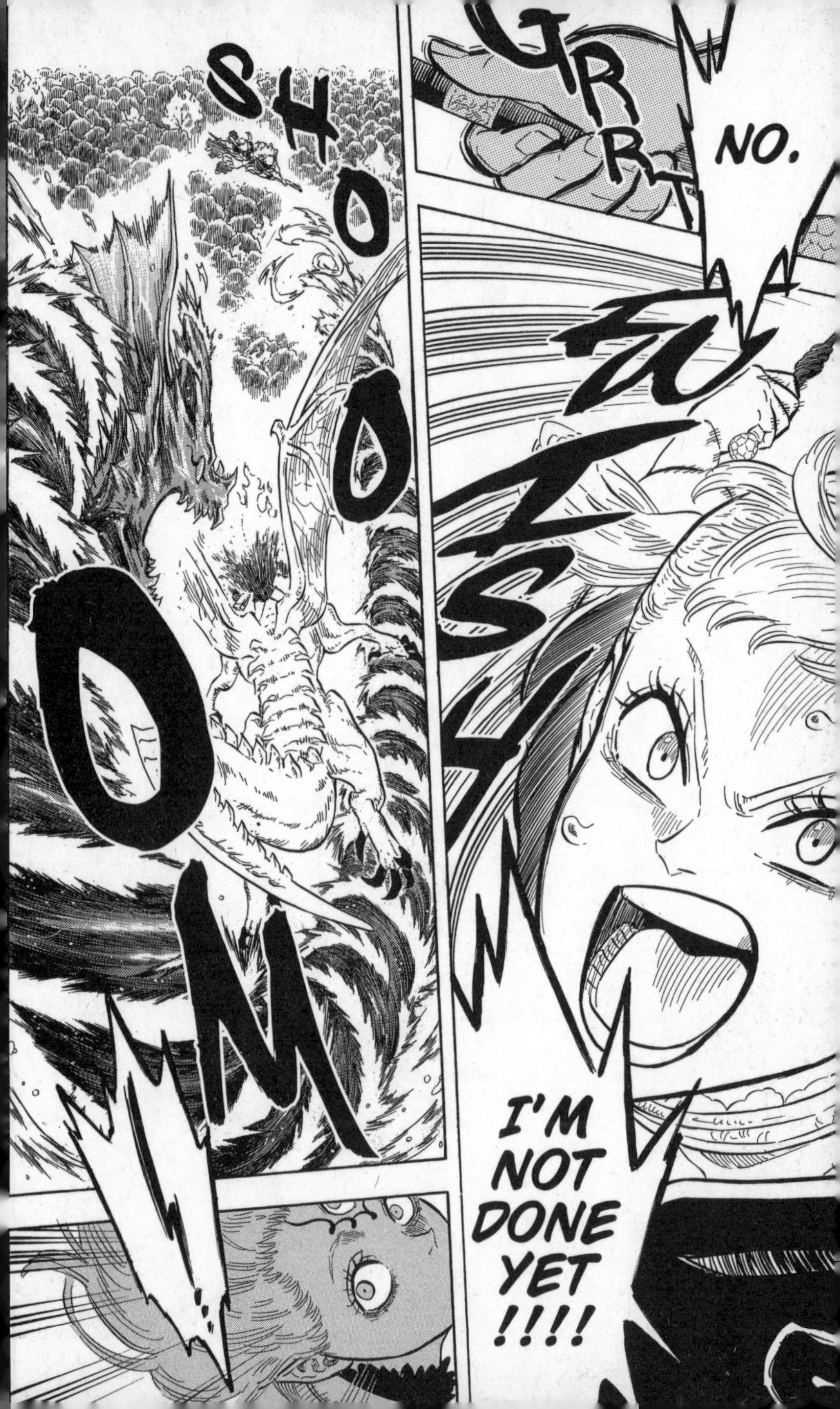
GRRT
NO.
WHSH
I'M NOT DONE YET!!!!
SHOOOM

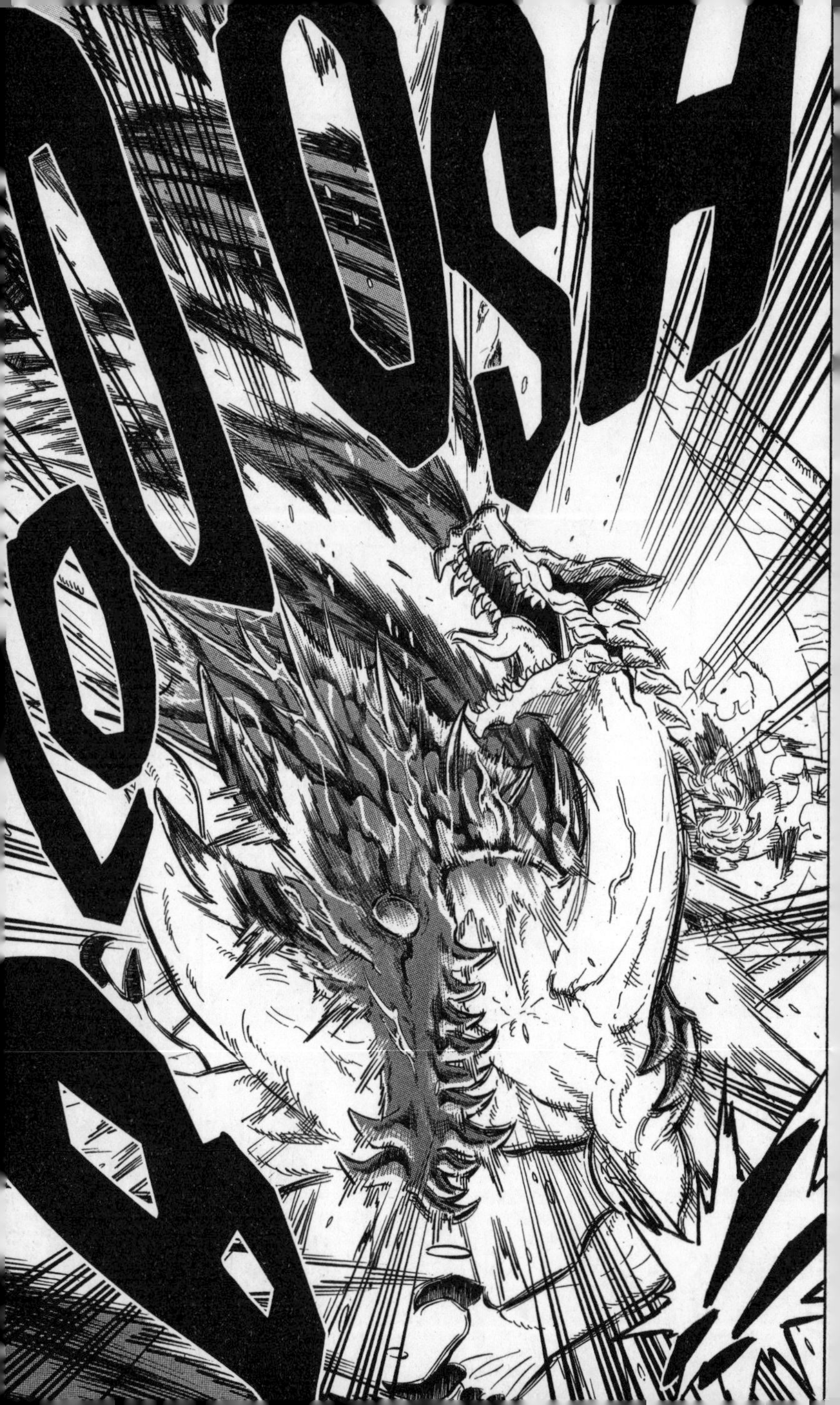
BOOSH!!

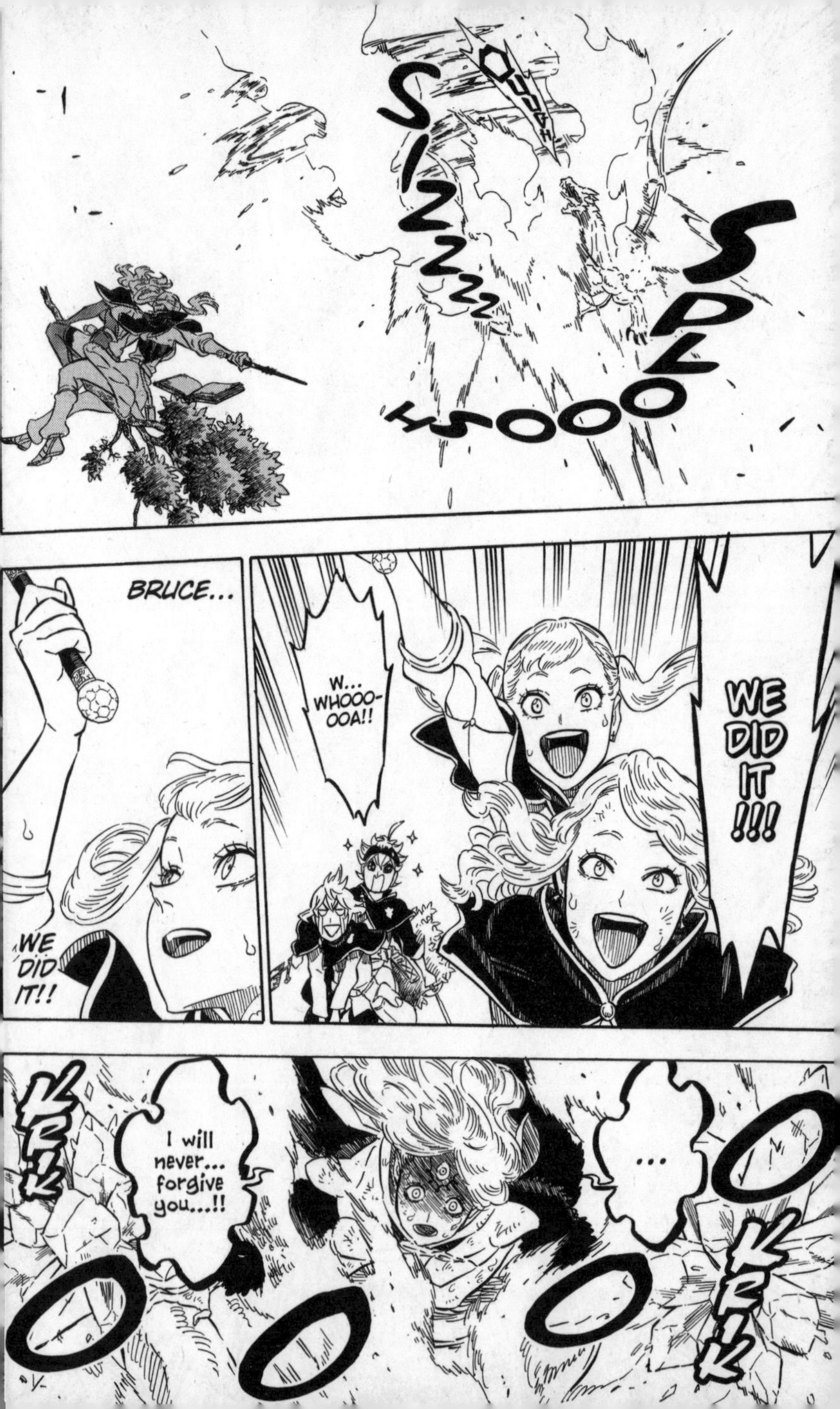
SIZZZZZ
OUUGH
SPLOOOOSH
WE DID IT!!!
W... WHOOOO-OOA!!
BRUCE...
WE DID IT!!
...
I will never... forgive you...!!
KRIK
KRIK

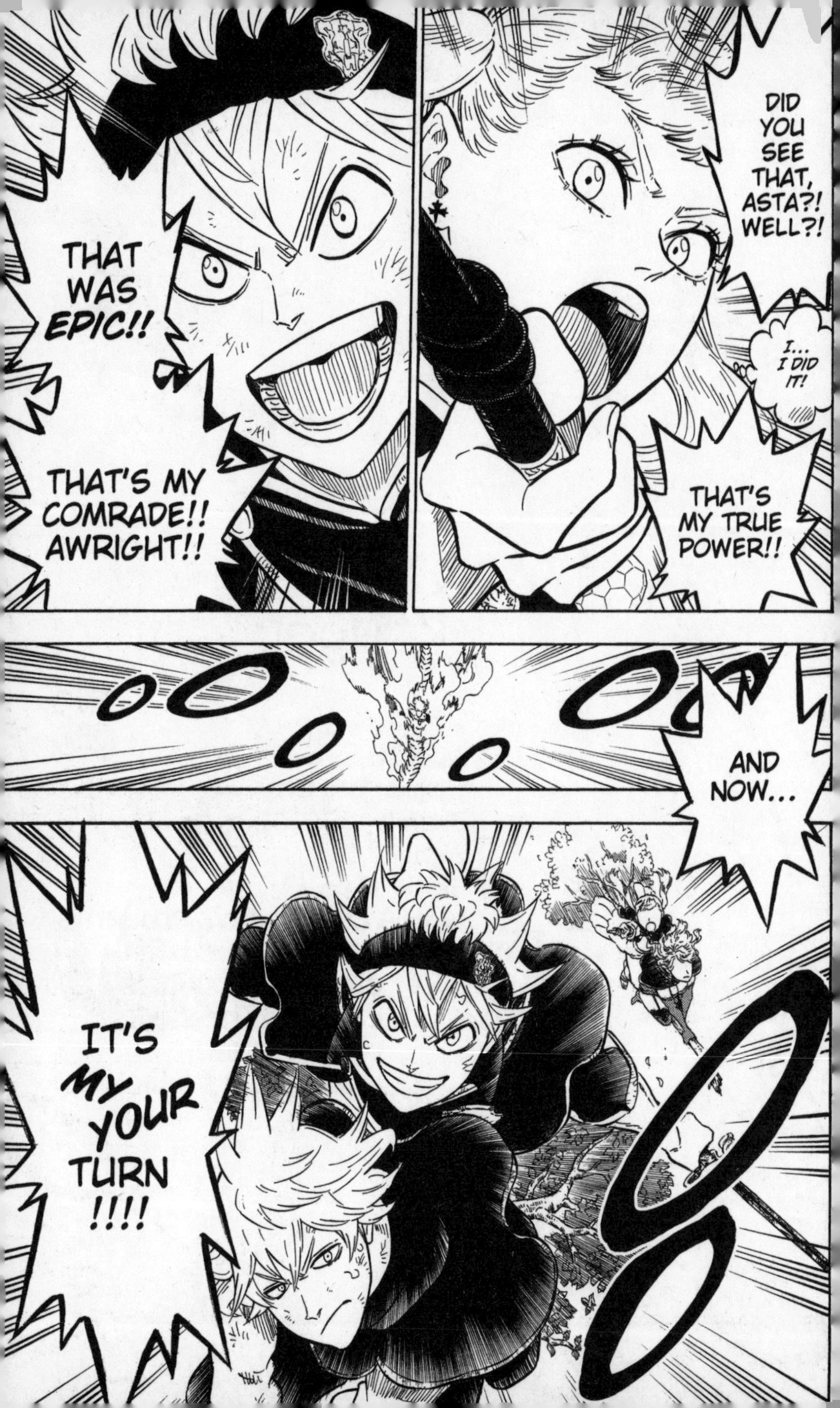
DID YOU SEE THAT, ASTA?! WELL?!
I... I DID IT!
THAT'S MY TRUE POWER!!
THAT WAS EPIC!!
THAT'S MY COMRADE!! AWRIGHT!!
AND NOW...
IT'S MY YOUR TURN !!!!

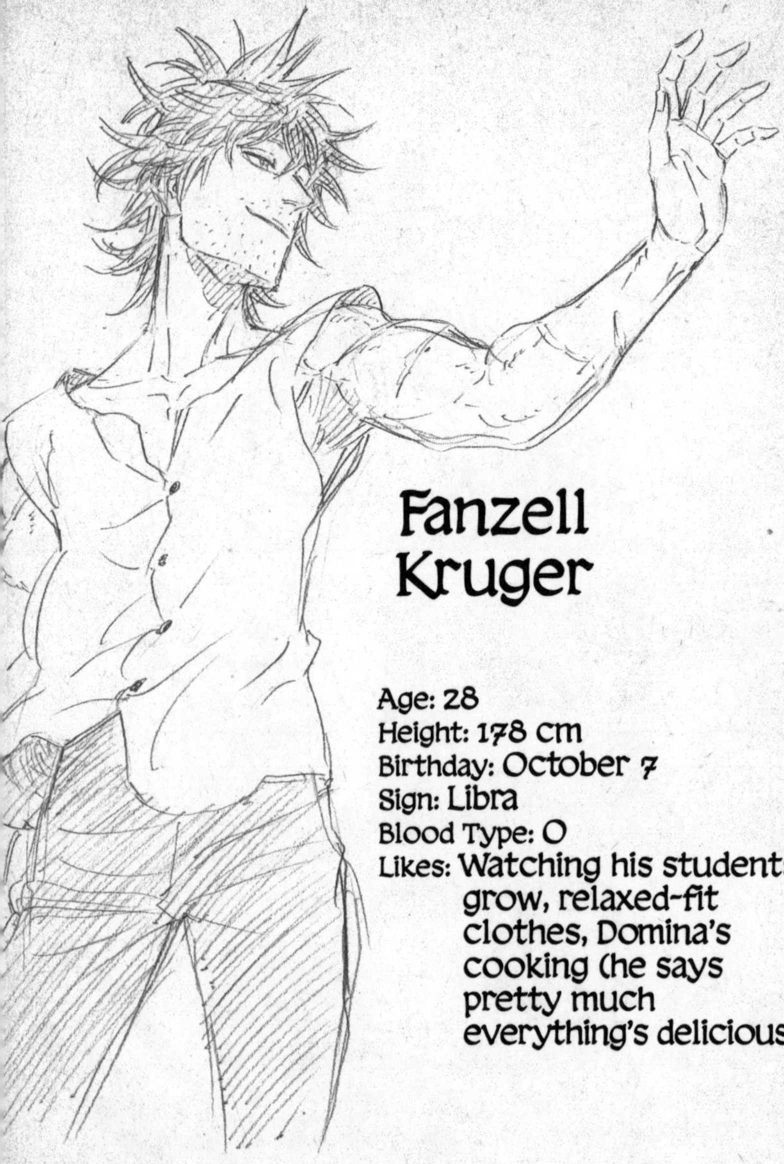

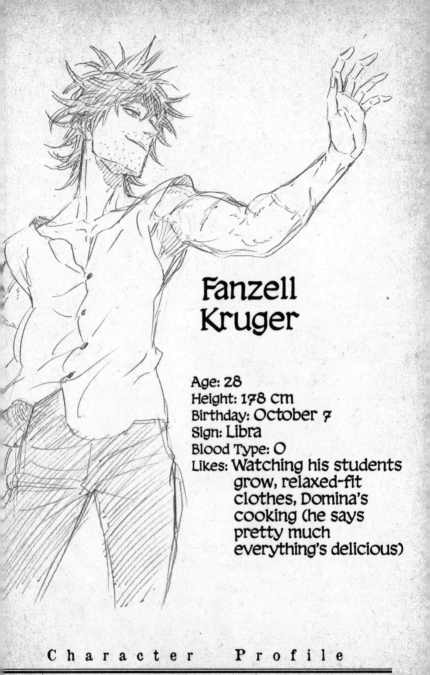

Fanzell Kruger

Age: 28
Height: 178 cm
Birthday: October 7
Sign: Libra
Blood Type: O
Likes: Watching his students grow, relaxed-fit clothes, Domina's cooking (he says pretty much everything's delicious)

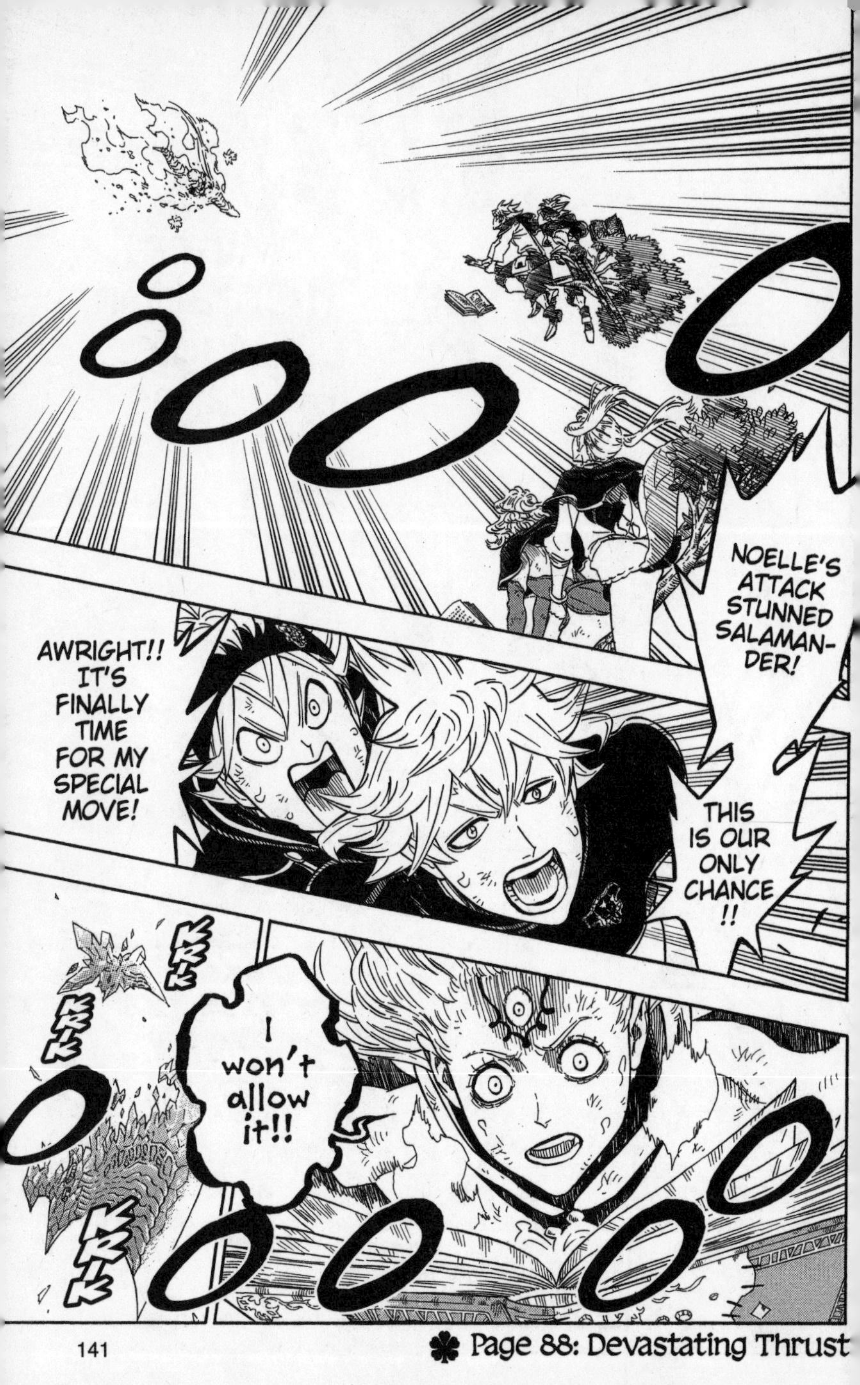
OOOOOO
NOELLE'S ATTACK STUNNED SALAMANDER!
THIS IS OUR ONLY CHANCE!!
AWRIGHT!! IT'S FINALLY TIME FOR MY SPECIAL MOVE!
I won't allow it!!
KRIK
KRIK
KRIK
OOOOOOO

Page 88: Devastating Thrust

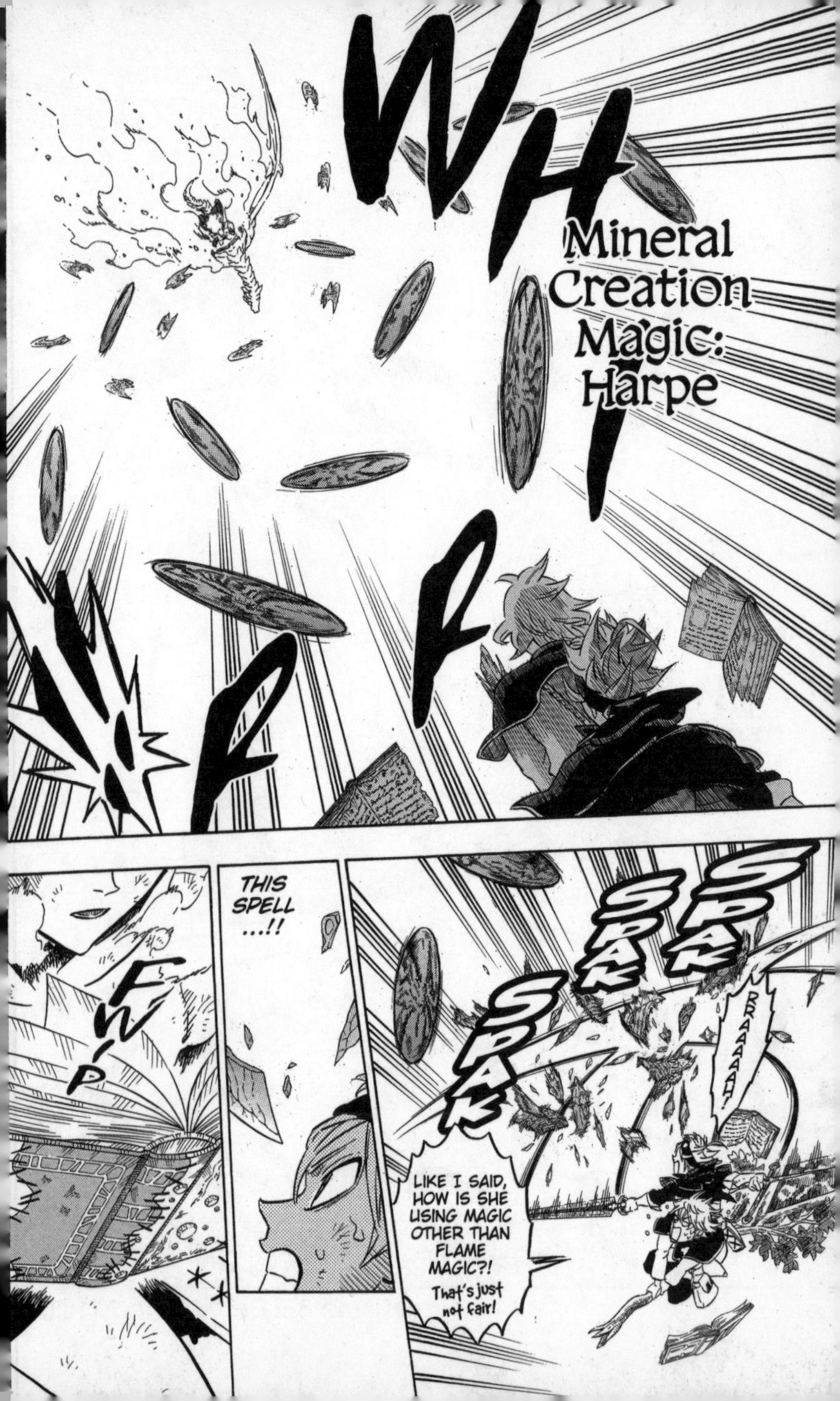
WHIRR
Mineral Creation Magic: Harpe
SPAK SPAK
SPAK
RRAAAAAH!
LIKE I SAID, HOW IS SHE USING MAGIC OTHER THAN FLAME MAGIC?!
That's just not fair!
THIS SPELL ...!!
FWIP

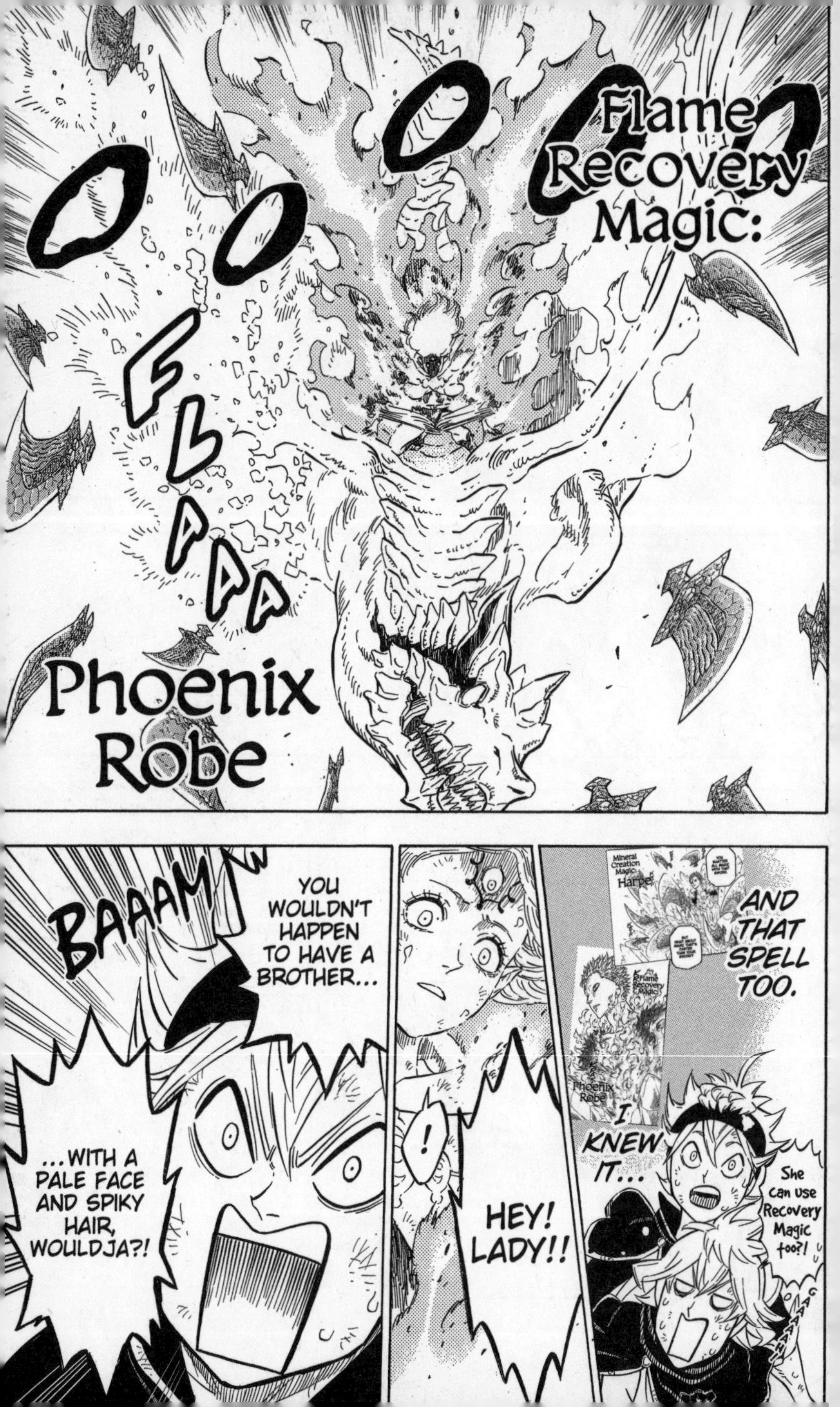
Flame Recovery Magic:
FLAPAA
Phoenix Robe
Mineral Creation Magic: Harpe
AND THAT SPELL TOO.
Flame Recovery Magic:
Phoenix Robe
I KNEW IT...
She can use Recovery Magic too?!
GAAAAAH!
!
HEY! LADY!!
BAAAM
YOU WOULDN'T HAPPEN TO HAVE A BROTHER...
...WITH A PALE FACE AND SPIKY HAIR, WOULDJA?!

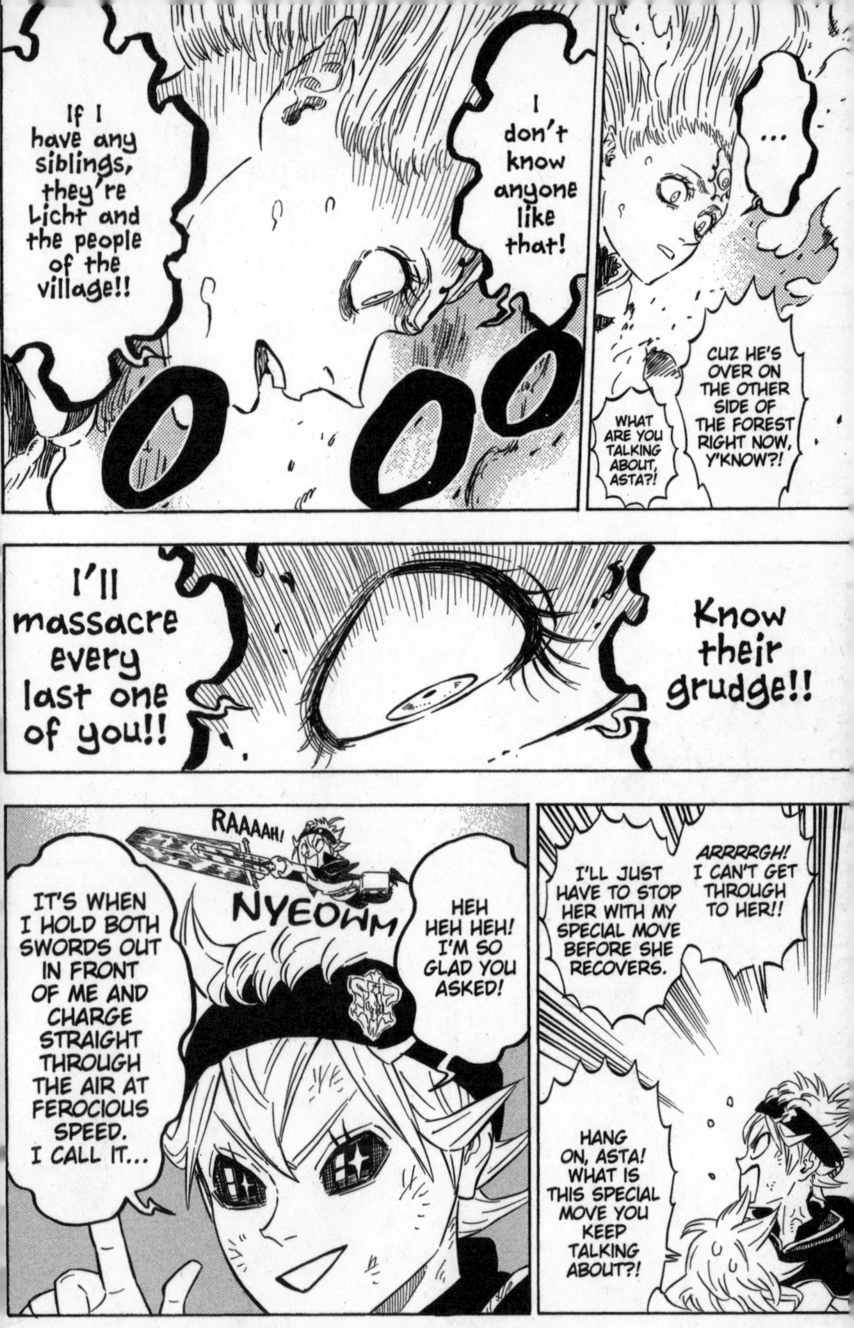
...
CUZ HE'S OVER ON THE OTHER SIDE OF THE FOREST RIGHT NOW, Y'KNOW?!
WHAT ARE YOU TALKING ABOUT, ASTA?!
I don't know anyone like that!
If I have any siblings, they're Licht and the people of the village!!
Know their grudge!!
I'll massacre every last one of you!!
ARRRRGH! I CAN'T GET THROUGH TO HER!!
I'LL JUST HAVE TO STOP HER WITH MY SPECIAL MOVE BEFORE SHE RECOVERS.
HANG ON, ASTA! WHAT IS THIS SPECIAL MOVE YOU KEEP TALKING ABOUT?!
HEH HEH HEH! I'M SO GLAD YOU ASKED!
RAAAAH!
NYEOWM
IT'S WHEN I HOLD BOTH SWORDS OUT IN FRONT OF ME AND CHARGE STRAIGHT THROUGH THE AIR AT FEROCIOUS SPEED. I CALL IT...

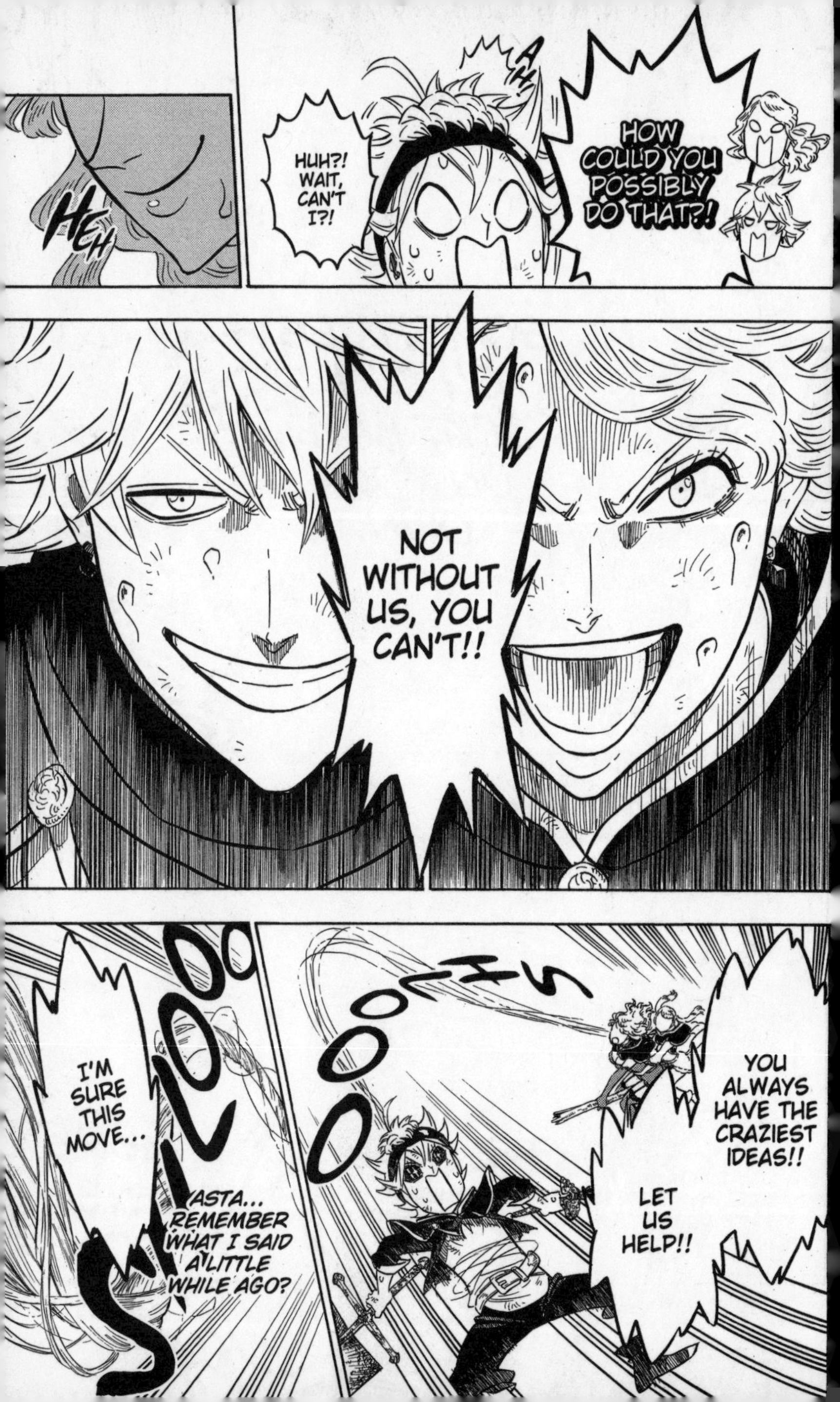
AH!
HOW COULD YOU POSSIBLY DO THAT?!
HUH?! WAIT, CAN'T I?!
HEH
NOT WITHOUT US, YOU CAN'T!!
YOU ALWAYS HAVE THE CRAZIEST IDEAS!!
LET US HELP!!
SHOOOO
I'M SURE THIS MOVE...
ASTA... REMEMBER WHAT I SAID A LITTLE WHILE AGO?
SHOOOO

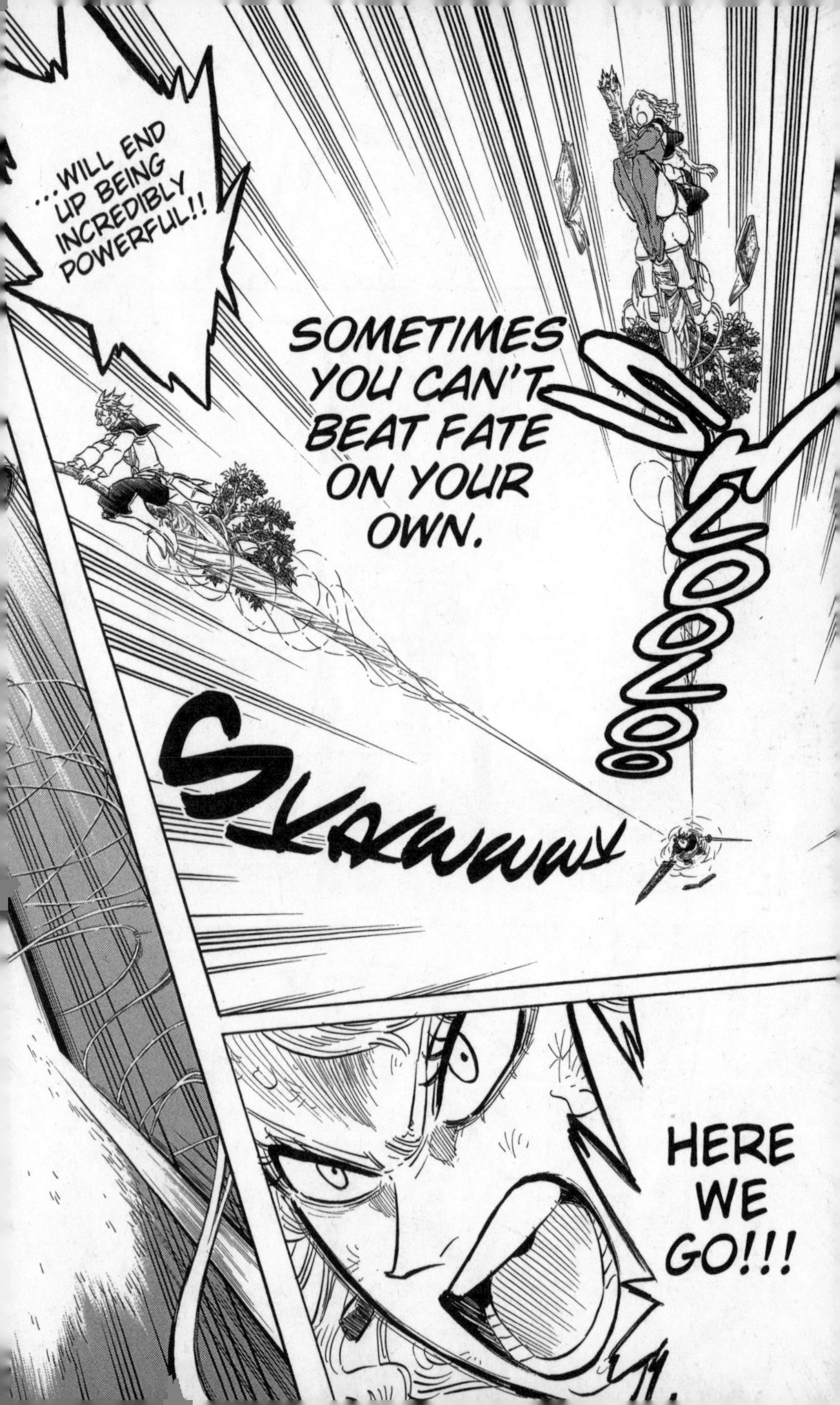
...WILL END UP BEING INCREDIBLY POWERFUL!!
SOMETIMES YOU CAN'T BEAT FATE ON YOUR OWN.
SHOOOOOO
SWAAAAAY
HERE WE GO!!!

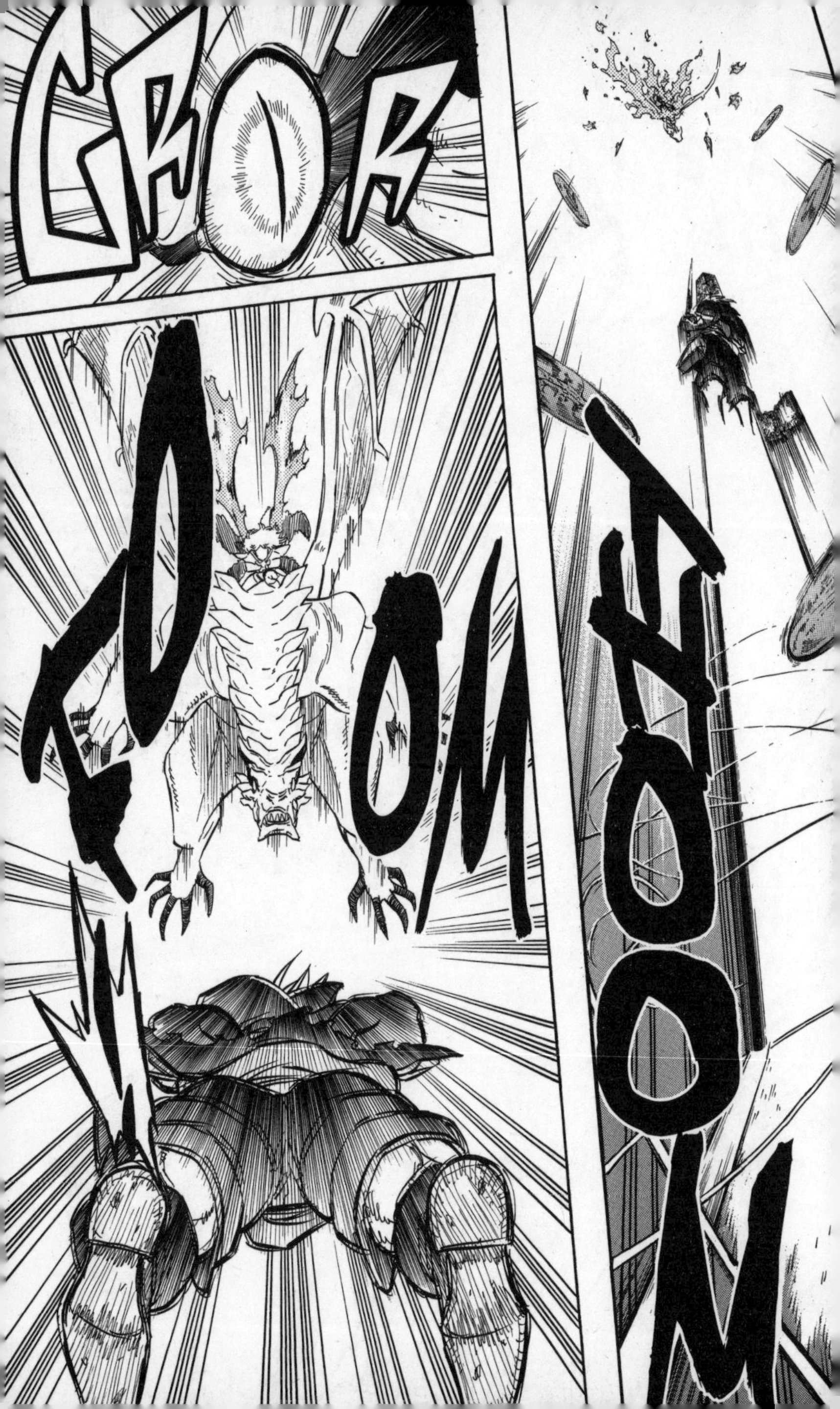
FOOM
GROR
FOOM

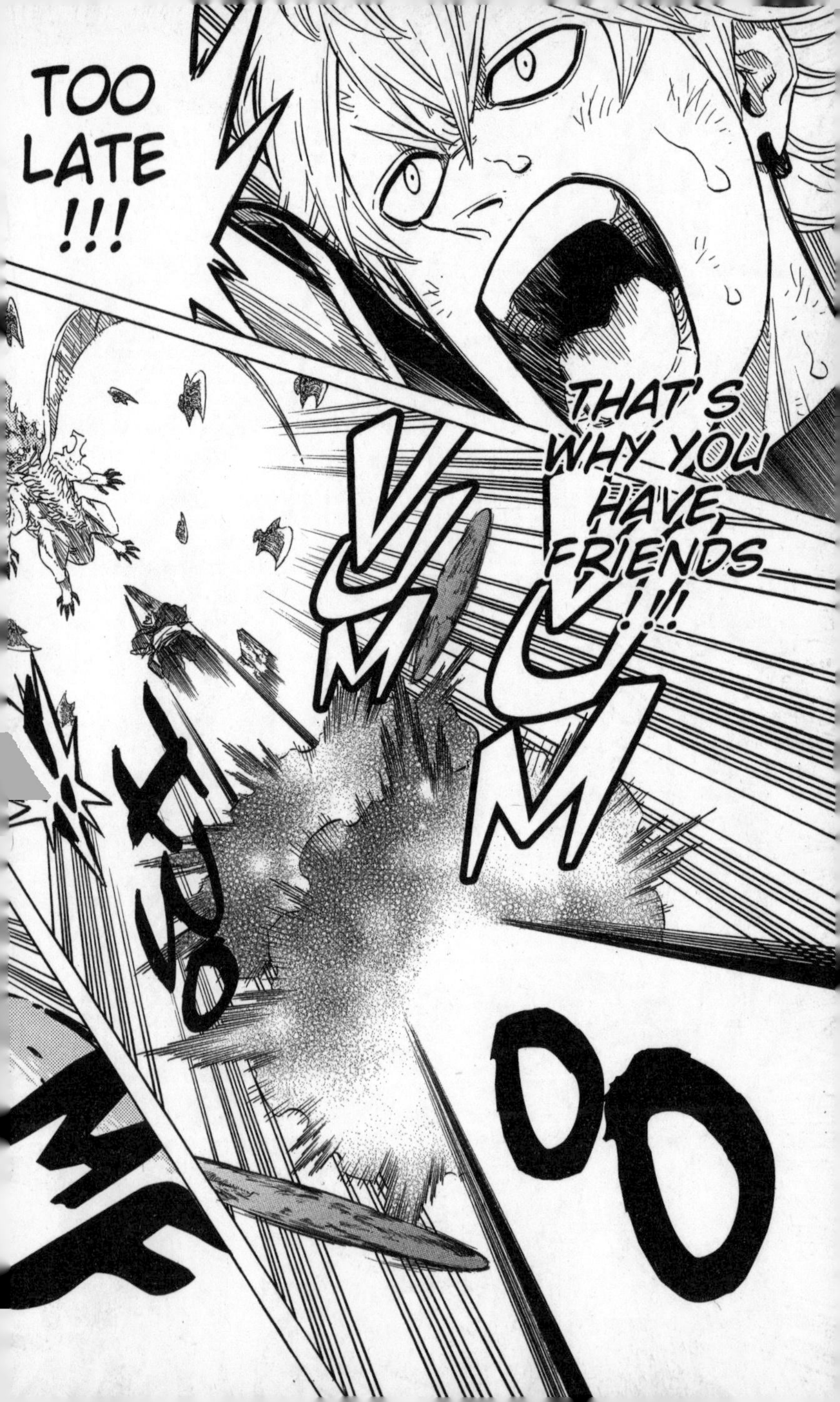
TOO LATE!!!
THAT'S WHY YOU HAVE FRIENDS!!!

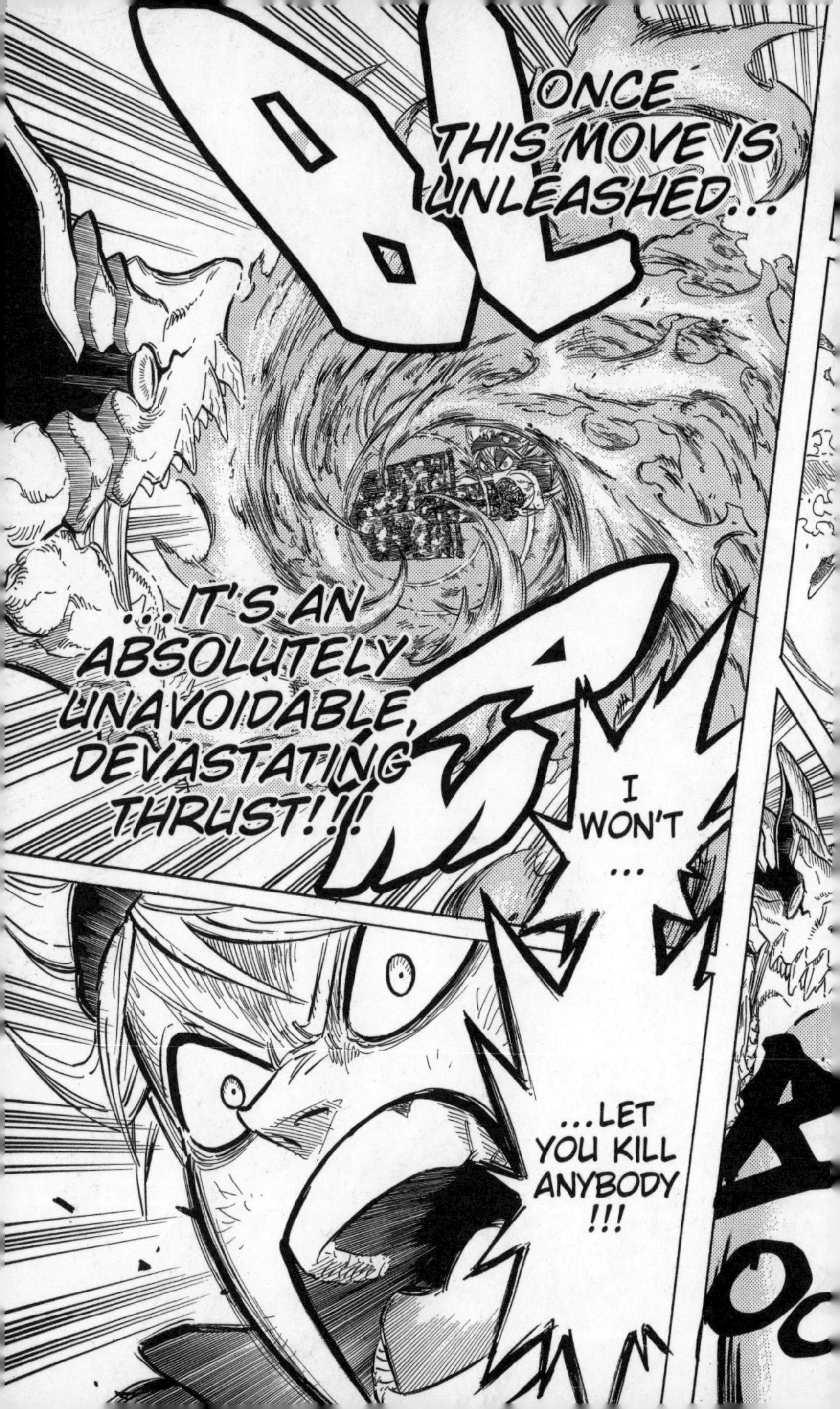

ONCE THIS MOVE IS UNLEASHED...
...IT'S AN ABSOLUTELY UNAVOIDABLE, DEVASTATING THRUST!!!
I WON'T ...
...LET YOU KILL ANYBODY !!!

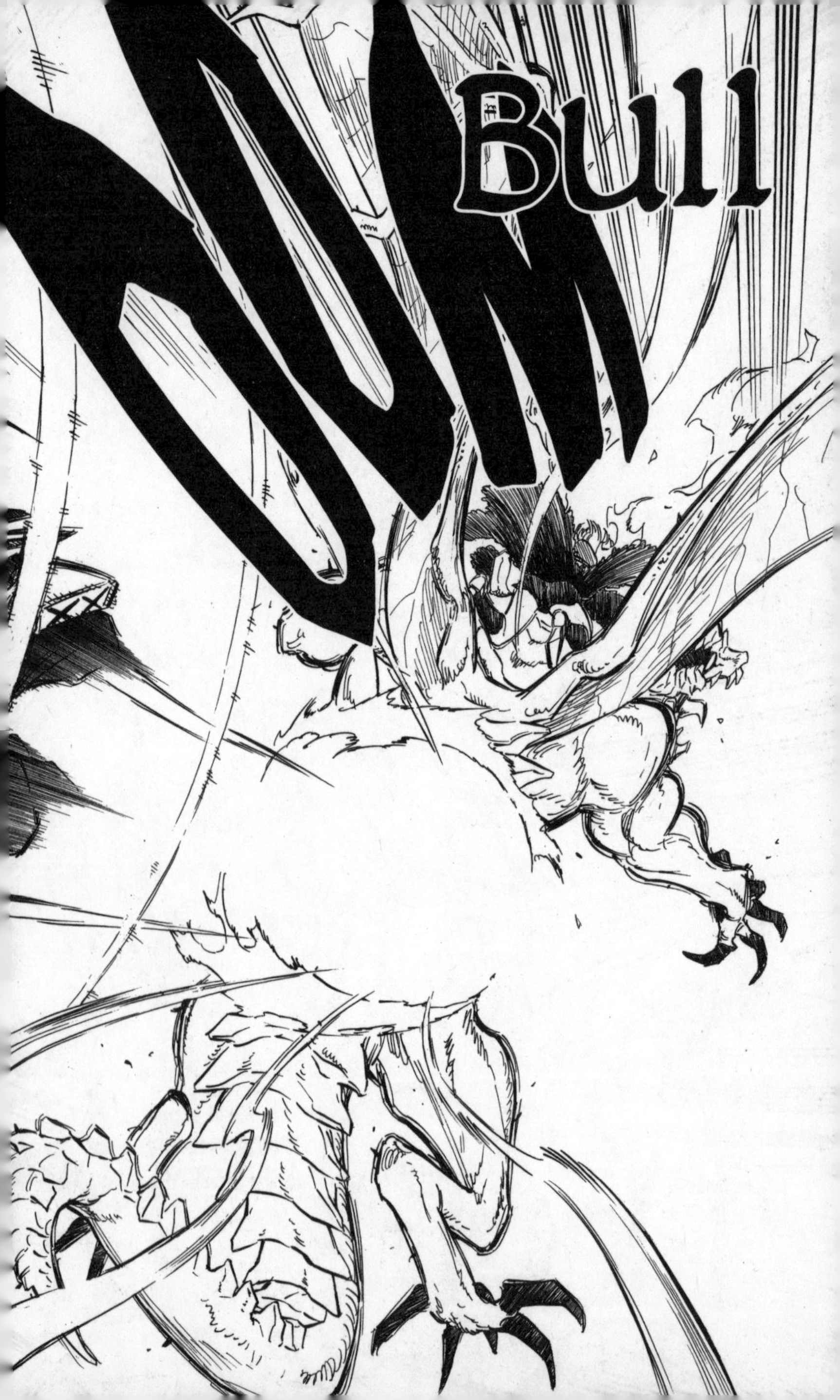
Bull

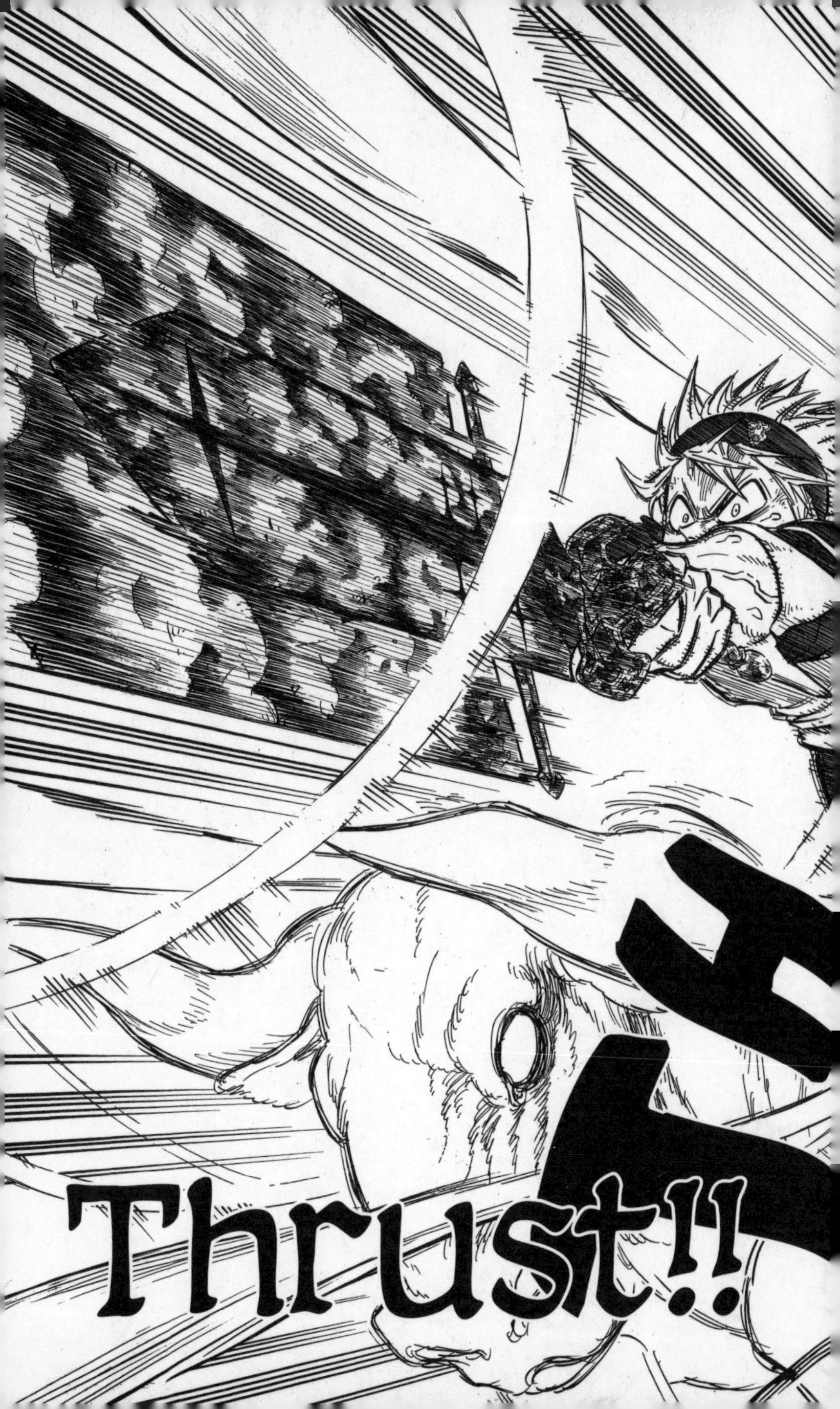
Thrust!!

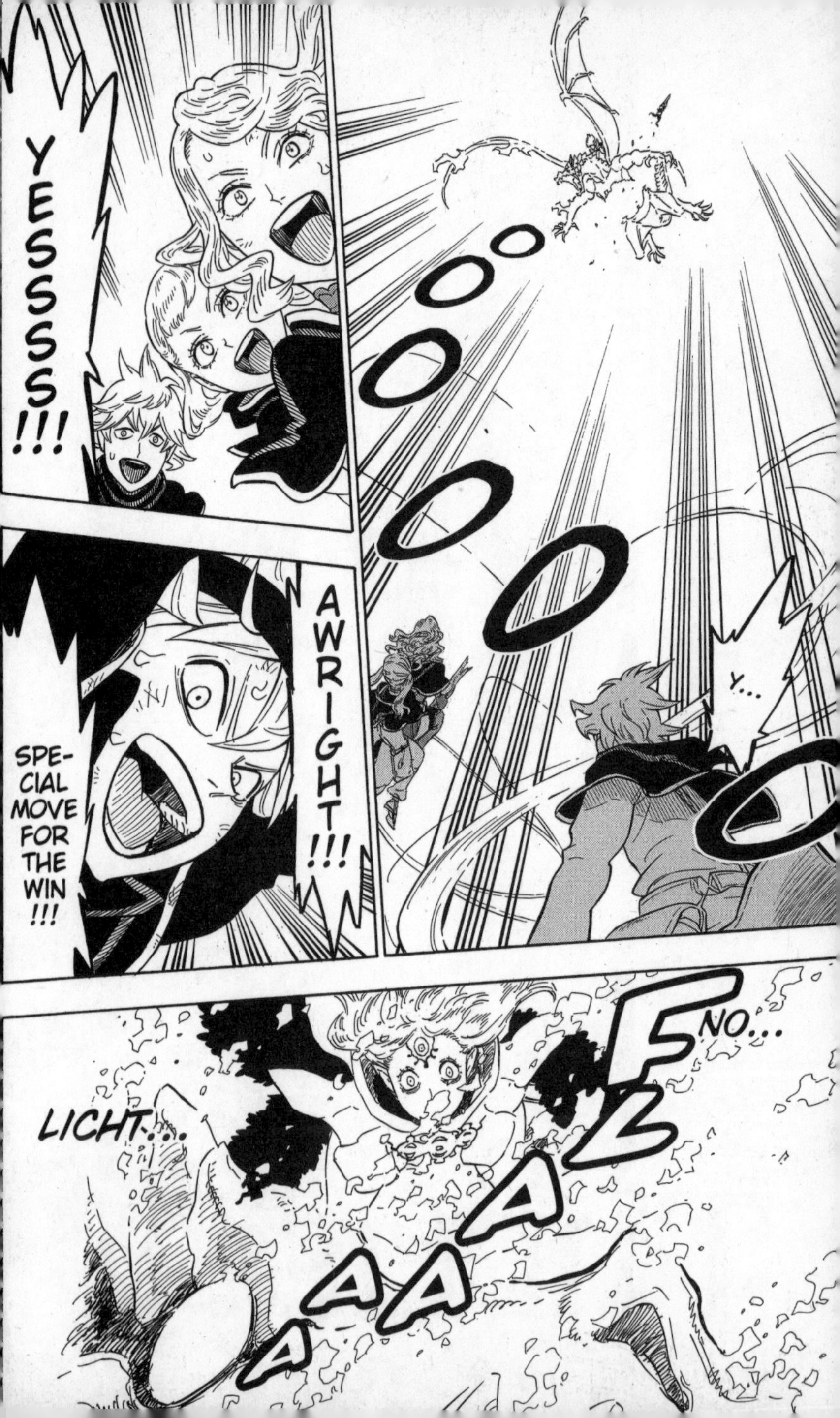

Y...
OOOOOOOO
YESSSSS!!!
AWRIGHT!!!
SPE-CIAL MOVE FOR THE WIN!!!
NO...
FZAAAAAA
LICHT...

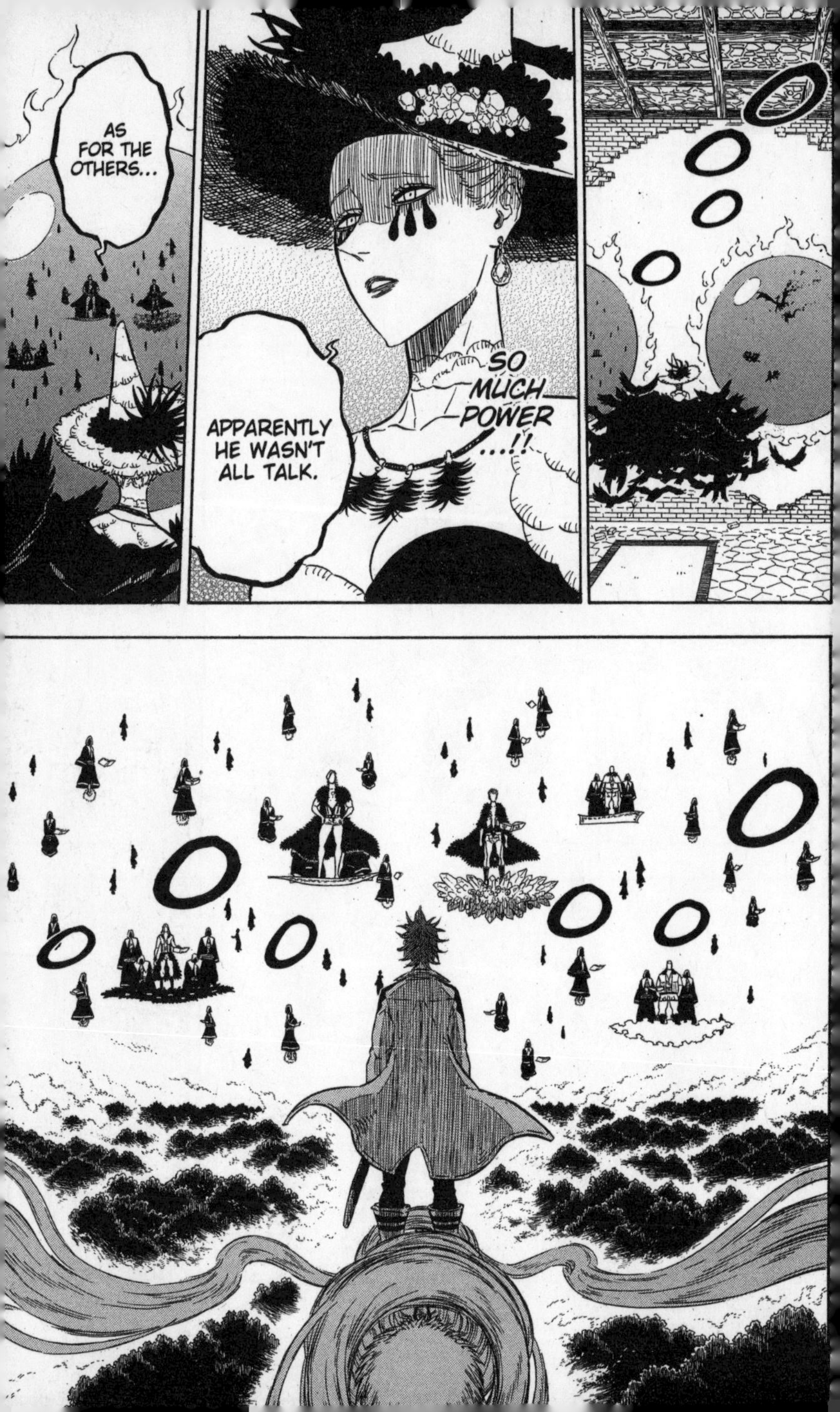
SO MUCH POWER...!!
APPARENTLY HE WASN'T ALL TALK.
AS FOR THE OTHERS...

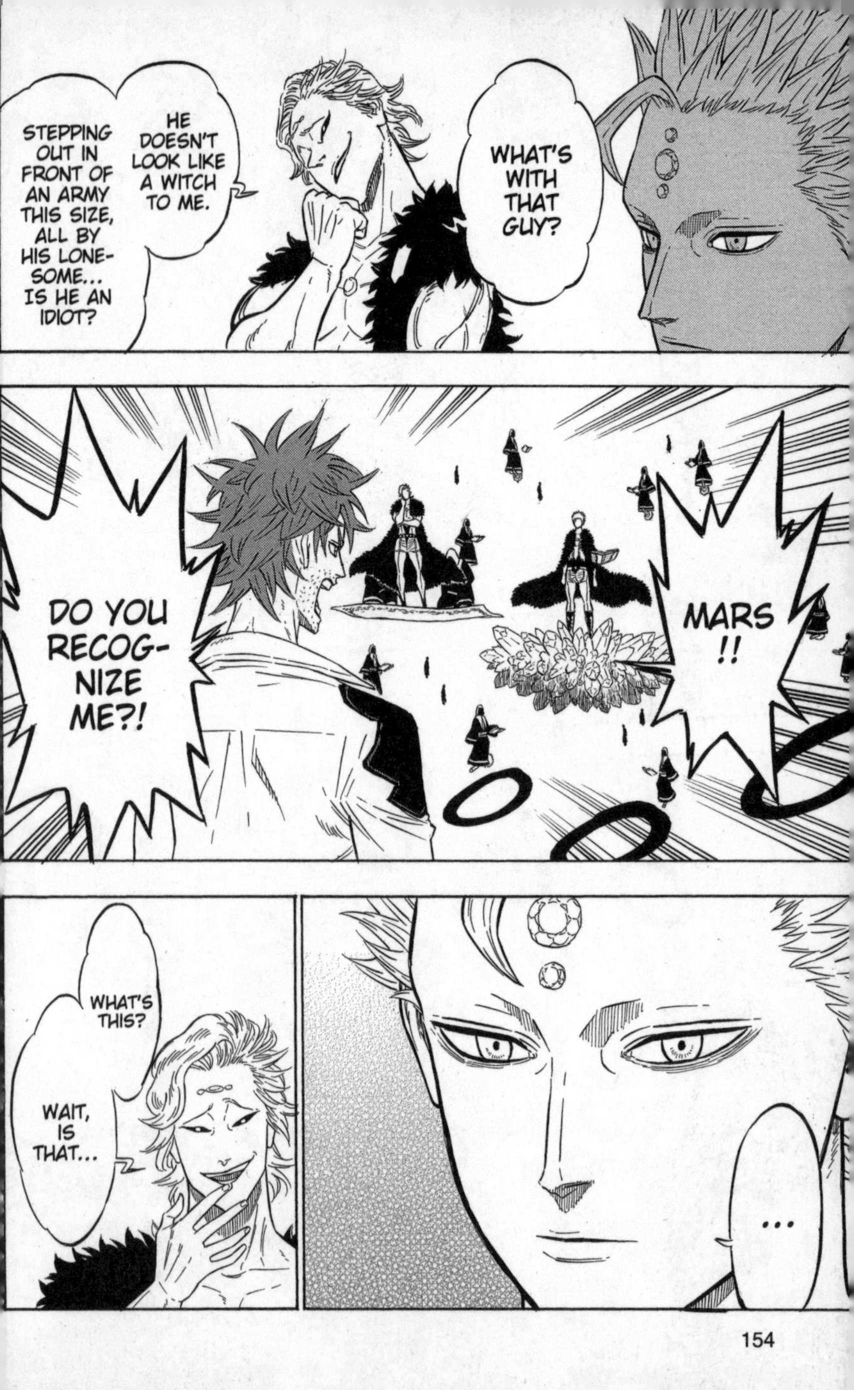
WHAT'S WITH THAT GUY?
HE DOESN'T LOOK LIKE A WITCH TO ME.
STEPPING OUT IN FRONT OF AN ARMY THIS SIZE, ALL BY HIS LONE-SOME... IS HE AN IDIOT?
MARS!!
DO YOU RECOG-NIZE ME?!
...
WHAT'S THIS?
WAIT, IS THAT...

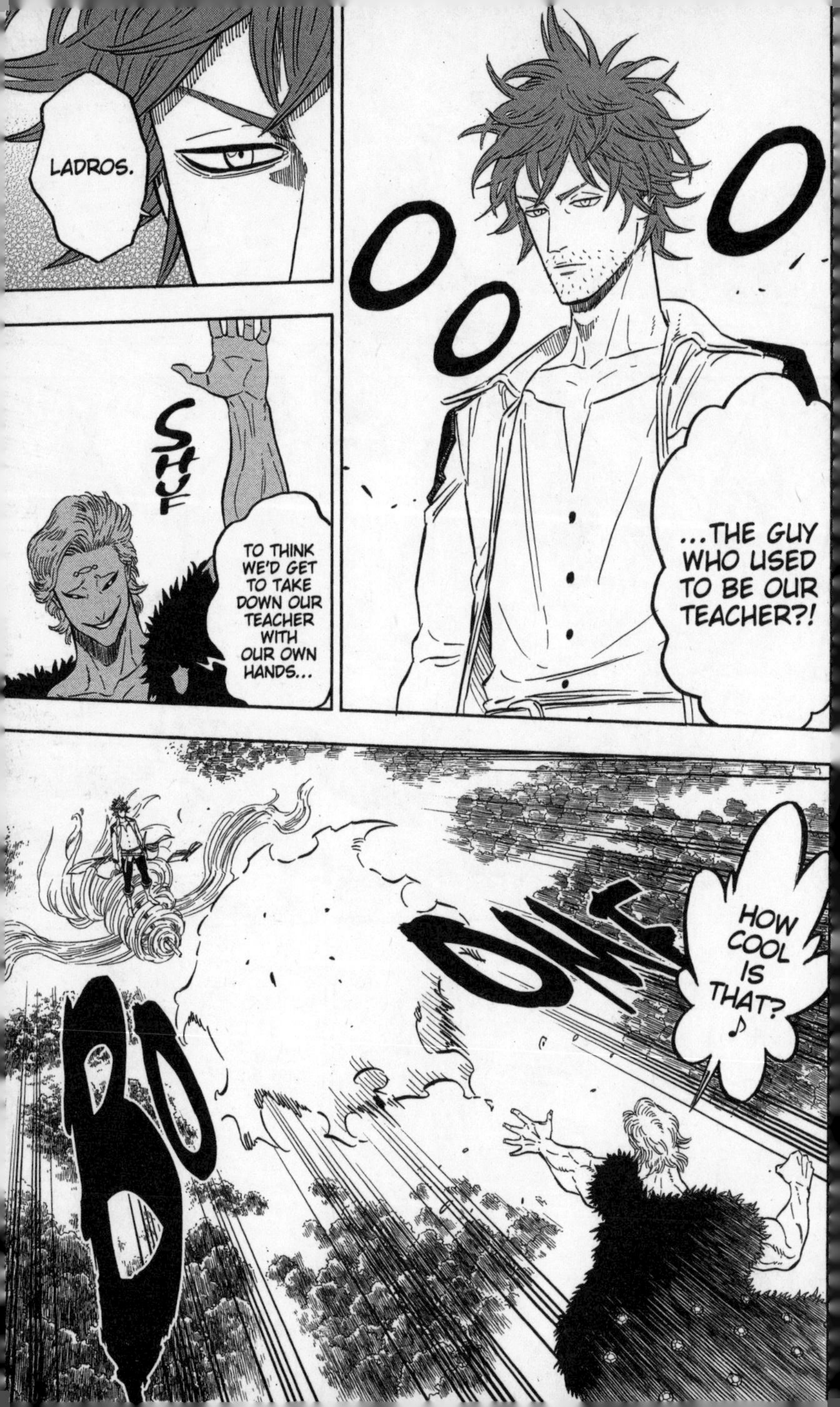
LADROS.
SHUF
TO THINK WE'D GET TO TAKE DOWN OUR TEACHER WITH OUR OWN HANDS...
OOOO
...THE GUY WHO USED TO BE OUR TEACHER?!
HOW COOL IS THAT? ♪
BOOM

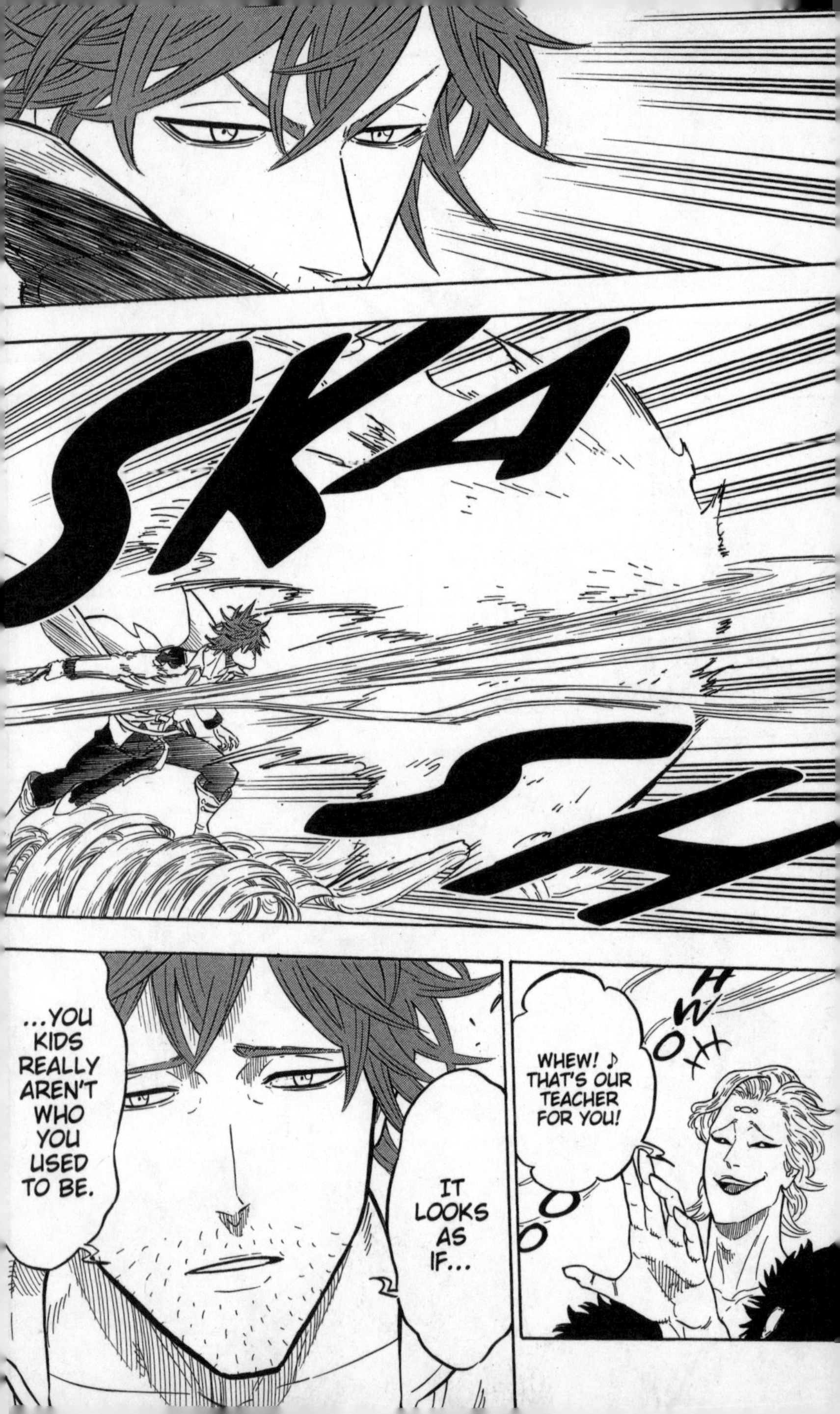
SKA
SH
WHEW! ♪ THAT'S OUR TEACHER FOR YOU!
IT LOOKS AS IF...
...YOU KIDS REALLY AREN'T WHO YOU USED TO BE.

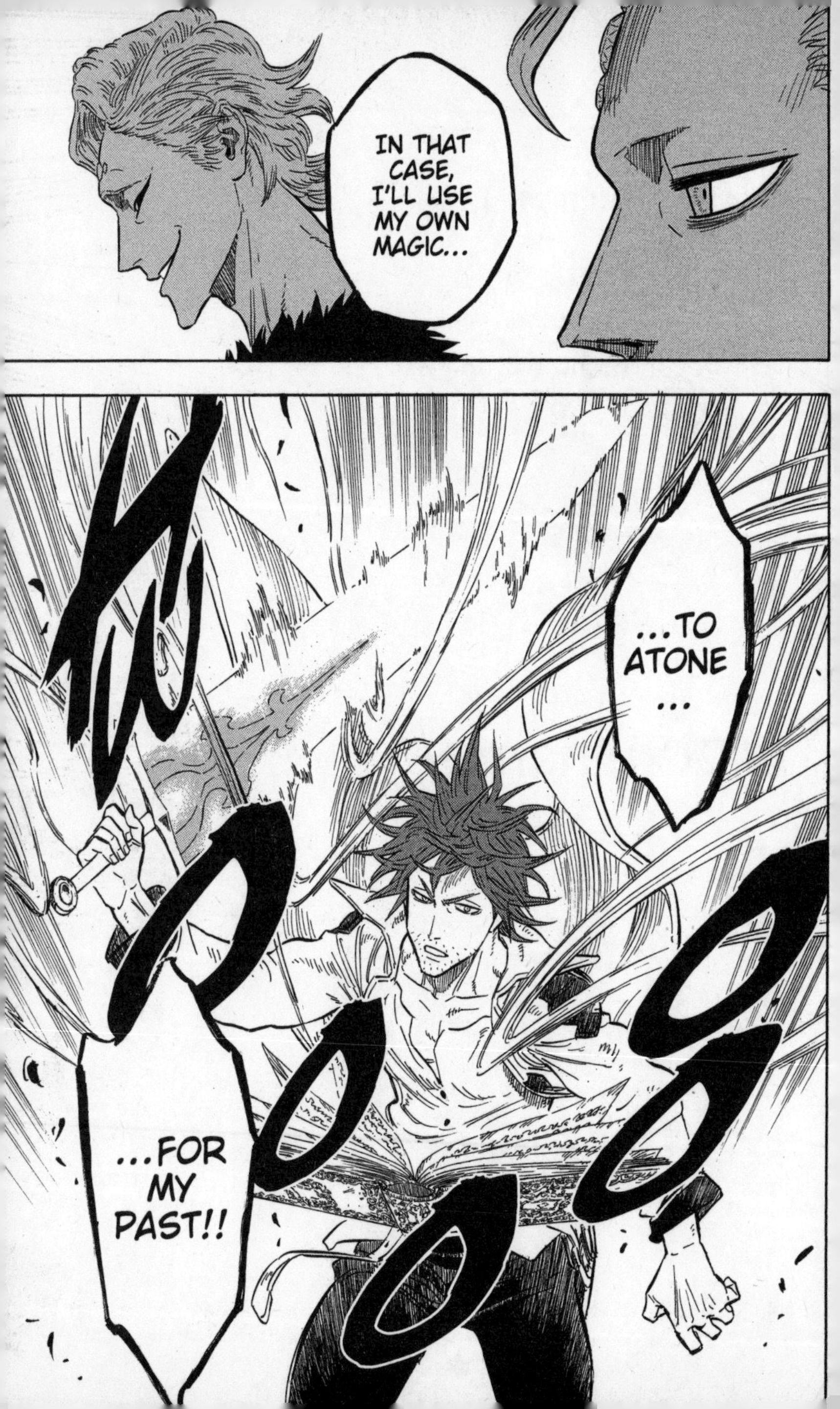
IN THAT CASE, I'LL USE MY OWN MAGIC...
...TO ATONE...
...FOR MY PAST!!

Age: 26
Height: 167 cm
Birthday: September 15
Sign: Virgo
Blood Type: O
Likes: Money, developing and tweaking magic items, all types of meat dishes

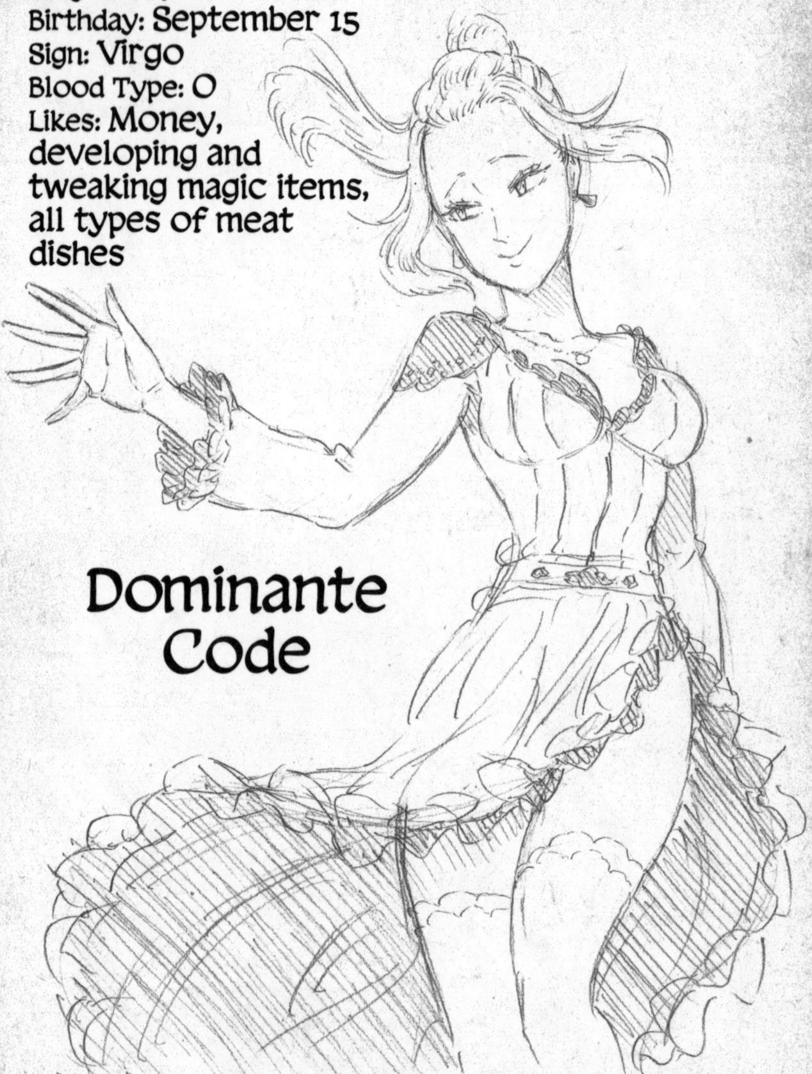

Dominante Code

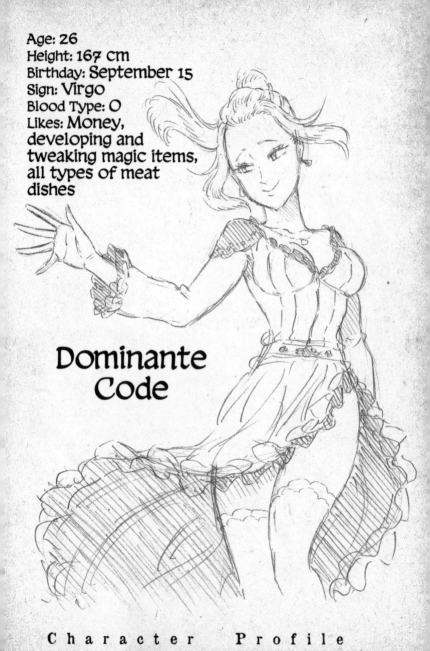

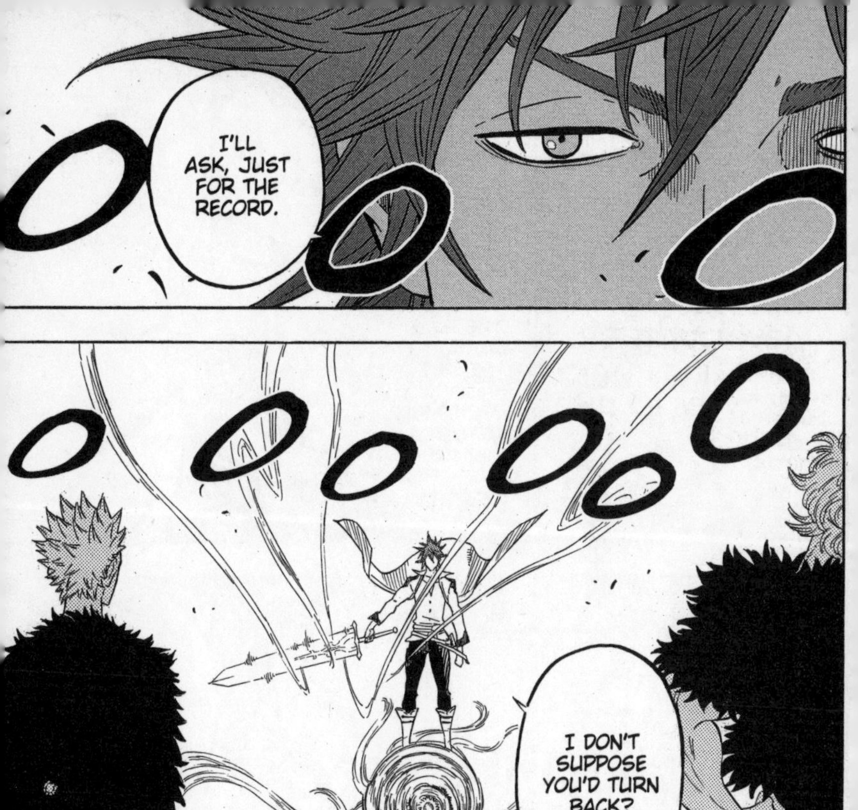
I'LL ASK, JUST FOR THE RECORD.
I DON'T SUPPOSE YOU'D TURN BACK?

Page 89: Defectors' Atonement

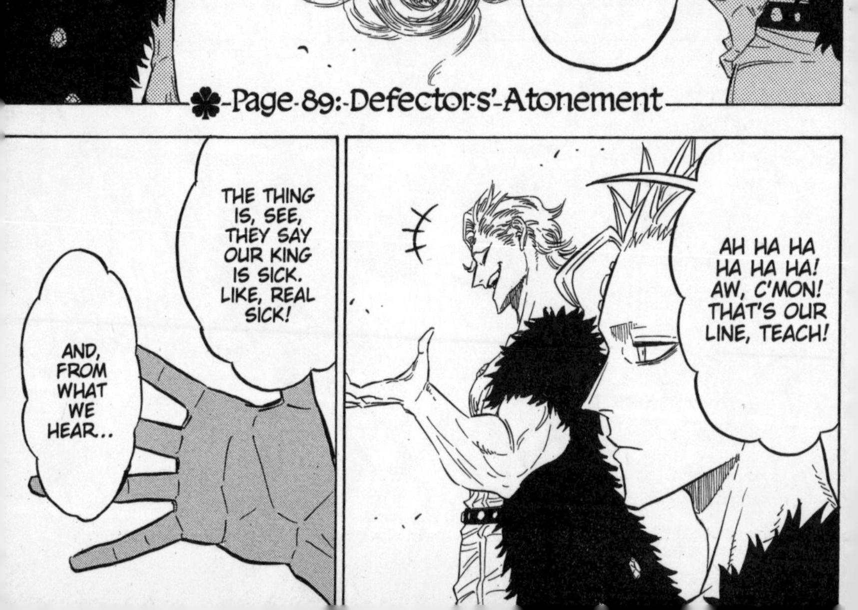
AH HA HA HA HA HA! AW, C'MON! THAT'S OUR LINE, TEACH!
THE THING IS, SEE, THEY SAY OUR KING IS SICK. LIKE, REAL SICK!
AND, FROM WHAT WE HEAR...

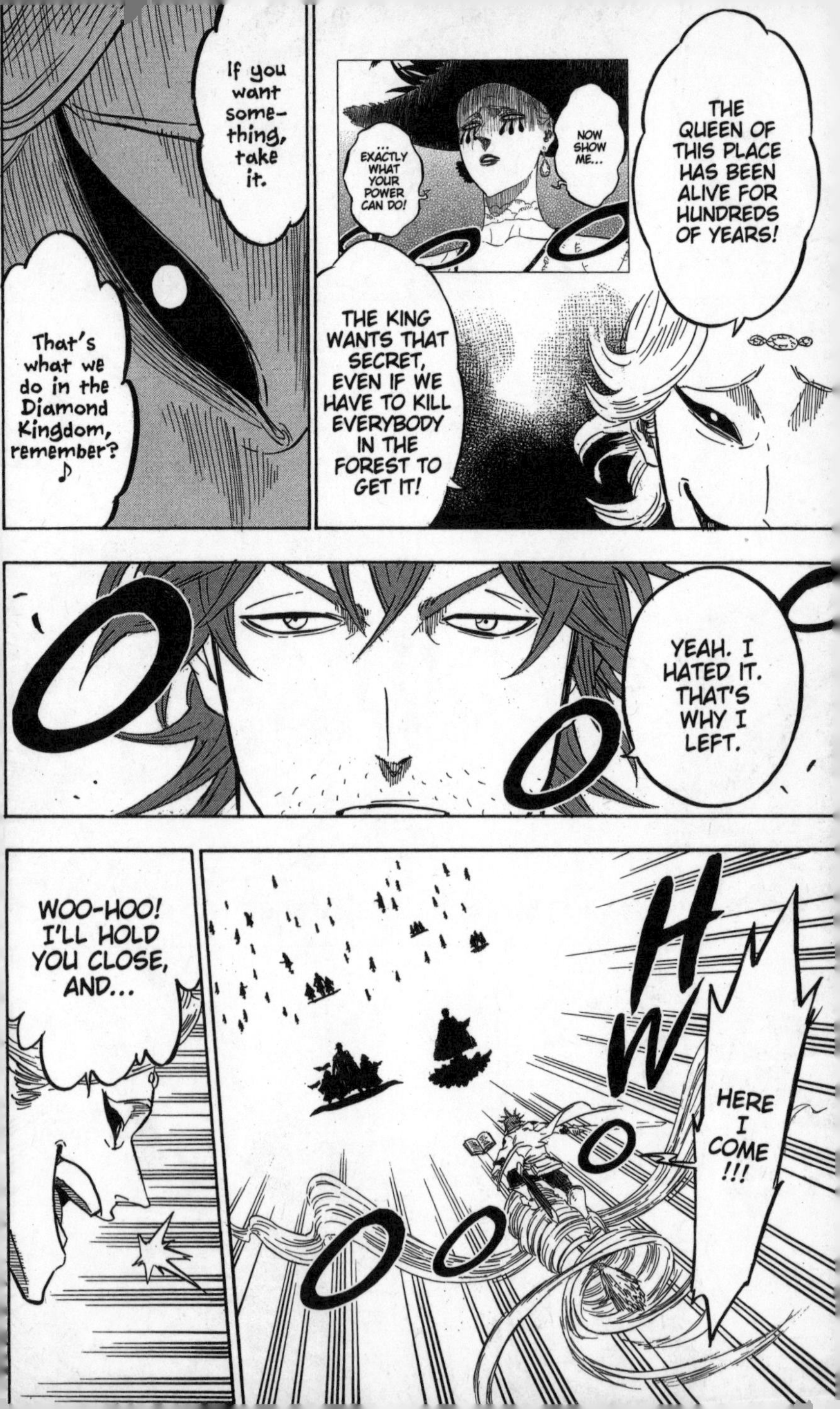
THE QUEEN OF THIS PLACE HAS BEEN ALIVE FOR HUNDREDS OF YEARS!
NOW SHOW ME...
...EXACTLY WHAT YOUR POWER CAN DO!
THE KING WANTS THAT SECRET, EVEN IF WE HAVE TO KILL EVERYBODY IN THE FOREST TO GET IT!
If you want some-thing, take it.
That's what we do in the Diamond Kingdom, remember? ♪
YEAH. I HATED IT. THAT'S WHY I LEFT.
HWOOOO
HERE I COME!!!
WOO-HOO! I'LL HOLD YOU CLOSE, AND...

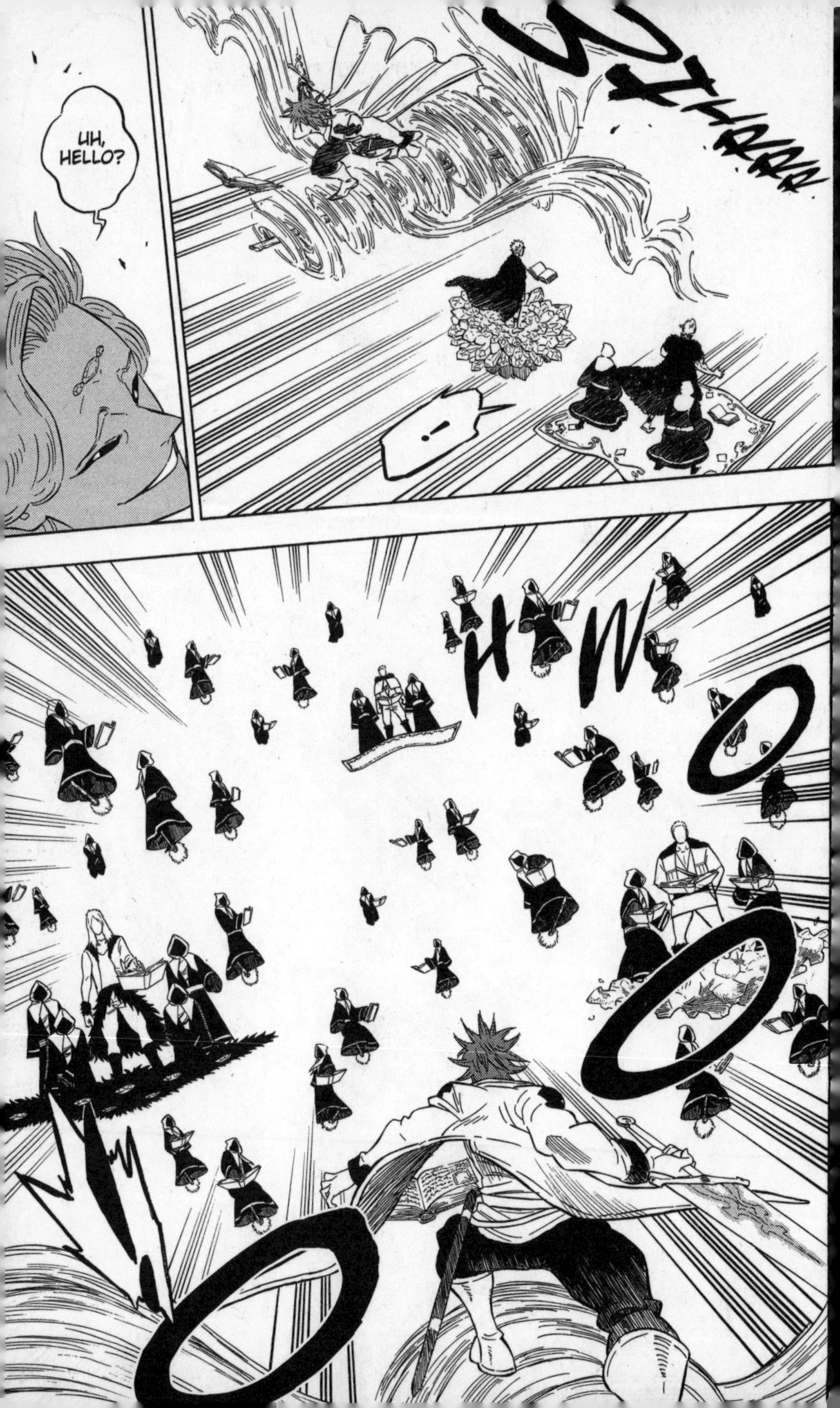
SWHIRRRR
!
UH, HELLO?
WHOOOM

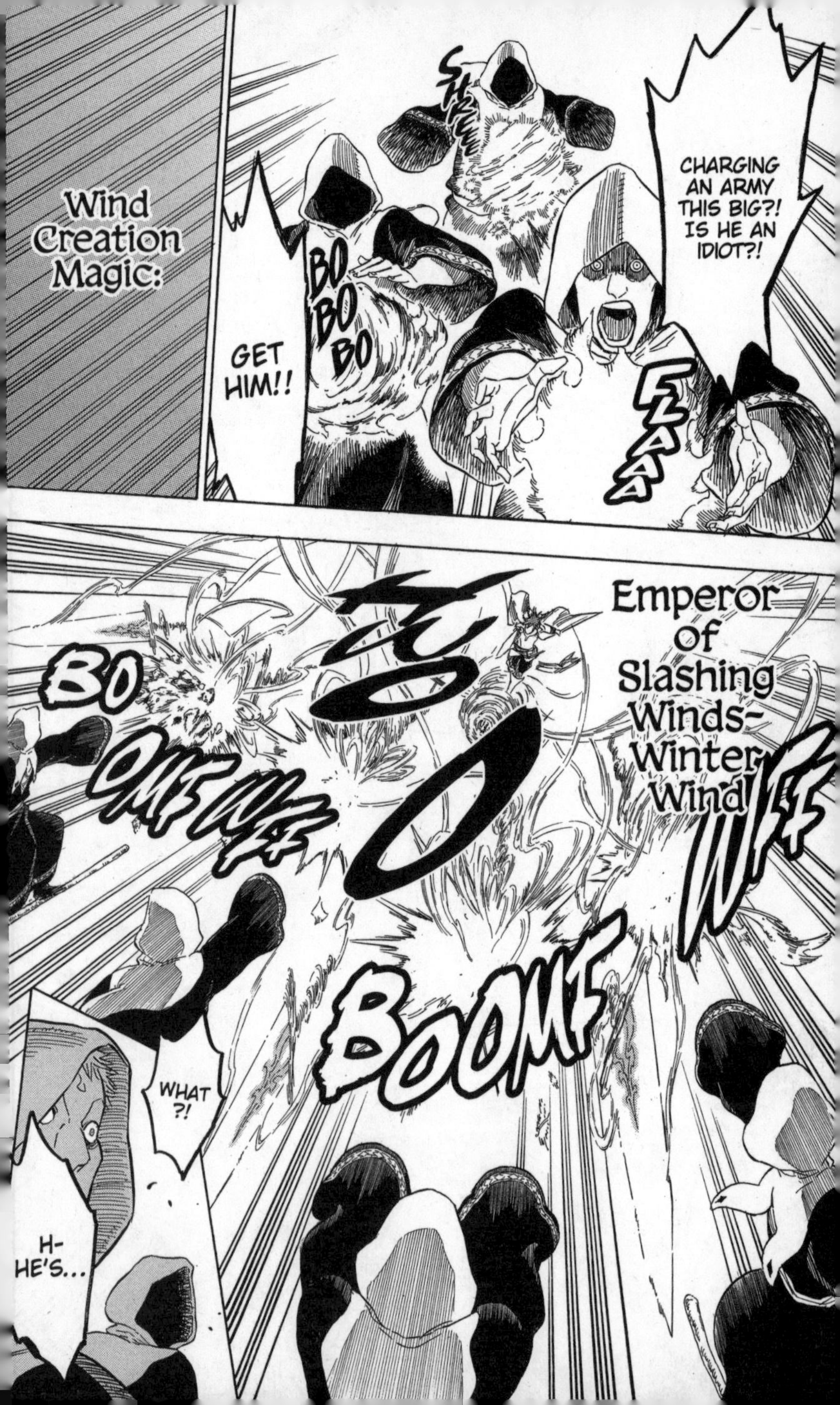
CHARGING AN ARMY THIS BIG?! IS HE AN IDIOT?!
FLAAA
BO BO BO
GET HIM!!
Wind Creation Magic:
Emperor of Slashing Winds- Winter Wind
BOOMF
WHAT?!
H- HE'S...

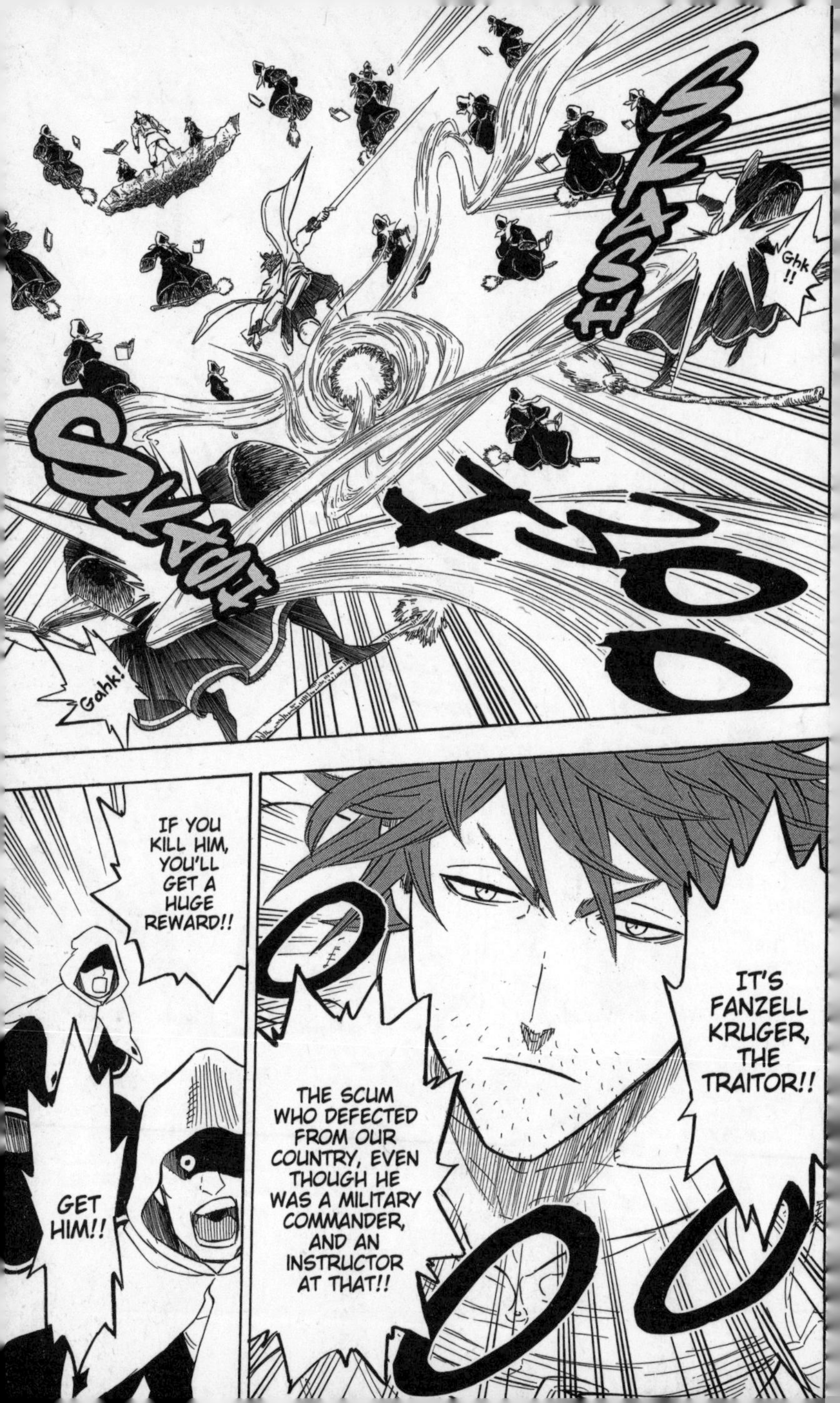
SHKASH
Ghk!!
SHKASH
Gahk!
IT'S FANZELL KRUGER, THE TRAITOR!!
THE SCUM WHO DEFECTED FROM OUR COUNTRY, EVEN THOUGH HE WAS A MILITARY COMMANDER, AND AN INSTRUCTOR AT THAT!!
IF YOU KILL HIM, YOU'LL GET A HUGE REWARD!!
GET HIM!!

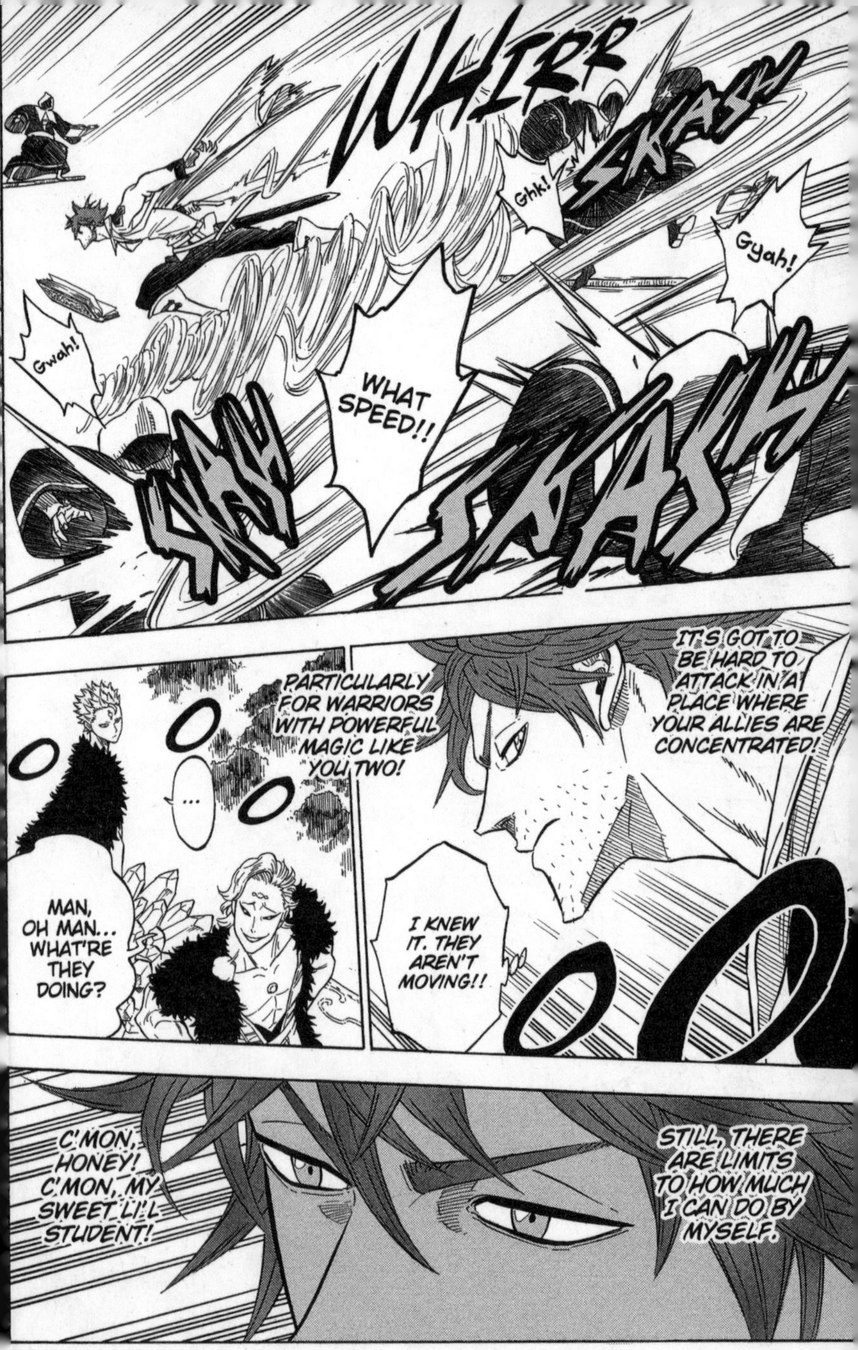
WHIRR
Ghk!
Gyah!
WHAT SPEED!!
Gwah!
IT'S GOT TO BE HARD TO ATTACK IN A PLACE WHERE YOUR ALLIES ARE CONCENTRATED!
I KNEW IT. THEY AREN'T MOVING!!
PARTICULARLY FOR WARRIORS WITH POWERFUL MAGIC LIKE YOU TWO!
...
MAN, OH MAN... WHAT'RE THEY DOING?
STILL, THERE ARE LIMITS TO HOW MUCH I CAN DO BY MYSELF.
C'MON, HONEY! C'MON, MY SWEET LI'L STUDENT!

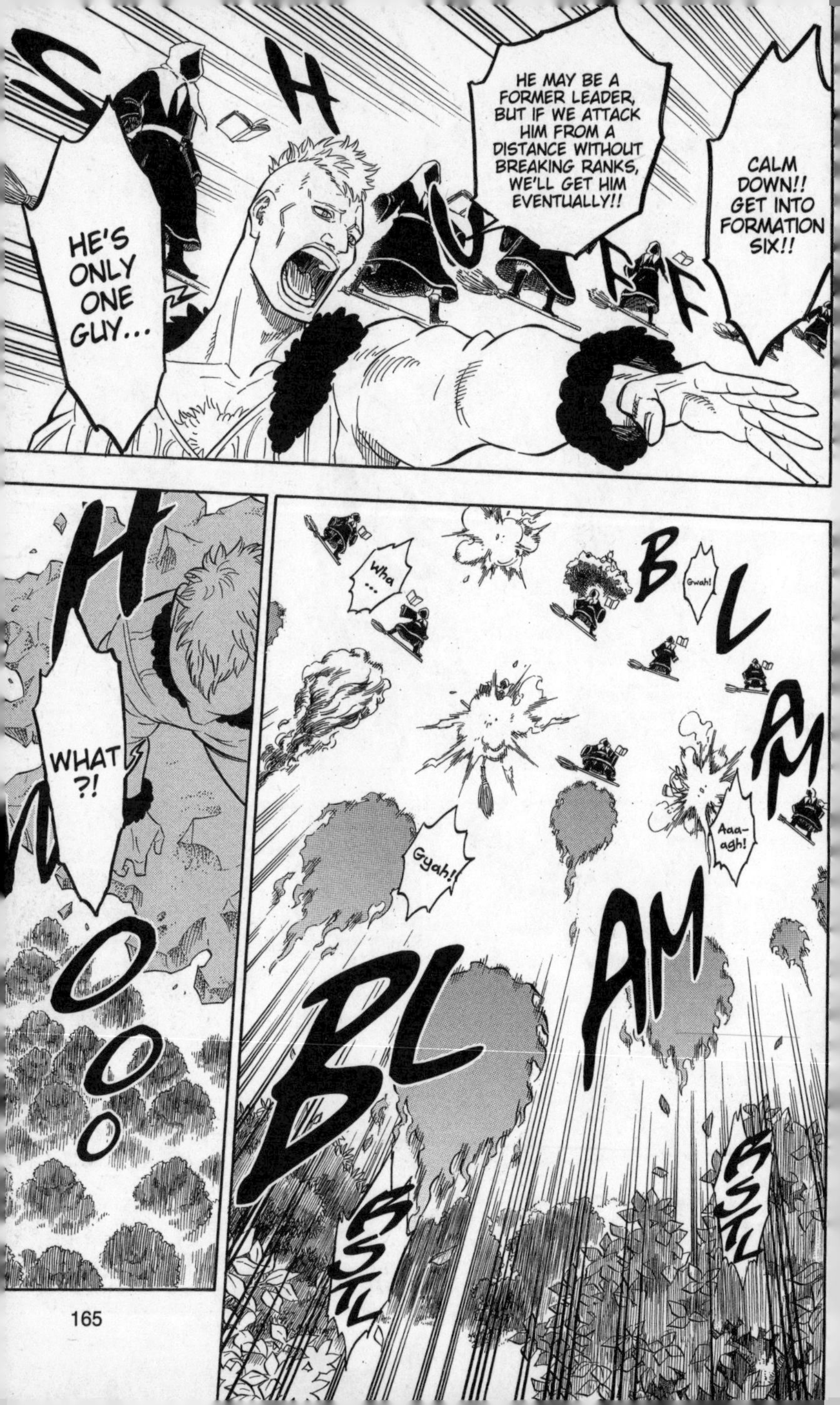

CALM DOWN!! GET INTO FORMATION SIX!!
HE MAY BE A FORMER LEADER, BUT IF WE ATTACK HIM FROM A DISTANCE WITHOUT BREAKING RANKS, WE'LL GET HIM EVENTUALLY!!
HE'S ONLY ONE GUY...
BLAM
Gwah!
Wha ...
Aaa-agh!
Gyah!
BLAM
RSTL
RSTL
WHAT?!

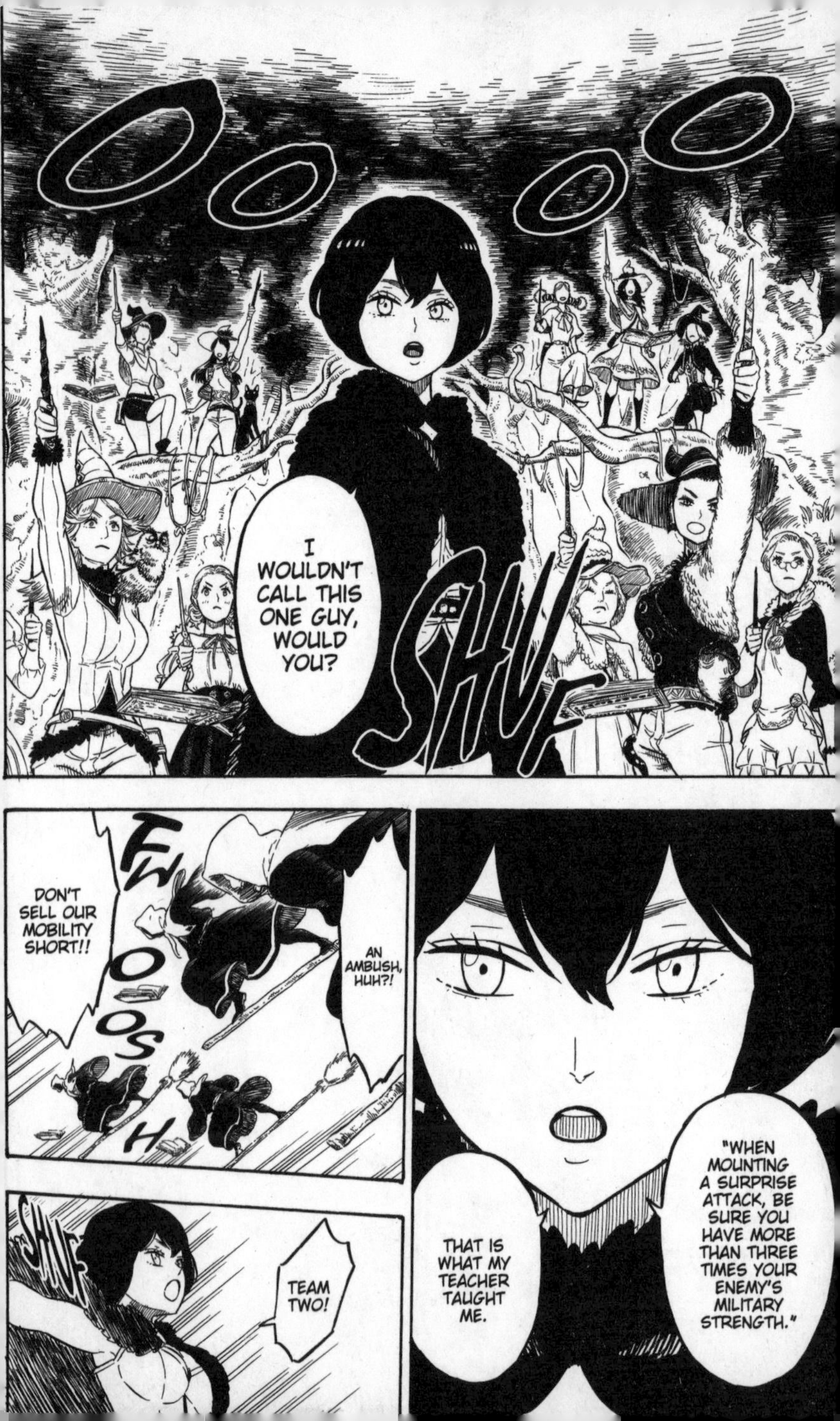
I WOULDN'T CALL THIS ONE GUY, WOULD YOU?
SHUF
"WHEN MOUNTING A SURPRISE ATTACK, BE SURE YOU HAVE MORE THAN THREE TIMES YOUR ENEMY'S MILITARY STRENGTH."
THAT IS WHAT MY TEACHER TAUGHT ME.
AN AMBUSH, HUH?!
DON'T SELL OUR MOBILITY SHORT!!
FWOOOSH
TEAM TWO!
SHUF

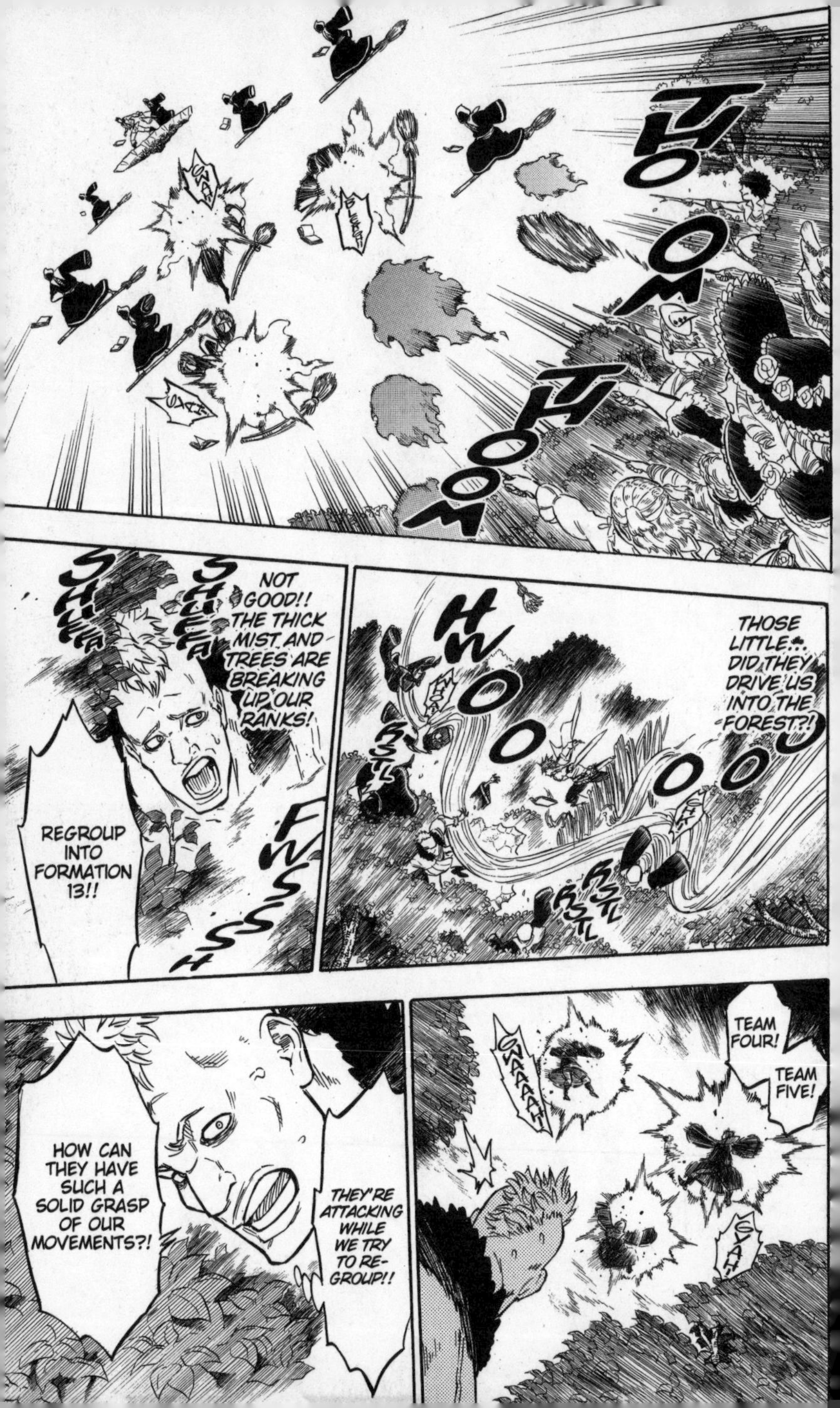
ZOOM
THOOOM
BLEGH!
WAH!
UXH!
THOSE LITTLE... DID THEY DRIVE US INTO THE FOREST?!
HWOOOOO
WHOA!
GHK!
RSTL
RSTL
RSTL
SHUFFA
SHUFFA
NOT GOOD!! THE THICK MIST AND TREES ARE BREAKING UP OUR RANKS!
REGROUP INTO FORMATION 13!!
FWSSSSH
TEAM FOUR!
TEAM FIVE!
GWAAAAH!
GYAH!
THEY'RE ATTACKING WHILE WE TRY TO RE-GROUP!!
HOW CAN THEY HAVE SUCH A SOLID GRASP OF OUR MOVEMENTS?!

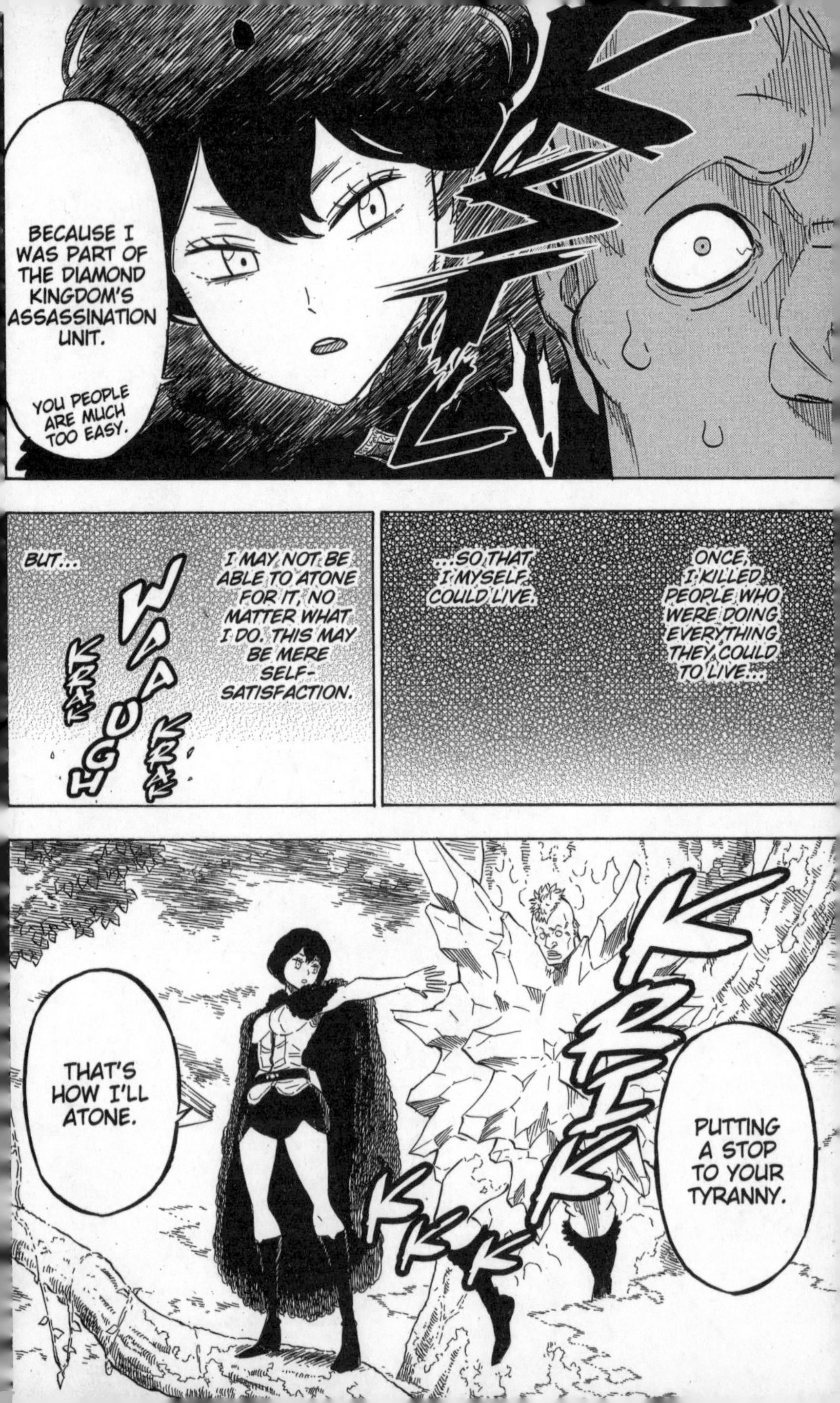
BECAUSE I WAS PART OF THE DIAMOND KINGDOM'S ASSASSINATION UNIT.
YOU PEOPLE ARE MUCH TOO EASY.
ONCE, I KILLED PEOPLE WHO WERE DOING EVERYTHING THEY COULD TO LIVE...
...SO THAT I MYSELF COULD LIVE.
I MAY NOT BE ABLE TO ATONE FOR IT, NO MATTER WHAT I DO. THIS MAY BE MERE SELF-SATISFACTION.
BUT...
WAAUGH
KRAK
KRAK
PUTTING A STOP TO YOUR TYRANNY.
KRRRK
KKK
THAT'S HOW I'LL ATONE.

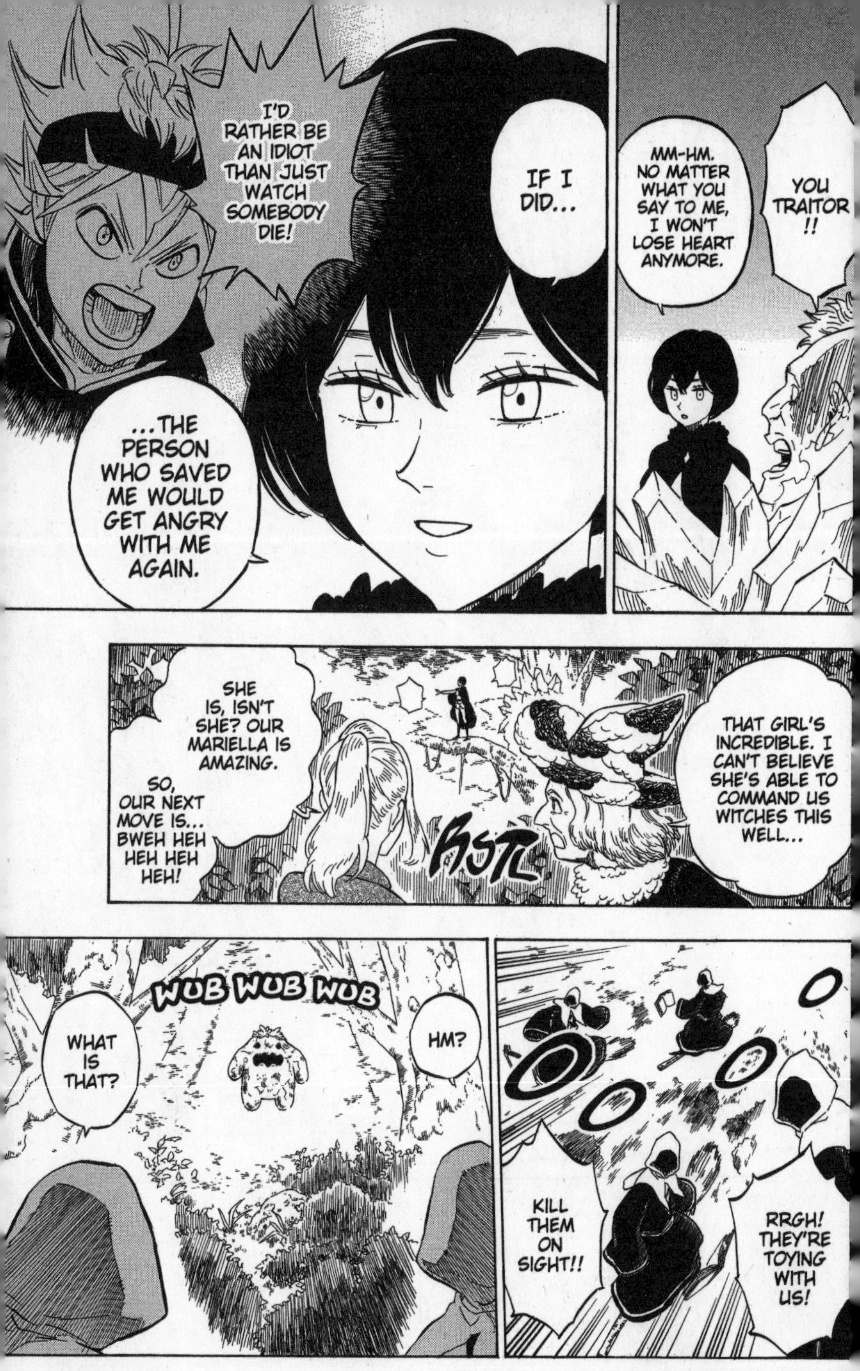
YOU TRAITOR!!
MM-HM. NO MATTER WHAT YOU SAY TO ME, I WON'T LOSE HEART ANYMORE.
IF I DID...
I'D RATHER BE AN IDIOT THAN JUST WATCH SOMEBODY DIE!
...THE PERSON WHO SAVED ME WOULD GET ANGRY WITH ME AGAIN.
THAT GIRL'S INCREDIBLE. I CAN'T BELIEVE SHE'S ABLE TO COMMAND US WITCHES THIS WELL...
SHE IS, ISN'T SHE? OUR MARIELLA IS AMAZING.
RSTL
SO, OUR NEXT MOVE IS... BWEH HEH HEH HEH HEH!
RRGH! THEY'RE TOYING WITH US!
KILL THEM ON SIGHT!!
HM?
WUB WUB WUB
WHAT IS THAT?

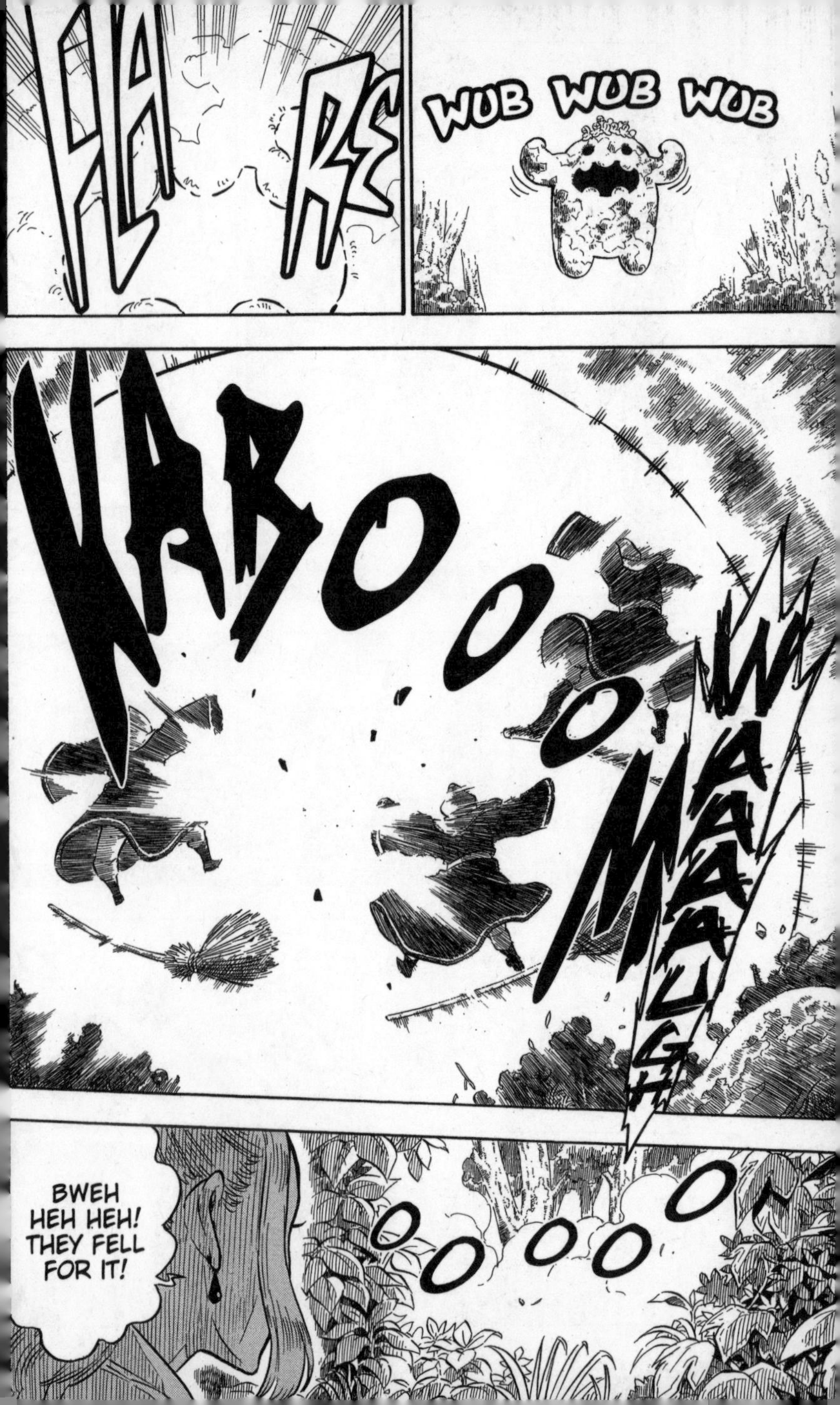
WUB WUB WUB
FLARE
KABOOOOM
WAAAAUGH
OOOOOO
BWEH HEH HEH! THEY FELL FOR IT!

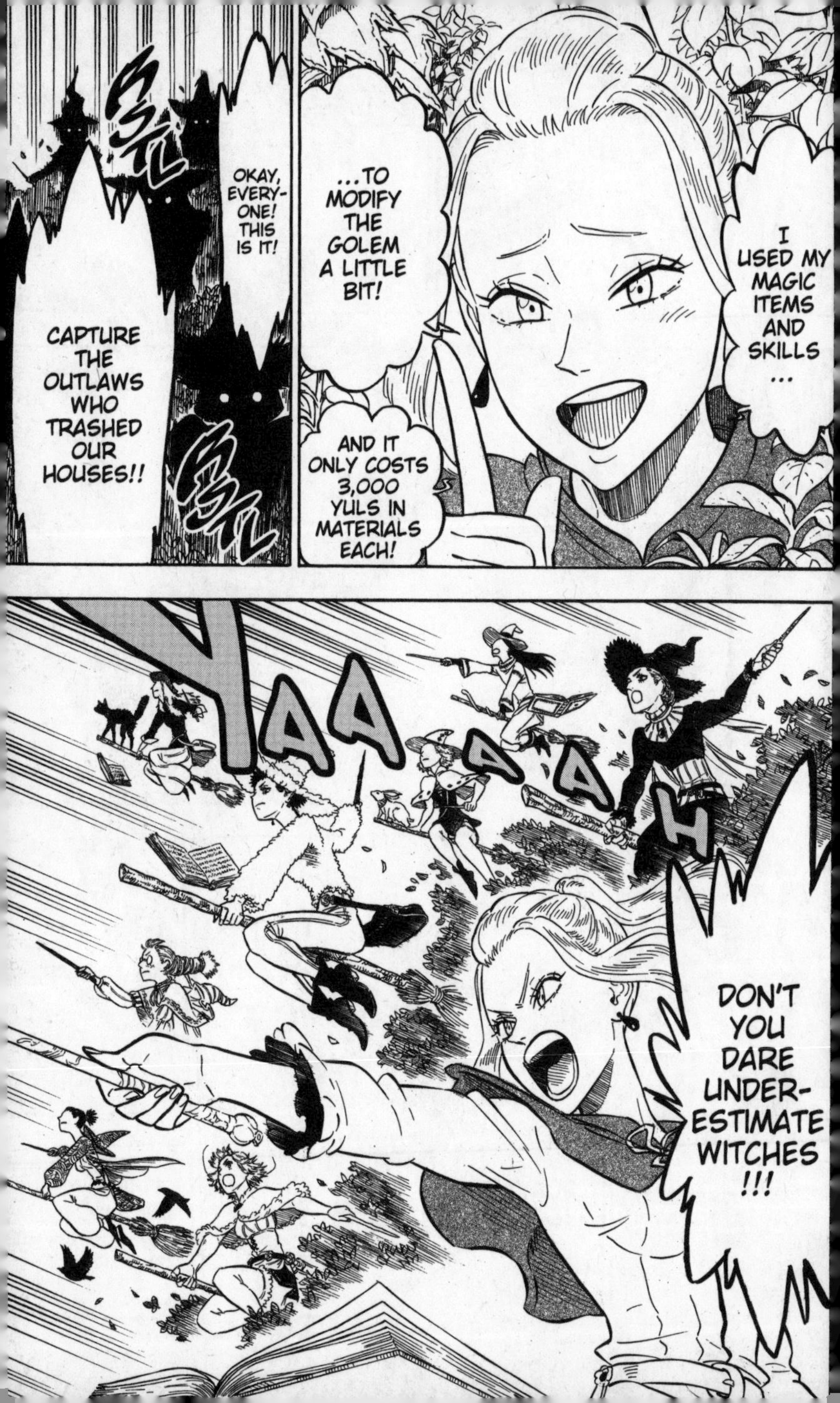
I USED MY MAGIC ITEMS AND SKILLS...
...TO MODIFY THE GOLEM A LITTLE BIT!
AND IT ONLY COSTS 3,000 YULS IN MATERIALS EACH!
OKAY, EVERY-ONE! THIS IS IT!
CAPTURE THE OUTLAWS WHO TRASHED OUR HOUSES!!
YAAAAAH
DON'T YOU DARE UNDER-ESTIMATE WITCHES!!!

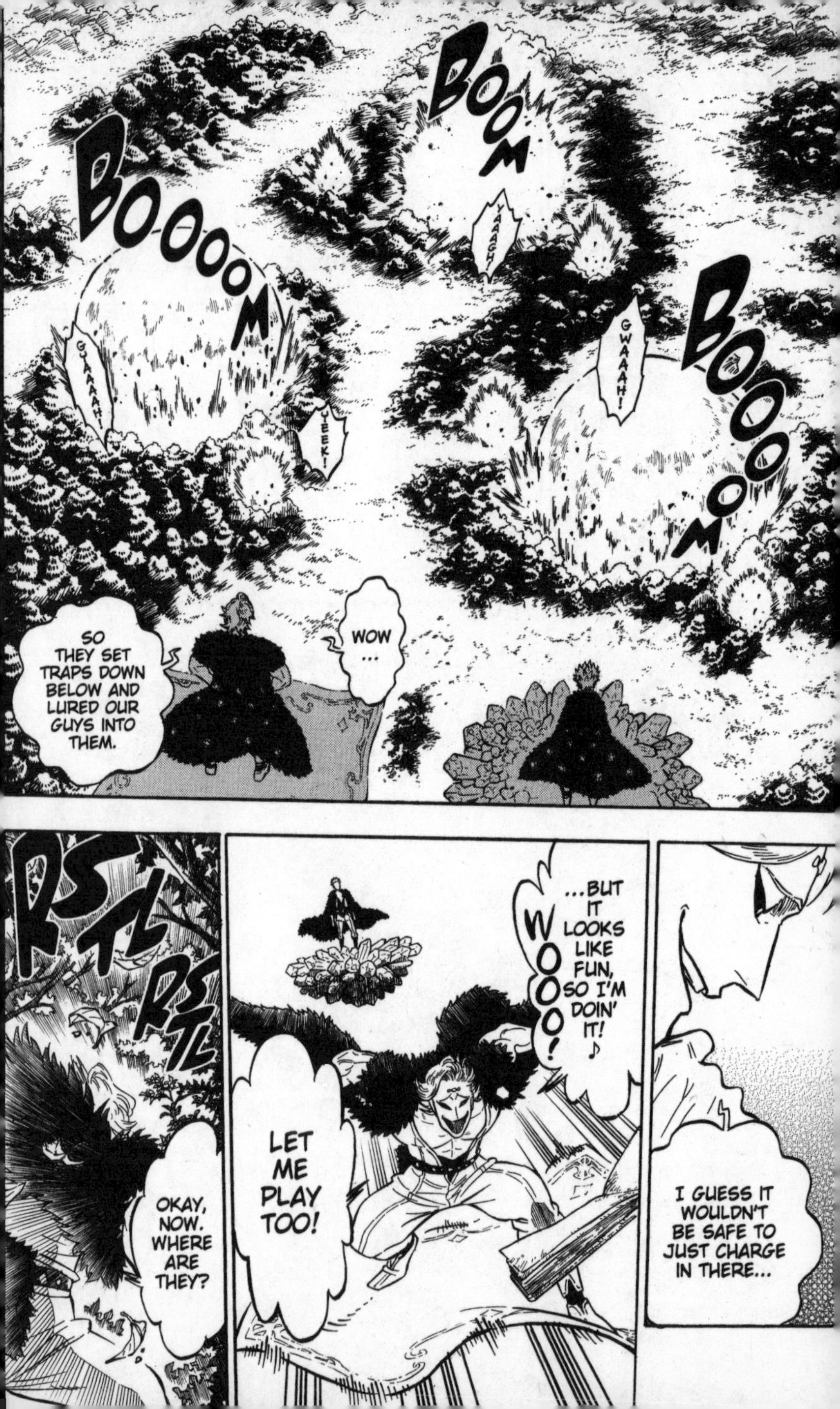
BOOM
YAAAGH!
BOOOOOM
GWAAAH!
BOOOOOM
GUAAAAH!
YEEK!
WOW...
SO THEY SET TRAPS DOWN BELOW AND LURED OUR GUYS INTO THEM.
I GUESS IT WOULDN'T BE SAFE TO JUST CHARGE IN THERE...
...BUT IT LOOKS LIKE FUN, SO I'M DOIN' IT! ♪
WOOOO!
LET ME PLAY TOO!
RSTL
RSTL
OKAY, NOW. WHERE ARE THEY?

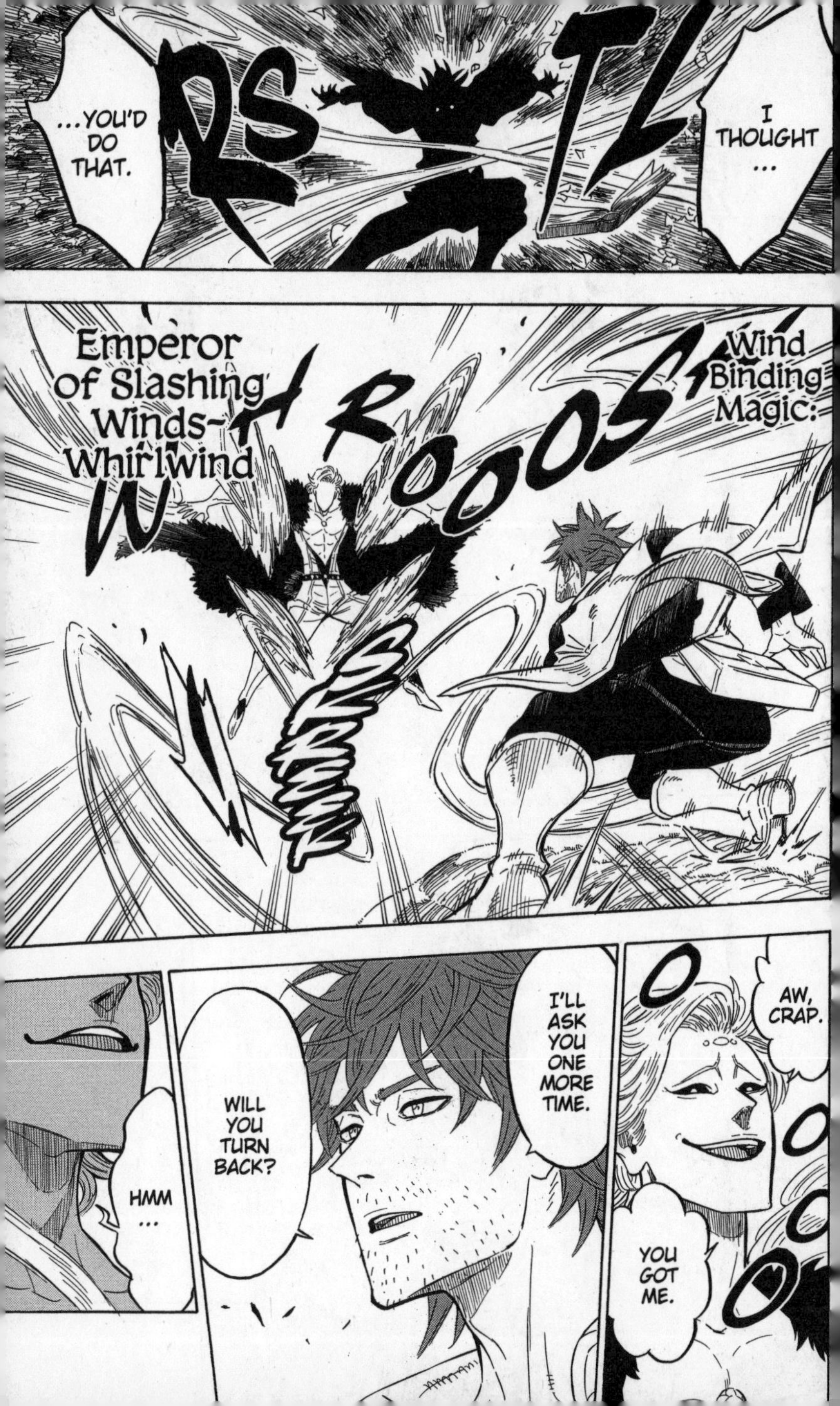
I THOUGHT...
...YOU'D DO THAT.
Wind Binding Magic:
Emperor of Slashing Winds~Whirlwind
AW, CRAP.
YOU GOT ME.
I'LL ASK YOU ONE MORE TIME.
WILL YOU TURN BACK?
HMM...

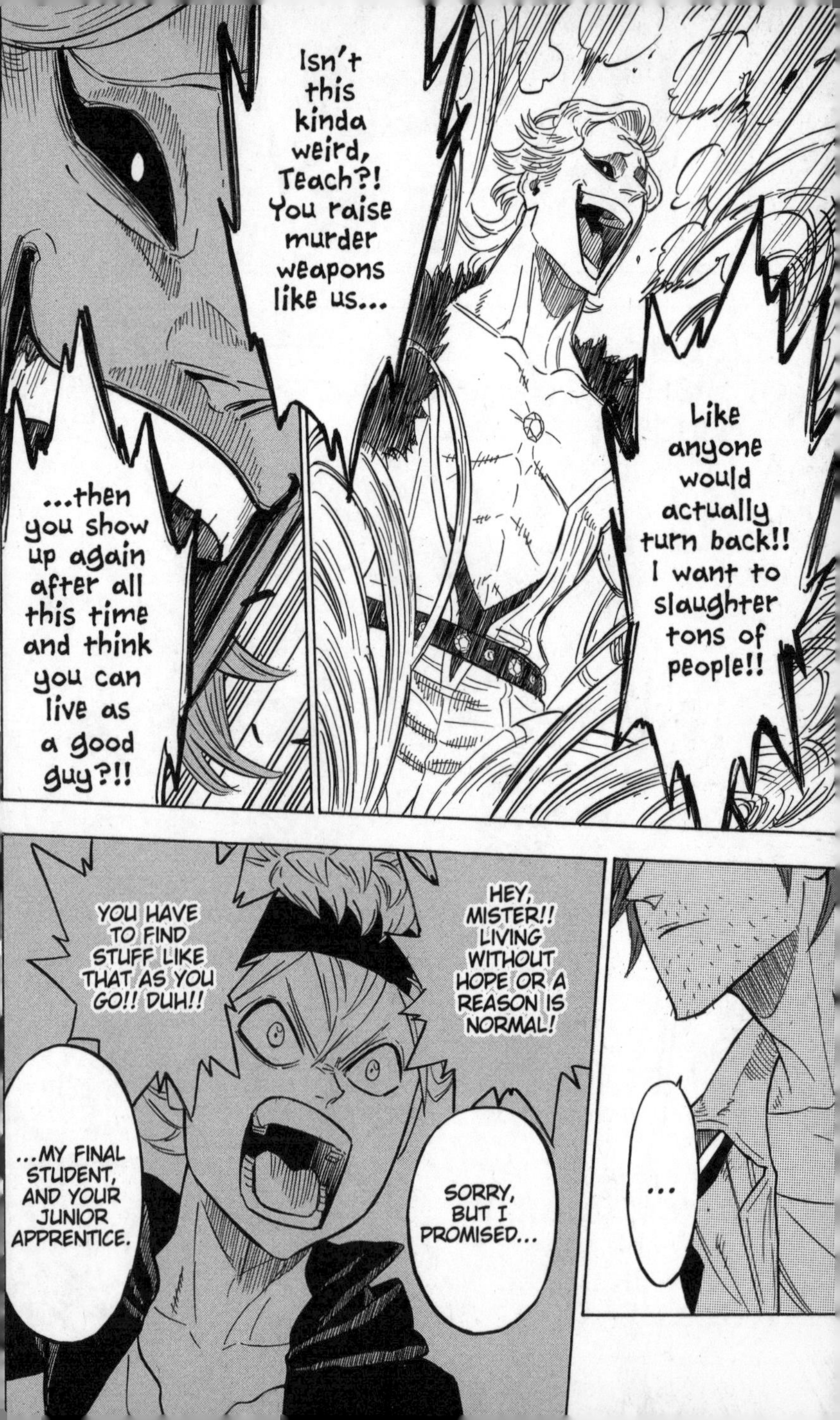
Isn't this kinda weird, Teach?! You raise murder weapons like us...
...then you show up again after all this time and think you can live as a good guy?!!
Like anyone would actually turn back!! I want to slaughter tons of people!!
...
HEY, MISTER!! LIVING WITHOUT HOPE OR A REASON IS NORMAL!
YOU HAVE TO FIND STUFF LIKE THAT AS YOU GO!! DUH!!
SORRY, BUT I PROMISED...
...MY FINAL STUDENT, AND YOUR JUNIOR APPRENTICE.

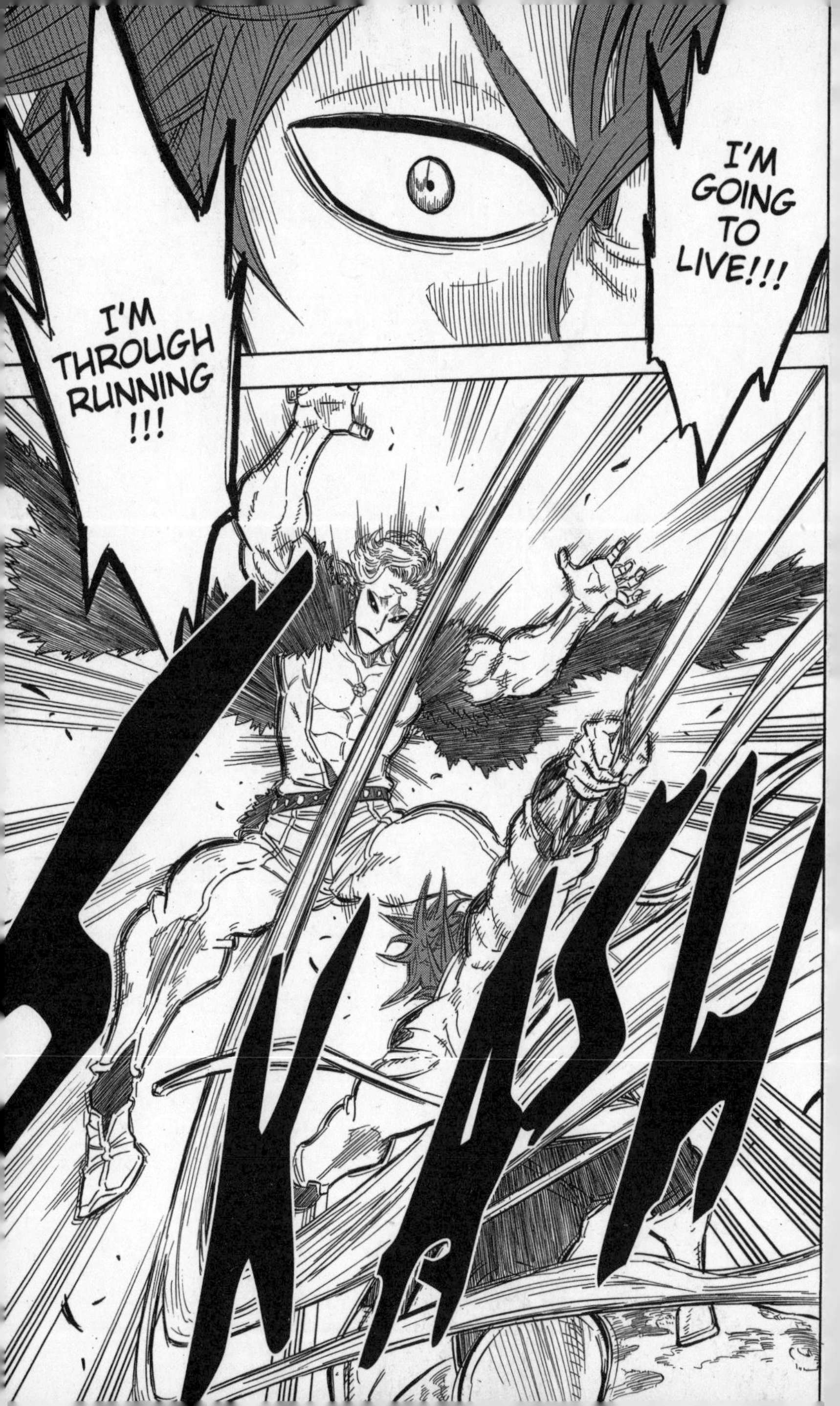
I'M GOING TO LIVE!!!
I'M THROUGH RUNNING!!!
SHASH

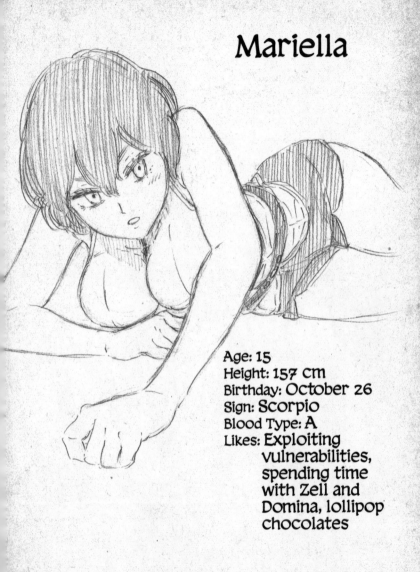

Mariella

Age: 15
Height: 157 cm
Birthday: October 26
Sign: Scorpio
Blood Type: A
Likes: Exploiting
    vulnerabilities,
    spending time
    with Zell and
    Domina, lollipop
    chocolates

C h a r a c t e r   P r o f i l e

✦

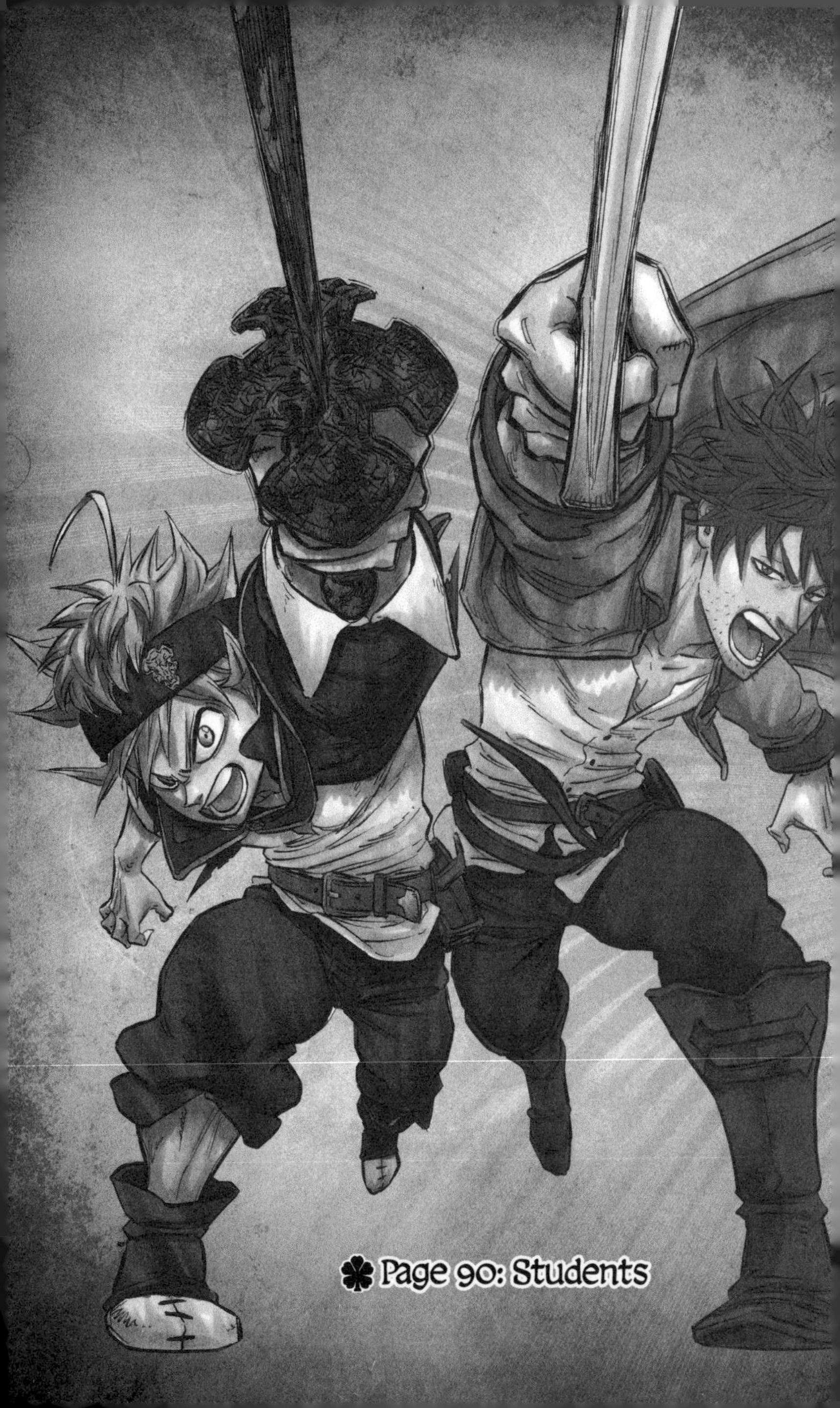
Page 90: Students

WEO WEO WEO

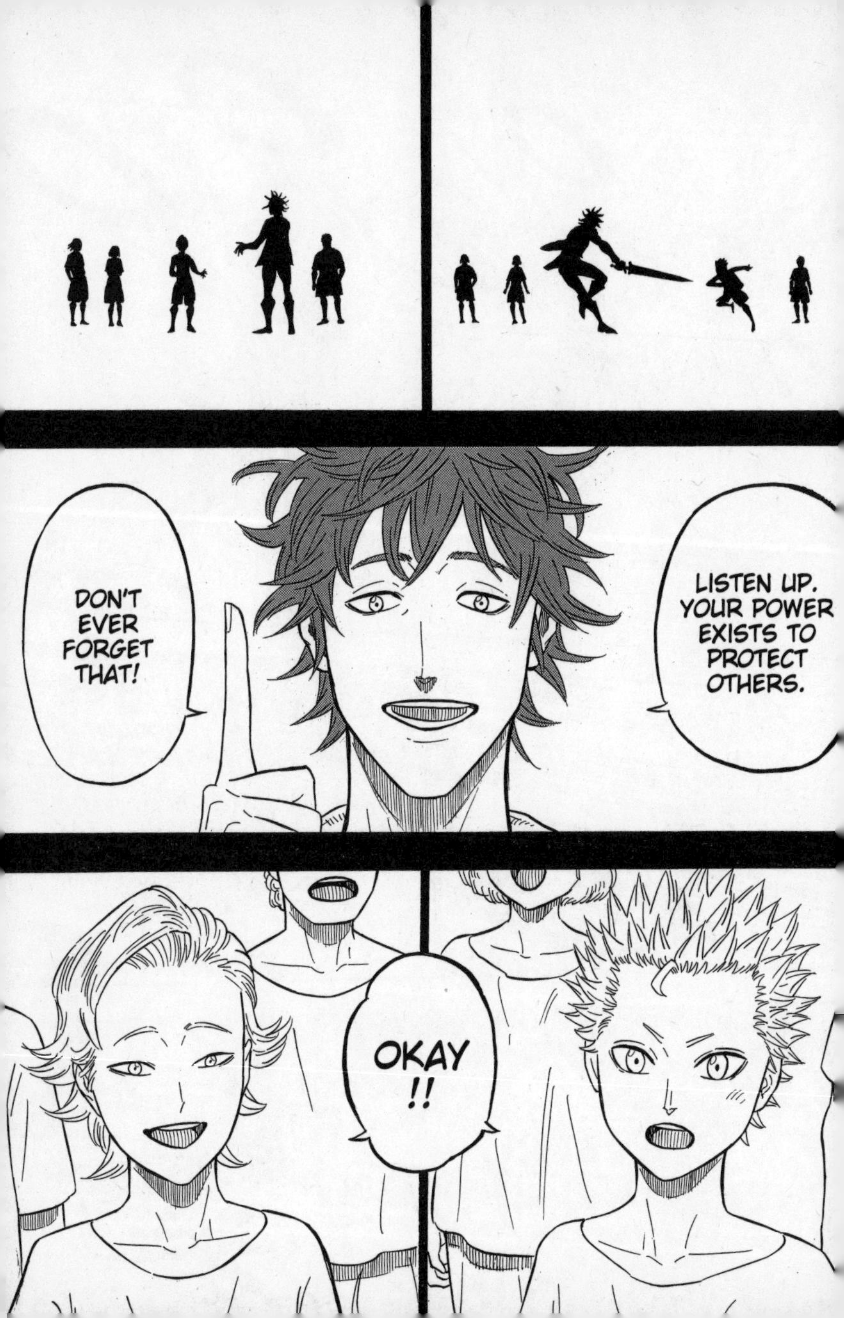
LISTEN UP. YOUR POWER EXISTS TO PROTECT OTHERS.
DON'T EVER FORGET THAT!
OKAY !!

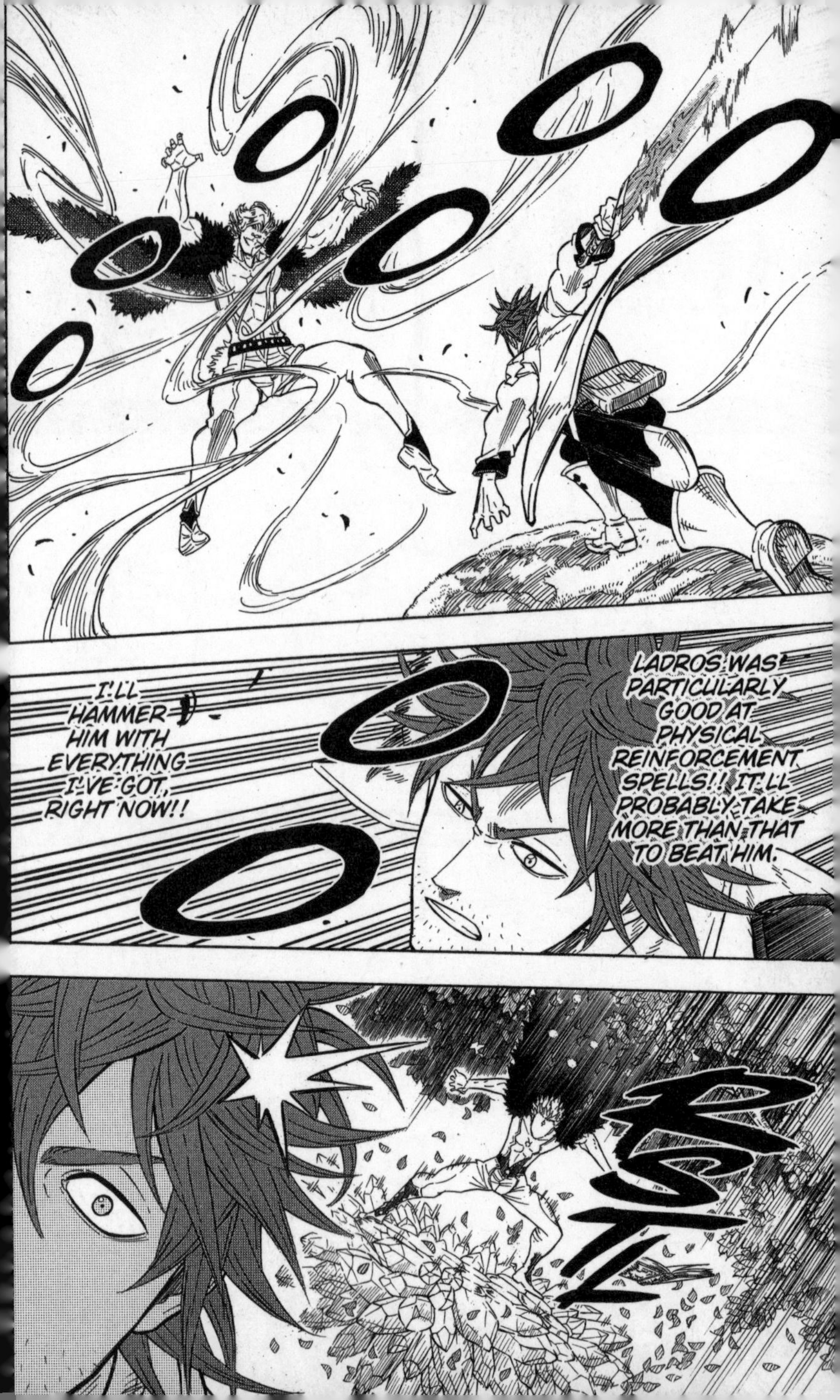
LADROS WAS PARTICULARLY GOOD AT PHYSICAL REINFORCEMENT SPELLS!! IT'LL PROBABLY TAKE MORE THAN THAT TO BEAT HIM.
I'LL HAMMER HIM WITH EVERYTHING I'VE GOT, RIGHT NOW!!

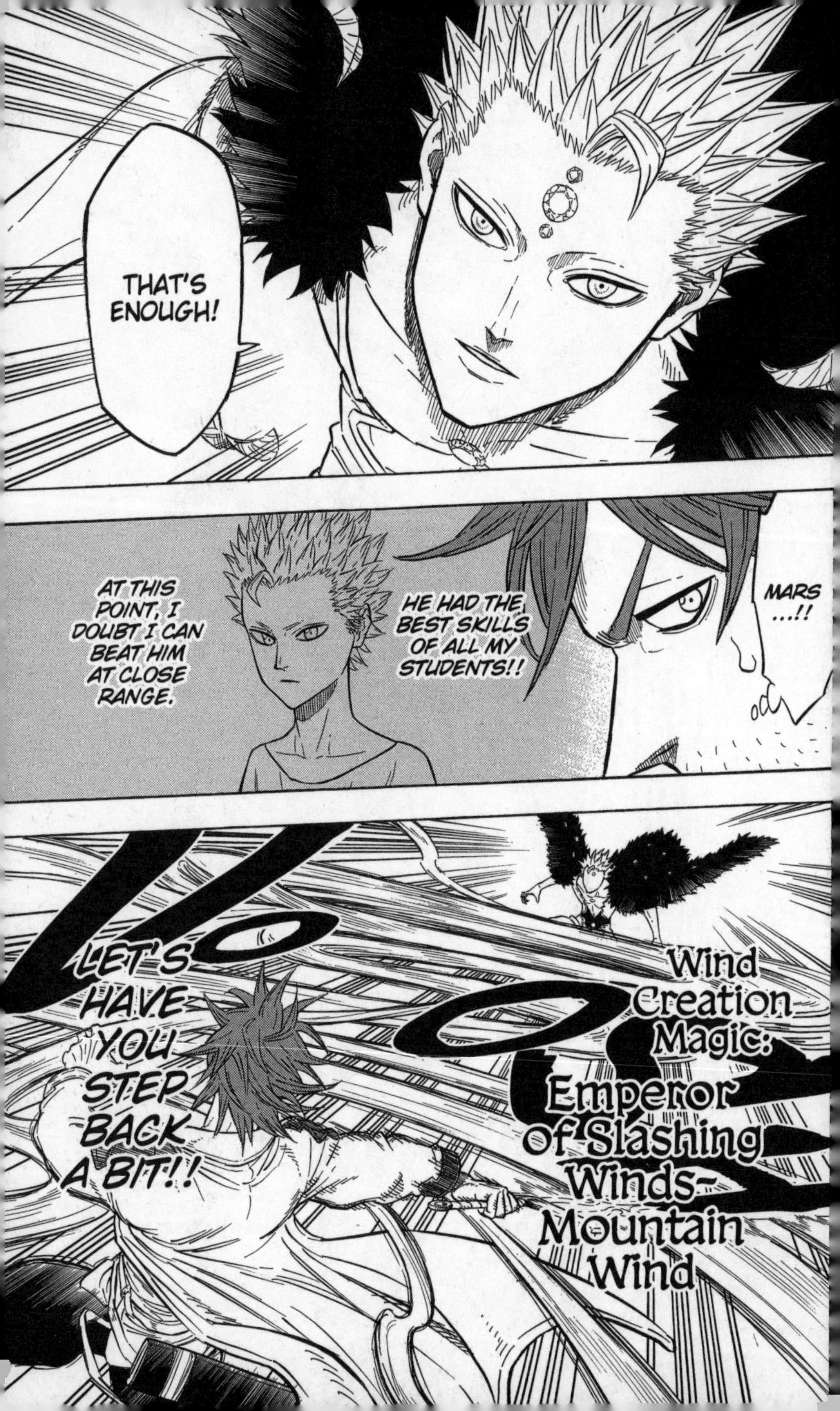
THAT'S ENOUGH!
MARS ...!!
HE HAD THE BEST SKILLS OF ALL MY STUDENTS!!
AT THIS POINT, I DOUBT I CAN BEAT HIM AT CLOSE RANGE.
Wind Creation Magic: Emperor of Slashing Winds- Mountain Wind
LET'S HAVE YOU STEP BACK A BIT!!

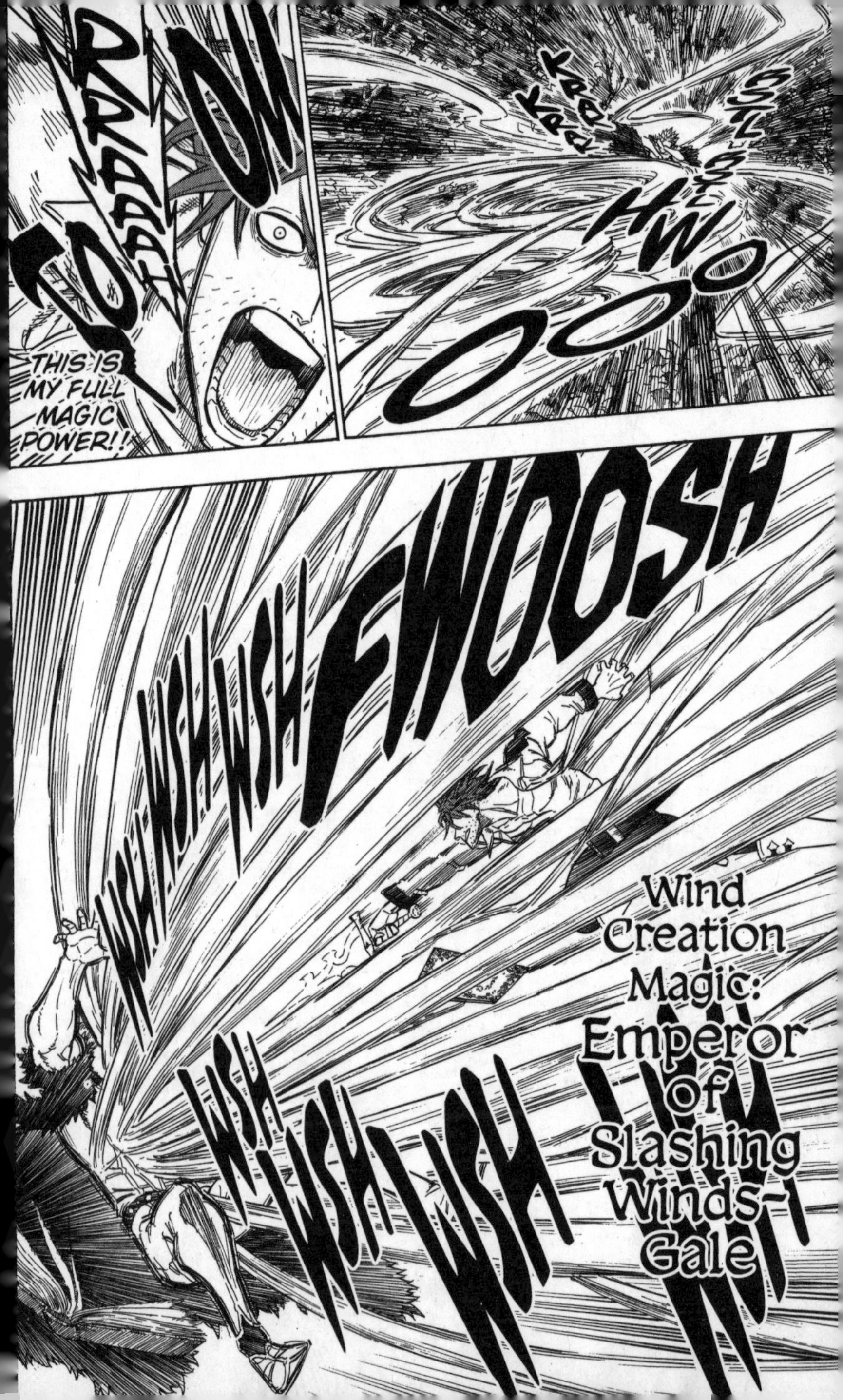
HWOOO
THIS IS MY FULL MAGIC POWER!!
FWOOSH
WSH WSH WSH WSH
Wind Creation Magic: Emperor of Slashing Winds—Gale
WSH WSH WSH

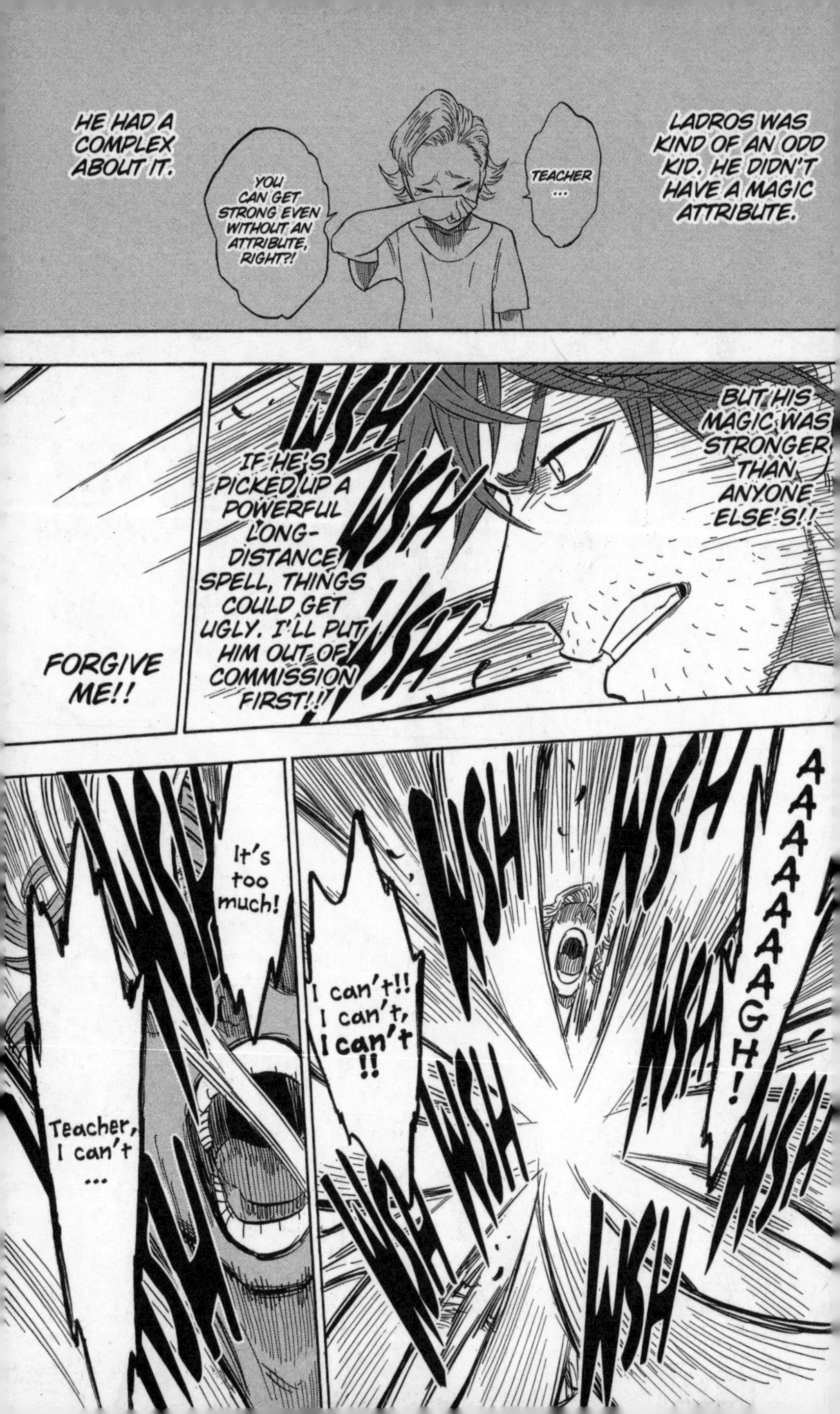
LADROS WAS KIND OF AN ODD KID. HE DIDN'T HAVE A MAGIC ATTRIBUTE.
TEACHER ...
YOU CAN GET STRONG EVEN WITHOUT AN ATTRIBUTE, RIGHT?!
HE HAD A COMPLEX ABOUT IT.
BUT HIS MAGIC WAS STRONGER THAN ANYONE ELSE'S!!
IF HE'S PICKED UP A POWERFUL LONG-DISTANCE SPELL, THINGS COULD GET UGLY. I'LL PUT HIM OUT OF COMMISSION FIRST!!
WSH WSH WSH
FORGIVE ME!!
AAAAAAAGH!
WSH WSH WSH WSH WSH WSH
I can't!! I can't, I can't !!
It's too much!
WSH WSH
Teacher, I can't ...

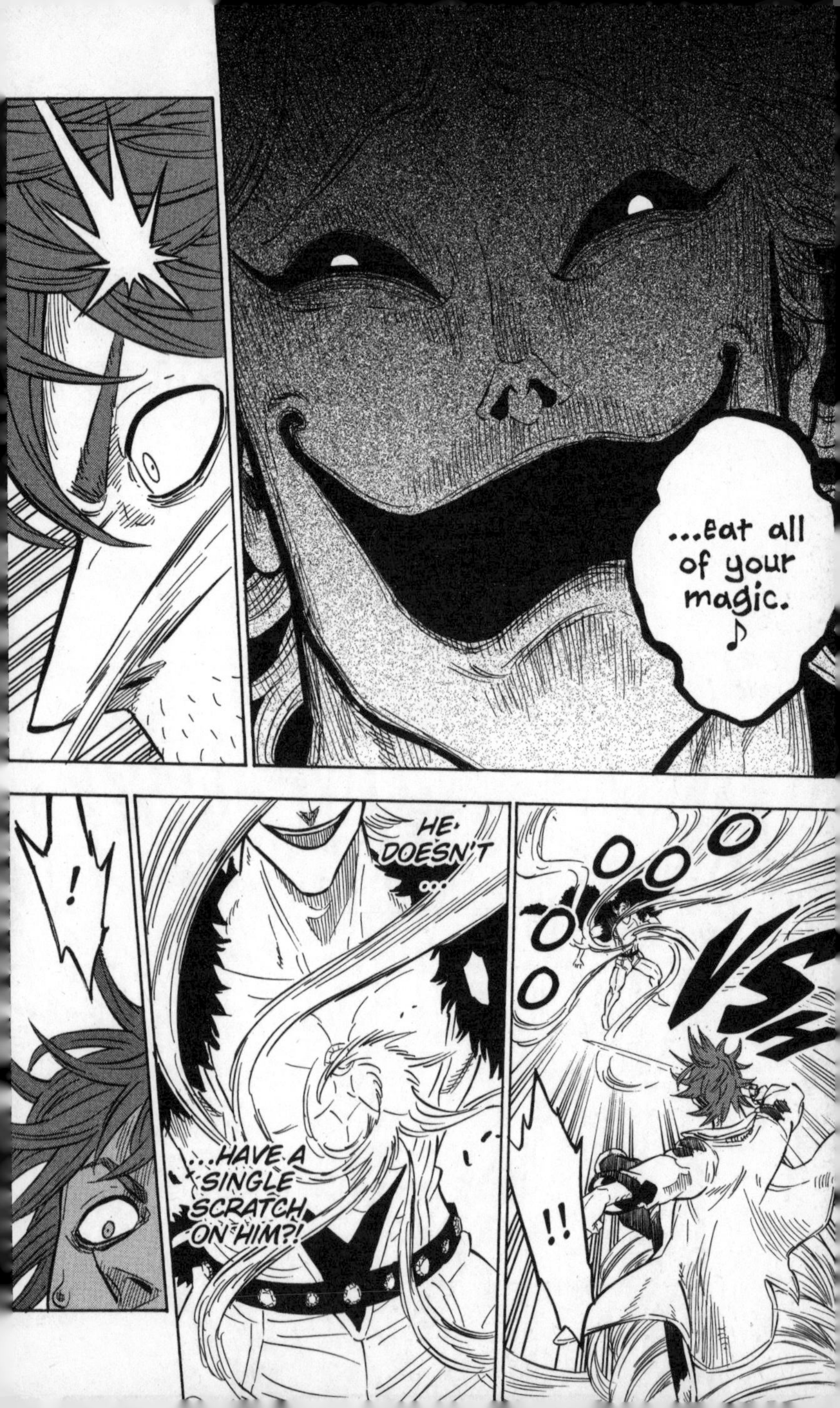

...eat all of your magic. ♪
VSHOOOOO
!!
HE DOESN'T...
...HAVE A SINGLE SCRATCH ON HIM?!
!

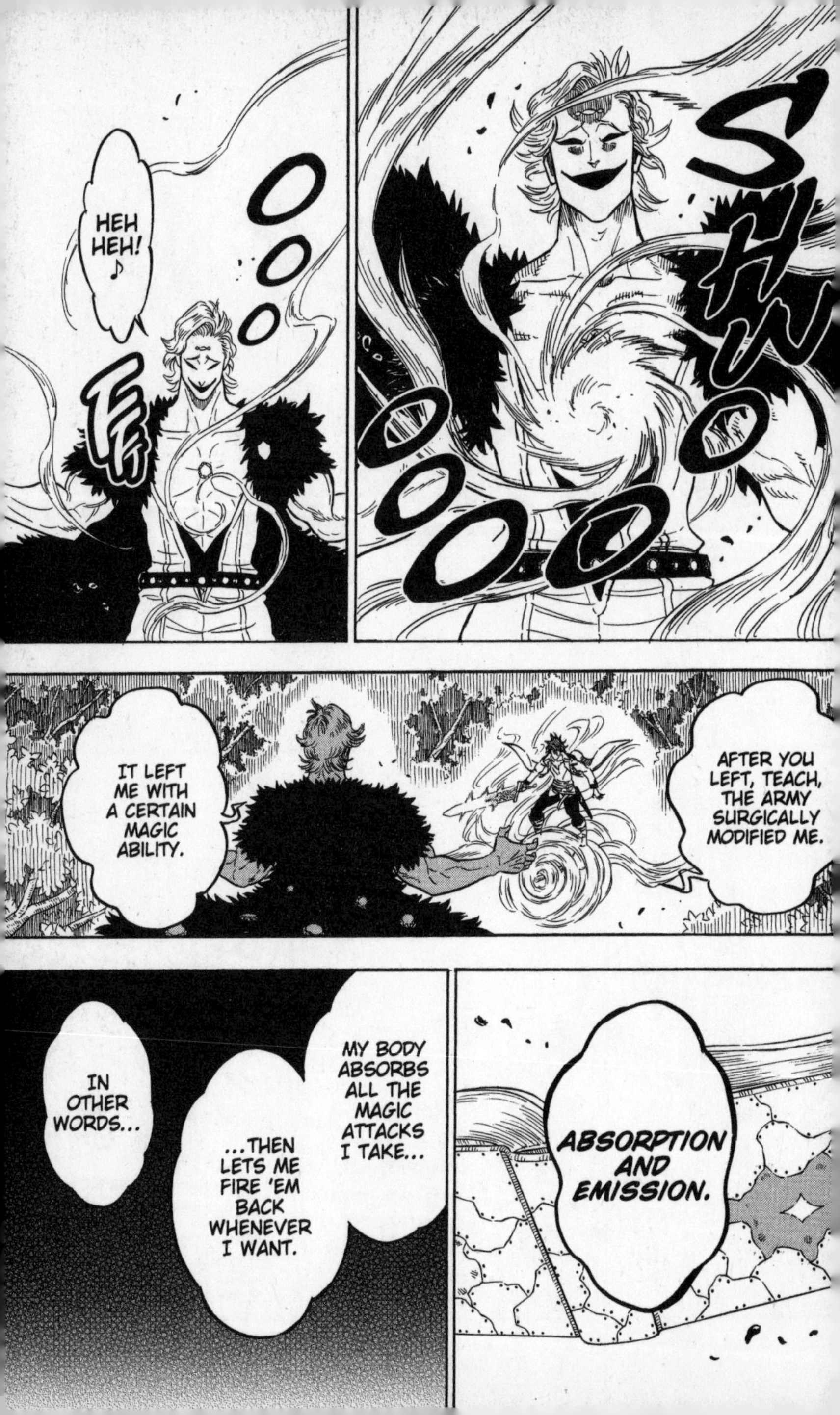
HEH HEH! ♪
AFTER YOU LEFT, TEACH, THE ARMY SURGICALLY MODIFIED ME.
IT LEFT ME WITH A CERTAIN MAGIC ABILITY.
ABSORPTION AND EMISSION.
MY BODY ABSORBS ALL THE MAGIC ATTACKS I TAKE...
...THEN LETS ME FIRE 'EM BACK WHENEVER I WANT.
IN OTHER WORDS...

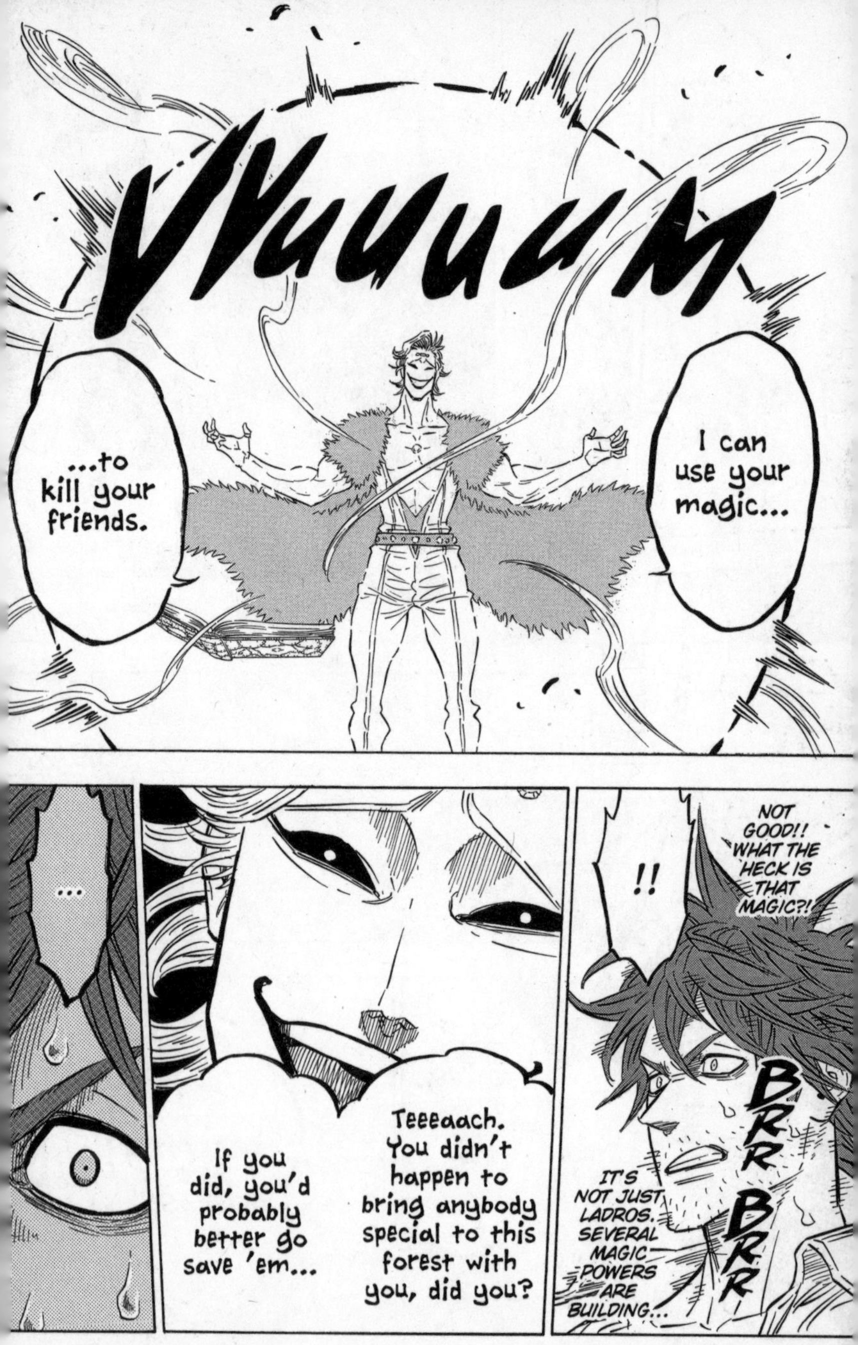
VVUUUM
I can use your magic...
...to kill your friends.
!!
NOT GOOD!! WHAT THE HECK IS THAT MAGIC?!
IT'S NOT JUST LADROS. SEVERAL MAGIC POWERS ARE BUILDING...
BRR BRR
Teeeaach. You didn't happen to bring anybody special to this forest with you, did you?
If you did, you'd probably better go save 'em...
...

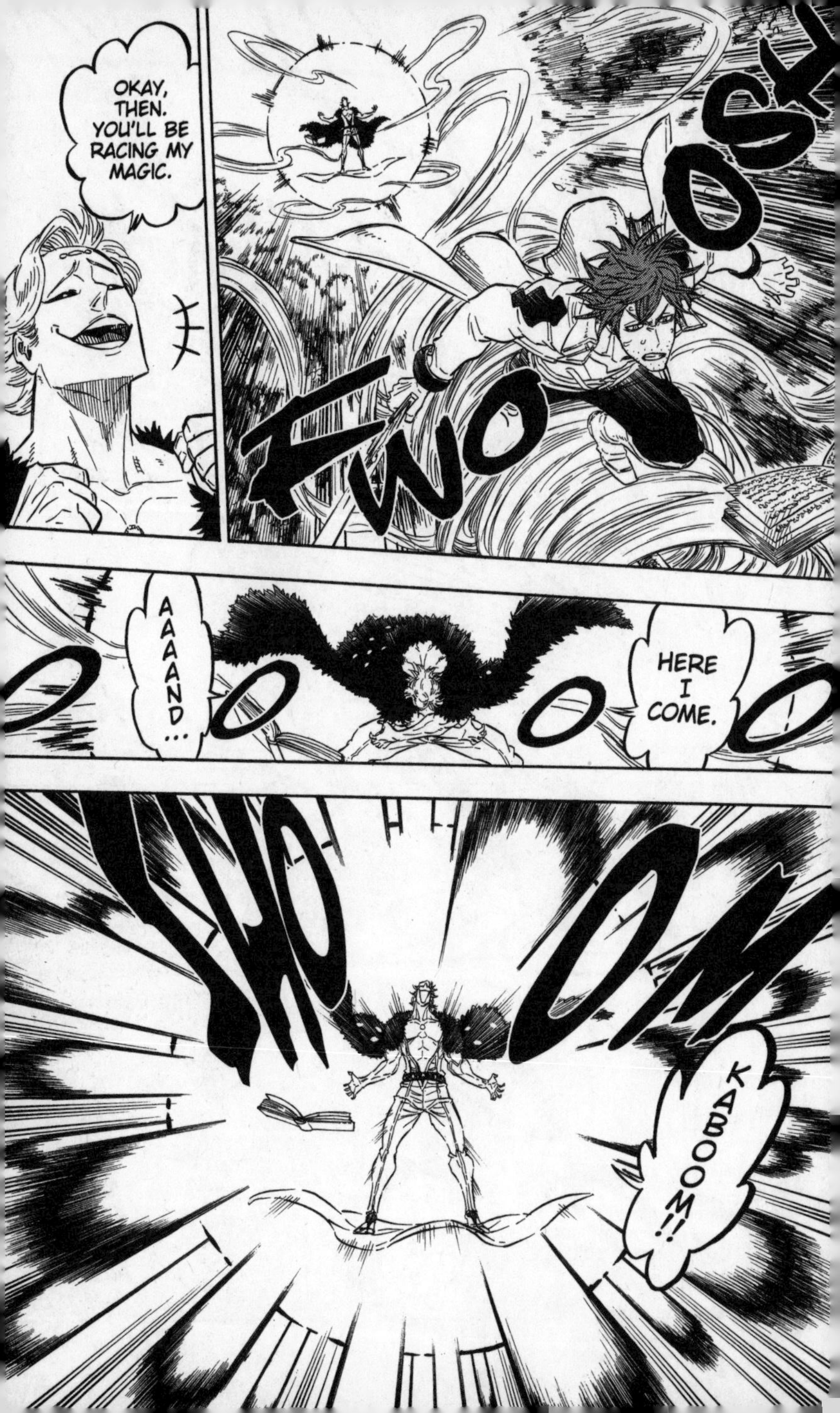
FWOOOSH
OKAY, THEN. YOU'LL BE RACING MY MAGIC.
HERE I COME.
AAAAND...
SHOOM
KABOOM!!

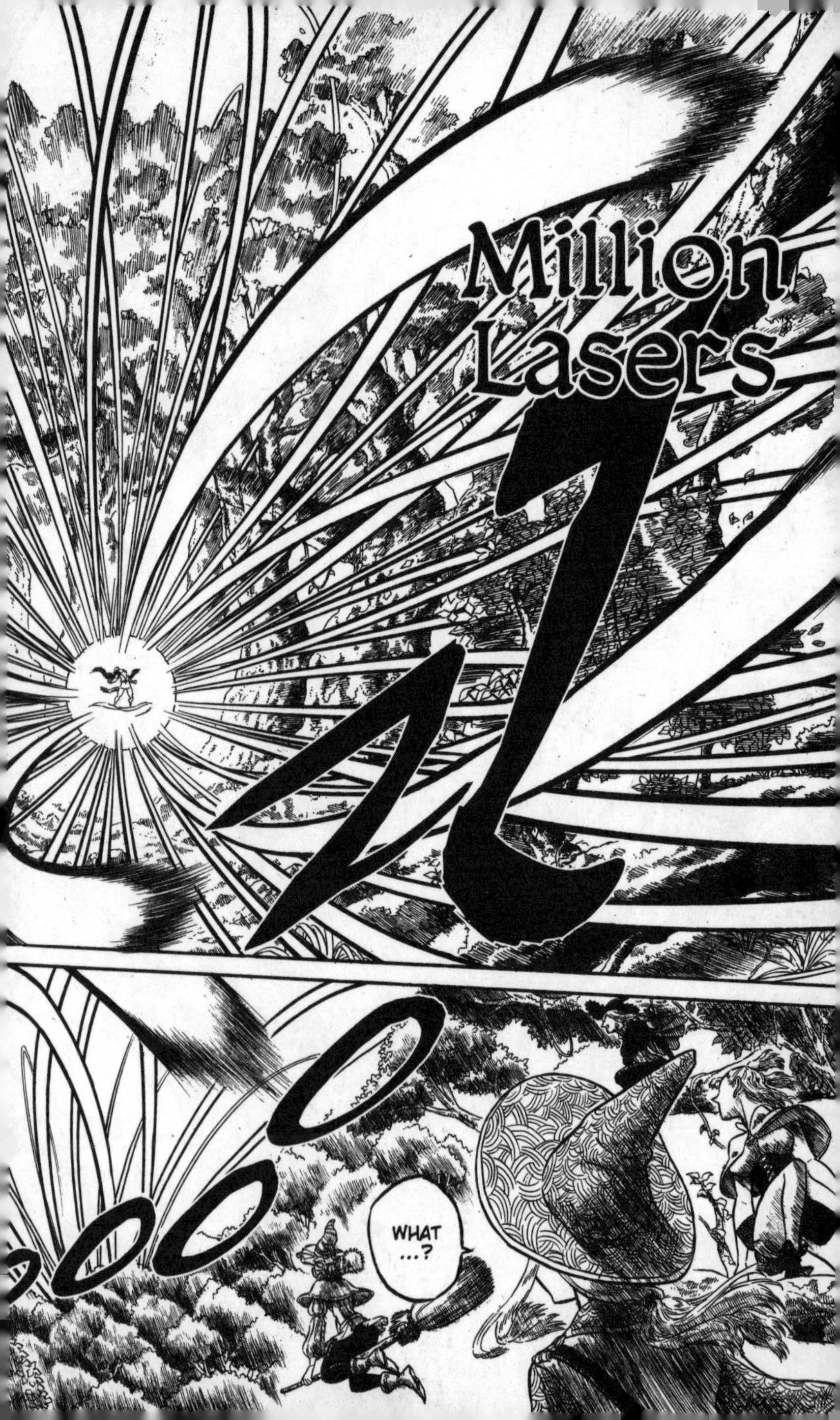
Million Lasers
WHAT ...?

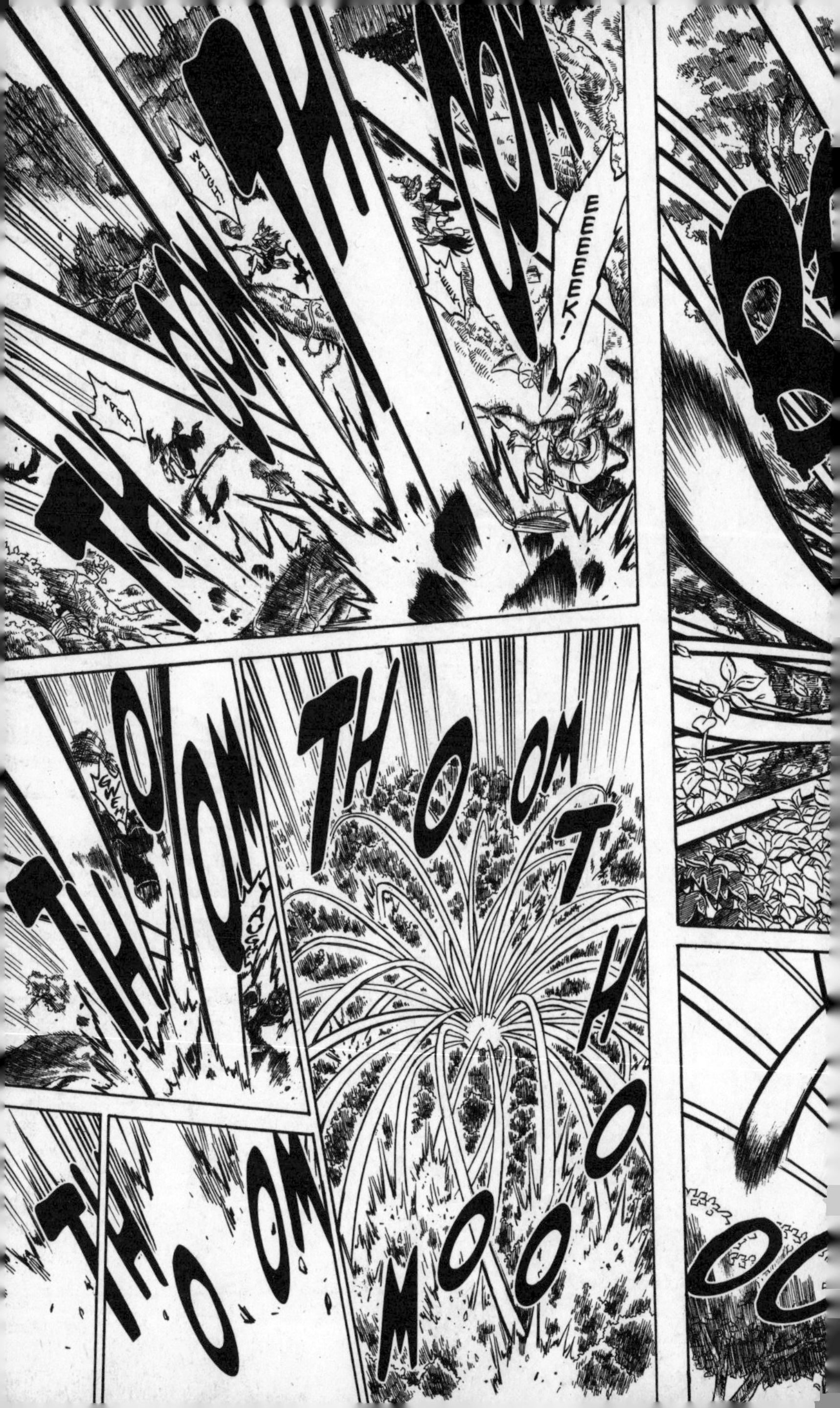
THOOM
EEEEEEK!
YUUK!
WAUGH!
THOOM
AAAA!
THOOM
THOOOOM
AUGH
THOOM
GWEH
THOOOM

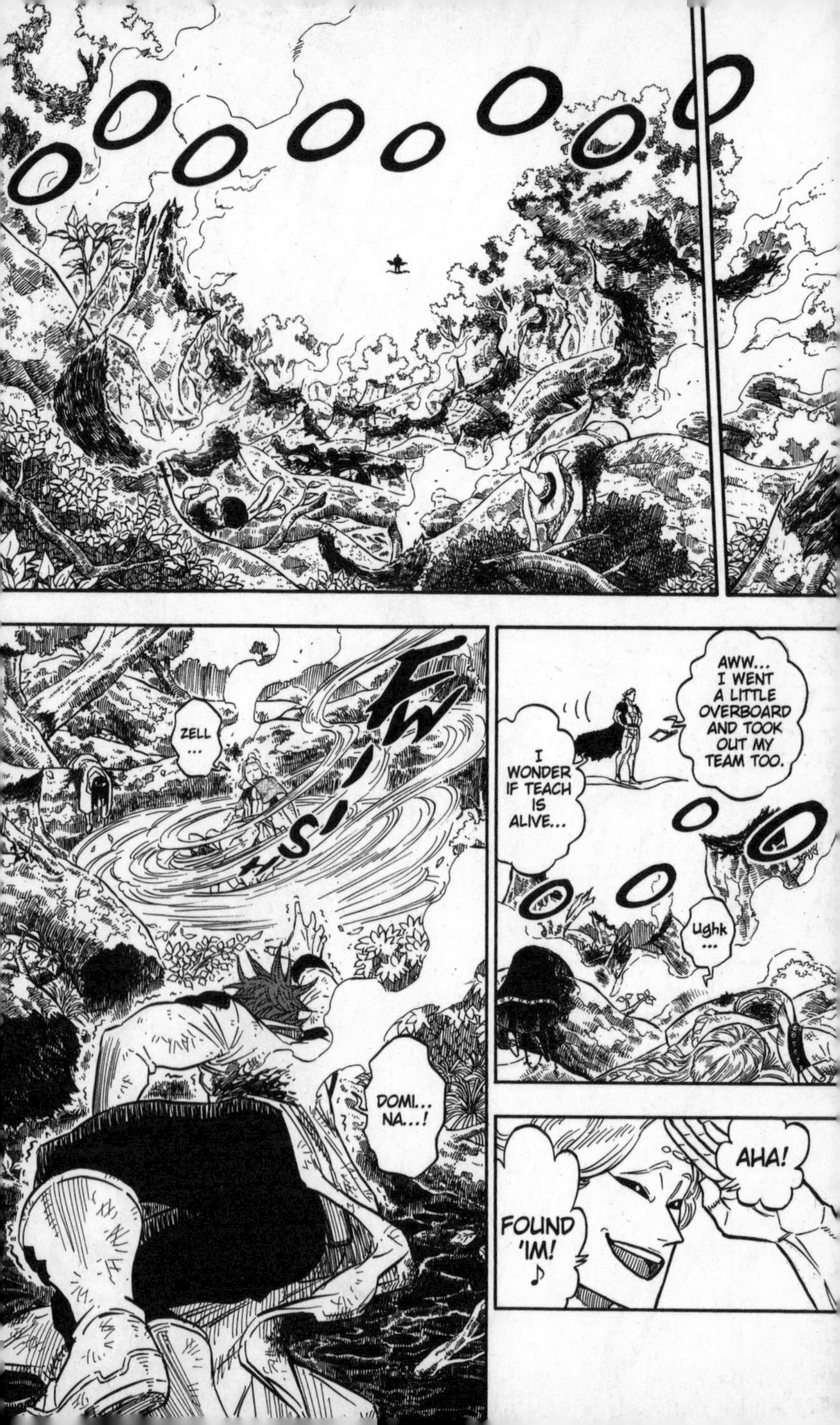
AWW... I WENT A LITTLE OVERBOARD AND TOOK OUT MY TEAM TOO.
I WONDER IF TEACH IS ALIVE...
Ughk...
AHA!
FOUND 'IM! ♪
ZELL...
DOMI... NA...!

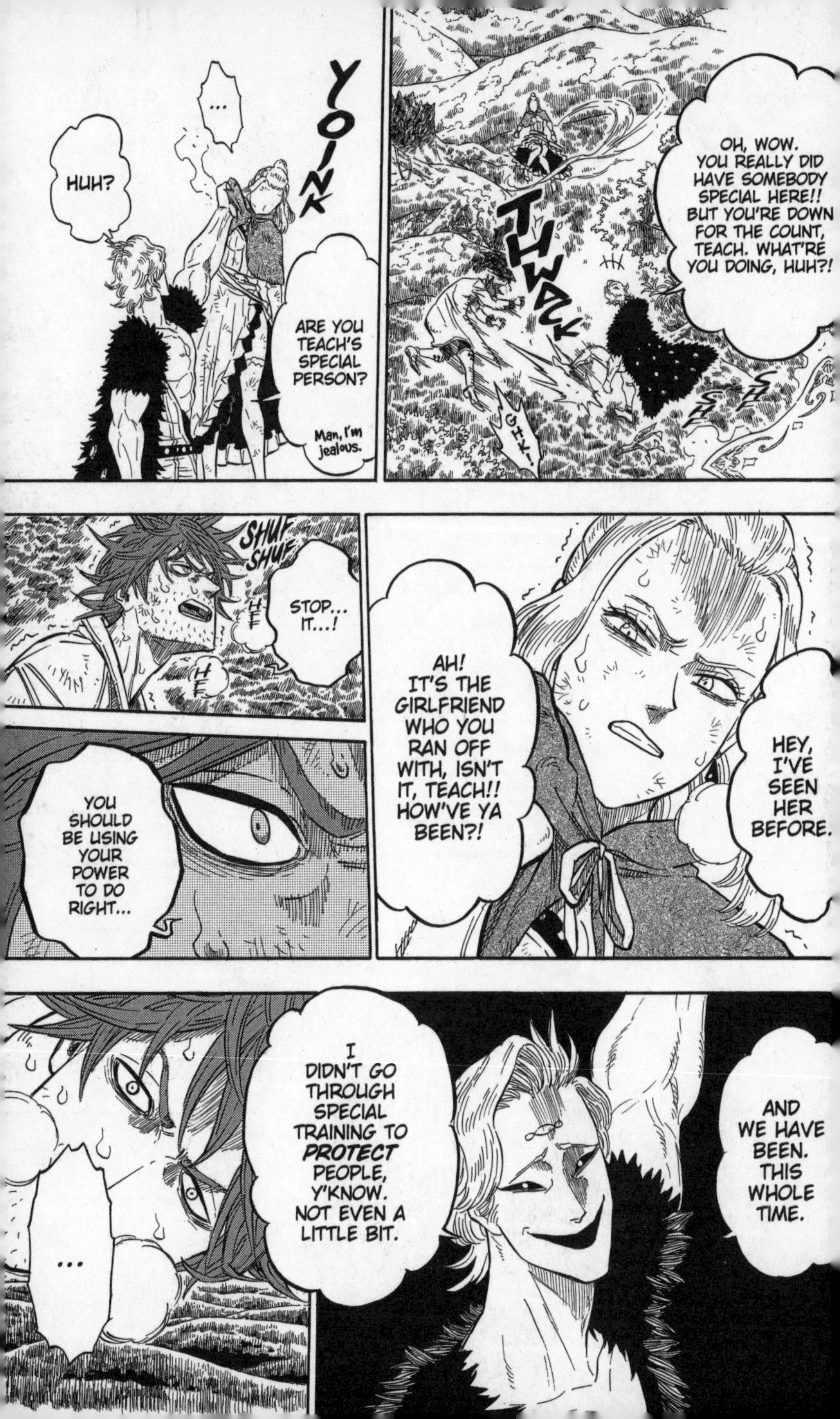
OH, WOW. YOU REALLY DID HAVE SOMEBODY SPECIAL HERE!! BUT YOU'RE DOWN FOR THE COUNT, TEACH. WHAT'RE YOU DOING, HUH?!
THWACK
GHK!
SHF SHF
YOINK
...
HUH?
ARE YOU TEACH'S SPECIAL PERSON?
Man, I'm jealous.
HEY, I'VE SEEN HER BEFORE.
AH! IT'S THE GIRLFRIEND WHO YOU RAN OFF WITH, ISN'T IT, TEACH!! HOW'VE YA BEEN?!
SHUF SHUF
STOP... IT...!
HF HF
YOU SHOULD BE USING YOUR POWER TO DO RIGHT...
AND WE HAVE BEEN. THIS WHOLE TIME.
I DIDN'T GO THROUGH SPECIAL TRAINING TO PROTECT PEOPLE, Y'KNOW. NOT EVEN A LITTLE BIT.
...

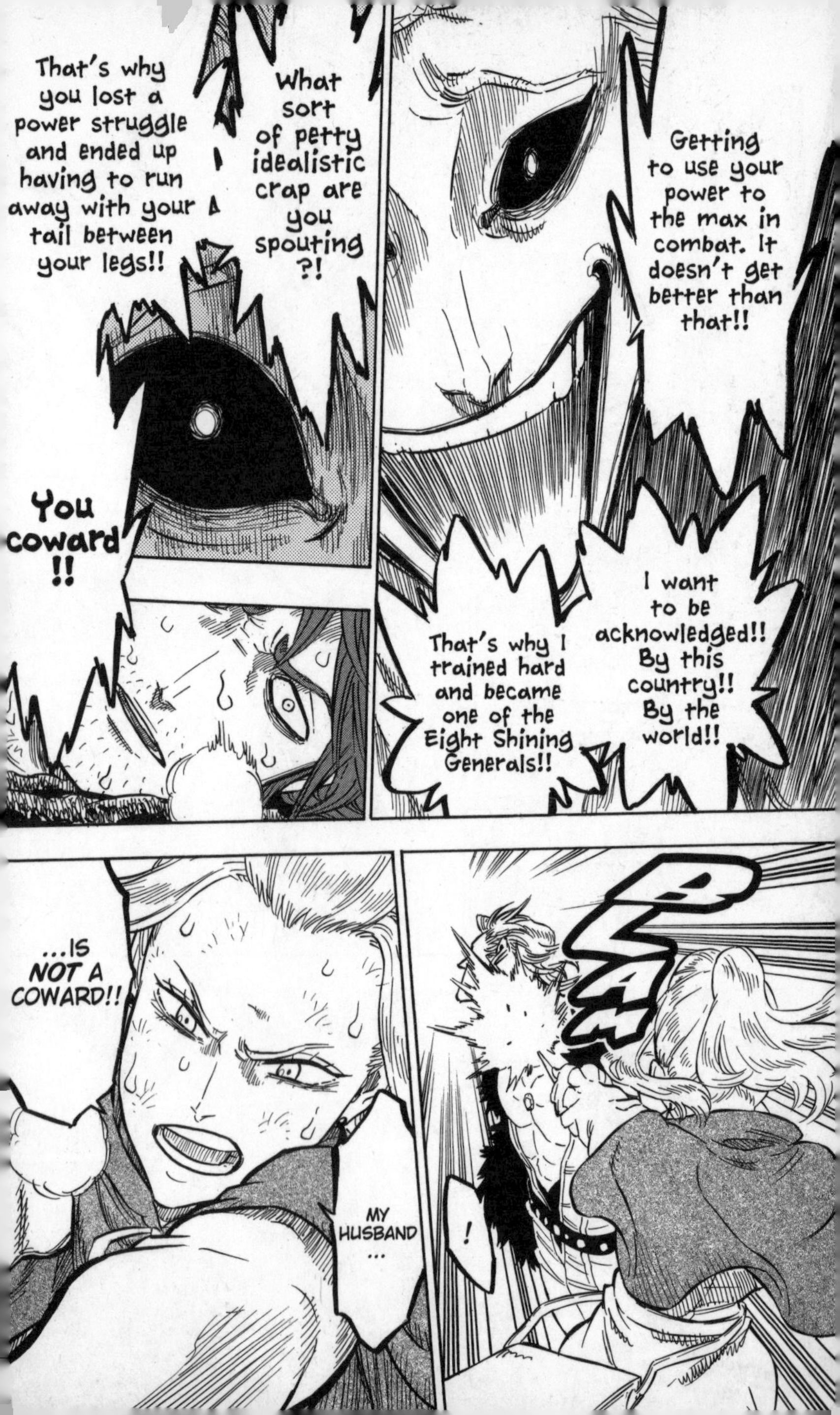
Getting to use your power to the max in combat. It doesn't get better than that!!
I want to be acknowledged!! By this country!! By the world!!
That's why I trained hard and became one of the Eight Shining Generals!!
What sort of petty idealistic crap are you spouting?!
That's why you lost a power struggle and ended up having to run away with your tail between your legs!!
You coward!!
BAM
!
MY HUSBAND...
...IS *NOT* A COWARD!!

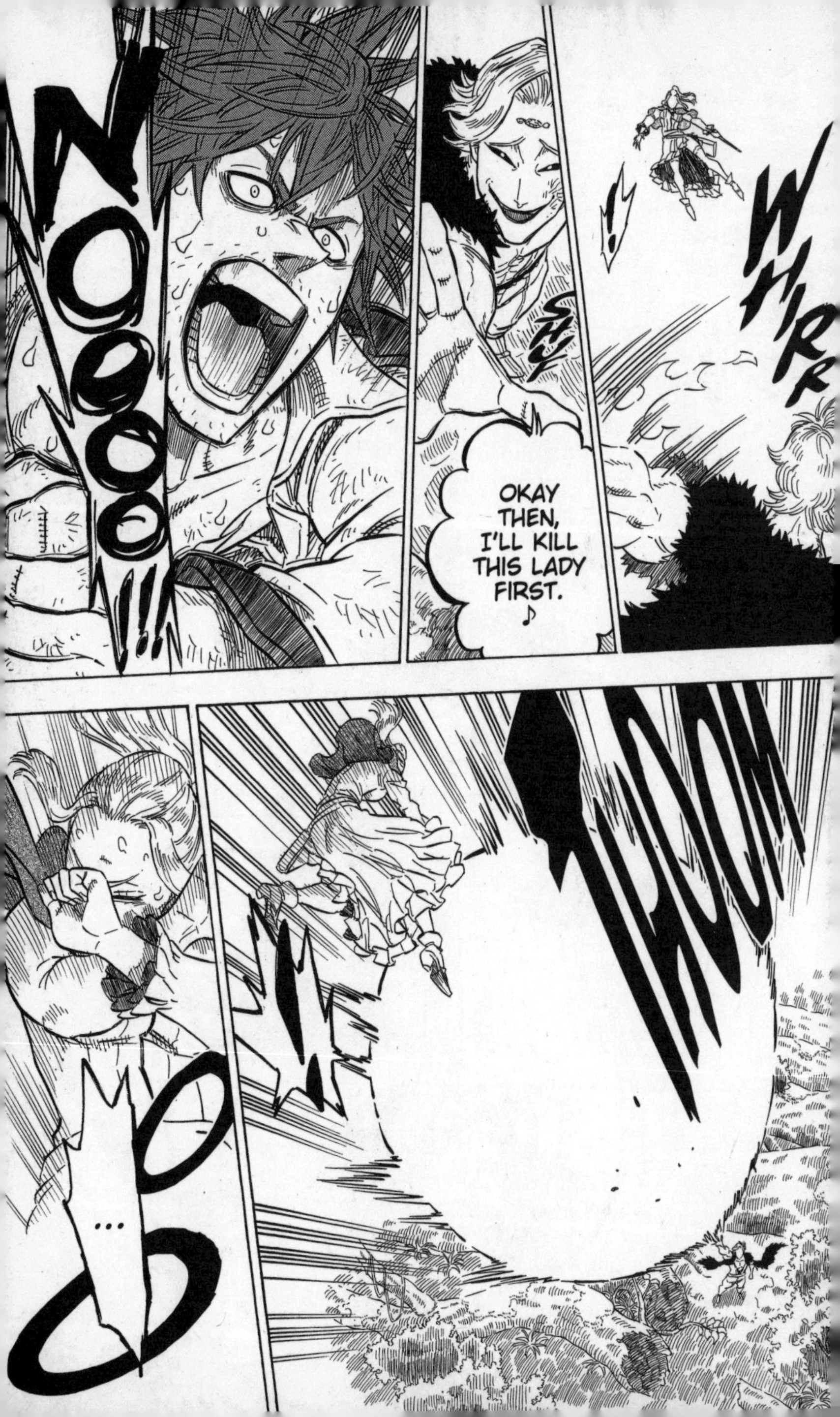
WHIRR
!
OKAY THEN, I'LL KILL THIS LADY FIRST. ♪
NOOOO!!!
THOOM
...

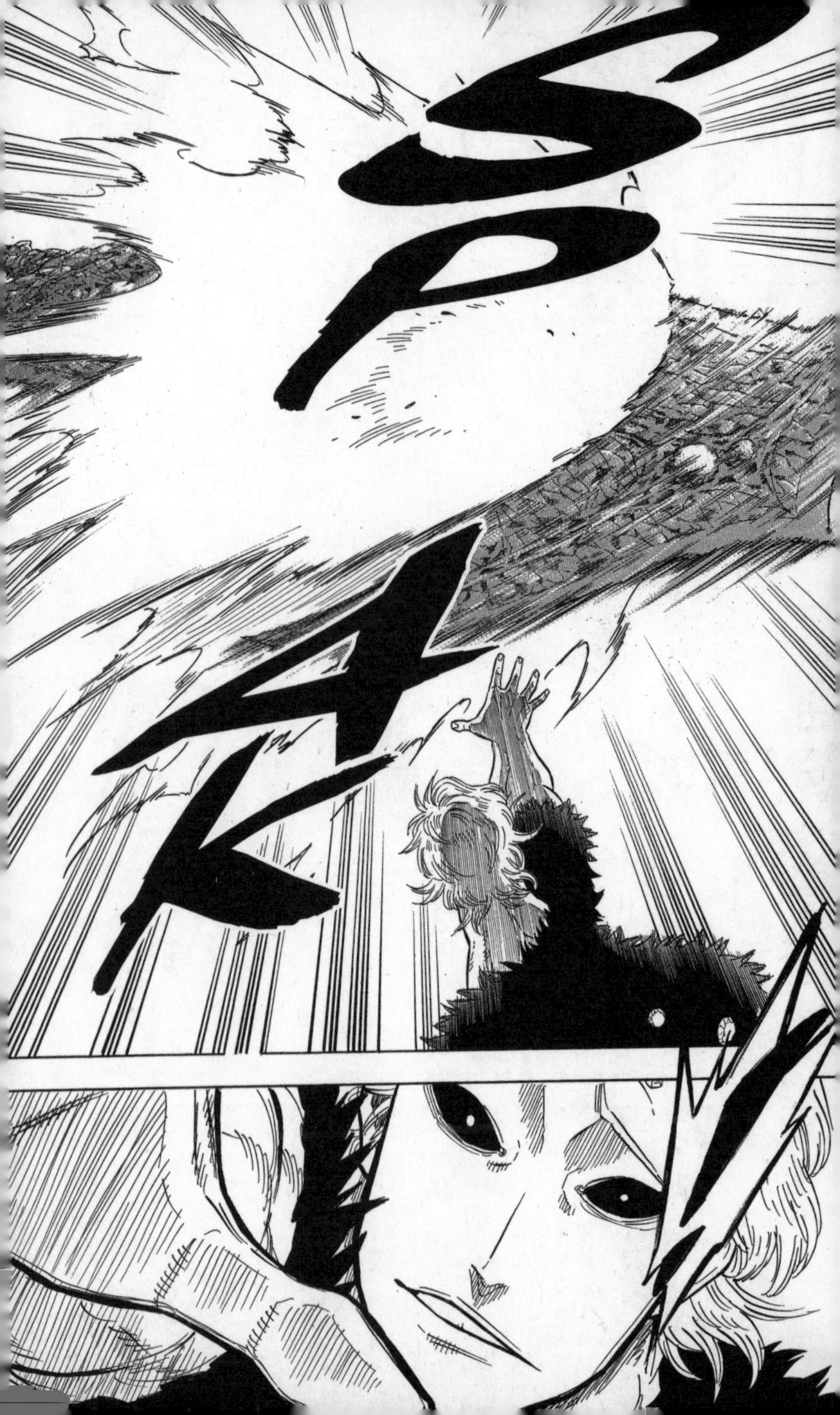
SPAK

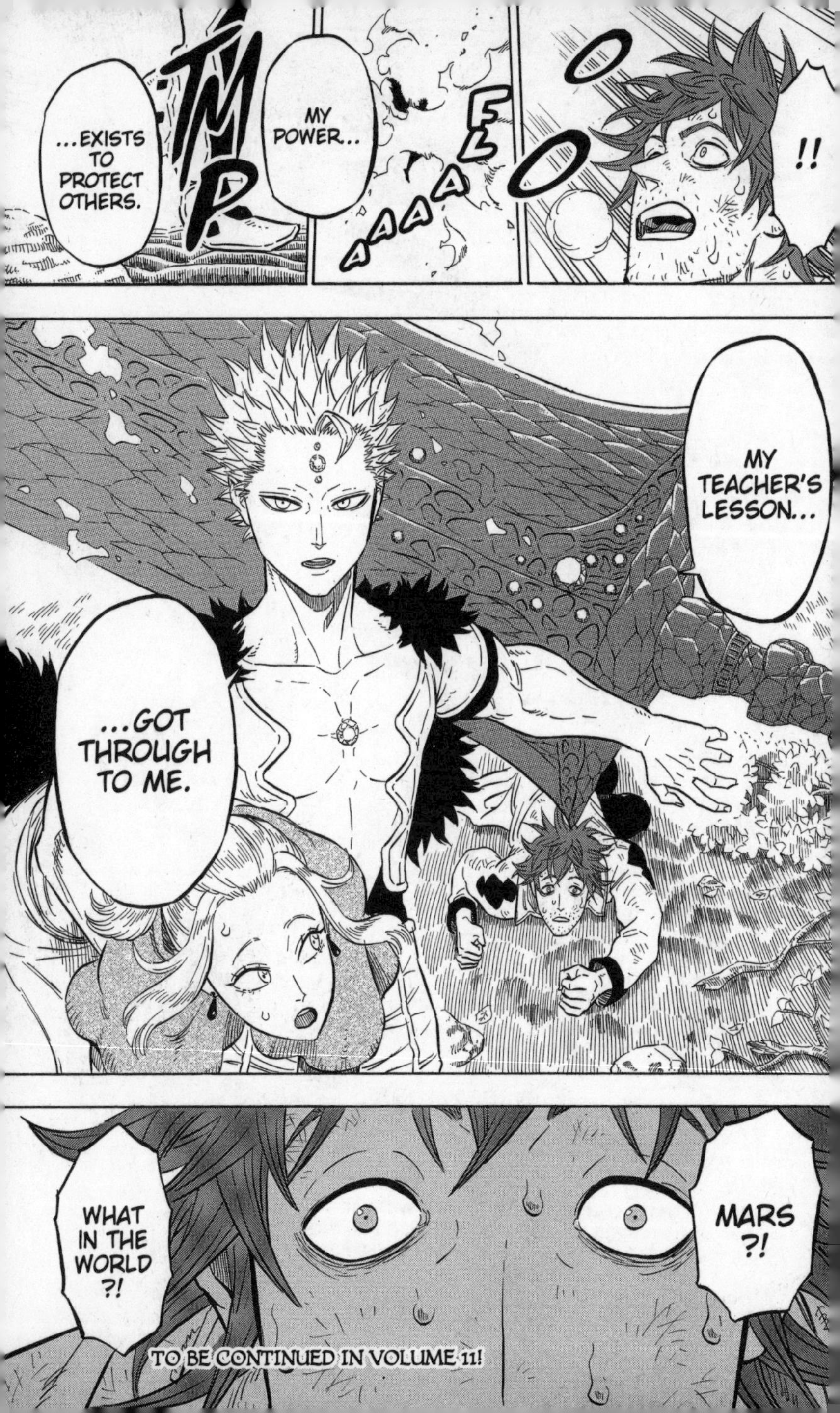
!!
MY POWER...
...EXISTS TO PROTECT OTHERS.
MY TEACHER'S LESSON...
...GOT THROUGH TO ME.
MARS?!
WHAT IN THE WORLD?!
TO BE CONTINUED IN VOLUME 11!

The Blank Page Brigade

This volume's topic: What made you think "You've gotta be kidding me..." recently? (Topic submitted by Candy Magician from Niigata Prefecture!)

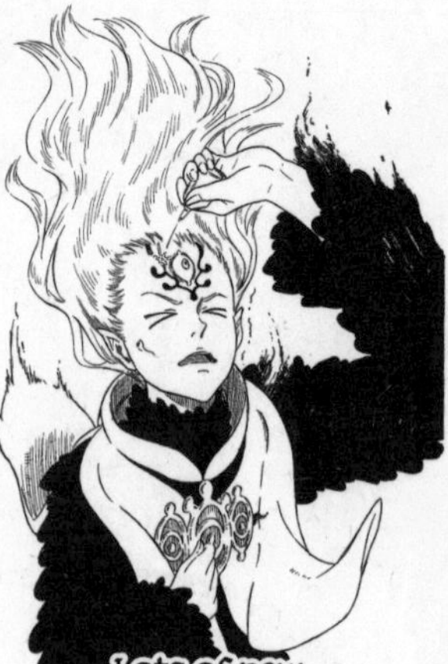

Lots of new people are joining the workplace.

Hayato Gotō

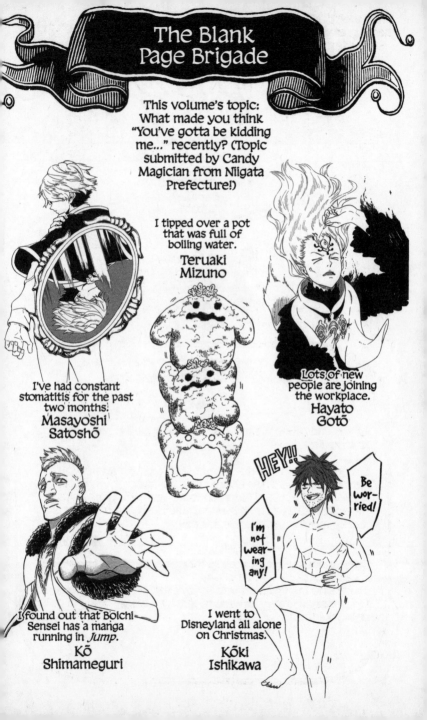

I tipped over a pot that was full of boiling water.

Teruaki Mizuno

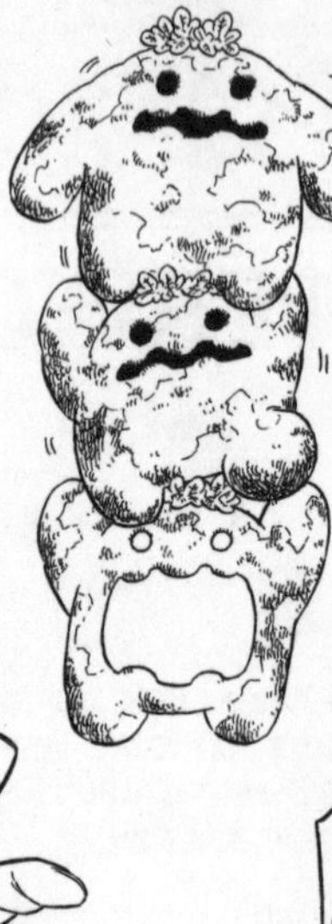

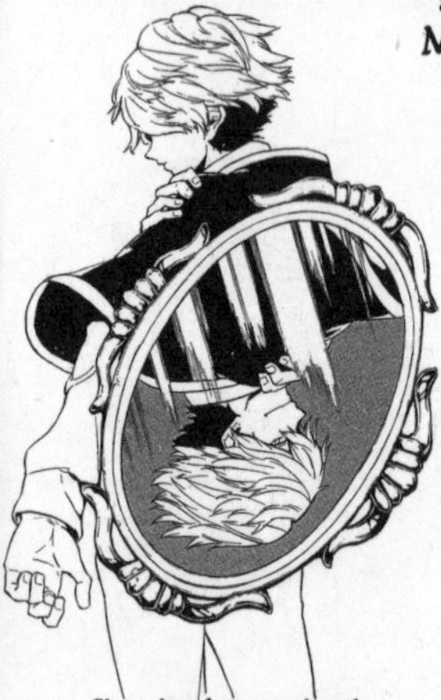

I've had constant stomatitis for the past two months.

Masayoshi Satoshō

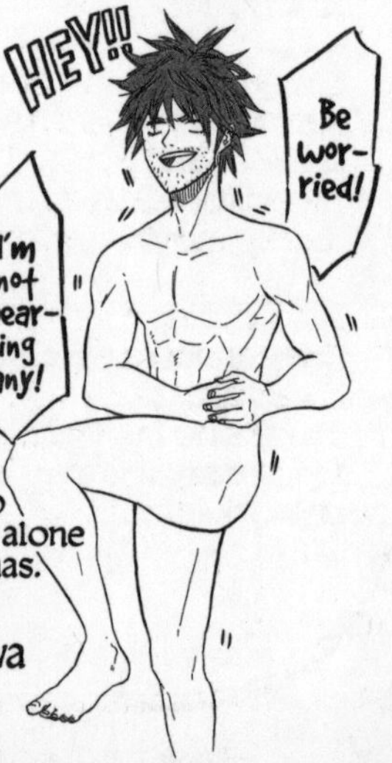
HEY!!
Be wor-ried!
I'm not wear-ing any!

I went to Disneyland all alone on Christmas.

Kōki Ishikawa

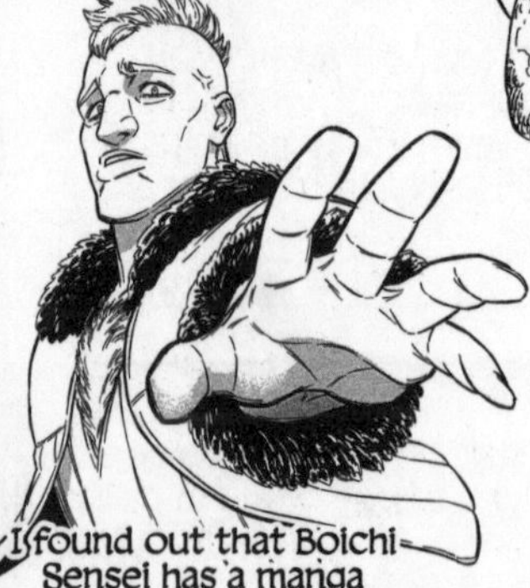

I found out that Boichi-Sensei has a manga running in *Jump*.

Kō Shimameguri

I saw a kingfisher at a nearby river when I was out walking. It was pretty.

©

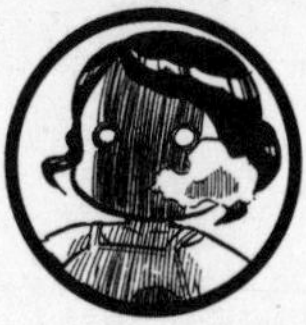

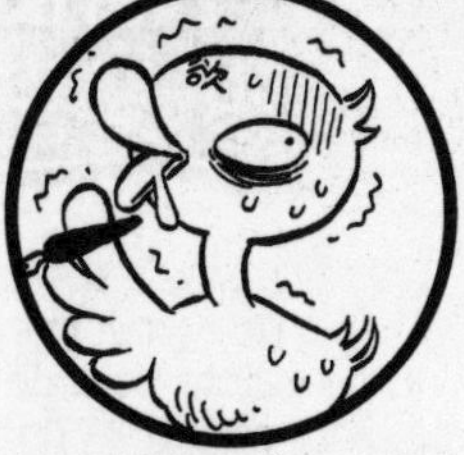

My wife and my dog were sleeping in the exact same position.

Captain Tabata

I had weird, single long hairs growing on both shoulders, my back, my shins and my butt.

Editor Katayama

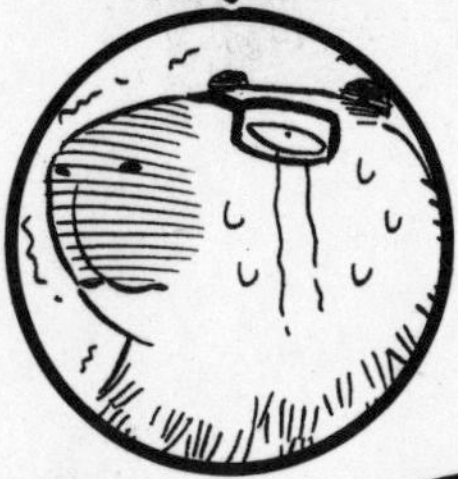

My stomach got smaller. (I think...)

Designer Iwai

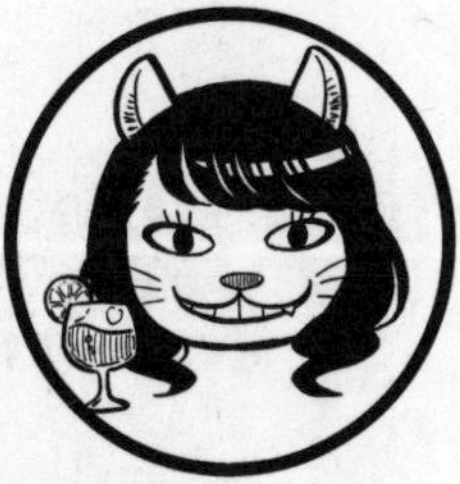

The fact that a trip that takes 40 minutes by train and on foot took ten minutes by car.

Comics Editor Koshimura

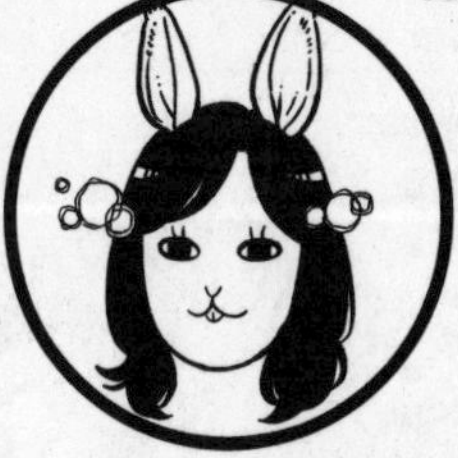

AFTERWORD

At the end of last year, I got to appear on Jump Super Stage at Jump Festa 2017!

Lots of people came to see me, and I was super-nervous, but thanks to Ryotaro Okiayu (the voice actor who acted as the MC) and Honoka Akimoto from Team Shachihoko (and my editor, Katayama), the event was lively. It was a fun and deeply moving experience for me!

Also, during that show, at last...
They announced that they're making a *Black Clover* anime!!
Yaaaaaaaaaaaaaaaaaaaaaaaaay!!!
There's no information yet, so it doesn't really feel real, but I'm already looking forward to seeing it on TV, and I'm going to work incredibly hard!

A money-type illustration
drawn as a present for the
prize giveaway in the 2016 17/18
double issue of *Shonen Jump*!
Let Asta's super laid-back
smile make you feel all
warm and fuzzy!!

Super rare!
An early sketch of
Vanessa!! Can you spot
anything that's a little
different from the way
it is now?

Special Bonus Materials

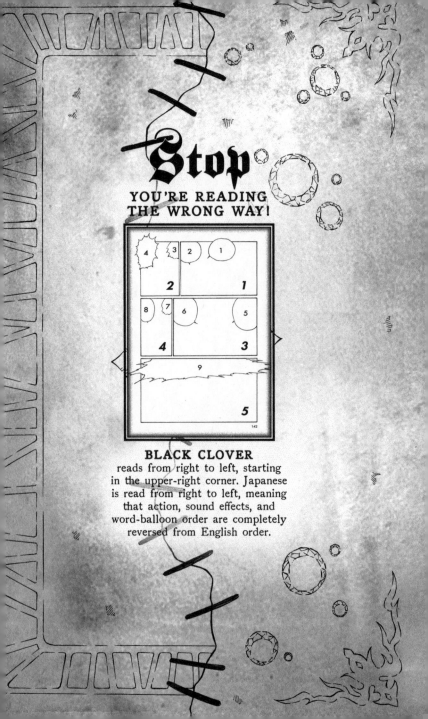

Stop

YOU'RE READING
THE WRONG WAY!

BLACK CLOVER

reads from right to left, starting
in the upper-right corner. Japanese
is read from right to left, meaning
that action, sound effects, and
word-balloon order are completely
reversed from English order.